*Shama Ramganesh*

# VENTURA 2.0

## 2ND EDITION

## ROB KRUMM

**MIS:** *PRESS*

*M A N A G E M E N T   I N F O R M A T I O N   S O U R C E ,   I N C .*

# COPYRIGHT

# DEDICATION

To Gerri, Kerri, and Mike:

Advance with confidence in the direction of your dreams. . .
and for God's sake pump your own gas.

# TABLE OF CONTENTS

# INTRODUCTION

If you are reading or browsing through this book, you probably have one question on your mind:

**How can I use Ventura to create the document I need?**

The answer is this book. That does not mean to say that this book contains everything there is to know about Ventura. That type of book would be a reference book for people who are already experienced Ventura users. There are several of those on the market. This book is not like those.

This book is designed as a structured educational experience. Its goal is to help you learn not just the techniques but the *concepts* the underlie Ventura. Learning concepts takes more time and effort than simply playing around with the software. Each chapter contains all of the commands, keystrokes, and mouse instructions that are required to create a specific document. Each example document demonstrates specific key concepts in Ventura desktop publishing. However, in the long run this approach will save you a tremendous amount of time because you will learn to use the tool — Ventura Desktop Publisher — in the most efficient way. Not only will you be more productive, but you will experience less frustration because you will be *working with* rather than *fighting against* the nature of the program.

Put another way, if you want to waste time with a computer in the long run, go fast; if you want to save time with a computer in the long run, go slow. It will take some time to work through each chapter in this book, but each chapter teaches a number of important concepts about Ventura that will make it easier for you to apply Ventura to your own needs.

The chapters are arranged in a hierarchy beginning with the most fundamental concepts in Chapter 1 and building to the more complex operations in the later chapters. You can begin creating your own documents after the first chapter. When you have finished the last chapter, you will have been exposed to the full breadth of Ventura's capabilities.

In writing a book of this type, it is necessary to make some assumptions about the reader. In this book, the assumption is made that the reader knows how to use a word processing program to create text files. While it is possible to create simple documents such as single flyers in Ventura without word processing, the more complex Ventura operations require word processing files.

# THE VENTURA PROFESSIONAL EXTENSION

Version 2.0 of Ventura is sold in two forms. The standard Ventura 2.0 program is discussed in the first eight chapters. The Professional Extension contains additional features that are not furnished with the standard program. Chapter 9 will focus on four additional typesetting features included in the Professional Extension version of Ventura 2.0.

- **Tables**. The Professional Extension edition contains special commands to create and format information tables. This makes it much simpler to prepare documents that contain column and row tables.

- **Equations**. The standard edition of Ventura 2.0 contains a fraction formatting function, which is discussed in Chapter 7. In the Professional Extension edition, this feature is expanded to cover creation of mathematical equations of all types and complexities.

- **Vertical Justification**. This feature is used to create text columns in which the text is aligned flush with the tops and bottoms of columns and pages.

- **Cross-References**. The Professional Extension edition allows you to create cross-references in documents. This feature is useful in large documents in which references are made to specific information, tables, or figures located on different pages. This feature allows Ventura to automatically update references with accurate page numbers.

In addition to these features, the Professional Extension edition supports EMS expanded memory. If you have this type of additional memory installed in your computer, the Professional Extension edition will use this memory to allow for longer documents and/or the loading of a hyphenation dictionary into memory to support dictionary hyphenation of words. The dictionary feature requires 1.2 megabytes of EMS expanded memory.

# CONVENTIONS

In this book there are two types of instructions:

- **Keyboard instructions.** These instructions tell you which keystrokes or key combinations to enter. The Return or Enter key will be represented by ⏎. The cursor arrow keys will be represented by ←, →, ↑, and ↓. All other special keys will be enclosed in square brackets, e.g. **[Ins]** stands for the Ins (insert) key. In addition, Ventura often uses the Ctrl (control) key in combination with letters to create shortcut commands. These commands require a keystroke combination. A combination of Ctrl and the letter "s" would be written as **[Ctrl/s]**. Note that the / (slash) is used as punctuation; it is not a keystroke to be entered. This convention is a bit different from the one used by Ventura, which lists the same keystroke as ^S, where ^ stands for Ctrl.

- **Mouse Instructions.** Mouse instructions are shown as follows:

  > **Point** the mouse at File
  > **Click**

  This instruction tells you where to point the mouse and when to click the left button on the mouse. Ventura uses only the left mouse button, even if your mouse has two or three buttons.

I hope you will find this book an effective way to learn Ventura and that the concepts learned in this book will make using Ventura as productive and enjoyable an experience as writing this book has been.

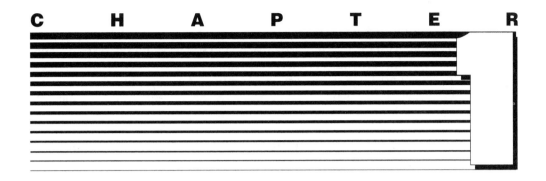

CHAPTER 1

# BASIC CONCEPTS

The term **desktop publishing** is used to describe the type of document production that is possible with even a modestly priced personal computer system. The "publishing" part of the term might be a bit misleading because it connotes images of printing presses and huge manuscripts. Ventura desktop publishing can be used for a wide variety of purposes from one-page documents to books such as the one you are reading. The significant word is "desktop" because it points to the fact that these documents can be produced on any desk or table top. This means that professional quality documents can be turned out by small businesses, schools, organizations, or individuals who know how to use personal computers.

The goal of this book is to teach you how to use Ventura to create a wide variety of documents in a series of step-by-step lessons in which you construct documents from scratch.

The book begins by creating a simple document in Ventura. Each succeeding chapter introduces another important group of concepts. By working through each of these chapters, you will learn more than just a list of commands. You will learn the basic philosophy behind Ventura. That understanding will enable you to create documents of your own design that are firmly rooted in the principles of Ventura. Put another way—this book is designed to get you thinking about Ventura document creation as well as the techniques required to operate Ventura.

Because each lesson contains a number of important points, you might find it beneficial to work through a chapter more than once in order to fully appreciate the concepts behind the techniques.

## INSTALLING VENTURA

Ventura 2.0 is supplied by Xerox in the form of a series of floppy disks (there are 19 disks in the Professional Extension version). The files on these disks must be installed on your hard disk before you can use the program.

Ventura is supplied with an installation program called **VPPREP**. This program will automatically guide you through the steps required to place Ventura on your hard disk. To begin this process, place disk #1 in drive A of your system and enter

**a:** ↵
**vpprep** ↵

The program will display messages that tell you when to change disks. After the first three disks have been copied onto the hard disk, you will be asked questions about the specific computer equipment you are using. You need to tell Ventura three things: the type of screen display you are using, the type of mouse you are using, and the printer or printers you intend to use. Note that you can have only one screen display or mouse but you can select more than one printer.

When installation is complete, you are ready to run Ventura. The installation process has created two new directories on your hard disk. The first is called **\VENTURA**. This directory holds the Ventura program and font files. Ventura allows you to store fonts in a separate directory from the Ventura program. Advanced users who purchase or create additional fonts for Ventura will use this option to reduce the amount of data stored in one directory.

The second directory is called **\TYPESET**. This directory is used to store the Ventura sample files, if you chose to install them. It is also the default directory for Ventura files. The term **default** refers to the option Ventura will use unless you specifically tell it differently. The term **default directory** refers to the directory on the hard disk into which Ventura will automatically place documents unless you specifically tell it otherwise. When you first load Ventura, it automatically defaults to this directory.

In addition to the two directories, Ventura places a batch file called VP.BAT or, if you are using the Professional Extension version, VPPROF.BAT. This file is used to issue the commands needed to run Ventura from the root directory of the hard disk. Enter

**vp** ⏎

or

**vpprof** ⏎

## THE SCREEN DISPLAY

After you have installed Ventura, you are ready to begin. The first series of concepts to learn is the organization of the Ventura screen. If you are used to working with PC applications such as WordPerfect or Lotus 1-2-3, you will find the Ventura screen a bit more complex to read.

Ventura presents you with a screen display that may seem unusual if you are used to the standard text display used by word processing and spreadsheet programs. Ventura uses high resolution graphics to create a screen display that displays text of various sizes and typefaces along with graphic images.

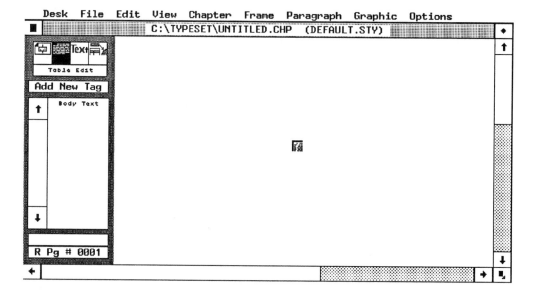

*Figure 1.1    Initial screen display of Ventura 2.0.*

It is important to understand that graphic screen displays such as those used by Ventura or Microsoft's Windows applications are device dependent. The term **device dependent** means that Ventura will display a similar but slightly different screen image, depending on what type of display and display adapter is used with your computer.

The key factor is the resolution of the screen display. **Resolution** refers to the total number of dots — called **pixels** — that your computer can display. The greater the number of dots, the higher the resolution. The main benefit of high-resolution displays is that they can draw characters and images more finely and therefore place more readable information on the same size screen than low-resolution displays. The figures used in this book are taken from a computer using an EGA (enhanced graphics adapter) display.

If you are using a different type of display, you will find that the amount of text displayed in the document window will vary from the amount in the figures shown in this book; however, these differences should not cause any problems in learning the technqiues discussed in this book.

Before you begin creating documents, you should become familar with the components of the Ventura screen display.

The screen is divided into a series of **bars** at the top, bottom, left and right sides of the display.  In the center is a blank area called the document window.  The **document window** is where you will see the pages of the document you are creating.

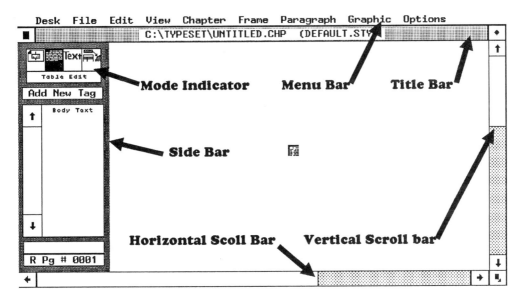

*Figure 1.2    Bars surrounding document window.*

The box in the center of the screen is the **mouse cursor**.  This cursor is used to indicate what part of the screen the mouse is pointing to.  You can change the position of the mouse cursor by moving the mouse.

The shape of the mouse cursor will change as you perform different operations. The current shape of the mouse cursor is a symbol that is supposed to resemble a block of paragraph text. This indicates that Ventura is currently in the **paragraph tagging** mode. You will learn more about Ventura modes later in this chapter and throughout the book.

The main features of the screen display are described as follows.

**Menu Bar**    At the very top of the screen display is the **menu bar**. The menu bar lists the major command topics used in Ventura. When you point the mouse at any of the words on the Menu bar, Ventura displays a box called a **drop-down menu**, which lists commands related to that menu topic.

**Title Bar**    This bar is located just below the menu bar. It shows the name of the current document and the style sheet file currently in use. Ventura displays the name UNTITLED.CHP when you do not have a document loaded. The style sheet is shown in parentheses. When Ventura is first installed, it displays the DEFAULT.STY style sheet.

**Document Window**    The center of the screen display consists of a blank square. This is called the **document window**. It is in this window that the text of your document will appear. This part of the screen display will change as you enter and format text.

**Side Bar**    The **side bar** consists of several items that display information needed to perform various operations. The side bar contains the mode indicator box, the add item box, the item list box, and the page number display box.

The **mode indicator** consists of four boxes, one for each of the operational modes available in Ventura. The four modes are the **Frame Setting** mode, the **Paragraph Tagging** mode, the **Text Editing** mode, and the **Graphic Drawing** mode.

The **add item** box is used to add an item to the list of items shown in the list box directly below the add item box. The wording of the add item box will change depending on which mode you are in. For example, in the Paragraph Tagging mode, the box reads **Add New Tag**; in the Frame Setting mode, it reads **Add New Frame**; and in the Text Editing mode, it reads **Set Font**.

The **page number** box displays the current page number and shows whether the page is a left or right page. Keep in mind that the distinction between right and left pages is important when you are creating documents that will eventually be printed on both sides of the page.

**Scroll Bars**  The right and bottom sides of the document window are bordered by **scroll bars** that indicate the relative position of the document window on the page because it is not always possible to display the entire page in the document window. The entire bar represents the length of the page. The solid, or white, part of the bar represents the section visible through the document window. The gray part shows the portion of the page not visible in the window. As you move up and down the page, the position of the solid part of the vertical bar will change to indicate how far the text displayed in the window is from the top or bottom of the page. The horizontal bar, displayed at the bottom of the window, shows the horizontal position of the display window on the page as you move left and right. At either end of the scroll bars are boxes that contain arrows. These boxes are used to scroll the display a set distance in the direction of the arrow.

# USING THE MOUSE

If you have not worked with a mouse before, there are several terms that you need to become familar with.

**Icon**  **Icons** are small pictures displayed on the screen. The Ventura display consists of words and icons. The mouse cursor is an icon, or picture, that moves around the screen when you move the mouse on the mouse pad. If you have not used a mouse before, it will take a few hours to get fully comfortable with one, but you will soon find the mouse quite natural and easy to use.

| | |
|---|---|
| **Point** | An instruction to **point** the mouse means that you should move the mouse so that the mouse cursor is positioned on the word, box, or bar you want to work with. Note that some of the mouse cursor icons are shapes without a clear point. The paragraph icon is a square. When you point with this icon, it is the top edge of the square you want to point with. |
| **Click** | **Clicking** refers to pressing down and then releasing the mouse button. If your mouse has more than one button, use the left button for clicking with Ventura. A **double click** refers to pressing the mouse button twice in rapid succession. When you first use the mouse, you may find that you have some problems double clicking fast enough for the double click to register with the program, but after a few hours of practice, this skill will seem quite natural. |
| **Drag** | **Dragging** refers to an operation that combines pointing and clicking. When you drag an item, you begin by pointing at it, and then you press and hold down the mouse button. While you are still holding down the button, you move the mouse to another position. A drag is completed when you release the mouse button. |

## USING THE MENUS

The menu bar in Ventura is really an outline of the major topics in Ventura. Each word on the menu bar is a heading for a series of commands listed under that topic. To display the commands listed for a menu bar topic, you simply point the mouse at that word.

---

**Point** the mouse at File

---

Two things happened when you pointed the mouse. First, the mouse cursor changed from a paragraph icon to an arrow. This happened because you pointed to an item outside the document window. Second, when you pointed the mouse at File, Ventura displayed the **File** menu.

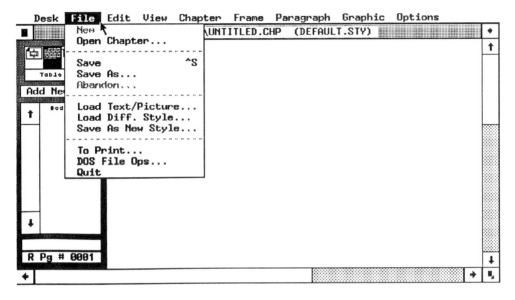

*Figure 1.3    File pull-down menu displayed.*

The menu lists the options under the topic File.  Note that not all of the menu items are displayed in exactly the same way.

**Grayed Items**    When a menu is displayed, some or all of the items on that menu may appear in gray rather than black.  The difference in color indicates which options are currently available — black — and which are not available — gray.  In the menu in Figure 1.3, the commands New and Abandon are in gray, indicating that you cannot perform these functions at this time, which makes sense because you haven't yet begun a document, so there is nothing to start over from or to abandon.

**Shortcuts**    Some of the more often used commands in Ventura have keyboard shortcut commands. In Figure 1.3, the **Save** command is followed by ^S. The ^S stands for a combination of the Control key, labeled **Ctrl** on most keyboards, and the letter **s**. This means that entering this keyboard combination is the same as selecting Save from the File menu.

In this book, shortcut key combinations will be written with a special notation. For example, ^S will appear as **[Ctrl/s]**, which means to press and hold the Ctrl key while simultaneously pressing the "s" key.

. . . When a menu item is followed by ellipses, they indicate that the item is associated with a submenu called a dialog box. The **dialog box** contains more details about that function and allows you to select options and enter specifications.

You can change menus by pointing at another word on the menu bar.

---

**Point** the mouse at Chapter

---

Ventura displays the drop-down menu for **Chapter**. To select an item from the drop-down menu, you must point and then click.

---

**Point** the mouse at Page Size & Layout

---

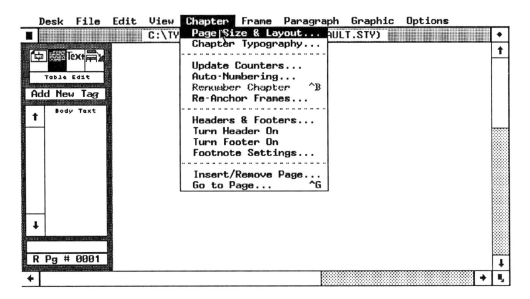

*Figure 1.4    Item highlighted on drop-down menu.*

Ventura highlights the item you point at on the menu.  You can select that item by clicking the mouse while that item is highlighted.

> **Click** the mouse

In this case, because the item has ellipses (. . .) after it, Ventura displays a dialog box in the center of the screen.  This box contains the settings and options related to the menu topic.

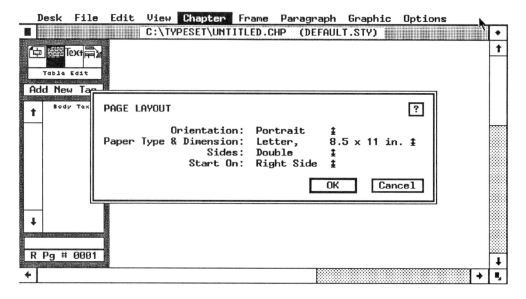

*Figure 1.5    PAGE LAYOUT dialog box.*

The box in Figure 1.5 contains a list of options, e.g., Orientation, Paper Type & Dimensions, etc. Next to each item is the current setting for that option. For example, the current paper size is standard letter size — 8.5" by 11".

Following each setting is a symbol with arrows pointing upward and downward. These symbols indicate that you can select from a list of options. To display this list you must point the mouse at any part of the item name or setting and hold down the mouse button. For example, to display different paper sizes you can point at any part of the **Paper Type & Dimensions** option and hold down the mouse.

> **Point** the mouse at Paper
> **Hold down** the button

Ventura displays a box with a list of options for paper size. The items will appear only as long as you continue to hold down the button. To return to the dialog box, simply release the button.

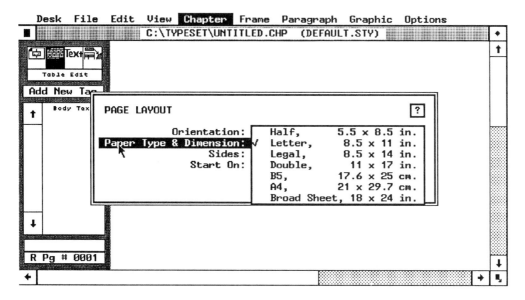

*Figure 1.6    Paper types and sizes listed.*

---

**Release** the button

---

There are three items that will appear in all Ventura dialog boxes:

**OK**          The OK box is used to tell Ventura that you have completed
                your selections and want to save the new settings as part of the
                document you are creating.  The ⌐ (Return) key can be used as
                a shortcut for the OK box.

**Cancel**      Cancel exits the dialog box without recording any of the changes.
                The [Ctrl/x] key combination can be used as a shortcut for the
                Cancel box.

**?**           In each dialog box a ? box appears.  This box is the **help box**,
                which provides information about the dialog box and its options.

To exit this dialog box, use the Cancel option.

---

**Point** the mouse at Cancel
**Click**

---

You have exited the dialog box and are returned to the normal screen display.

## CHANGING MODES

The mode icons located at the top of the side bar display can be used to place Ventura into different operational modes.

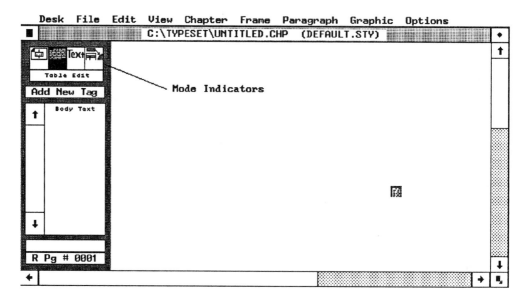

*Figure 1.7    Mode indicators displayed in the side bar.*

To change to the Text Editing mode, point at and click on the Text icon.

---

**Point** the mouse at the Text icon
**Click**
**Point** the mouse anywhere in the document window

---

Note what happened when you changed the mode. First, the Add New Tag box changed to read Set Font. The side bar changed to display a list of text attributes such as bold, italic, underline, etc. Also, the shape of the mouse cursor has changed to an "I" shaped icon. The information displayed in the side bar is mode dependent, meaning that it will change depending upon the current mode.

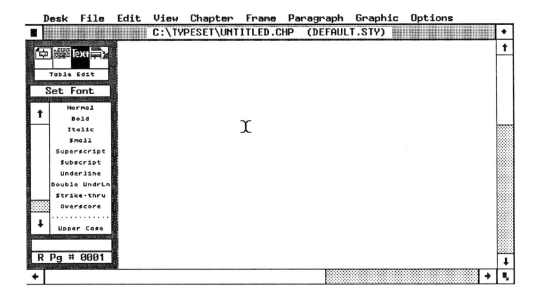

*Figure 1.8    Text mode changes mouse cursor and side bar displays.*

Also note that the main menu bar at the top of the screen is unchanged. In Ventura, the menu bar is a constant; that is, it stays the same in all modes.

Having different modes allows you to use the same basic screen display to carry out different tasks. Because mode changes are a common operation in Ventura, you can also change modes, using keyboard shortcuts or pull-down menus. (These commands and their keyboard shortcuts are located on the **View** menu.) The keyboard shortcuts for mode changes are as follows:

| Mode | Shortcut |
|------|----------|
| Frame Selection | [Ctrl/u] |
| Paragraph Tagging | [Ctrl/i] |
| Text Editing | [Ctrl/o] |
| Graphic Drawing | [Ctrl/p] |

To return to the Paragraph Tagging mode, enter

**[Ctrl/i]**

The side bar changes to display the option for the Paragraph Tagging mode. Note that the mouse cursor has disappeared from the display. You can return the mouse cursor by simply moving the mouse in any direction.

> **Move** the mouse

## VIEWING THE DOCUMENT

The largest single area on the display is the document window. In this area, the page or portion of the page you are working on will appear. That area is blank at the moment because you have not created anything or loaded any information into Ventura.

If you examine the scroll bars to the right and at the bottom of the window, you will see that part of the bar is white while the rest is gray. This indicates the document window is showing only part of the blank page.

In addition to the **operational modes** — Frame Setting, Paragraph Tagging, Text Editing, and Graphic Drawing — Ventura has **view modes**. These modes are used to reduce or enlarge the view of the document in the document window. Ventura has four viewing modes:

**Reduced**    This view reduces the text so that an entire page can be displayed at one time. This view is used to examine full-page layout, including headers and footers.

**Normal**    This view shows the text at about half the size of the enlarged view. Because the text is smaller, you can see twice as much of the page as you can in the enlarged view. This view is the most commonly used view and can be used for making format changes to text at the paragraph level.

**Enlarged**    This view shows the text at maximum enlargement and is used when you need to see and work with small details in the text.

**Facing Pages**    This view reduces the text even farther so that two pages — a left and a right — can be seen at one time. This view is used to compare formatting differences between left and right pages.

The keyboard shortcuts for view modes are as follows:

| Mode | Shortcut |
| --- | --- |
| Reduced (full page) | [Ctrl/r] |
| Normal | [Ctrl/n] |
| Enlarged | [Ctrl/e] |
| Facing Pages | none |

The current view mode is the **normal** mode. Change to the reduced mode by entering

**[Ctrl/r]**

You now have the page displayed in the **reduced** mode. In this mode, you can see the entire page displayed. Note also that the scroll bars are solid white, indicating that you are seeing all of the page in the document window.

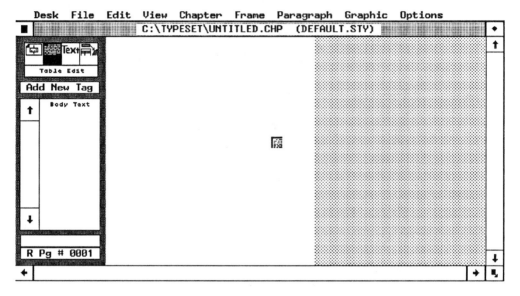

*Figure 1.9    Reduced display mode.*

The right side of the document window is gray, indicating that the page fills only the left side of the document window.

## Column Guides

The blank window that Ventura shows may be a bit misleading when it comes to entering or formatting text. Ventura is a highly structured program and automatically sets margins on the page. When you enter text, it is forced to fit inside the margins in the same way word processing programs can automatically wrap lines of text.

If you want to see those margins, you can have Ventura display a guide that shows you where on the page the top, bottom, left, and right margins can be found. You can do this by using one of Ventura's screen display options. The options are located on the Options menu.

---

**Point** the mouse at Options

---

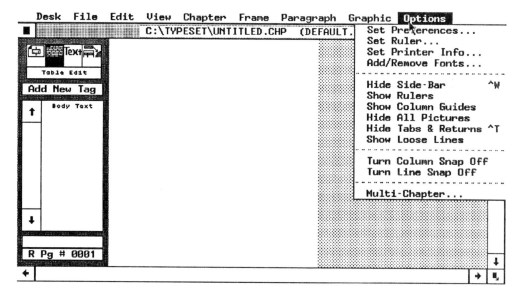

*Figure 1.10    Options drop-down menu.*

In the center of the list you will find **Show Column Guides**. The name "column guides" refers to the fact that Ventura will display one set of margin guides for each column on the page. Currently, there is only one column set for this page.

---

**Point** the mouse at Show Column Guides
**Click**

---

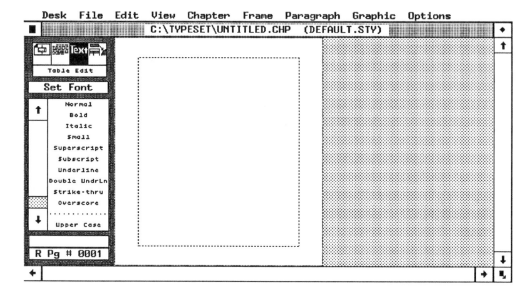

*Figure 1.11   Column guides displayed.*

These lines show the margins on the page. Currently, the lines form a right angle, indicating that this is the upper left corner of the page. As you move the cursor around the page, the column guides will appear whenever the cursor comes near one of the margins. Keep in mind that there will be times during which you will not see the column guides in the document window even though you have turned them on because your document window is positioned in the center of your document — too far from any margin for the column guides to be displayed. You also can confirm your position by looking at the position of the white block on the horizontal and vertical scroll bars.

The lines are called "column" guides because Ventura can display text in more than one column on the page. When you have selected multiple-column layouts, you will see several sets of column guides, each set indicating the margins for one of the columns of text. For now, all text will be entered into a single column, so there will be only one set of column guides on each page.

# VENTURA DOCUMENTS

Before you begin to enter text into a Ventura document, you should understand some important concepts that are fundamental to all Ventura operations.

## How Ventura Differs from Word Processing

Many people using Ventura have had some previous experience with microcomputer software (e.g., WordStar, MultiMate, WordPerfect, PFS Write, or Microsoft Word.) All these programs allow you to create and revise documents easily, as well as check spelling. Ventura is not meant to replace your word processing program. Word processors can edit, revise, move, and copy text and check spelling more efficiently than Ventura.

Ventura is a **page layout** program. Its features allow you to arrange and format the text on the page. Ventura also has the advantage of a graphics screen display so that the text on the screen accurately represents the way the final printed page will look. Changes in print size and style, lines, boxes, drawings, and other images will appear on the screen as they will appear on the page. Also keep in mind that most printers will print at a higher resolution than the screen display. For example, the HP LaserJet printers have a resolution of 90,000 dots per square inch. An EGA screen display will have only about 5,625 dots per square inch. For this reason the screen image will not be as sharp as the printed image but will provide a reasonable preview of the final printed page.

Ventura is a **highly structured** program. This means that all of the information placed onto any of the pages in a document is related to one of the units of organization in Ventura. The program has three levels of organization:

**Chapter**  A **chapter** is the largest unit of organization in Ventura. All of the information that creates a single document is coordinated by the chapter. In Ventura, each document is called a chapter because a Ventura document can use several text and graphics files to create a single document. In this book, the words "document" and "chapter" will have the same meaning. The term **file** is used to refer to units of information stored on the disk, which can contain any type of information.

Chapter operations cover items such as page headers and footers, footnotes, and page size and orientation.

**Frame**

Within each chapter, Ventura organizes information into **frames**. A frame can contain information drawn from a single text or graphics file. The simplest Ventura chapter has only one frame. This frame is called the **underlying** or **master** frame, and it is automatically created when you start a Ventura document. The column guides currently displayed on the screen outline the underlying frame of the current chapter. When you add information such as text, drawings, or graphics from other files, you will add more frames to the chapter. In this book, the terms "master frame" and "underlying frame" are equivalent.

Frame operations cover topics such as margins, columns, lines, and boxes.

**Paragraph**

If a frame contains text, as opposed to a drawing or graphic image, the text is organized in **paragraphs**. In Ventura, each paragraph is assigned a complete set of typographical settings for font, spacing, alignment, tab settings, etc. Unlike word processing programs, such as WordPerfect, in Ventura, the settings for each paragraph are not stored within the text of the document. Instead, each group of unique settings is given a special name, called a **tag**. Every paragraph in the document must be assigned a tag. Instead of allowing you to format an individual paragraph, Ventura requires that you format the paragraph tag. Ventura then searches the document for all of the paragraphs assocated with that tag and updates their format to match the current tag definition.

Ventura automatically creates a tag called **Body Text**. This tag is automatically assigned to all paragraphs unless you select a different tag.

This system is more structured than the average word processing program. (Microsoft Word is an exception. Like Ventura, it uses tags to define paragraph formatting.) The advantage is that your documents will have greater consistency because the program will automatically update the text when formatting changes take place.

If you use a free-form word processing program such as WordPerfect, you will find that at first the highly structured approach of Ventura is a bit confining, but after you create a few chapters, you will see that Ventura's approach to document creation has a number of important advantages that simplify the complicated process of page layout.

You are now ready to begin creating your first document in Ventura. This first document will be the simplest document you create in Ventura. In each succeeding chapter, you will create increasingly more complex documents.

## Entering Text

As you progress in using Ventura you will almost always prepare the text of the document with your favorite word processing program; however, it is possible to create a document directly in Ventura.

When you execute a document in this way, Ventura creates a separate file for your text. This is a helpful feature because the text entered into the master frame is saved in a file that can be easily accessed by a word processor even though it was entered directly into Ventura. At some later point, you can use your word processor to edit or spell check the document that was begun in Ventura.

To enter text, you must first place Ventura in the Text Editing mode. In this mode, Ventura allows you to enter and delete text. You can also underline, bold, italicize, and change the capitalization of text. The Text Editing mode operates in a manner similar to the editing modes in most word processing programs. The main difference is that Ventura allows you to use the mouse to edit text.

You can tell what mode you are in by looking at the mode indicator box in the upper left corner of the screen display. Currently, the Paragraph Tagging mode is active. Change to the Text Editing mode by selecting the Text icon.

---

**Point** the mouse at Text icon
**Click**

---

The mode indicator highlights the Text icon. Also note that the cursor has changed to a new "I" shape for text editing.

## Zooming onto a Page

When you are in a reduced display mode, you can change to one of the more detailed display modes by using the cursor and key combination shortcuts. The trick is to indicate which part of the page you want to display in the enlarged window by placing the mouse cursor on the part of the page that you want to enlarge.

In this case, you want to enlarge the upper left corner of the page. The area within the column guides is the text area on the page. The area outside the column guides is the margin space.

**Point** the mouse at upper left corner of the column guides

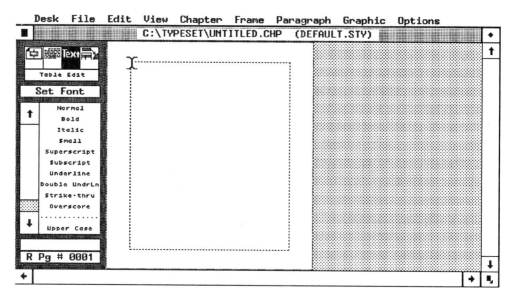

*Figure 1.12   Mouse cursor positioned on column guides.*

Use the key combination shortcut to place the display in the enlarged mode. Enter

**[Ctrl/e]**

Ventura enlarges the upper left corner of the screen.

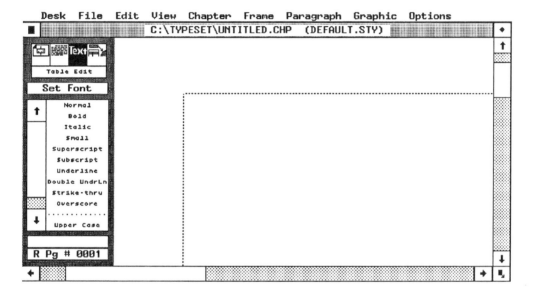

*Figure 1.13    Enlarged view of page.*

To begin the actual text editing, you need to activate the frame. This is done by pointing the mouse anywhere inside the frame outlined by the column guides and then clicking the mouse.

**Point** the mouse inside the frame
**Click**

Ventura responds by displaying two new items on the screen. The first is a thin vertical line that is blinking in the upper left corner of the screen. This line is the **text cursor**, and it functions like the cursor in a standard word processing application. Next to the text cursor is a box, which is the **end-of-file marker**. This box is displayed to show you where the end of the text file is located, which is useful in determining if all of the text from the file is contained in a given frame. Note also that the box in the side bar just above the page number box reads **End of File**, which confirms that the text cursor is located at the end of the text file.

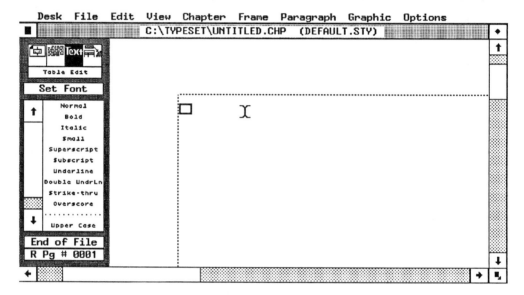

*Figure 1.14   Text cursor and end-of-file marker displayed.*

You can now enter text into the frame:

**Microcomputer Software** ⏎

The text appears on the screen as you enter it. The text cursor moves along with the text just like a word processor cursor does, while the mouse cursor's position is unaffected. Ventura also displays a ¶ (paragraph end) character at the end of the line, indicating that a return was entered at the end of the line. These symbols are displayed to help you determine were paragraph endings are placed into the text.

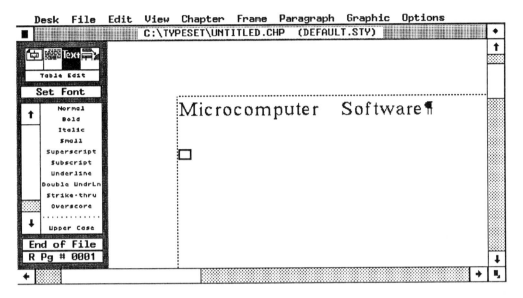

*Figure 1.15    Text entered into window.*

The special symbols displayed for the paragraph end and end of file are not printed as part of the document.  Ventura allows you to turn the display of these special characters off or on, using the [Ctrl/t] keyboard shortcut.  Enter

**[Ctrl/t]**

The document appears as it will print — without the special characters.  Turn the display of special characters back on by entering the [Ctrl/t] command a second time.

**[Ctrl/t]**

Continue by entering the following text:

**Since 1981 when the IBM PC was introduced**

Note what happened to the end of the line. As you typed, the line extended until it ran past the edge of the window. If you are using an EGA screen display, you should lose sight of the text following "IBM PC."

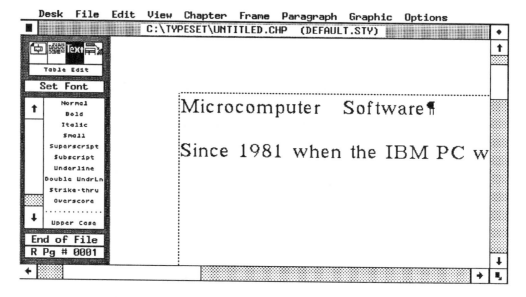

*Figure 1.16   Text extends past edge of document window.*

You might be surprised to see that Ventura does not automatically scroll the screen display to follow the text you are typing. Note that even though you cannot see it at this moment, the text is entered into the document frame. There are three ways you can deal with this problem:

**Scrolling**      Scrolling means that you change the relative location of the document window on the page. In this case, you would scroll the window to the right to see the right side of the line. Keep in mind that when you do, the left side of the text will be hidden from view.

**Reduce View**   Another method is to reduce the view to the normal or reduced display modes. This will reduce the size of the characters and show more of the page inside the document window.

**Side Bar**   The side bar display can be removed from the left side of the screen, providing more room for the document window. The disadvantage of this method is that you cannot access the items in the side bar when it is not displayed.

To see how these methods work, begin by scrolling to the right, using the bottom scroll bar. You can do this in two ways. One method is to click on the arrow at the right end of the bar. This will move the white portion of the scroll bar a fixed amount to the right for each click. To make a larger change, you can point the mouse at the white portion of the scroll bar and **drag** it to the right.

---

**Point** the mouse at the scroll bar right arrow
**Click**

---

The document window scrolls to the right, revealing more of the characters you typed. To move farther, repeat the action.

---

**Point** the mouse at the scroll bar right arrow
**Click**

---

On most screen displays, you should now have enough room to see the end of the line and continue text entry.

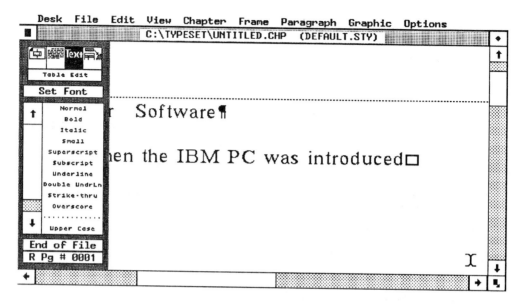

*Figure 1.17   Screen scrolled to the right.*

Note that scrolling the document window left the text cursor in the same place. You can now continue the entry. Remember to put a space after the word "introduced," and enter

**the quality and**

It seems that once again you are typing beyond the screen display. This time you can change the display mode to reveal more of the page. First, place the mouse cursor on "introduced."

---

**Point** the mouse at "introduced"

---

This will give Ventura a point of reference so that when you zoom out you will still see the part of the page you are currently concerned with. Change the display to the normal mode by entering

**[Ctrl/n]**

You can now see twice as much of the screen display as before.

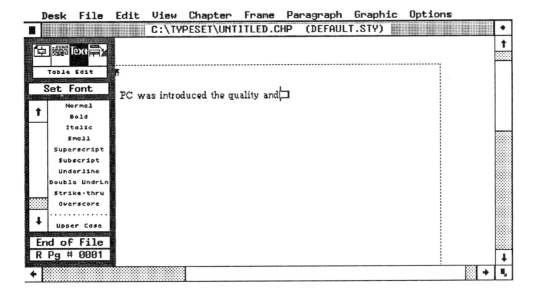

*Figure 1.18    Display mode changed to normal mode.*

Continue by entering the following text:

**quantity of software programs has increased dramatically.**

Note what happened this time. The text that you were typing reached the right column guide, which is the right margin of the page. Ventura, like most word processing programs, automatically created a new line, but because the document window was centered on the right side of the page, you couldn't see the text wrapped around to the left side of the page.

You can enlarge the size of the document window by suppressing the display of the side bar. Enter

**[Ctrl/w]**

Scroll the window to the left by clicking on the left scroll bar arrow.

| |
|---|
| **Click** twice on the scroll bar left arrow |

Now the text is a bit too far to the left because you cannot see the right column guide. To adjust the document window display more precisely, you can drag the white portion of the horizontal scroll bar until you have centered the text in the window. On an EGA monitor, it is possible to display both the left and right column guides at the same time while the side bar is turned off.

| |
|---|
| **Drag** the horizontal scroll bar |

Release the mouse button when you have centered the display so you can see the left and right column guides.

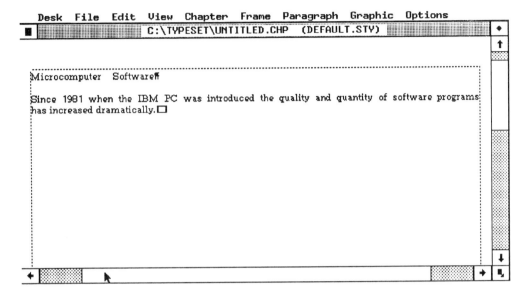

*Figure 1.19   Column guides displayed.*

Now enter the following:

**Examples are:** ⌐
**Lotus 1-2-3 Release 2**

Before you continue, take a careful look at the vertical spacing of the lines on the screen display. Notice that the two lines that make up the paragraph are spaced closely together; however, after each return, Ventura has automatically inserted additional space to separate paragraphs from one another.

This is another difference between Ventura and most word processing programs. In word processing programs, you must enter two returns at the end of a paragraph in order to create the space between the paragraphs, but Ventura takes a more sophisticated approach to the problem of vertical spacing. Ventura assumes that each time you enter a return you want to create a new paragraph. If you are using the default style sheet, DEFAULT.STY, Ventura automatically inserts additional space to mark the start of a new paragraph. (If you aren't familiar with the term "style sheet," don't worry; style sheets will be discussed in detail later in the book.)

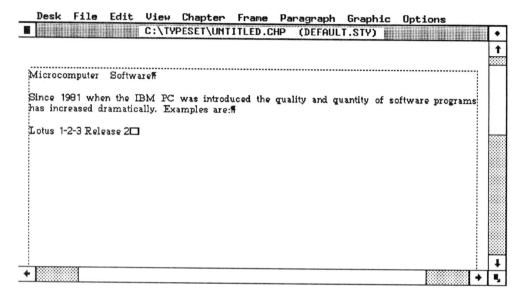

*Figure 1.20    Ventura adds space following paragraph ends.*

This approach to the space between paragraphs eliminates the need to enter an extra return at the end of each paragraph.  Keep in mind that when you prepare a document with a word processing program for use with Ventura, you must remember to eliminate the extra return characters normally inserted between paragraphs.

## Line Endings

In the current document you are about to make a list of items.  The items will consist of short lines that do not reach the right margin.

The problem is how to end each line.  For example, if you end the line with a return, Ventura will assume that you want to start a new paragraph and automatically insert the additional vertical spacing required between paragraphs.

But suppose you want to list the items with the same type of vertical spacing used to separate lines of text within the same paragraph. How could this be done when the lines you are typing are not long enough to reach the right margin?

Ventura allows a type of line ending different from the return. It is called a **line ending** in contrast to a **paragraph ending**. While a paragraph ending is entered simply by pressing the ⏎ (Return) key, the line ending is entered with the [Ctrl/⏎] key combination. When a line is ended with [Ctrl/⏎], Ventura spaces the next line as if it were part of the same paragraph. Enter

**[Ctrl/⏎]**
**WordPerfect 5.0 [Ctrl/⏎]**
**dBASE III Plus Version 1.1 ⏎**

Ventura spaces the short lines with the same vertical spacing used to separate lines in a paragraph and displays the ⏎ character on screen at the end of each line you ended with the [Ctrl/⏎] key combination. (Note that most word processing programs do not have a line-ending keystroke. The exception is Microsoft Word. However, Word uses [Shift/⏎] instead of [Ctrl/⏎] as the line-ending keystroke.)

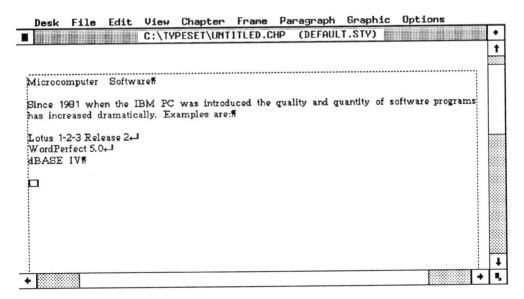

*Figure 1.21   Line endings used to control spacing.*

Enter the following paragraph, but do not press the Return key at the end of the paragraph:

**These programs have evolved through several versions and will continue to change as the computer industry provides faster and more powerful computers on which to run applications.**

## Cut and Paste

Ventura does not possess the sophisticated editing capabilities of full-powered word processing programs; however, with Ventura you can insert, delete, move, and copy text.

Ventura's text entry is in an **insert mode**, which means that any characters you add to the document are automatically inserted where the text cursor is positioned. The Del (Delete) and Backspace keys will remove individual characters. You can also move or copy larger blocks of text.

Suppose you wanted to insert the word "software" between the words "These" and "programs." You can move the text cursor with the arrow key or by clicking the mouse.

> **Point** the mouse at "p" in "program"
> **Click**

The text cursor now is positioned to the left of the letter "p." Enter

**software [Space bar]**

The word is inserted into the paragraph. Note that Ventura automatically adjusts the rest of the paragraph to accomodate the new entry.

Ventura also permits you to copy or move text. Suppose that you want to copy the text "Lotus 1-2-3 Release 2." The first step is to select the text you want to copy. Selecting is done by pointing the mouse at the beginning of the text you want to copy and dragging the mouse to the end of the selection. As you drag the mouse, Ventura will highlight the text.

---

**Point** the mouse at "L" in "Lotus"
**Drag** the mouse to "2"

---

The phrase is now highlighted.

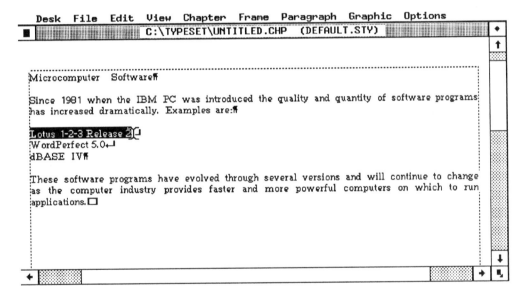

*Figure 1.22   Text selected with the mouse.*

To remove the text, you would enter [Del]. To copy the text, you would enter [Shift/Del]. Enter

**[Shift/Del]**

The highlighted text is copied in the memory of the computer. You can retrieve a copy of the text by entering [Ins]. Note that you can retrieve as many copies as you like. Position the text cursor at the end of the text by clicking on the end-of-file symbol.

> **Point** at the end-of-file symbol
> **Click**

Enter

**[Space bar]**
**[Ins]**

The text is copied to the new position in the document.

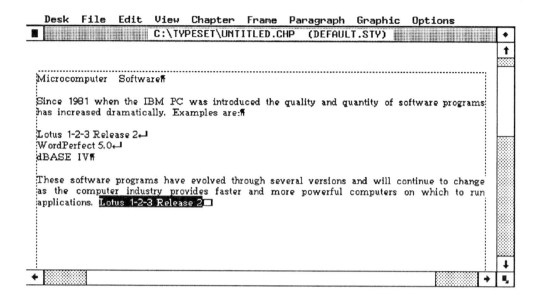

*Figure 1.23    Text copied to a new position.*

Complete the sentence by entering

→
**[Space bar]**
**is scheduled to be updated in 1989.**

## Text Enhancements

So far, you have created a document in which all the text looks fairly similar. Ventura allows you to add a number of enhancements to text, such as bold, italic, underline, or changes in font typeface and size. These options are listed in the side bar. Recall that you turned off the side bar display to enlarge the document window. In order to add text enhancements, you will not need to turn on the side bar display. Enter

**[Ctrl/w]**

There are two ways to enhance text in the text entry mode. You can use the side bar list to create bold, italic, small, underline, superscript, or subscript effects or change the case (upper and lower) of text. Ventura also provides an option called Capitalize. **Capitalize** makes the first letter of each highlighted word uppercase and the remaining letters lowercase. These enhancements will leave the size and typeface of the characters the same.

The other option is to select the **Set Font** box. This option permits you to change the print character typeface and point size. The term **fonts** refers to the shape and style of the letters. Some print styles vary the thickness of the lines used to make up the characters. Dutch, Times-Roman, or Text fonts feature this type of character. Other fonts use a uniform line thickness for their characters. Swiss and Helvetica fonts use this style. **Point size** refers to the size of the letter. The larger the point size, the larger the letter. Keep in mind that when you change the point size of a character in Ventura, you change both horizontal and vertical spacing.

Suppose that you want to bold the words "IBM PC." The first step is to highlight the words you want to change.

---

**Point** the mouse at "I"
**Drag** to "C"

---

To change the highlighted text to bold, select **Bold** from the side bar list.

---

**Point** the mouse at Bold
**Click**

---

Because the text is still highlighted, the effect may be hard to see. You can remove the highlight by pointing the mouse cursor anywhere in the document window and clicking the mouse button.

The next step is to change the names of the software program to italic text. Use the mouse to highlight all of the text beginning with "Lotus" to the end of "dBASE IV." When you point at a block of text, you don't need to be exact. For example, you can begin highlighting by pointing the mouse cursor to the left of the word "Lotus" in the margin area on the left side of the screen. Next, hold down the mouse button and move diagonally toward the lower right corner of the text block. As you move the mouse, you will see that the highlighting covers all text between the two points.

> **Point** the mouse at "L"
> **Drag** to "V"

Change the text to italic by selecting Italic from the side bar.

> **Point** the mouse at Italic
> **Click**

The text is italicized.

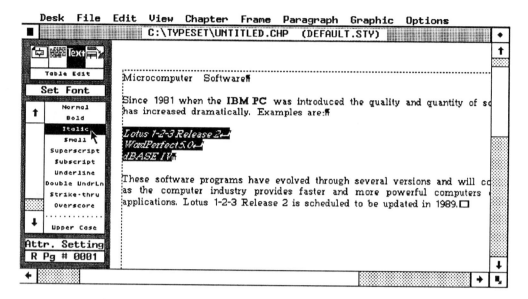

*Figure 1.24   Italicized text.*

Another option presented in the text mode is to change the case of text. You might want the title "Microcomputer Software" to appear as all uppercase characters.

Note that the term **highlight**, when used as an instruction, will refer to the process of highlighting text, using the mouse as discussed in this chapter.

> **Highlight** "Microcomputer Software"

The next step is to choose the case enhancement you want to use. At this point, only one case option — Upper Case — is visible on the side bar display; however, you will notice that the side bar display contains its own scroll bar with arrows at the top and bottom of its left side. This bar works in the same way as horizontal and vertical window position bars. Its purpose is to display additional options in the side bar display.

Note that a small portion of the bar just above the down arrow is shown in gray. This indicates that the list you currently see in the side bar display is only a partial list of all the possible options. Some options below Upper Case are not visible at this time.

To display the options,

> **Point** the mouse at the side bar's down arrow
> **Click**

The display shifts down one line, revealing a new option, Capitalize.

> **Click**

Another option — Lower Case — appears. Also notice that the solid portion of the bar has now reached the bottom of the bar, indicating that you have reached the end of the option list. The gray portion of the bar is now at the top, indicating that there are options at the top of the list that are not currently visible.

The bar system, as used throughout Ventura, enables Ventura to display options in windows of a fixed size. By looking for the gray portions of the bar, you can tell if parts of the list are currently hidden from your view. If the bar is completely solid, then you can assume that the list you see is a complete list of all options.

In this case, you want to change the text to all uppercase.

> **Point** the mouse at Upper Case
> **Click**

The text is changed to all uppercase.

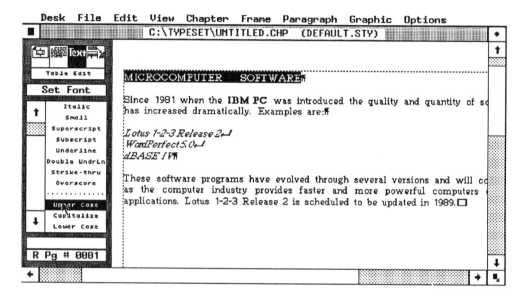

*Figure 1.25   Uppercase text.*

Ventura does not automatically remove the highlight from the text after you have selected a text enhancement. Rather, the highlight remains on the same portion of text until you select some other area by clicking the mouse. This is useful because you can easily change your mind about a text enhancement by selecting a different option.

Suppose that you are not sure which way you like the title. To see the title with only the first letter of each word in uppercase, you can select the Capitalize option.

---

**Point** the mouse at Capitalize
**Click**

---

The text is altered according to your selection. You can switch back and forth as many times as you like. Change the text back to all uppercase.

> **Point** the mouse at Upper Case
> **Click**

In addition, you might want the text underlined.

> **Point** the mouse at Underline
> **Click**

The text is underlined. Suppose you want to remove a text modification. The first option on the list, not currently visible, is Normal. To display the top of the option list,

> **Point** the mouse at side bar up arrow
> **Click** twice

To remove the underline,

> **Point** the mouse at Normal
> **Click**

Changing text to Normal removes all print modifications previously assigned to a section of the text. For example, suppose you had selected underline and italic but wanted only italic. When you change the text to Normal both the underline and italic are removed. You will then need to select Italic once again to get the text displayed as you want.

The Normal side bar option has no effect on the case (upper, lower, or capitalized) you have selected. Note that the text is still highlighted, meaning that it is still selected for further modifications.

## Changing Fonts

In addition to enhancing the existing text, you can change the font of a select group of characters by using the Set Font box. Font changes allow you to change the size and shape of the characters entered into the document. The heading is already selected, so you can choose a new font by clicking on the Set Font box. (The keyboard shortcut to activate Set Font is the [Ctrl/2] key combination.)

---

**Point** the mouse at Set Font
**Click**

---

Ventura displays the **FONT SETTING FOR SELECTED TEXT** dialog box.

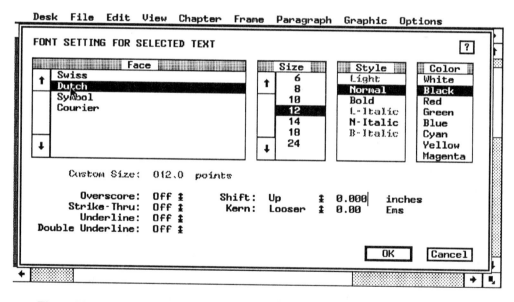

*Figure 1.26    FONT SETTING FOR SELECTED TEXT dialog box, HP LaserJet.*

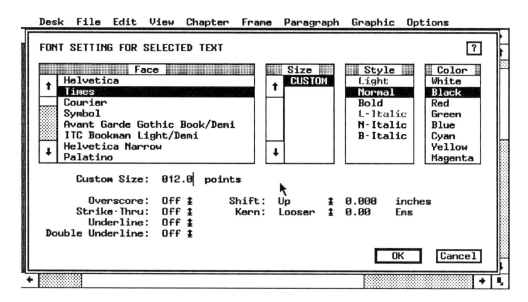

*Figure 1.27   FONT SETTING FOR SELECTED TEXT dialog box, Postscript printer.*

There are four specifications you can select for the highlighted text: Face, Size, Style, and Color. The first two, Face and Size, will be discussed here.

**Face**   This selection refers to the style and shape of the characters. The Face box lists the names of the fonts available. The list will vary depending on the specific printer you have. Figure 1.26 shows the dialog box for an HP LaserJet or compatible printer. Figure 1.27 shows the dialog box for a Postscript printer. In this example, four fonts — Swiss, Dutch, Courier, and Symbol — are listed. Your printer may cause a different list of fonts to be displayed. When fonts selected in this book are not available on your printer, choose the closest font as a substitute. To simplify selection, only two font types are used in this book: Dutch (also called Times or Roman) and Swiss (also called Helvetica). Most laser printers support at least these two fonts.

**Size**   The size of the letters in the fonts is measured in points (a term used in printing and typesetting). Points are measured as follows: Printers divide an inch into 6 parts. Each part is called **pica**. A pica is then divided into 12 parts, called **points**.

1 inch = 6 picas
1 pica = 12 points
1 inch = 72 points

While these measurements may seem strange to individuals not acquainted with printing terminology, many computer users are familiar with the fact that most computer printers print 6 lines of text in each inch of vertical space. Put another way, each line is 1/6th of an inch in height. Printers and typesetters reference each line as one pica, or 12 points, in height.

Suppose you want the title to stand out from the rest of the text. Swiss fonts are usually good for headings and titles because the lines are of uniform thickness. To select the Swiss font,

```
Point the mouse at Swiss
Click
```

The highlight moves from Dutch to Swiss. Now, change the point size to 18.

```
Point the mouse at 18
Click
```

Note that the Style box changes to display fewer style options. The large fonts are usually limited to one or two style options. In this case, the Swiss 18-point font is supplied in bold only, so there is no need to select Bold. The screen reflects the selections you have made.

Accept the changes by entering

↵

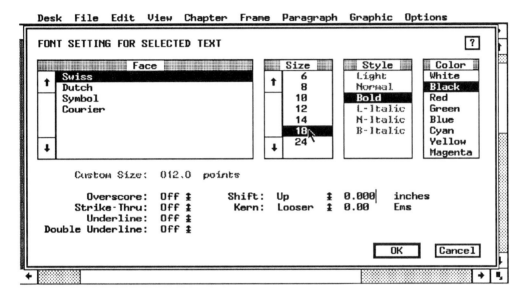

*Figure 1.28    Font set for Swiss 18-point bold.*

The document display shows the selected text as Swiss 18-point bold, while the unselected text remains as it was.

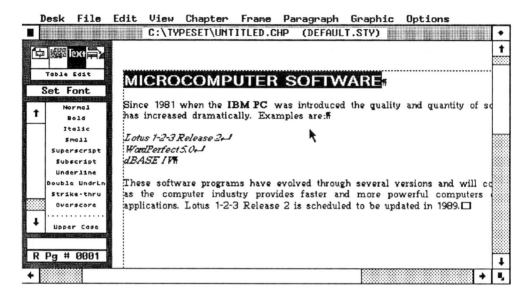

*Figure 1.29    Text is displayed with new font.*

Ventura displays the text as closely as possible to the final printed product. Text that is set for large fonts appears in proportion to the small text just as it will when it is printed.  This ability is often referred to by the acronym WYSIWYG, which stands for "What You See Is What You Get."  Keep in mind that the correspondence between the screen display and the final product is only approximate.  The screen display used on most computers does not contain a sufficient amount of pixels to emulate the resolution of a laser printer; however, the text does appear in the approximate proportions that it will have in the final printed product.

Note how increasing the point size of the title increased both its height and width. Ventura is an intelligent program when it comes to changes in fonts because it adjusts the layout of each page to accommodate changes in the size and shape of any part of the text.  As you learn to create more complex formats, you will appreciate this ability even more.

## The Text and Mouse Cursors

Normally, when Ventura is in the Text Editing mode, two cursors appear on the text display. The mouse cursor is controlled by the mouse, and the text cursor is controlled by arrow keys.

The text cursor allows you to enter and edit text just as you would in a word processing program in which the Left and Right Arrow keys move character by character, and the Up and Down Arrow keys move line by line.

The mouse cursor is independent of text lines and columns and responds to any movement you make with the mouse; however, there may be times when you want to achieve the character-by-character control offered by the text cursor instead.

For example, in the name "dBASE IV" the letters "BASE IV" are usually printed in a larger font than the "d" character, which means that you would highlight just those seven characters — "BASE IV" (remember that the space is also a character) — to change their font. You can use the mouse cursor, but it might be easier for some people to use the arrow keys to control selection. This is especially true when the existing font is a small point size.

> **Point** the mouse between the "d" and "B" in "dBASE"
> **Click**

To select text, you can use a [Shift/Click] combination, which means that instead of dragging the highlight, you point at the end of the selection. Press and continue to hold down the Shift key, and click the mouse button. The text between the two points will be selected.

> **Point** the mouse at the end of the line
> **[Shift/Click]**

The text is highlighted. The font can be changed from the FONT SETTING FOR SELECTED TEXT dialog box, which can be accessed by using a keyboard shortcut ([Ctrl/2]) or by pointing at the Set Font box. Enter

**[Ctrl/2]**

The FONT SETTING FOR SELECTED TEXT dialog box appears. To change the font size,

```
Point the mouse at 14
Click
```

Then enter

⏎

The highlighted text is enlarged to 14-point size.

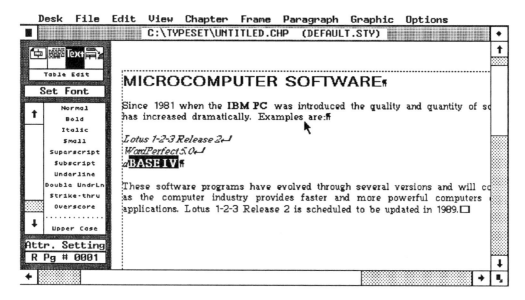

*Figure 1.30   Point size changed for selected characters.*

# PRINTING A DOCUMENT

You have now explored the basic editing and text enhancement functions in Ventura and are only beginning to tap the power of this program. Once you have established a good understanding of the basic techniques used by Ventura, the next logical step is to print the document you have created and see the final results of your work.

The Print command is found on the File menu. The File menu is used for all commands involving the input or output of information. Because printing is considered an output operation, it is included on the File menu.

---
**Point** the mouse at File
---

The File menu is displayed.

---

**Point** the mouse at To Print
**Click**

---

The PRINT INFORMATION dialog box appears.

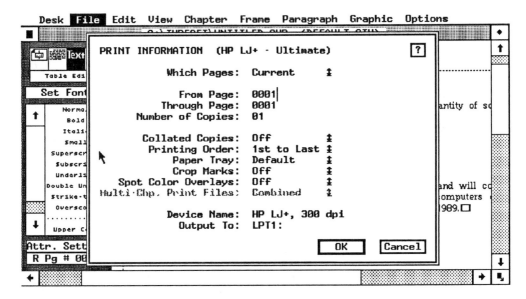

*Figure 1.31   PRINT INFORMATION dialog box.*

Ventura is set to automatically print the page that is displayed on the screen. Because the document consists of only one page, you can accept this setting. If you were working with a larger document you could choose to print all pages or a select range of pages, or you could choose to print the currently displayed page. To begin printing, enter

↵

Ventura loads the files needed to print the document and then displays a box that tells you which page is being printed.

When you are printing large documents, this feature is handy. It helps you keep track of how far the printing has progressed. Pressing [Esc] cancels the printing and returns to the document display. Note that pressing [Esc] does not cause Ventura to instantly terminate printing. It will stop when it completes the current page.

When the printing is complete, the normal display appears.

## SAVING A CHAPTER

The final step in the document cycle is to save the document in a chapter file you can use later.

The Save command is located on the File menu.

> **Point** the mouse at File
> **Point** at Save
> **Click**

Ventura displays the ITEM SELECTOR dialog box.

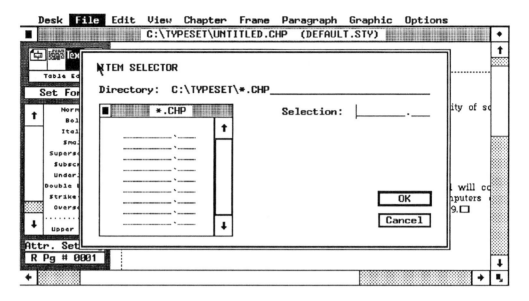

*Figure 1.32    ITEM SELECTOR dialog box for saving a file.*

This dialog box is displayed whenever you must select or enter filenames. Ventura automatically displays the directory specification **C:\TYPESET\*.CHP**. The **TYPESET** directory is automatically created by Ventura when you run the VPPREP installation program. If you copied the sample files during installation, you will see them listed in this display.

You can enter a standard DOS eight-character filename. Ventura automatically adds the CHP extension to the chapter files. Enter

**software** ⌐

The chapter file is saved and Ventura returns to the screen display, exactly as you left it. The only change is that the name of the chapter — **SOFTWARE.CHP** — appears at the top of the display.

When Ventura saved the SOFTWARE chapter, it also created a separate file called **software.txt**. This file contains the text you entered into the frame. Ventura does this so that you can edit, revise, or expand the text of the document without having to use Ventura. The **software.txt** file is formatted in standard ASCII text format. This file can be edited with most word processing programs. You will learn in the next chapter how to load a document created with a word processing program into Ventura.

To clear the work area so that you can start a new document, select New from the File menu. If you want to exit Ventura, choose Quit from the File menu.

To complete this first chapter, clear the work area or exit the Ventura program. If you select New, Ventura displays a new frame. If you select Quit, Ventura returns you to the operating system level.

---

**Point** the mouse at File
**Point** at New or Quit
**Click**

---

You have now completed your first Ventura document.

## SUMMARY

- **Display Modes**. Ventura's screen display has four modes. Each mode displays a different amount of text.

     **Facing Pages**   This mode displays two adjacent pages at one time.

     **Reduced**       This mode displays an entire page, including margins. This view is used to evaluate the overall layout of the text on the page.

**Normal**    The normal display mode is used for text entry and formatting. The amount of text displayed in this mode depends on the type of screen display attached to the computer. The higher the resolution, the more text you can view in the normal mode.

**Enlarged**    This mode displays the document at double the size of the normal mode. This mode is used to examine details of the document.

The modes can be changed by using the Views menu or, with the exception of the Facing Pages mode, by entering a Control key combination from the keyboard.

| Mode | Shortcut |
|------|----------|
| Reduced (full page) | [Ctrl/r] |
| Normal | [Ctrl/n] |
| Enlarged | [Ctrl/e] |
| Facing Pages | none |

- **Operational Modes**. Ventura has four basic operational modes. You can activate a mode by clicking on the mode's icon or by using Control key combinations.

**Frame Selection**    This mode allows you to add, change, or modify frames that contain text. Ventura automatically establishes a master frame for each chapter you create. You can use the master frame by itself or add more frames to the chapter. [Ctrl/u] places Ventura in the Frame Selection mode.

**Paragraph Tagging**    This mode is used to create and modify paragraph style tags. Tags are discussed in more detail in Chapter 2. [Ctrl/i] activates the Paragraph Tagging mode.

**Text**
**Editing**

This mode allows you add, edit, and revise actual text. This mode operates like a typical word processor. You can add enhancements to the text such as bold, italic, and underline in this mode. [Ctrl/o] activates the Text Editing mode.

**Graphic**
**Drawing**

This mode allows you to add non-text items such as lines and boxes to your chapter. [Ctrl/p] activates this mode.

- **Highlighting**. In the Text Editing mode, Ventura selects text for modification by highlight. Once text is highlighted, you can select enhancements from the side bar display. Text Editing mode modifications include font changes, print modifications, and capitalization options.

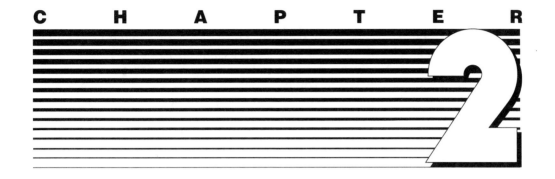

# PARAGRAPH FORMATTING

In Chapter 1, you learned about the basic structure of Ventura and how to enter and enhance text in a Ventura document. In this chapter, you will learn the next important concept in Ventura — paragraph formatting. **Paragraph formatting** refers to the techniques by which you can control various aspects of paragraph layout, including indents, alignment, spacing, tab settings, and character attributes. Ventura also allows you to add ruling lines and boxes to paragraph formats. (Ruling lines are straight lines that are added to the text to visually mark off different sections of text.)

The primary difference between the way Ventura formats paragraphs and the way standard word processing programs format paragraphs is that Ventura introduces the concept of paragraph tags and style sheets.

It is with the concepts of tags and styling that Ventura most dramatically departs from the standard word processing concepts found in programs such as WordStar, MultiMate, and WordPerfect. (Microsoft Word contains a styling feature that operates in a similar manner to Ventura. If you understand Word style sheets, you will find that Ventura operates in an almost identical fashion.) Most word processing programs allow for formatting of paragraphs, tabs, indents, and, to some degree, changes in font and point size. But all of these features are implemented manually. You must manually enter the commands to change each paragraph format or group of paragraph formats each time you want to vary from the default margins and tabs. If you want to replicate identical formats in two different places in one document, you must remember the exact settings and enter them manually each time you want that particular format.

This system has a number of drawbacks. Because it is your memory, not the computer's, that keeps track of the settings, it is hard to consistently format a document, let alone a series of related documents such as chapters in a book. Even worse, if you decide to change a format, you must search manually for each location in which the formatting occurs. You must change the setting in each location to match the new setting.

Ventura takes a different approach. With style sheets and tags, it separates the settings used to create a specific format from any specific area of the text. Ventura stores the settings in a file separate from the text, called a **style sheet** file. This means that a Ventura chapter is the result of the combination of two files: one that holds the text and another that holds the style specifications.

This chapter will show you how style sheets and paragraph tags are created, used, and stored and what advantages they provide over the manual formatting concept found in most word processing programs.

# THE TEXT FILE

In Chapter 1, you created a document by entering text directly into the master frame. While it is possible to create documents directly in Ventura, it is generally recommended that you initially prepare text by using a word processing program, preferably one that is directly compatible with Ventura. Such word processing programs include WordStar, WordPerfect, Microsoft Word, Multi-Mate, Displaywrite III or IV, XyWrite, and Xerox Writer. If you use a different word processing program, you can still import text into Ventura by converting your text into ASCII format. For example, PFS Write allows you to store text in an ASCII format. Another method is to convert your word processing files to a format Ventura recognizes. For example, WordStar 2000 users can convert their files to WordStar, which can then be used by Ventura.

There are many advantages to creating text with a word processor as opposed to the direct entry method discussed in Chapter 1. Word processing programs have better facilities for making entries and corrections, for example, search and replace functions, spell checking, and block move and copy operations. Word processing programs can handle files faster than Ventura because they use the built-in character set of the computer. Ventura uses its own typographical fonts, which operate more slowly. Word processing programs can generally handle larger files than can Ventura. Also, some advanced programs, such as Microsoft Word and WordPerfect, allow you to work on more than one document at a time.

With that explanation in mind, the next step is to use a word processing program to create the text of the document. As an example, the document you will create is a balance sheet showing the assets and liabilities of a business. This type of document normally requires figures aligned into columns. However, in a word processor, you need only enter the bare text without being concerned with text alignment. The alignment of the columns can be left for Ventura and will be accomplished after the document has been loaded into Ventura from the word processor.

Following is the text of the document to be prepared. The arrows show the places in the document where ⏎ (returns) should be entered. Notice that you should not leave blank lines between paragraphs. In Ventura, spacing between paragraphs is handled as part of the paragraph formatting options you will learn about as the chapter, as well as the book, progresses. The example assumes you are using WordPerfect 5.0 as the text processor. However, you can still prepare the same text in WordPerfect 4.2, Word, WordStar, or MultiMate. The default margins may be different from those in WordPerfect, but that is irrelevant as long as the returns are entered at the correct positions. Ventura will reformat the lines to match its own margins.

If you are using WordPerfect, save the file as **INVIT.WP**. Remember that Word-Perfect does not automatically add the WP extension; you must do so manually. While it is not necessary to add this extension to a document prepared with Word-Perfect, it is a good habit to get into so you can identify WordPerfect document files when they appear in a directory display. Note that the assumption is also made that you are storing your WordPerfect files in a directory called **c:\WP50**.

---

A PERSONAL INVITATION ⏎
VARIMATH 4-D ⏎
We would like to introduce you to what we believe is the new look and feel of Spreadsheet software for the year 2000. ⏎
Your hosts are Walter LaFish and Carl LaFong of Independent Computer Support Associates. ⏎
This is a personal invitation to a private preview for very important computer users at the ICSA hospitality suite 8657. ⏎
The Regal Regency Marquis Hotel ⏎
1770 Main Street ⏎
Fort Wayne, Indiana ⏎
Buffet and bar from 12:00 noon to 12:00 midnight, Tuesday, Wednesday and Thursday, September 1st, 2nd and 3rd. ⏎
Come and enjoy our hospitality and our ongoing product demonstration. ⏎

---

*Figure 2.1    INVIT.WP text file.*

Once you have completed and saved the document, return to the root directory by entering

**cd\** ⏎

Start Ventura by entering

**vp** ⏎

or

**vpprof** ⏎

## Loading a Text File

The benefit of using your favorite word processor to create a document is that you can take advantage of its text editing, thesaurus, and spelling features and reserve Ventura for the formatting tasks.

Most word processors use the text mode of the IBM PC and compatibles to display text because that display is usually easier to read. The computer can display large amounts of text more quickly in a word processor than it can in Ventura, which must calculate the exact visual proportions of all the characters it displays.

Now that you have the text file prepared, you can load it into a Ventura page.

```
Point the mouse at File
Point the mouse at Load Text/Picture
Click
```

Ventura displays the LOAD TEXT/PICTURE dialog box.

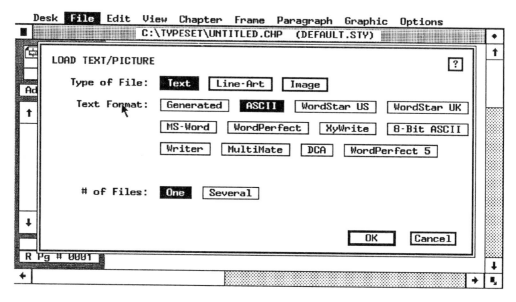

*Figure 2.2    LOAD TEXT/PICTURE dialog box.*

This is an important display that you will see quite often when working with Ventura. The menu allows you to load three types of files:

**Text**      These are files created with a word processor, a text editor, or applications that convert data to standard ASCII text files. The ASCII setting on the LOAD/TEXT PICTURE dialog box refers to files that end paragraphs with two carriage returns. Most PC applications create ASCII files with single carriage returns. These files should be loaded using the WordStar format. Many popular programs can create ASCII text files that contain at least part of the information they usually store in their own file format. For example, Lotus 1-2-3 can copy spreadsheet values and labels (not formulas) to a print file with a PRN extension. These files can be loaded as WordStar files. The procedure used to format Lotus 1-2-3 print files is covered in detail later in this book.

Other file types supported are WordStar, Microsoft Word, XyWrite, MultiMate, IBM DCA format, and Wordperfect 4.2 and 5.0.

| | |
|---|---|
| **Line-Art** | Line-art refers to a special type of graphic structure used to create picture files. Line-art comes from programs such as Lotus 1-2-3, AutoCad, MacPaint, and Gem Draw and consists of vector instructions that can be calculated to create an image. Line-art images can be scaled up or down with little loss of resolution. |
| **Image** | Image files are bit-mapped images that consist of a pixel-by-pixel description of the image. Ventura will support GEM image files and PC Paintbrush, MacPaint, and TIFF formats. |

To load a text file, you must make sure the Text box is highlighted. The initial setting in Ventura is to automatically highlight the Text box. If Text is not highlighted,

```
**Point** the mouse at Text
**Click**
```

Note that when you select Text, the options for text file formats appear.

Once text is selected, the next step is to select file type. As mentioned previously, in this book the assumption is made that you are working with WordPerfect 5.0. If you use a different word processor, select the file type for the word processor you used to create the text file.

```
**Point** the mouse at WordPerfect 5
**Click**
```

With the setting correctly selected, enter

⏎

Ventura displays the **ITEM SELECTOR** dialog box.

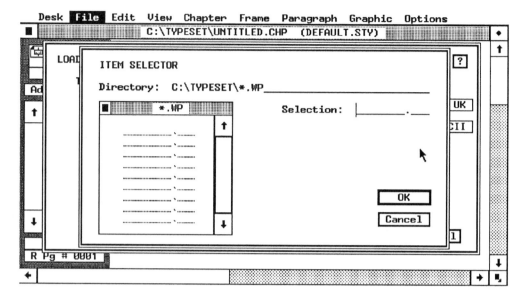

*Figure 2.3     ITEM SELECTOR dialog box for loading a text file.*

The ITEM SELECTOR dialog box is also an important one to understand because Ventura uses it to represent the DOS concepts of drives, directories, and files. The box on the left side of the ITEM SELECTOR dialog box lists the names of the files. Note that the top of the list box shows the title **\*.WP**, which means that only files with a WP extension will be displayed in the list. The list is probably empty at this point unless someone else has used the program.

The top line, labeled **Directory**, shows the name of the active DOS disk directory. In this example, the active directory is C:\TYPESET. The next line, labeled **Selection**, is used to enter the name of the file you want to load. It is not actually necessary to fill in this line by typing. You can select the name of the file with the mouse.

The upper left corner of the box contains the up level button, which is used to move back one DOS directory level. The center includes a listing of files that qualify under the current file specification. On the left side is a bar that indicates whether the list is longer than the nine files that can appear in the window at any one time.

In most cases, your word processing program is stored in its own directory on the hard disk. For example, WordPerfect is usually stored in a directory called \WP or \WP50, Microsoft Word in a directory called \WORD, and WordStar in a directory called \WS. Of course, you can install these programs into any directory you like; the ones suggested are only those typically used.

Ventura currently displays the contents of the **TYPESET** directory, which was created automatically when you installed Ventura. Ventura always defaults to the last directory used during the last session. If your directory display does not show **TYPESET**, it is because the last person using Ventura accessed some other directory.

Because you saved your text document, INVIT.WP, in the directory \WP50 — not \TYPESET — change the directory display by using the up level button.

---

**Point** the mouse at the up level button
**Click**

---

The display in the selector box changes to display the contents of the root directory of your hard disk. Note that your directory's contents will differ from the contents of the one displayed.

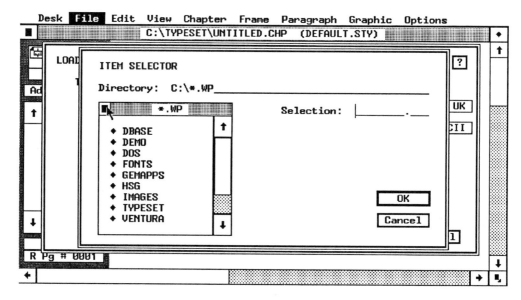

*Figure 2.4    Directories displayed in ITEM SELECTOR dialog box.*

The diamond that appears in front of the items indicates that these items are directories, not individual files. The file you want is located in the WP50 directory. If the WP50 directory is not visible, scroll the display in the ITEM SELECTOR dialog box. To do this,

---

**Point** the mouse at the down arrow
**Click**

---

Continue clicking until the WP50 directory is visible.

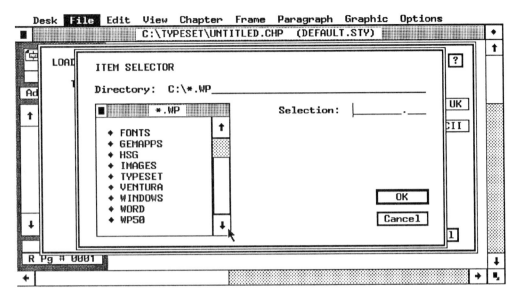

*Figure 2.5    Display scrolled to reveal WP50 directory.*

When you select the directory, you will display its contents in the ITEM SELEC-
TOR dialog box:

```
Point the mouse at WP50
Click
```

The selector displays those files in the WP50 directory with the WP extension,
one of which should be INVITE.WP. If your file doesn't appear on the screen,
scroll the display by clicking on the down arrow at the bottom of the selector window bar. Select the INVITE.WP file:

```
Point the mouse at INVITE.WP
Double Click
```

The two clicks must be issued in rapid succession. If the program fails to react when you click twice, try it again entering the click a little faster, or simply press Return (⏎).

Ventura loads your text file and switches into the Frame Setting mode. You can confirm that your file has been loaded by examining the side bar display, where you can see the name of the text file listed in the box.

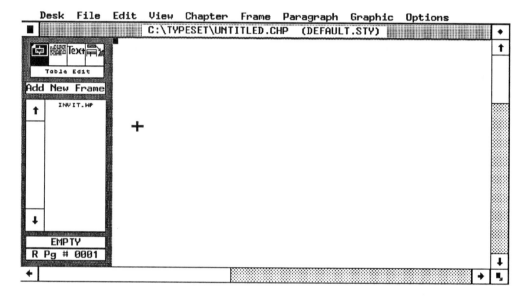

*Figure 2.6    File added to side bar list.*

The text is not automatically displayed on the page. Instead, Ventura waits for an indication as to which frame to insert the text in. Ventura uses the frames concept to place text and pictures at specific locations in a chapter. All chapters have at least one frame, which is automatically generated whenever work is begun on a chapter document. This frame is referred to as the **underlying** or **master frame** because it is the basic frame to which all the elements of Ventura are attached. In this book, the terms "underlying frame" and "master frame" are used interchangeably. The Ventura manual only uses the term "underlying frame."

In a simple document, all the text can be placed directly into the master frame by selecting the name of the text file from the side bar display.

> **Point** the mouse at INVITE.WP
> **Click**

The text is displayed in the page frame exactly as if you had typed it there.   Save
INVITE.WP as a Ventura chapter file.

> **Point** at File
> **Point** at Save
> **Click**

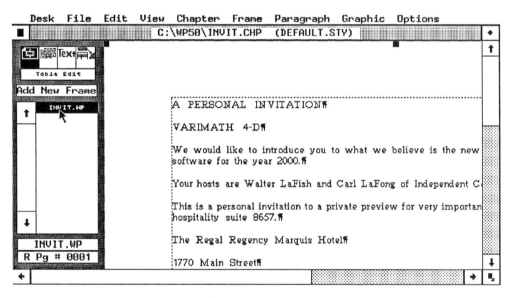

*Figure 2.7    Text loaded into Ventura document and saved as chapter file.*

Text loaded from a word processing file can be edited by placing Ventura into the Text Editing mode — [Ctrl/o] — and using the methods discussed in Chapter 1. Any changes made in Ventura will be saved in the text file. This means that Ventura editing changes will appear in the text if it is later edited again with the word processor.

## CREATING A STYLE TAG

You have already correctly entered the text, so the objective now is to change the text from plain text to a more dramatic presentation. This requires changing the format of some of the paragraphs.

For example, the first two lines of the text should be more vivid than the rest. There are a number of ways this can be done: change fonts, center the text, increase the amount of space between lines, or add ruling lines. All of these options require that you create a style tag. A **style tag** is a specification that communicates to Ventura how you want the text to appear.

Style tags are created and altered in the Paragraph Tagging mode. Change to this mode by entering

**[Ctrl/i]**

The mode indicator shows that the Paragraph symbol is highlighted. In addition, the side bar displays a style tag called **Body Text**. Ventura creates a master style tag that is automatically assigned to every paragraph unless another tag is assigned instead. You will always have a Body Text style tag; however, you can change the format of that tag any way you like.

For the moment, leave the Body Text style tag as it is. Your objective is to create some new styles for the parts of the text that need to stand out. Begin with the first line of the text, and select it for formatting. Because formatting affects an entire paragraph, you can point at any part of the paragraph to select it. The term "paragraph" is used in the same sense as in word processing, that is, to indicate all the text from one return to the next. The term "paragraph" has no grammatical significance in computer terminology. A short line, such as the first line in the example, is considered a paragraph because it ends with a return.

> **Point** the mouse at "A" in the first line of text
> **Click**

The entire paragraph is highlighted.

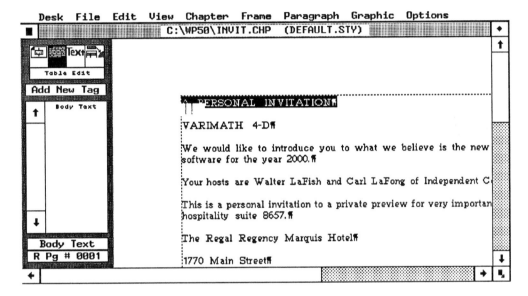

*Figure 2.8    Paragraph highlighted in Paragraph Tagging mode.*

Now, tell Ventura that you want to establish a new style tag by selecting the Add New Tag option from the box that appears just above the side bar display.

> **Point** the mouse at Add New Tag
> **Click**

Ventura displays the **ADD NEW TAG** dialog box.

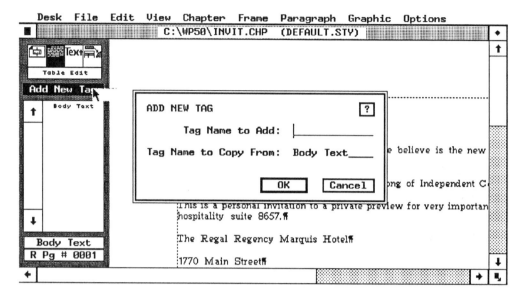

*Figure 2.9    ADD NEW TAG dialog box.*

You can now type in the name of the new style tag. The box also has a line for the name of the style tag you want to copy from. The two specifications indicate that new tags are never created from scratch. Instead, a new tag always begins as a copy of an existing tag. Ventura usually inserts the name of the tag for the currently highlighted paragraph as the tag to copy from. In this case, that tag is the only existing tag, **Body Text**.

The names of the tags can be up to 13 characters long and can contain spaces. Tag names can be entered with either upper- or lowercase letters; however, for reasons that will be discussed later in the book, it is better not to enter tag names as all uppercase characters.

Don't confuse tag names with filenames. Tag names can contain spaces because they are used only by Ventura. Filenames are used by Ventura and DOS, and must therefore conform to DOS filename conventions, which forbid the use of spaces in filenames.

The names should reflect as much as possible the purpose or appearance of the tag. This is not always easy to do in 13 characters, but don't be too concerned. Ventura allows you to rename tags if you think of a better name later. In this case, enter

**Greeting** ⌐

If you look only at the text, you won't see that much has been accomplished, but there are some other important changes. The side bar now shows two names, **Body Text** and **Greeting**, indicating that a new style tag has been added to the chapter. Also, the box above the page number reads **Greeting**, revealing that the paragraph currently highlighted is formatted using the Greeting style.

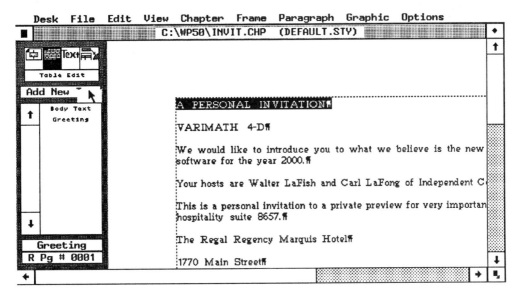

*Figure 2.10   New tag added to tag list.*

The highlighted paragraph looks the same as the other text because when the Greeting tag was created it copied all of its format settings from the only other tag that existed, Body Text. At this point, both tags consist of the same settings. This is always the case in Ventura. Now that you have tagged the first paragraph with the new tag, you can change the settings for that tag and, subsequently, the look of the text. Tag settings are controlled from the **Paragraph menu**.

---

**Point** the mouse at Paragraph

---

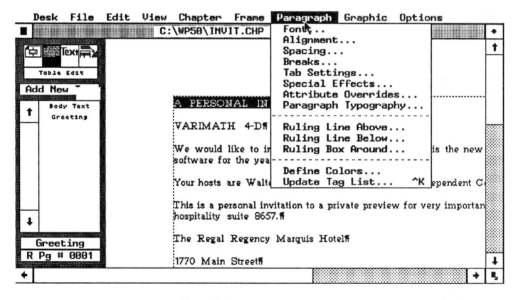

*Figure 2.11   Paragraph menu.*

Ventura displays the Paragraph menu, which consists of three types of operations (these types are separated by dotted lines when the menu is displayed):

**Paragraph Format**     These operations stress paragraph items such as margins, tabs, line spacing, text alignment, and some special paragraph formats available in Ventura.

| | |
|---|---|
| **Ruling**<br>**Lines** | Ventura can add ruling lines to your text. The lines can be placed above, below, and around text. If the text is divided into multiple columns, vertical lines can be added between the columns. |
| **Tag-Related**<br>**Operations** | These functions allow you to remove, rename, or print a style tag. To assign commonly used tags more quickly, you can also assign a specific style tag to a function key . If you are using colors, you can also define the exact shade and hue of colors used in Ventura. |

Begin by changing the font of the text.

> **Point** the mouse at Font
> **Click**

Ventura displays the Greeting FONT dialog box, which is exactly the same as the one that appeared when you used the Set Font option in Chapter 1. The only difference is that this time, the font you select will affect all of the text in any paragraph with the selected style tag, in this case Greeting. To select Swiss 14-point,

> **Point** the mouse at Swiss
> **Click**
> **Point** the mouse at 14
> **Click**

To complete the selection, enter

↵

The paragraph now appears as Swiss 14-point text.

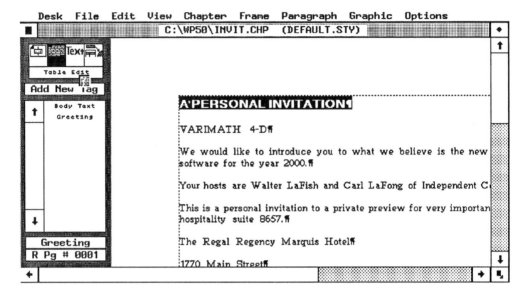

*Figure 2.12    Swiss font applied to Greeting tag.*

For this example, center the greeting. Centering is a characteristic that Ventura groups with alignment. To center the text,

---

**Point** the mouse at Paragraph
**Point** the mouse at Alignment
**Click**

---

Ventura displays the ALIGNMENT dialog box.

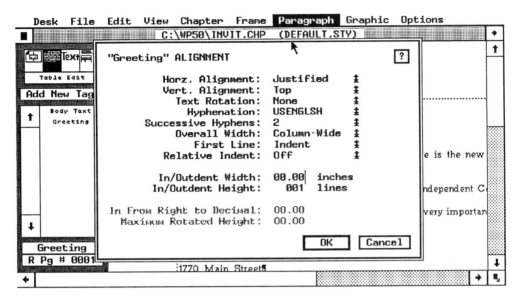

*Figure 2.13    ALIGNMENT dialog box.*

The first series of options on the menu controls the horizontal alignment of the text. To display the options for this item, you must point at the item and hold down the mouse button.

---

**Point** the mouse at Horz. Alignment
**Hold down** the mouse button

---

A box is displayed that lists left, center, right, justified, and decimal alignment.

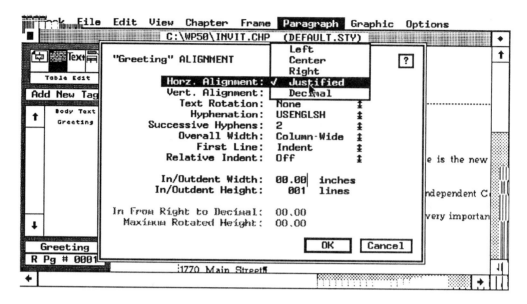

*Figure 2.14    Horz. Alignment options displayed.*

Select center alignment.

---

**Drag** the mouse to Center
**Release**

---

The word **Center** appears in the dialog box on the Horz. Alignment line, which tells you that you have selected center alignment for this paragraph tag. Complete the entry by pressing

⤶

The paragraph is now centered.

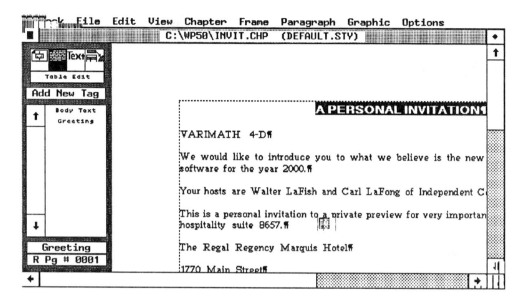

*Figure 2.15   Paragraph centered.*

## APPLYING A STYLE TAG

You have now prepared a style tag that carries with it the specifications you have selected from the Paragraph menu. The advantage of creating a style tag, as opposed to formatting just the highlighted paragraph, is that you can apply that tag to other paragraphs.

Suppose that you want the next line of text to have the same formatting. You can accomplish this by applying the style tag you have already created.

First, highlight the paragraph you want to tag.

---

**Point** the mouse at "VARIMATH"
**Click**

---

The highlight is removed from the first paragraph and placed on the second. To apply a style tag, you will use the mouse to select one of the names displayed on the side bar.

> **Point** the mouse at the tag name Greeting
> **Click**

Now the second paragraph has the same font and alignment as the first paragraph.

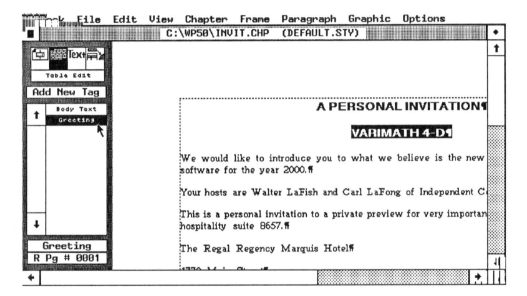

*Figure 2.16 Greeting tag applied to another paragraph.*

Tag the next paragraph.

> **Point** the mouse at "introduce"
> **Click**
> **Point** the mouse at Greeting
> **Click**

The text now is formatted exactly like the two preceding paragraphs. However, this is probably not the look you want. This paragraph is probably better off as body text. Fortunately, Ventura makes it easy to correct blunders. Simply select the Body Text style tag, and the text reverts to its previous format.

---

**Point** the mouse at Body Text
**Click**

---

Reassigning the paragraph its original tag causes the text to return to its previous format and style.

## SAVING A NEW STYLE

Because you have created a special style tag to format this document, you can save it as part of a **style sheet** so you can use it again.

Ventura allows as many style sheets as you want to create. The current style sheet, called DEFAULT, was created by the manufacturer. While it is possible to change this style sheet, it is a good idea to leave it as is. The DEFAULT should be used to start new styles from scratch. It is a good idea to create a new style sheet with a new name to store the formats that are used with this invitation.

You could wait until you have completed the document to save the style, but there is a compelling reason to do it now. When you get to the end of your work, it is easy to forget that Ventura saves the style under DEFAULT. To prevent this from happening, you should create a new style sheet as soon as you begin to alter an existing style sheet.

---

**Point** the mouse at File

---

To save the style sheet,

---

**Point** the mouse at Save as New Style
**Click**

---

The ITEM SELECTOR dialog box appears. You need to enter the name for the new style sheet you are creating. In this case, you will use the same name for the style sheet as you used for the text file, **INVIT**. Enter

**invit** ⏎

The new style sheet is created. Note that the top of the screen shows the name of the style sheet as **INVIT.STY**. Ventura automatically assigned the name **INVIT.CHP** as the name of the chapter file.

Now, save the chapter you are working on so you won't lose what you have accomplished so far. Ventura allows you to save the chapter at any point without removing the document from the screen. The **Save** command can be found on the File menu, or you can use the [Ctrl/s] keyboard shortcut. Enter

**[Ctrl/s]**

The top of the screen shows the name of the file, **INVIT.CHP**, and the style sheet, **INVIT.STY**.

## CHANGING THE BODY TEXT STYLE

Because this document is an invitation, you may want to create a standard body text that is different from normal body text.

For example, you may decide to center all the lines and print them in a font different from the one in which they are now displayed. All the paragraphs in the text, except the first two, are formatted as body text, so you can change the format of all of these paragraphs by changing the style of the Body Text paragraph tag. Remember, you should alter the Body Text style only when you are certain that you want to alter the format of a document's standard text paragraphs. Ventura automatically formats a paragraph as body text unless you specifically request a different tag. In this example, the change is acceptable because printing on invitations is often centered for the entire text.

The first paragraph is currently highlighted. To check for the style that is currently in effect for this paragraph, look at the box directly above the page number box. You can see the tag's name, **Body Text**. To change the alignment of Body Text to centered,

---

**Point** the mouse at Paragraph
**Point** the mouse at Alignment
**Click**

---

To select centered text from the menu,

---

**Point** the mouse at Horz. Alignment
**Click** and **Drag** to Center

---

Complete the entry by pressing

↵

All paragraphs currently tagged as Body Text are now centered.

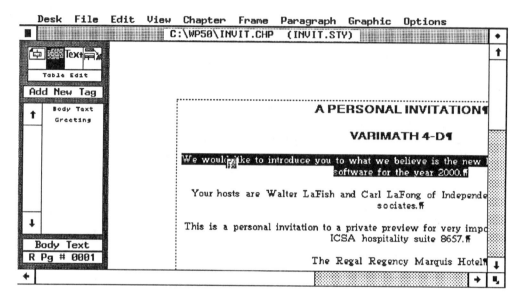

*Figure 2.17    Body Text changed to center alignment.*

Note that when the format of the highlighted paragraph was changed, the format of all the paragraphs that had the same style tag was also changed. Any changes made to a single paragraph with the Body Text style in turn affects all of the paragraphs in the document with that style tag. Also, keep in mind that any other documents that use the same style sheet will also be affected the next time they are loaded. It is important to remember which styles are used in which documents so that you do not accidentally change the format of a document. You can see how powerful changes in style tags can be when a tag is applied to a large portion of the text.

Next, change the font of the Body Text tag.

---

**Point** the mouse at Paragraph
**Point** the mouse at Font
**Click**

---

To change all the text to italic,

---

**Point** the mouse at N-Italic
**Click**

---

The "N" before Italic stands for Normal Italic. Some printers offer Light-Italic and Bold-Italic print as well. To complete the change, enter

↵

Now the text appears centered and italicized.

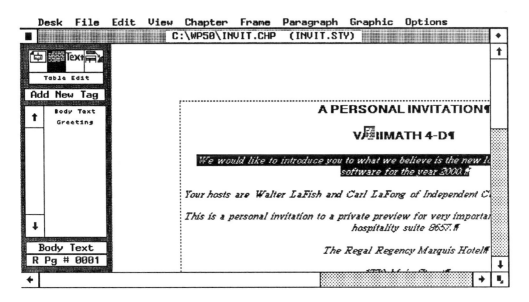

*Figure 2.18   Body Text changed to italic font.*

You have used styles to lay out the basic look of your document by using the Font and Alignment options. Ventura offers a number of other options that can change a document's appearance. Two very important ways to enhance the look of a document are to add spacing and ruling lines to vary the texture.

As an example, examine the second paragraph, the one that begins "Your hosts are. . . ."

To emphasize the names of the hosts, it might be advantageous to split the text into two parts following the word "are." Doing so allows the names of the hosts to be more noticeable because they begin a new line of text. To make this change, place Ventura into the Text Editing mode by entering

**[Ctrl/o]**

---

**Point** at the space between the words "are" and "Walter"
**Click**

---

Create a new line by entering

↵

Next, you will want to start a new line following the name "LaFong."

---

**Point** at the space between "LaFong" and "of"
**Click**

---

This time, enter a new line, not a new paragraph, command. Enter

**[Ctrl/⏎]**

Note that the two lines are spaced as if they are part of the same paragraph when the [Ctrl/⏎] key combination is used to split the lines.

Because the current paragraph is meant to have a different appearance from the rest of the text, it will need to have its own tag. In Ventura, every time you want a paragraph to have a different format from any of the other paragraphs, you must create a new tag. Change the mode to Paragraph Tagging by entering

**[Ctrl/i]**

> **Point** the mouse at "Walter"
> **Click**

To create the tag name,

> **Point** the mouse at Add New Tag
> **Click**

Enter the name of the new tag:

**Hosts ⏎**

Because the **Hosts** tag was copied from Body Text, the format of the new tag is identical to the way it was when it was tagged Body Text, but now you can use the Paragraph menu to change the appearance of the Hosts tag.

> **Exercise 1:** Change the point size of the font to 14-point. Try this on your own. The correct commands can be found under EX-1 at the end of this chapter.

Note that the fonts Ventura supplies have only a bold style for 14-point Dutch text. Ventura automatically changed the text from italic to bold because there was no italic option available for the typeface and point size you selected.

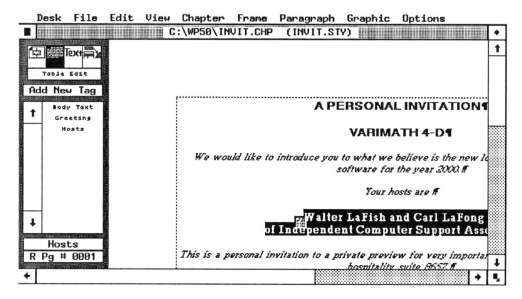

*Figure 2.19   Text with three tags defined.*

## RULING LINES

Another way of attracting attention to an area of a document is to divide the space, using ruling lines. A **ruling line** is simply a straight line that is drawn in the text area. Ventura allows you to create horizontal and vertical ruling lines, which you can specify to be drawn above and/or below or around a paragraph. Vertical ruling lines are used with text that is formatted in several columns. Ruling line commands are found on the Paragraph menu.

> **Point** the mouse at Paragraph

Ventura offers three types of ruling lines with paragraph text.

**Above**          This option draws a ruling line above the first line of the paragraph.

**Below**          This option draws a ruling line below the last line of a paragraph.

**Box**            This option is used to draw a box around the entire paragraph. Note that although Ventura will allow you to draw a box around any paragraph, this feature is really meant for use with paragraphs that consist of one or two lines only. This is because long paragraphs may be split between pages. If this happens, the ruling box is drawn around the part of the paragraph that falls on the first page but not around the part of the paragraph that appears on the second page.

In this case, you will want to draw lines both above and below the Hosts paragraph. Begin by adding a ruling line above the paragraph.

> **Point** the mouse at Ruling Line Above
> **Click**

Ventura displays the dialog box for drawing a line above a paragraph.

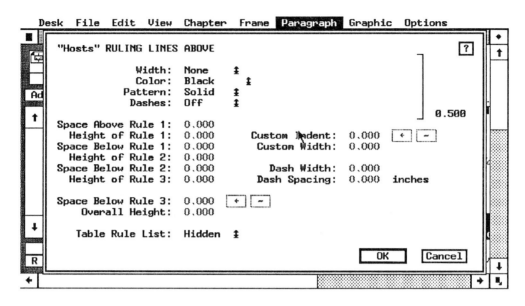

*Figure 2.20   RULING LINES ABOVE dialog box.*

The four options listed at the top of the display are as follows:

**Width**        This option is one of the two most important items in this dialog box. The width option tells Ventura how wide the ruling line should appear when it is drawn above the paragraph. The default setting is None. The width of the line is not set in specific distances but in relation to some other aspect of the paragraph such as the width of the text, margins, column, or frame.

**Black**        This option allows you to select the color of the line. The default is Black.

**Pattern**      This option allows you to select a gray tone pattern for the line. The default setting is Solid for a solid colored line.

**Dashes**       The line can appear as a series of dashes if this item is set On. The default setting is Off for a continuous line.

The first decision is how wide the line should be. In this particular case, you have two choices: text width or frame width. Note that in this case the frame, column, and margins all have the same width because this is a single frame, single column paragraph with no indents. Set the width for **Text** width.

---

**Point** the mouse at Width
**Drag** to Text
**Release**

---

The word **Text** appears next to the width option. You should also note that when you select a width option other than None, the number values listed in the center of the box change from gray (not available) to black (available). This is important because you need to fill in a value for the height of the line, or no line will appear even though you have selected Text as the width.

Position the dialog box cursor on the **Height of Rule 1** line by entering

↓

Clear the value from this line by entering

**[Esc]**

You can now enter the height of the ruling line. The value you enter is the number of inches in height for the ruling line. In traditional typography, the height of lines is expressed in points. For example 10- or 12-point text would typically use a 1-point ruling for standard, 3-point for heavy, or 1/2-point for light lines. Suppose you wanted to draw a standard height line. It takes a little arithmetic to translate points to inches. Recall that a point is 1/72 of an inch. If you divide 1 by 72, you get approximately 0.014 (0.0138888888889). Thus, a one-point line would be .014" high, a three-point line .042", and a half-point line would be .007". Enter a one-point line:

.014

When you enter the value, Ventura displays a line in the upper right corner of the screen that corresponds to the one you have selected. The display is drawn to a .5-inch scale. To see how the line looks within the context of the document, enter

⌐

Above the first line of the paragraph, Ventura draws a line that is exactly as wide as the text.

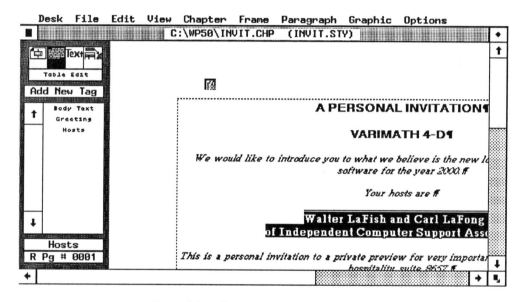

*Figure 2.21   Ruling line drawn above text.*

**Exercise 2:**     Because the paragraph consists of two lines of different lengths, it might look better if the ruling line were as wide as the column guides. Change the width setting to Frame width. Try this on your own. The correct commands can be found under EX-2 at the end of this chapter.

As a result of Exercise 2, the ruling line is drawn from left to right margins all the way across the frame.

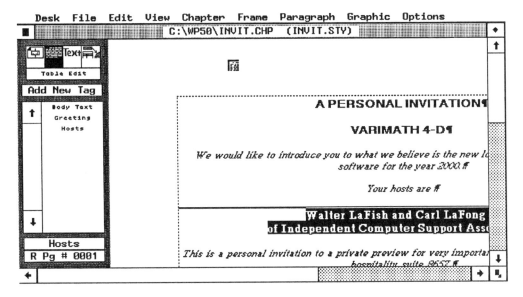

*Figure 2.22    Ruling line drawn across frame.*

## Space Above and Below Ruling Lines

In many cases, you might be content to simply draw the ruling line above the text and go on, but Ventura allows you to delve into the details of line placement. One factor that you might simply take for granted is the space above and below the ruling line. When you added the line, Ventura automatically placed the line a short distance above the text; however, Ventura allows you to change the spacing by adding more space above and/or below the ruling line.

To clearly understand why the text and ruling line look the way they do, it is necessary to ask some general questions about vertical spacing and learn some of the basic concepts of typography Ventura uses to format paragraph text.

If you examine any of the paragraphs that contain more than one line, you will notice that Ventura automatically places a specific amount of space between each line. That space is called inter-line spacing. **Inter-line spacing** is the distance between the bottom of one line and the bottom of the other. Naturally, that distance should be a bit larger than the point size of the characters. For example, if the point size of the text is 12 points, the spacing between the lines must be more than 12 points. A good rule of thumb is that the inter-line spacing should be at least 20% larger than the character size. Thus, if the text is 12 points, then the inter-line spacing should probably be at least 14.5 points high.

Ventura uses a special method to calculate the amount of space needed between lines; it takes into consideration the look of the typeface as well as other considerations, such as letters with descenders. A **descender** is a part of a letter that is printed below the bottom of the line. For example, the letter "g" in "LaFong" prints the tail of the "g" below the base line of the text. The same is true of the letters "p" and "y."

Exactly how much space is Ventura allowing between lines? You can find the exact value by looking at the SPACING dialog box on the Paragraph menu.

> **Point** the mouse at Paragraph
> **Point** at Spacing
> **Click**

The dialog box shows the current spacing settings used for the Hosts tag.

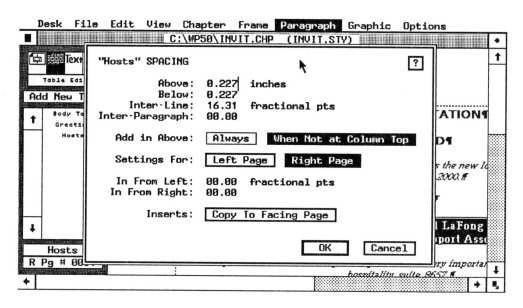

*Figure 2.23    SPACING dialog box for Hosts tag.*

The box displays four values used by Ventura to determine the spacing between lines and paragraphs.

**Above**        The value set for Above controls the amount of space inserted above a paragraph.

**Below**        This value sets the amount of space that follows a paragraph.

**Inter-Line**   This spacing is used to separate lines of text within the same paragraph and is similar to the line spacing specifications used by word processing programs.

**Inter-**       This option is used to add additional space between specific
**Paragraph**    paragraphs in addition to the normal inter-paragraph spacing. This option is not often used but adds flexibility to documents that have complicated spacing requirements.

The values displayed in the dialog box show the current values used by Ventura for the Hosts tag. The number you are most interested in at this point is the Inter-Line value, which is set at 16.31 fractional points. A **fractional point** is simply a precise measurement of the standard point size. Note that 16.31 is slightly larger than the 14.5 minimum inter-line value dictated by the 20% larger rule.

This display also tells you something about the placement of the ruling line. At this point, it is placed approximately four points (16.31 minus 12) above the top of the characters. This is the minimum amount of space allocated for the placement of the ruling line.

To improve the appearance of the line, you might want to increase both the space below and above the ruling line. Exit the SPACING dialog box without making any changes by entering

**[Ctrl/x]**

Suppose that you want to increase the amount of space between the ruling line and the text. Return to the RULING LINE ABOVE dialog box.

> **Point** the mouse at Paragraph
> **Point** the mouse at Ruling Line Above
> **Click**

In addition to setting the height of the ruling line, you can also enter values for space before and after the ruling line. To increase the space that separates the text from the ruling line, you can increase the Space Below Rule 1 value. In this case, increase the spacing by 6 points ($6 \times .014 = .084$). Enter

↓ ↓
**[Esc]**
**.084** ↵

The space between the ruling line and the text increases.

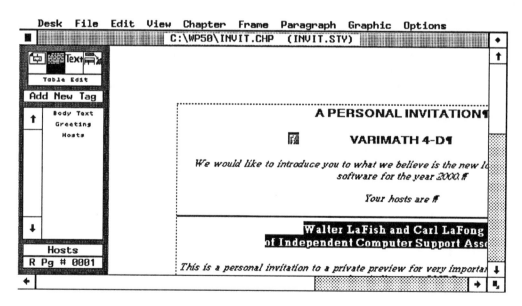

*Figure 2.24   Space increased between text and the ruling line.*

## Multiple Ruling Lines

Ventura allows you to add multiple ruling lines — up to three at a time — to the paragraph format so you can create rulings composed of several lines of different thicknesses.

Display the RULING LINE ABOVE dialog box.

---

**Point** the mouse at Paragraph
**Point** at Ruling Line Above
**Click**

---

To create a second ruling line, move the cursor to the line labeled **Height of Rule 2** by entering

↓ (3 times)

Make the ruling line about half the height of the first ruling line. Enter

**[Esc]**
**.007**

The upper right portion of the box shows the two ruling lines separated by .084". The separation between the lines is now controlled by the value entered for Space Below Rule 1. Recall that the value .084 was originally used to separate the first ruling line from the text, but now that you have added a second ruling line, the purpose of the first ruling line is to set the amount of space between the two ruling lines. The value entered for Space Below Rule 2 now controls the space between the lines and the text. If you were to add a third ruling line, then the Space Below Rule 3 would control line/text separation.

In this case, the value .084" is probably too large a separation for ruling lines of .014" and .007". Reduce the space between the lines to one point (.028") by entering

↑
**[Esc]**
**.028**

You can see that the space between the two lines, as shown in the upper right corner of the dialog box, has been reduced so that the two lines appear to form a single ruling pattern.

Before you exit the RULING LINE ABOVE dialog box, you need to remember that to create space between the text and the pair of ruling lines, the value of the Space Below Rule 2 setting should be increased. In this case, enter a value equal to 8 points, 0.112". Enter

↓ ↓
**[Esc]**
**.112**

Note that Ventura automatically calculates the overall height of the ruling lines and spacing in the **Overall Height** line displayed near the bottom of the dialog box. The sum of all the settings is .161", which means that the ruling lines and spaces will create .161" more distance between the Hosts paragraph and the preceding paragraph. This value helps you gauge how much space the ruling lines will add to the vertical layout of the document. Recall that the current inter-line spacing is 16.31 points. Converted to inches, this value is 0.227". You can see that the ruling lines you are adding to the paragraph are a little over 2/3 (.161") of the height of a normal line in the paragraph.

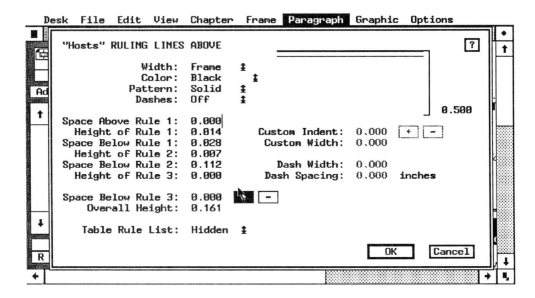

*Figure 2.25   Two lines defined for Hosts paragraph.*

Return to the document window display to see how the modified paragraph appears by entering

↵

The double ruling lines appear above the Hosts paragraph.

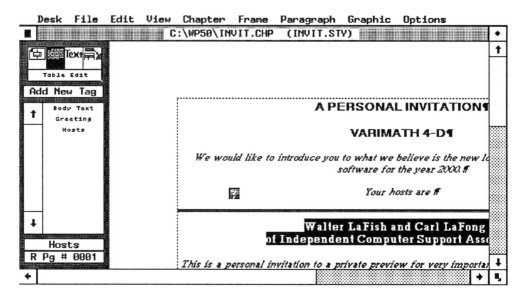

*Figure 2.26   Double ruling lines appear above Hosts paragraph.*

## Ruling Lines Below

In order to complete the tag definition for the Hosts paragraph, you will need to add a pair of ruling lines below the paragraph that is similar to the pair above the paragraph.

> **Point** the mouse at Paragraph
> **Point** the mouse at Ruling Line Below
> **Click**

Note that this dialog box appears to be exactly the same as the RULING LINE ABOVE dialog box. The key idea to remember is that the logic of the ruling lines and spacing is turned upside down. To create a symmetrical appearance, you would want to make rule 1 the thin half-point line and rule 2 the thicker one-point line. Also, consider how the space between the text and the ruling lines would be controlled. In this case, the value you enter for Space Above Rule 1 will create the space between the bottom of the text line and the beginning of the ruling line that is closest to the text.

Select Frame as the width for the ruling lines.

| |
|---|
| **Point** the mouse at Width<br>**Drag** to Text<br>**Click** |

**Exercise 3:** Enter the values for the lines and spaces. The goal is to create a ruling pair below the paragraph that is a mirror image of the ruling lines above the paragraph. Try this on your own. The correct commands can be found at the end of this chapter under EX-3.

Complete the entry by pressing

↵

The text now shows the ruling lines above and below the text.

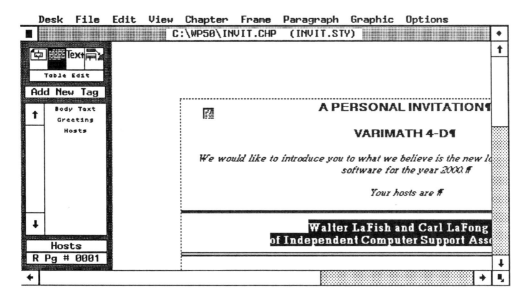

*Figure 2.27    Ruling lines added above and below Hosts paragraph.*

Now that you have created a complicated tag like Hosts, you can apply that tag and its settings to any paragraph. Suppose you wanted the paragraph that begins "We would like. . ." to be formatted with the Hosts formatting. Duplicating a paragraph format is easy once you have created a tag for that format.

---

**Point** the mouse at "We would like. . ."
**Click**

---

This highlights the paragraph you want to format. Next, select from the side bar list the tag you want to apply to this paragraph.

---

**Point** the mouse at Hosts
**Click**

---

The paragraph is automatically formatted to the specifications recorded for the Hosts tag.

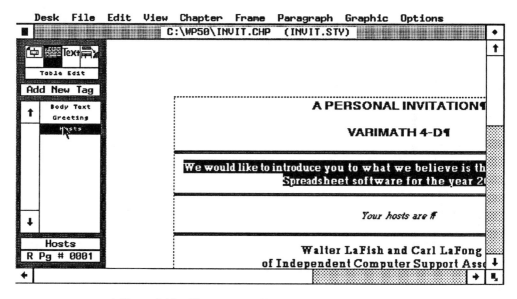

*Figure 2.28   Hosts tag applied to another paragraph.*

## Defining Shortcut Keys

Ventura provides another way to assign tags that does not involve using the mouse or the side bar. You can assign tags by using the function keys.

Ventura automatically assigns the Body Text tag to the F10 key. Enter

**[F10]**

The paragraph you just formatted with the Hosts tag is now formatted as Body Text. You can assign other tags in the style sheet to function keys F1 through F9. You can even override the setting for the F10 key if you do not want that key to be Body Text.

The operation that allows you to define function keys as tag commands is found on the Paragraph menu.

**Point** the mouse at Paragraph

The last option on the menu is called **Update Tag List**. Note that this option can also be accessed by entering the [Ctrl/k] keyboard shortcut.

**Point** the mouse at Update Tag List
**Click**

Ventura needs to know if changes in the chapter or the style sheet should be saved before you enter the Update Tag List information. Enter

↵

Ventura displays the UPDATE TAG LIST dialog box. This box contains five commands that help you manage your style operations.

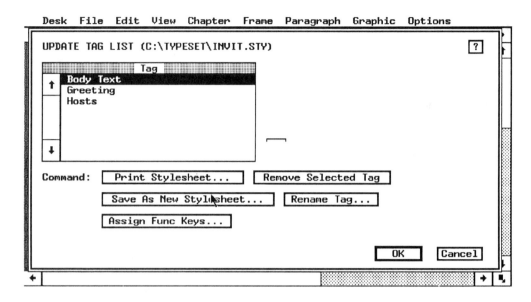

*Figure 2.29   UPDATE TAG dialog box.*

**Print Style Sheet**    This option is used to create a document that lists information about the current style sheet. Keep in mind that this option does not actually send any information to the printer. Rather, it creates a text file in the Ventura Generated text file format. The text file contains the style sheet information, and after it has been created, you can load this information as a Ventura document and then print the results. The text is tagged, but you must format that text with your own tags if you want to see the style sheet data printed in a specific style.

Keep in mind, however, that even with this option it is not possible to print a style sheet while you are working with a document.

**Remove**    You can use this option to remove a tag from the style
**Selected Tag**    sheet. You must also specify a tag to assign to the all of the paragraphs that formerly used the tag name that you are removing. In this way, no paragraph is ever without a tag.

**Rename Tag**  This option allows you to change the name of a tag. All paragraphs assigned to the renamed tag are tagged with the revised name.

**Save As**  This option stores a copy of the current style sheet under
**New Style Sheet**  a new style sheet name. This option is the same as the Save as New Style option on the File menu.

**Assign**  This option allows you to assign tag names to function
**Function Keys**  keys.

Select the Assign Function keys option.

---

**Point** the mouse at Assign Func. Keys
**Click**

---

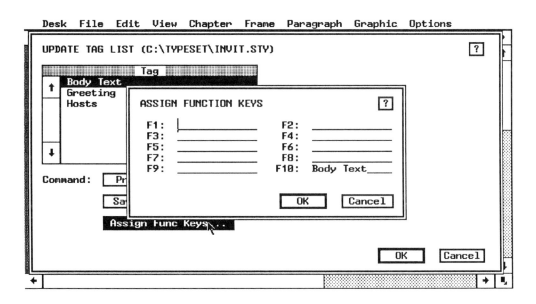

*Figure 2.30  ASSIGN FUNCTION KEYS dialog box.*

Ventura displays the function keys box. You can see that the F10 key is already assigned to Body Text. You can fill in the other nine with the names of tags from your style sheet. Enter

**Greeting** ↓
**Hosts** ↵

Accept these changes and exit the UPDATE TAG LIST dialog box by entering

↵

Ventura warns you that you have made modifications to the style sheet. Assigning the tags to function keys qualifies as a modification of the style sheet.

---

**Point** the mouse at Save
**Click**

---

You can now change the format of paragraphs by using the function keys. Enter

**[F1]**

The format changes to that of the Greeting tag. Enter

**[F2]**

The format is once again changed, this time to that of the Hosts tag.

# MANUAL KERNING

Most characters displayed and printed in Ventura fonts are proportionally spaced characters. This means that Ventura automatically allocates different amounts of horizontal space according to the size of each character. For example, the letter "M" is usually the widest letter in any typeface. It is naturally assigned the widest amount of space. The letter "l" is much narrower and is therefore assigned less space. This technique, known as **kerning**, creates the professionally typeset look you expect from Ventura documents.

In most cases, the spacing between characters is left to Ventura to automatically generate. However, in some cases, usually in headings that use large point sizes (for example, 18 or more points), you may find that the automatic spacing that looks fine in 10- or 12-point text leaves too much or too little space between certain pairs of letters.

To see how this problem occurs and how you can alter the spacing between characters, change the font of the Greeting tag to 24-point text.

---

**Point** the mouse at "VARIMATH"
**Click**
**Point** the mouse at the Paragraph menu heading
**Point** the mouse at Font
**Click**
**Point** the mouse at 24
**Click**
**Point** the mouse at OK
**Click**

---

The text tagged as Greeting is enlarged to 24-point.

When you look at the text, you may see that Ventura's automatic character spacing produces some character pairs whose spacing could be adjusted to produce a more pleasing appearance. Keep in mind that people who have never been involved in graphic arts may look at the text and see nothing that needs to be improved.

To understand kerning, you can look at some specific examples. The most commonly used example occurs in the word **VARIMATH**. The first two letters, "V" and "A," consist of vertical lines drawn on a slant; however, because they slant in opposite directions, there appears to be more space between V and A than between most of the other letters in the word. A similar spacing problem occurs later in the word with the letters "A" and "T." Because "A" slants away from "T," there appears to be too much space between those letters.

Ventura allows you to manually adjust the distance between characters, using the manual kerning operations. These operations take place in the Text Editing mode. Enter

**[Ctrl/o]**

Select a pair of letters whose spacing you want to adjust.

| **Highlight** the letters "VA" |
|---|

With the letters highlighted, you can change the spacing by using a combination of [Shift] and the ← or → keys. The [Shift/←] key combination reduces the amount of space, while the [Shift/→] key combination increases the amount of space. Enter

**[Shift/←]** (10 times)

The space between the "V" and the "A" is reduced.

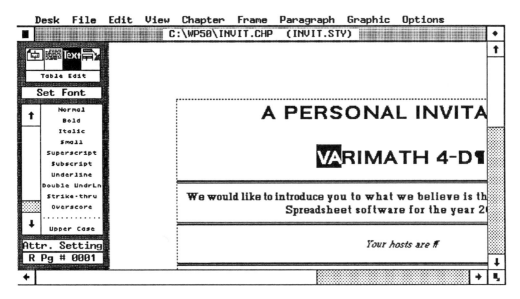

*Figure 2.31   Manual kerning used to move characters together.*

Perform the same operation on the "AT" pair in the same word.

---

**Highlight** the letters "AT"

---

Enter

**[Shift/←]**  (12 times)

Your screen should resemble the following:

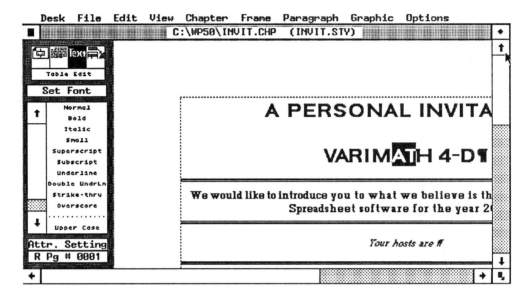

*Figure 2.32 "VARIMATH" kerned manually.*

## Spacing Between Paragraphs

The spacing between paragraphs is automatically generated by Ventura when you select the font for the style tag. Ventura automatically increases the amount of space between lines and paragraphs according to the point size of the font.

In the case of small point sizes (for example, 9, 10, or 12 points), there is seldom a need to change the spacing values, but when larger fonts are used, you may want to alter the way lines and paragraphs are spaced.

When you look at the current document, you can see that the amount of space between the first two paragraphs is larger than the distance between paragraphs with smaller fonts. In this sense, it can also be said that vertical spacing is set proportionally — according to the size of the font selected for that paragraph tag.

Suppose that you wanted to vary the spacing used by a particular paragraph tag. Recall that the Spacing dialog box that was previously displayed contained settings that controlled the amount of space used by the tag. Those settings can be used to alter the spacing between lines and paragraphs.

For this example, suppose you wanted to use spacing to make the first two lines of the document more distinct from the rest of the text. One way to do that is to increase the amount of space below the tag.

> **Point** the mouse at Paragraph
> **Point** the mouse at Spacing
> **Click**

The screen displays the spacing settings for the current tag, Greeting. Note that Ventura displays the space above and below in terms of inches but displays the inter-line spacing in terms of points. You may find this confusing. The reason is that entering fractional points is the most accurate measurement in Ventura. For example, the smallest value you can enter in inches is .001". But you can enter a value for points as small as 0.01 (remember, points are much smaller than inches). When you convert 0.01 points into inches, you get a value of 0.00014". It is recommended that inter-line spacing be entered as points rather than inches so that you get the best pagination possible in Ventura.

To increase the amount of space below the paragraph to 1", enter

↓
**[Esc]**
**1**
↵

The new spacing setting increases the separation between paragraphs that have been assigned the Greeting tag.

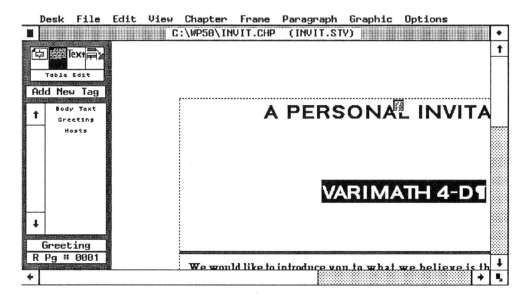

*Figure 2.33    Spacing increased below paragraph.*

Exactly how far are the paragraphs from each other? In typography, the distance is measured from the bottom of one line to the bottom — not the top — of the next. In this case, the space below is set for 1", and the inter-line spacing is set at 27.97 points. The total space between paragraphs in this case is *below space + inter-line space*. However, to make this calculation, you need to convert points to inches or inches to points so that you can add them together.

You can avoid actually calculating the values by getting Ventura to convert the values displayed in the dialog box.

---

**Point** the mouse at Paragraph
**Point** the mouse at Spacing
**Click**

---

To change the unit of measurement, point at the unit name and click.

> **Point** the mouse at fractional points
> **Click**

The value label changes to inches, and the value appears as .388. Thus, 27.97 points is equal to approximately .388 inches. This also reveals that Ventura usually sets the inter-line, above, and below spacing to the same value initially; however, that fact is not obvious because the inter-line spacing is displayed in points rather than inches. Thus, the distance between paragraphs is 1.000" + 0.388" = 1.388".

> **Point** the mouse at inches
> **Click**

This time, the unit of measurement changes to centimeters.

> **Point** the mouse at centimeters
> **Click**

The unit of measurement changes back to picas and points. Remember, a pica is a unit that consists of 12 points.

> **Point** the mouse at picas & points
> **Click**

The measurement returns to fractional points, the most precise measurement. You can toggle through these conversions as much as you want.

In examining the settings in this dialog box, you might wonder why the Below setting is the one that controls the space between paragraphs. What about the Above spacing? With the exception of the first and last paragraphs on a page, each paragraph will have another paragraph both above and below it. What happens to the value set for space above?

Ventura uses a rule to determine whether the above or below spacing setting is to be used in calculating the distance between paragraphs. When Ventura prepares to space paragraphs, it compares the below spacing of the first paragraph to the above spacing of the second paragraph. The setting with the largest measurement is used.

In the case of the Greeting tag, the Below paragraph setting is greater than the Above setting, so it is used for spacing, and because the 1" Below setting in Greeting is also larger than the Above setting for the Hosts tag, the spacing between these two paragraphs is 1.388".

The exception to this rule is the first paragraph on the page or at the top of a column in a multiple-column layout. The dialog box contains an **Add in Above** setting. This setting determines whether or not the Above spacing value is used at the top of a page or column. The default setting is to ignore above spacing when the paragraph falls at the top of a page or column, but selecting Always will cause blank space to appear above a paragraph at the top of a page or column.

Exit the dialog box by entering

**[Ctrl/x]**

## Reducing Vertical Spacing

In the previous section, you used increased vertical spacing to change the appearance of the text. In other cases, you might want to reduce the amount of space between paragraphs.

Although you cannot see them in the window, there are lines of text farther down on the page that need to have the spacing between them reduced. These lines contain the address.

Scroll down so that you can see the address of the hotel.

---

**Point** the mouse at the scroll bar down arrow
**Click** (5 times)

---

You can now see the three lines that give the address of the hotel.

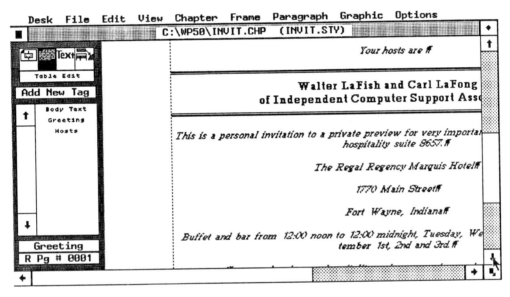

*Figure 2.34   Address visible after scrolling downward.*

In this case, you want to reduce the amount of space between the three lines that make up the address. You could simply delete the paragraph endings at the ends of the lines and replace them with line ending—[Ctrl/↵]—characters, which would cause Ventura to use the normal inter-line spacing for the text lines.

But suppose you wanted to reduce the amount of space so that the lines were spaced about a 1/2 a line farther apart than single-spaced lines, i.e., line-and-a-half spacing? In that case, you would need to create a new tag and alter the line spacing values. Create a new tag called **Address**.

Point the mouse at Add New Tag
Click

Enter

**Address** ⏎

Note that you created the new tag without having to highlight any of the paragraphs first; however, if you want to define attributes for that tag, you must select a paragraph first.

**Point** the mouse at "Regal"
**Click**
**Point** the mouse at the Address tag
**Click**

Display the SPACING dialog box.

**Point** the mouse at Paragraph
**Point** the mouse at Spacing
**Click**

The current line spacing settings for above, below, and inter-line are all for the same value. Note that .194" is approximately equal to 13.98 points. This setting helps you figure out the amount of space Ventura will insert between paragraphs. That distance would be the inter-line spacing plus the space above or below: 0.194"+0.194" = 0.388".

Recall that 0.388" was the line height of the lines in the Greeting tag. This makes sense because you selected 24-point characters for that tag. The current Address tag uses 12-point characters and has a line height that is exactly half as high as the Greeting tag lines. The values confirm the idea that Ventura increases or decreases line height according to the point size of the font used in that tag.

In this case, you want to reduce the above and below values by half, to 0.097". Enter

**[Esc]**
**.097 ↓**
**[Esc]**
**.097 ↵**

Nothing has happened to the document. All of the lines are spaced exactly as they were before. Your changes have not altered the spacing because the Address paragraph is surrounded by Body Text paragraphs. When Ventura calculates vertical spacing, it first compares the Below value of the Body Text tag with the Above value of the Address tag. In this case, Body Text has a larger value of .194" compared to the .097" Above value you set for the Address tag. Ventura therefore uses the Body Text Below value for the spacing. The same thing happens in reverse at the end of the paragraph. The Body Text Above value is greater than the Address below spacing value.

But suppose you tagged two consecutive paragraphs as Address paragraphs. What would be the result?

```
Point the mouse at "1770"
Click
Point the mouse at the Address tag
Click
```

The spacing between the two paragraphs with the same tag is reduced. This happens because when Ventura calculates the distance between two paragraphs tagged as Address, the Below value of the first paragraph and the above value of the second are both .097". The spacing between these paragraphs is displayed as .097".

Again, you must understand the spacing between the paragraphs tagged as Address and those tagged as Body Text is not reduced but stays the same. This is an important concept in Ventura. The calculation of vertical spacing may seem very complicated, but it is designed to create a system that can accommodate a large number of paragraph formats with a minimum of spacing problems. In this example, the system allows you to reduce space between paragraphs with the same tag while maintaining the correct spacing between paragraphs with different tags.

Add another line to the Address tag.

---

**Point** the mouse at "Fort"
**Click**
**Point** the mouse at the Address tag
**Click**

---

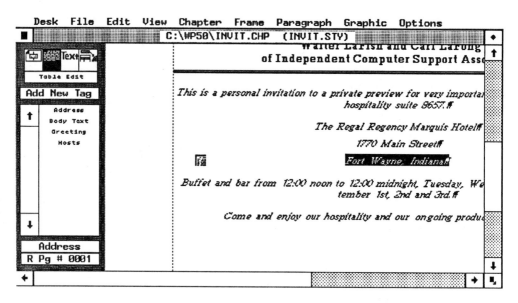

*Figure 2.35   Spacing adjusted with the Address tag.*

## Left/Right Spacing

In addition to the vertical spacing values that can be set for each paragraph, Ventura also allows you to create additional space on the left and right sides of paragraphs. These indents can be added to a paragraph tag from the SPACING dialog box, which is opened from the Paragraph menu.

For example, the Body Text paragraphs in this document tend to consist of one very long line followed by a very short line. It might improve the appearance of the document if you place additional space on the left and right sides of the paragraph to create more evenly distributed lines.

Select a Body Text paragraph.

> **Point** the mouse at "personal invitation"
> **Click**

Display the SPACING dialog box.

> **Point** the mouse at Paragraph
> **Point** the mouse at Spacing
> **Click**

If you look at the bottom half of the box, you will see two settings — one for **In From Left** spacing and the other for **In From Right** spacing. You can indent the paragraph from the current margins by entering values for these settings. Enter

↓ (4 times)

Note that the default unit of measurement for these settings is points. Change this measurement to inches.

---

**Point** the mouse at fractional pts
**Click**

---

You can now enter the indents in terms of inches. In this case, indent 1" from both the left and right margins. Enter

**[Esc]**
**01**
↓
**[Esc]**
**01** ⏎

The Body Text paragraphs are indented one inch from the left and right margins.

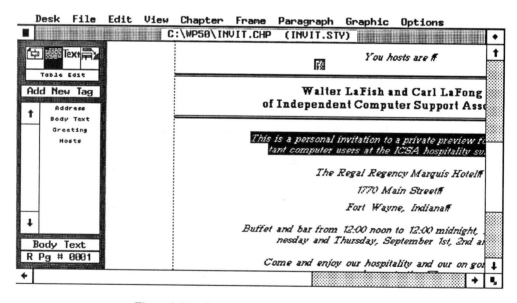

*Figure 2.36   Body Text indented from margins.*

## Side-by-Side Paragraphs

The use of indents allows you to indent paragraphs from the left and right margins. But indents can also be used to create a simple but useful type of column layout called **side-by-side** paragraphs.

Display the end of the document by scrolling downward.

---

**Point** the mouse at the scroll bar down arrow
**Click**
**Point** the mouse at scroll bar right arrow
**Click** twice

---

The last two paragraphs are centered between the margins with left and right indents.

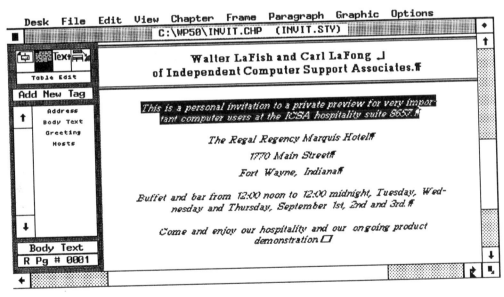

*Figure 2.37   Bottom of INVIT.CHP document.*

Suppose that in order to add more visual variety to the document, you want to print the two paragraphs not consecutively but side by side in columns. Ventura allows you to add column-aligned text to any document, even if you have not created a column layout for the page. The columns are created by using the left and right indent settings in the SPACING dialog box, which you can select from the Paragraph menu.

For an example of side-by-side paragraphs, you will create two tags, **Left Col** and **Right Col**, that will display and print paragraphs side by side instead of consecutively.

Begin by creating a left column paragraph format for the next-to-last paragraph in the document.

---

**Point** the mouse at "Buffet"
**Click**
**Point** the mouse Add New Tag
**Click**

---

Enter

**Left Col** ⏎

The first step is to change the alignment of the text to left alignment rather than center alignment to allow two paragraphs to be displayed side by side.

---

**Point** the mouse at Paragraph
**Point** the mouse at Alignment
**Click**
**Point** the mouse at Horz. Alignment
**Drag** to Left

---

Enter

↵

To create a column of text on the left side of the page, you can simply increase the amount of the right indent.  For example, if you increased the right indent from 1" to 3.5", all of the lines in that paragraph would end at about the middle of the page.  Change the right indent spacing to 3.5".

---

**Point** the mouse at Paragraph
**Point** the mouse at Spacing
**Click**

---

Enter

↓ (5 times)
**[Esc]**
**03.5** ↵

The text of the paragraph is formed into a column on the left side of the page.

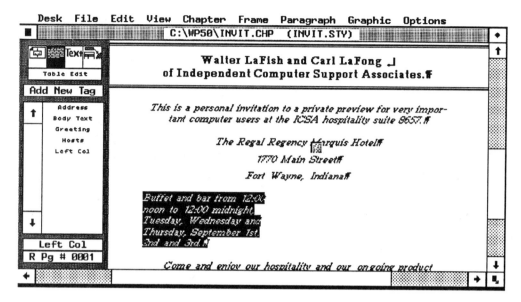

*Figure 2.38   Column created by paragraph indents.*

The next task is to perform the same type of operation on the last paragraph, except that this time the left indent will be increased to create a column of text on the right side of the page.

| |
|---|
| **Point** the mouse at "enjoy"<br>**Click** |

To make the operation simpler, you can format this paragraph as **Left Col** to start with and automatically pick up the change in alignment entered for the **Left Col** tag.

| |
|---|
| **Point** the mouse at the Left Col tag<br>**Click** |

**Exercise 4:**    Create a new tag called **Right Col**. Try this on your own. The correct commands can be found under EX-4 at the end of this chapter.

You can now adjust the settings copied from the Left Col tag to define the indents for the Right Col tag.

**Point** the mouse at Paragraph
**Point** the mouse at Spacing
**Click**

This time you need to indent the text far enough from the left so that the lines will begin at a point on the page that is past where the Left Col text ends. In this case, simply reverse the values. If Left Col is indented 1" left and 3.5" right, then indent Right Col 3.5" left and 1" right. Enter

↓ (4 times)
**[Esc]**
**03.5** ↓
**[Esc]**
**01** ↵

You have created two columns, one on the left side of the page and the other on the right, but they are not side by side. They are still displayed one after the other.

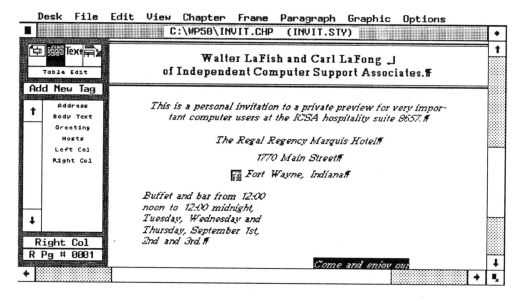

*Figure 2.39    Columns still displayed consecutively.*

## Line Breaks

The solution to this problem requires the use of a feature that has no direct equivalent in any word processing program. Until this point, most of the features used to format paragraphs had rough equivalents in full-powered word processing programs such as Microsoft Word and WordPerfect; however, you now need to use a feature that does not exist in those programs.

To understand this feature you need to return to the subject of paragraph ending characters created when you use the Return (⏎) key. In most cases, the assumption is made that following each return, the text should begin another paragraph. Put another way, each paragraph begins with a line break. This is always the case in word processing programs.

In Ventura, the default setting for paragraphs causes them to begin with a line break. What is different about Ventura is that you can choose to suppress that line break. Suppressing line breaks causes consecutive paragraphs to be displayed and printed on the same line. In ordinary conditions this would simply cause a mess because lines of text would be printed over each other; however, in the Left Col and Right Col paragraphs, the indents used would allow them both to start on the same line and not interfere with each other. The result would be two paragraphs that are displayed and printed side by side, exactly the effect you are hoping to achieve.

The line break quality can be changed for a paragraph by selecting **Breaks** from the Paragraph menu. Display the BREAKS dialog box.

---

**Point** the mouse at Paragraph
**Point** the mouse at Breaks
**Click**

---

The BREAKS dialog box appears.

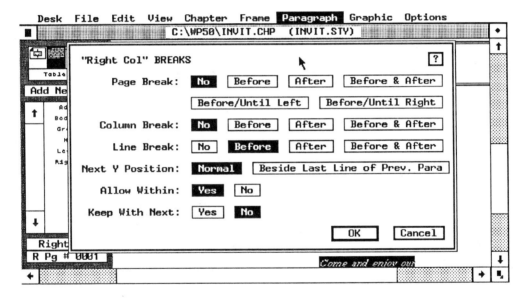

*Figure 2.40    BREAKS dialog box.*

Ventura recognizes three types of breaks: page, column, and line. Note that the line break setting is set for a break *before* the beginning of a new paragraph.

To suppress that line break, select No for the line break setting.

> **Point** the mouse at No
> **Click**

Then enter

↵

The paragraphs now appear side by side rather than consecutively.

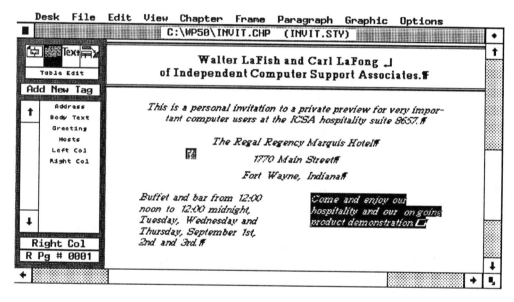

*Figure 2.41   Paragraphs aligned in side-by-side columns.*

Save the document and style sheet by entering

**[Ctrl/s]**

Now, print the chapter.

> **Point** the mouse at File
> **Point** the mouse at To Print
> **Click**

Enter

↵

Ventura prints the document.

This document shows the most common ways in which paragraph formatting can be used to improve the appearance of a document. All of the effects shown on this page are the result of settings selected from the Paragraph menu. Prepare Ventura to create another document by selecting the New document option from the File menu.

> **Point** the mouse at File
> **Point** the mouse at New
> **Click**

# SUMMARY

This chapter was designed to show you how Ventura implements paragraph-level formatting through the use of paragraph tags and style sheets.

- **Paragraph Tags.** Ventura uses a highly structured approach to text formatting. Every paragraph in a document must be assigned a paragraph tag. That tag name refers to a complete set of formatting specifications. Ventura automatically creates and assigns the tag name **Body Text** to all paragraphs in a document. Additional paragraph tags can be added to the document. Each tag is independent of the other tags and can contain a unique set of formatting specifications. Once tags have been created, you can apply any of the tags to any of the paragraphs in the document. The text is then formatted according to specifications used for a particular tag. If a tag is revised, any paragraphs in the document that are assigned to that tag are automatically reformatted to the revised specifications.

- **Style Sheets.** A style sheet is a list of all of the tags created for a given document. The style sheet can contain up to 128 different tag names. All style sheets begin with the Body Text tag. Style sheets are not stored in the same disk file as the text or the chapter information. Each style sheet is stored in a file with an STY extension. This system allows you to use the same style sheet with as many documents as you like. Tags can be added, removed, or renamed by using the Paragraph menu's Update Tag List options. You can also assign tag names to function keys to create keyboard shortcuts for tagging paragraphs.

- **Loading Text.** While Ventura does allow you to create new files and edit text, the most common way of adding text to a Ventura document is to create a text file with a word processing program. Ventura will read word processing files from most popular applications as well as files in general ASCII text format. Text files must be placed in a Ventura frame — usually the master frame — in order to have the text displayed. Editing changes made during a Ventura session will be written into the source file when the Ventura chapter is saved.

- **Font Changes.** Ventura allows you to select a base font for each tag you create. You can still use the Set Font option in the text editing mode to select fonts or text attributes for specific characters or words within the paragraph that deviate from the base font for that tag.

- **Ruling Lines.** You can instruct Ventura to draw ruling lines above, below, or around each paragraph with a specified tag name. The ruling line can consist of one to three lines in which width and spacing can be specified individually. The height of the ruling lines and any spacing used between lines or between a line and text is added to the overall height of the paragraph tag. Note that multiple-line paragraphs that are split between two pages will not have the box drawn properly. Boxes around multiple-line paragraphs should only be used be used when you are sure that the entire paragraph will appear on one page.

- **Alignment.** The text of a paragraph can be aligned as left, center, right, or justified.

- **Spacing.** Ventura allows you to adjust the amount of space above, below, to the left, or to the right of a paragraph. In addition, you can control the height of the lines within a single paragraph. The Inter-Line, Above, and Below spacing values are initially set to a value based on the point size of the font used for that tag. When spacing above or below a paragraph is changed, the effect of that change depends on the tag settings of the paragraphs above and below the selected paragraph. Ventura compares the Below value of one paragraph to the Above value of the next and uses the *larger* value as the actual spacing value. The actual space used by Ventura is the result of the interaction of the tag settings for pairs of paragraphs.

- **Side-by-Side.** Side-by-side column formats are useful when you want column-formatted text for only a small portion of the document. The column widths and horizontal location are controlled by the left and right spacing settings. The paragraphs can be placed side by side on the page by suppressing the line break that Ventura usually inserts before every paragraph. To create a side-by-side column layout, you must define one tag for each column. The tags should have left and right spacing settings that format the text into columns that do not overlap. The left-most column should maintain the default setting of a line break before the paragraph. All column tags to the right of that tag should have their line break setting turned off.

- **Manual Kerning.** Ventura automatically creates proportionally spaced text based on the font selected for the paragraph tag. However, in large fonts, certain pairs of characters will appear to have too much or too little space between them. This usually occurs when characters that slant in opposite directions are placed next to each other. Manual kerning is a process by which the space between pairs of characters can be increased or decreased to improve the appearance of the text. Manual kerning takes place in the Text Editing mode. When a pair of characters is highlighted, the [Shift/←] key decreases the space between them, while [Shift/→] increases the space between them.

## Answers to Exercises

**EX-1 (see p. 91):** Change font.

> **Point** the mouse at Paragraph
> **Point** the mouse at Font
> **Click**
> **Point** the mouse at 14
> **Click**

Then enter

↵

**EX-2 (see p. 96):** Set ruling line width.

> **Point** the mouse at Paragraph
> **Point** the mouse at Ruling Line Above
> **Click**
> **Point** the mouse at Width
> **Drag** to Frame
> **Release**

Enter

⏎

**EX-3 (see p. 105):** Create ruling line.

Enter

**[Esc]**
**.112** ↓
**[Esc]**
**.007** ↓
**[Esc]**
**.028** ↓
**[Esc]**
**.014**

**EX-4 (see p. 129):** Create new tag.

```
Point the mouse at Add New Tag
Click
```

Enter

**Right Col** ⏎

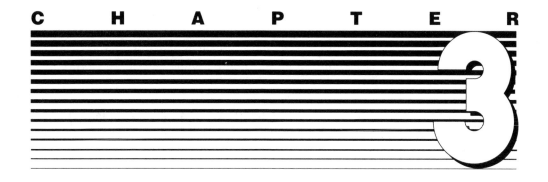

# FINANCIAL DOCUMENTS
# AND TABLES

Chapters 1 and 2 covered some very general but fundamental concepts in Ventura document creation. This chapter concentrates on a specific type of formatting problem and then goes into greater detail about several of Ventura's paragraph formatting abilities.

In particular, this chapter focuses on how text is aligned into columns and how tabs are handled in Ventura. As an example, a financial balance sheet document will be created.

This type of document raises an important point about the relationship between the work you do in your word processing program and the way Ventura formats documents. Because of Ventura's advanced formatting capabilities, you may need to vary the way you prepare documents in your word processor if those documents are meant to be used as text files for Ventura chapters.

Load your word processing program and prepare to create a document, which you will name BALANCE.WP if you are using WordPerfect. If you are using another word processor, you should adjust the name of the file accordingly. For example, Microsoft Word users should call the document BALANCE.DOC, while WordStar users should name it BALANCE.WS.

The document to be prepared, a financial balance sheet, will contain indented headings as well as text aligned in three different columns. Financial statements typically use three columns of numbers. The first column is used to show subtractions, such as depreciation values; the second is used for account totals; and the third is used for totals and subtotals.

In creating the text for this document, you should not be concerned with the actual physical location of the items. For example, if you wanted to place a value into the second column, typical word processing requires that you create three tab stops and that those tabs be decimal-aligned. Most word processing programs allow you to distinguish between normal tabs and left-aligned, decimal-aligned, and right-aligned tab stops.

When you enter the text in a word processor, pressing the Tab key positions you at the appropriate tab stop. Pressing the Tab key also inserts a special character into the text that tells the word processor to align the text on the next tab stop; however, this is not true of all word processing programs. WordPerfect and Microsoft Word do insert tab characters that Ventura also recognizes, but Word-Star does not actually insert tab characters (i.e., ASCII character #9) when the Tab key is used. Instead, it inserts a series of spaces (ASCII character #32) between tab stops. Ventura reads these spaces as space characters, not as tab instructions, so if you are using WordStar, your text document will not be formatted correctly when loaded into Ventura. To correct this, you can edit the spaces out of the text after loading it into Ventura and replace them with tab characters. Also, if you use WordPerfect, note that WordPerfect 4.1, 4.2, and 5.0 all use slightly different methods to establish decimal tabs. In this chapter's example document, it will not be necessary to use a right- or decimal-aligned tab. In WordPerfect, pressing the Tab key is quite sufficient.

When you create the following document, you must understand that the alignment of the text in WordPerfect, or whatever word processing program you are using, is not important. In most cases, the text will not line up correctly in your word processor. That is quite all right. All you need to do in the word processor is make sure that a tab character is inserted between the column items on the same line, as in the example document for this chapter (see Figure 3.1). Ventura, not your word processor, determines the actual physical location of the heading and the value when you create the style tags for various lines. When using the word processor, you need only be concerned that the proper characters — text and tabs — are inserted in the proper order.

Following is the text of the document you will need to create. The text is shown in the form of the keystrokes you need to enter. The tabs to be entered are represented by the ⇒ symbol. The tab character referred to is entered by pressing the Tab key.

```
Central Hardware
Balance Sheet
December 31, 1986
Assets
Current Assets
Cash⇒1,000
Accounts Receivable⇒3,000
Notes Receivable⇒1,500
Inventory⇒40,000
Supplies⇒1,000
Total Current Assets⇒46,500
Plant Assets
Land⇒5,000
Buildings⇒76,000
Less Accumulated Depreciation⇒3,000⇒73,000
Store Equipment⇒20,000
Less Accumulated Depreciation⇒6,000⇒14,000
Total Plant Assets⇒92,000
Investments⇒50,000
Patents⇒10,000
Good Will⇒5,000
Total Assets⇒203,000
Liabilities
Current Liabilities
Accounts Payable⇒15,000
Notes Payable⇒5,000
Accrued Taxes⇒3,000
Total Current Liabilities⇒23,000
Long-term Liabilities
Mortgages Payable⇒50,000
Notes Payable⇒20,000
Total Long-term Liabilities⇒70,000
Total Liabilities⇒93,000
Capital
Walter La Fish, Capital⇒110,500
Total Liabilities and Capital⇒203,500
```

*Figure 3.1   BALANCE.WP document text.*

When you have completed the document, save it as BALANCE.WP if you use WordPerfect, BALANCE.DOC if you use Word or MultiMate, or BALANCE.WS if you use WordStar. Once you have created and saved the text, you can exit the word processor. You are now ready to format the document in Ventura. Load the Ventura program in the usual manner.

## LOADING THE TEXT

The chapter name currently displayed is UNTITLED.CHP, but the style sheet INVIT.STY has been loaded. Note that if you or someone else loaded a chapter with a different style sheet after you worked with the INVIT.CHP chapter discussed in Chapter 2, your style sheet may be different. Ventura remembers the last style sheet you worked with and automatically loads that style sheet the next time the program is loaded. It also remembers the operational and view modes and settings, such as the display or removal of column guides, that were last used. Also, the last directory used to select various files from the file selctor boxes is recorded. This information is stored in a file or files with INF extensions, which are written in the \VENTURA directory when you quit the program. If you were to delete these files, Ventura would start with the default settings used the first time you loaded Ventura.

First, load the text from the BALANCE.WP file into the master frame.

---

**Point** the mouse at File
**Point** the mouse at Load Text/Picture
**Click**

---

The LOAD TEXT/PICTURE dialog box retains the last set of options entered, for example, **Text** as the file type and **WordPerfect 5** as the text format. If you are using a different word processor, the selections should reflect that program. If the options displayed on your screen are different, use the mouse to select those just mentioned.

To continue, enter

⏎

The ITEM SELECTOR dialog box indicates the last directory used to load a text file. This should be the same directory — in this example C:\WP50 — that you used to load the INVIT.WP file in the previous chapter.

---

**Point** the mouse at BALANCE.WP
**Double Click**

---

To load the text into the master frame, you need to select the file name from the frame list.

---

**Point** the mouse at BALANCE. WP
**Click**

---

The text is loaded into the master frame. To save it as a Ventura chapter file, enter

**[Ctrl/s]**

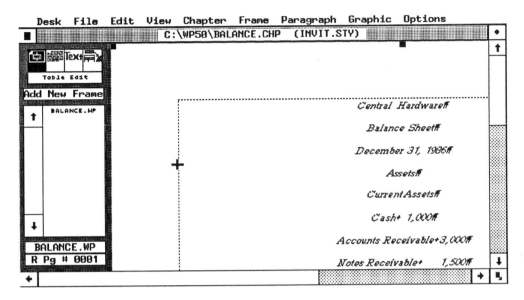

*Figure 3.2    Document loaded into master frame and saved as chapter file.*

The current style sheet file, INVIT.STY, uses a center-aligned, italic font for the Body Text style tag, so the text is formatted according to those specifications. Any text loaded into the master frame will be automatically formatted according to the Body Text settings for the active style sheet.

This financial document is different in purpose from the invitation created in Chapter 2, so you should create a new style sheet for it.  Begin by loading the DEFAULT style sheet.  Loading the DEFAULT.STY file will start you off with an empty style sheet with Body Text set to the default font, alignment, and spacing settings.

---

**Point** the mouse at File
**Point** the mouse at Load Diff. Style
**Click**
**Point** the mouse at DEFAULT. STY
**Double Click**

---

The DEFAULT. STY style sheet file is loaded.  The text now appears aligned to the left and in a normal text font, as it did in the word processor.

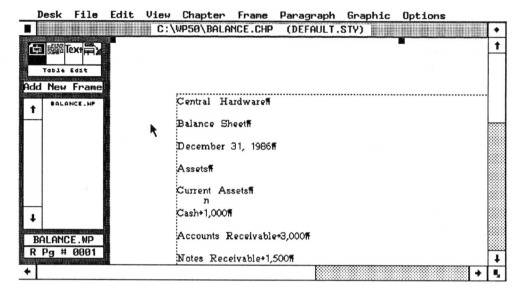

*Figure 3.3    The DEFAULT. STY style sheet formats text to the default settings.*

After you load the DEFAULT. STY style sheet, save a copy of it under a new name so that any new style tags you create will not be saved as part of the default style sheet. This is important because if you don't modify the DEFAULT. STY style sheet, you can always use it to create new style sheets from scratch. Note that should you accidentally add tags or change the settings on the default style sheet you can recover the default by loading a new copy of the style sheet from the original Ventura disks.

---

**Point** the mouse at File
**Point** the mouse at Save As New Style
**Click**

---

Enter the name of the new style sheet file:

**finance** ⏎

The tags you create will now be stored in the FINANCE.STY file. You are now ready to begin formatting the text.

# DRAWING A BOX

The first three lines of the document function as a kind of title for the rest of the document. Suppose that you wanted to center those lines and draw a box around the text. Using the options on the Paragraph menu, you can add both of those characteristics by creating a style tag and defining the format you want. Note that the ruling box will be drawn around several lines. This is okay because the format used for the document title will only appear at the top of the first page, so there is no danger that the paragraph will be split between two pages.

Begin by creating a new style tag. Change the mode to Paragraph Tagging by entering

**[Ctrl/i]**

Select the first pargraph in the document.

```
Point the mouse at Central
Click
```

Exercise 1:     Create a new tag called **Title**. Try this on your own. The correct commands can be found under EX-1 at the end of this chapter.

Change the font to 14-point.

> **Point** the mouse at Paragraph
> **Point** the mouse at Font
> **Click**
> **Point** the mouse at 14
> **Click**

Enter

⏎

The text is now displayed in 14-point characters.

**Exercise 2:** The next change is to set the alignment as centered. Try this on your own. The correct commands can be found under EX-2 at the end of this chapter.

The Title tag's format has changed the paragraph to 14-point, centered text.

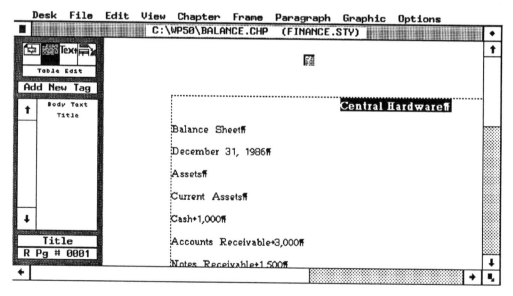

*Figure 3.4    Title tag formatted as 14-point, centered text.*

The final change to the format is to add a box around the text. This procedure is similar to drawing a ruling line above a paragraph except that the rule extends all the way around the text.

---

**Point** the mouse at Paragraph
**Point** the mouse at Ruling Box Around
**Click**

---

The dialog box for this option is essentially the same as for the Ruling Line Above or Below options. The only difference will be the effect of the entries on the text in the document.

Ruling boxes have the same width and height options as ruling lines. Select Text width for the ruling box.

---

**Point** the mouse at Width
**Click**
**Drag** to Text

---

To complete the specifications, you must enter the values for the height and spacing of the line or lines you want to draw. It is important to remember that the spacing relationship for Ruling Box Around corresponds to the Ruling Line Above option. This means that the Space Above Rule #1 setting is used to separate the rule line from other paragraphs. Because you are drawing a box, the direction of the spacing adjusts for each side of the box. The Space Below Rule #1 setting would be used to increase the spacing between the box and the text it encloses. In most cases, you will want to enter a value for the Space Below Rule #1 setting that prevents the ruling lines from coming in contact with descender characters such as "g" and "p." In this case, draw a two-point — .028" thick — line around the text and add six points — .084" — of space between the text and the box by entering

↓
**[Esc]**
**. 028** ↓
**[Esc]**
**. 084** ↵

The text of the paragraph is surrounded by a ruling box.

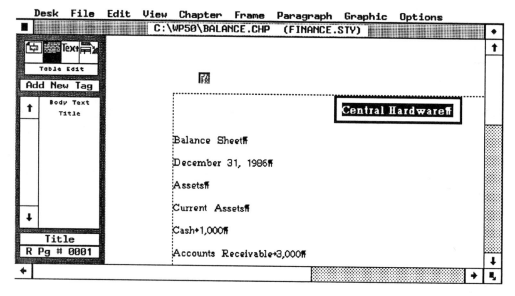

*Figure 3.5    Ruling box drawn around text.*

## Multiple Selection

The first three lines of text should all be part of the page title. This means that you must tag all three paragraphs with the Title tag. To simplify the task of formatting a group of paragraphs on the same page with the same tag, Ventura allows you to highlight more than one paragraph at a time. The trick is to use the Shift key in combination with the mouse button. The procedure is to hold down the Shift key and then click the mouse button while continuing to press the Shift key. This technique is called **[Shift/Click]**.

Begin by selecting one paragraph in the normal manner.

```
Point the mouse at "Balance"
Click
```

Now select the next paragraph.

```
Point the mouse at "December"
Click
```

Ventura shifts the highlight from the first paragraph to the one you have just clicked. To highlight other paragraphs at the same time (i.e., to use **multiple selection**), use the [Shift/Click] technique just discussed. With the "December" paragraph still highlighted,

```
Point the mouse at "Balance"
[Shift/Click]
```

This time, the highlight does not switch to a different paragraph but is extended to cover both paragraphs.

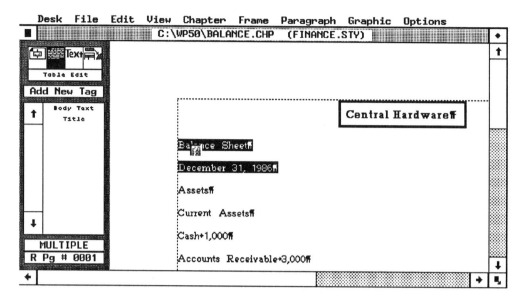

*Figure 3.6    Two paragraphs highlighted using multiple selection.*

You can continue to add paragraphs to the selection until you have selected all the text you want to include. Keep in mind that the paragraphs do not have to be consecutive.

---

**Point** the mouse at "Cash"
**[Shift/Click]**

---

A nonadjacent paragraph is now included in the selection. If you include too many paragraphs in a selection, you can deselect a paragraph by applying the [Shift/Click] a second time.

---

**Point** the mouse at "Cash"
**[Shift/Click]**

---

The paragraph's highlight is removed without removing the highlight from the other paragraphs. Remember that if you click without the [Shift], Ventura will select the specified paragraph and deselect all of the other paragraphs. Also, multiple sections can only occur on one page at a time.

Once you have selected all the paragraphs you want to include, you can apply a tag to all of the paragraphs in one command.

> **Point** the mouse at the Title tag
> **Click**

Now all three paragraphs display the Title format.

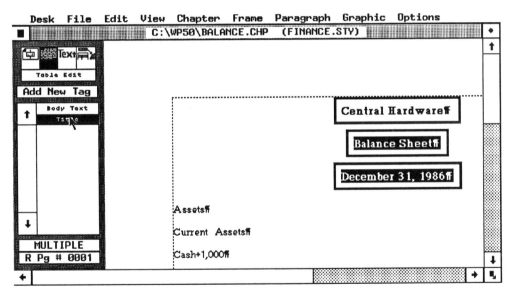

*Figure 3.7    Multiple paragraphs tagged in one step.*

However, there is a problem. It would make more sense to have a single box that surrounds all of the title lines. Ventura generates a box for each line because all three lines end with paragraph end characters. To draw a single box around all of the lines requires replacing paragraph-end (¶) characters with line-end (⏎) characters. Place Ventura in the Text Editing mode by entering

**[Ctrl/o]**

> **Point** to the right of "Hardware"
> **Click**

Remove the paragraph end and replace it with a line end by entering

**[Del]**
**[Ctrl/⏎]**

These commands cause Ventura to treat both lines as part of the same paragraph and draw the box around both lines. Repeat the process to include the third Title line.

> **Click** to the right of "Sheet"

Enter

**[Del]**
**[Ctrl/⏎]**

The three lines are surrounded by a single ruling box.

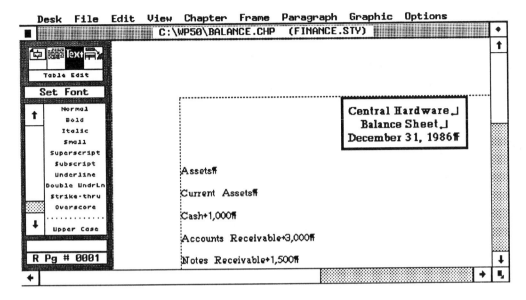

*Figure 3.8     Line ends replace paragraph ends.*

## Spacing with Boxes

Now that you have created the box around all three title lines, there are some special spacing considerations that apply mainly to boxed paragraphs.

To create a single box around the three lines, you removed the paragraph end characters from two of the lines. In addition to solving the box problem, this procedure also reduced the amount of space between the lines to equal the inter-line spacing used in multi-line paragraphs. The space between the lines could be increased by changing the inter-line spacing value. For example, to return the lines to the same spacing that they had as individual paragraphs, you would double the inter-line spacing value.

Return to the Paragraph Tagging mode and select the boxed text. Enter

**[Ctrl/i]**

> **Point** the mouse at "Central"
> **Click**

Display the SPACING dialog box.

---

**Point** the mouse at the Paragraph menu heading
**Point** at Spacing
**Click**

---

The current value for inter-line spacing is 16.31 fractional points, approximately .227". The line spacing between paragraphs would be 16.31 points × 2, which is 32.62 points. If you change the inter-line spacing to that value, the lines will appear with the same spacing they had when they were individual paragraphs. Enter

↓ (2 times)
**[Esc]**
**32.62** ↵

The spacing between lines increases to the spacing they had when they were separate paragraphs.

## Margins vs. Frame Width

When a ruling box is drawn around a paragraph, the issue of spacing between the text and rule lines may be of significance. In the current document, you might want to widen the box so that the sides are not so close to the text. If you choose the Frame, Column, or Margin box width option, the sides of the box would extend to the column guides. You need some way to control the width so you can extend the box to a width between the frame width and the text width.

How this can be done is not obvious. You must understand what Ventura means by **margin** width. To see how margin width operates, change the width setting for the ruling box to **Margin**.

> **Point** the mouse at Paragraph
> **Point** at Ruling Box Around
> **Click**
> **Point** at Width
> **Click**
> **Drag** to Margin

Enter

⏎

The box widens to a width equal to the column guides and the margins for the entire document frame; however, the margin width setting takes into consideration any left or right spacing added to the paragraph tag. For example, if you add 1" of spacing on the left and 1" on the right for this tag, the ruling box would be moved in from the left and right by 1". Display the Paragraph Spacing menu.

> **Point** the mouse at Paragraph
> **Point** at Spacing
> **Click**

Add 1" of spacing in from the left and right sides by entering

↓ (4 times)
**[Esc]**
**01** ↓
**[Esc]**
**01** ⏎

The ruling box adjusts to the new paragraph spacing values.

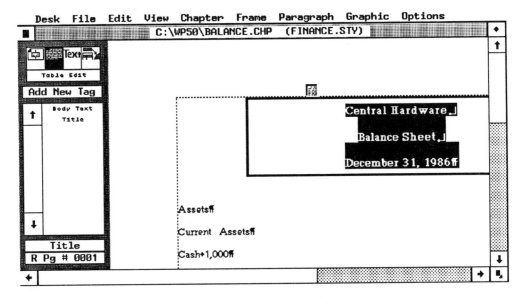

*Figure 3.9    Ruling box indented from left and right margins.*

You can see that the Margin width setting for ruling lines is quite flexible because you can use the left and right spacing values to limit the width of the box or lines.

The next action is to create a style for the major headings that occur in financial statements, such as Assets, Liabilities, and Capital. The tag you create for these paragraphs is similar to the tags you have already learned to create. Begin by creating a style tag for headings.

---

**Point** the mouse at "Assets"
**Click**
**Point** the mouse at Add New Tag
**Click**

---

Enter the name of the new tag.

**Heading** ⏎

Change the font for this heading to Swiss, 12-point bold.

**Point** the mouse at Paragraph
**Point** the mouse at Font
**Click**
**Point** the mouse at Swiss
**Click**
**Point** at 12
**Click**
**Point** the mouse at Bold
**Click**

Enter

⏎

The **Heading** paragraph is now formatted as Swiss, 12-point bold text.

# TABS

The next line in the text is **Current Assets**. It is formatted as Body Text. In this case, you can leave that line as it is.

The next line, which begins with "Cash," is different from the others you have worked with because the text contains a tab. The tab was entered in order to separate items on the same line with a unit of space, but the tabs don't show up because the current paragraph tag for that text, Body Text, is not correctly set for tabs.

The financial statement you are working on traditionally uses three columns in which numeric values are displayed. The first column is used for raw values that need to be added or subtracted to form a total. The second column is used for totals. These totals can represent the result of values in column 1 or simply be entered as totals for a category. The third column is used for grand totals that consolidate a group of totals. Your task is to create tags that align the tabbed values in the correct columns. The tabs are already inserted into the text. You need to create tags that will tell Ventura exactly where the values should be placed.

To align text by using tabs, you need to consider two settings.

**Alignment**     The default style sheet automatically sets the alignment of the Body Text tag to Justified. **Justified** alignment means that Ventura will make sure that each full line of text aligns flush with both the left and right column guides. Justification is achieved by inserting additional spaces between the words in a line. Justified alignment is wrong for this document because none of the lines are long enough to extend across the width of the page or are meant to be long enough to be wrapped around. In addition, tab spacing cannot be used if the alignment is justified. Left alignment is the typcial choice for text with tabs.

**Tab Stops**     In addition to setting the text to left alignment, you will usually need to specify the locations in which you want the tabbed text to be aligned. Ventura automatically sets tab stops every .5". In most cases, you will need to adjust the locations to fit the document you are working with.

Select the "Cash" paragraph. This paragraph is an example of a total on the balance sheet. The numbers should be aligned in column 2.

---

**Point** the mouse at "Cash"
**Click**

---

Create a new tag called **Col 2** for this paragraph.

---

**Point** the mouse at Add New Tag
**Click**

---

Enter

**Col 2** ⤶

**Exercise 3:** To align the text correctly, you must change the alignment to left alignment. Try this on your own. The correct commands can be found under EX-3 at the end of this chapter.

The next step is to specify the horizontal location at which the tabbed text should be aligned. Tab settings are always entered in inches. You need to estimate the location in inches that should be used for the tab stop. To help you gauge the distances on the page, Ventura can display ruler bars that help you measure distances on the page. The ruler bars can be turned on from the **Options** menu.

---

**Point** the mouse at Options
**Point** the mouse at Show Rulers
**Click**

---

Ventura displays two bars — one at the top and one to the left of the document window. The bars are marked off in .1" increments.

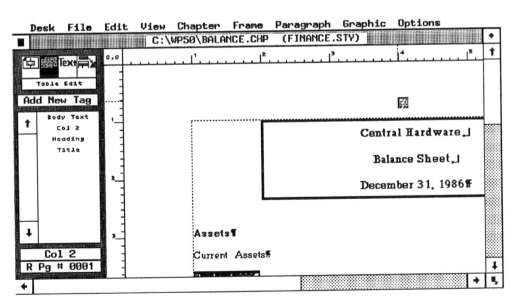

*Figure 3.10   Ruler bars displayed.*

If you look at the ruler lines while you move the mouse, you will see that two thin dotted lines move along with the mouse. These lines indicate the location of the mouse on the page. With the rulers displayed, you can reduce the view to get a feel for the dimension of the entire page. Enter

**[Ctrl/r]**

The ruler lines now border the entire page. You can see from the rulers that your document is placed on an 8.5" by 11" page with 1" margins at the top, bottom, left, and right. These dimensions were set as part of the default style sheet from which the current style sheet was copied.

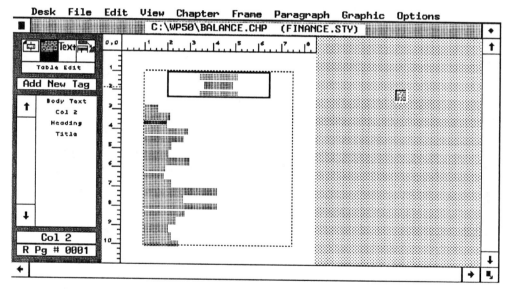

*Figure 3.11    Rulers border entire page.*

The rulers begin measuring from the upper left corner of the page. However, it is sometimes useful to adjust the starting point to some other reference point on the page. For example, when you enter values for tab locations, the distance of the tab is measured from the left column guide not from the edge of the paper. In attempting to estimate the correct placement of tabs, you might want to adjust the rulers to measure from the column edge rather than from the edge of the paper.

The **Set Ruler** command, found on the Options menu, allows you to change the starting position of the rulers.

```
Point the mouse at Options
Point the mouse at Set Ruler
Click
```

Ventura allows you to enter a value for repositioning both the horizontal or vertical axis of the rulers. In this case, you want to move the horizontal axis 1" inward. Enter

**[Esc]**
**01** ⌐

The horizontal ruler begins measuring at the left column guide. The ruler now shows that the column guides are 6.5" apart. This means that you could, for example, place column 1 at 4.5", column 2 at 5.5", and column 3 at 6.5", but there are many ways you could place these tabs. Return to the normal view by entering

**[Ctrl/n]**

Scroll down and to the right so you can see more of the document.

> **Point** at the scroll bar down arrow
> **Click**  (3 times)
> **Point** at the scroll bar right arrow
> **Click**

To see the full width of the page, turn off the side bar display by entering

**[Ctrl/w]**

You are now ready to set a tab at 5.5" from the column border.  Begin by displaying the **TAB SETTINGS** dialog box.

> **Point** the mouse at Paragraph
> **Point** the mouse at Tab Settings
> **Click**

Ventura displays the TAB SETTINGS dialog box.

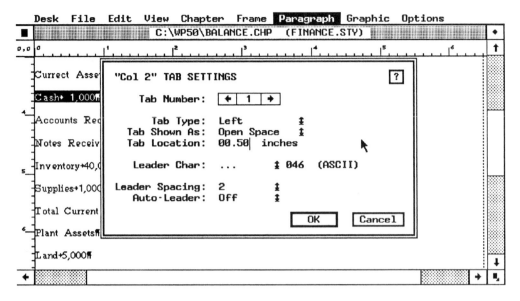

*Figure 3.12    TAB SETTINGS dialog box.*

At the top of the box is the tab number display. The box begins by displaying the settings for tab number 1. You can use the arrows to increase or decrease the tab number. You can define up to 16 different tabs on one line.

Setting a tab requires you to set three specifications:

**Tab Type**  The tab type determines the type of alignment that will be used at the tab location. You can select left, center, right, or decimal. Right alignment is used for numbers that contain no decimals or that have a fixed number of decimal points. For example, financial values that are always expressed as dollars and cents should be right aligned — not decimal aligned. Decimal alignment should be used when the number of decimal places used in the numeric values varies.

**Tab**
**Shown As**  This option is used to determine how the space left by the tab should be shown. The default is to show the space as blank. You can choose to fill the space with periods (the default fill character) or any other character.

**Tab**
**Location**
The tab location is the horizontal distance from the left column border to a tab stop. The default unit of measure is inches, but you can set tabs with any other unit of measurement available in Ventura.

Change the tab type to right aligned.

---

**Point** the mouse at Tab Type
**Click**
**Drag** to Right

---

Enter the value of 5.5" for the tab location.

**05.5** ⤶

The text following the tab is right aligned at 5.5" from the column border.

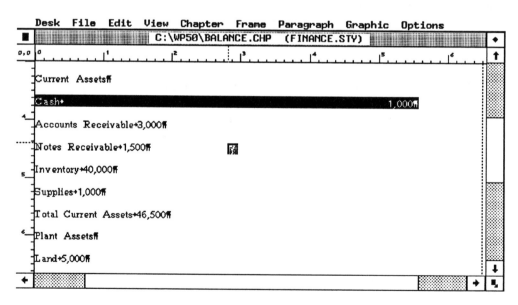

*Figure 3.13    Text aligned at tab stop.*

You can use the [Shift/Click] technique to tag the other items under "Current Assets" as Col 2 paragraphs.

---

**Point** the mouse at "Accounts"
**[Shift/Click]**
**Point** the mouse at "Notes"
**[Shift/Click]**
**Point** the mouse at "Inventory"
**[Shift/Click]**
**Point** the mouse at "Supplies"
**[Shift/Click]**

---

Display the side bar so you can select a tag from the side bar list.  Enter

**[Ctrl/w]**

Apply the Col 2 tag to these paragraphs.

---

**Point** the mouse at Col 2
**Click**

---

Suppress the side bar display again so you can see the text aligned at the tab stops. Enter

**[Ctrl/w]**

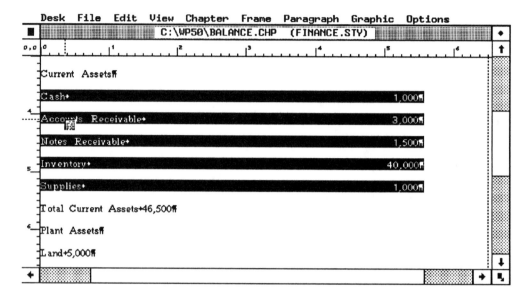

*Figure 3.14   Text aligned at tab stops.*

In addition to the tab alignment, you can use spacing to more clearly define the items under the "Current Assets" heading.  You might want to reduce the amount of space between the lines and indent the lines .5" from the left.  Display the SPACING dialog box.

---

**Point** the mouse at Paragraph
**Point** at Spacing
**Click**

---

The dialog box reveals that the inter-line height for the Col 2 tag is set at 13.98 points.  Recall that in the previous document the inter-line spacing for 12-point italic text was set at 16.31 points.  Ventura adjusts the inter-line spacing according to the weight, i.e. bold, italic, normal, etc., as well as the point size.

You can cause the paragraphs to appear as single-spaced lines by removing the above and below spacing values.  Enter


**[Esc]**
↓
**[Esc]**


Set the In From Left value to .5" to indent the left end of the line.  Enter


↓ (3 times)
**[Esc]**
**.5** ↵


The Col 2 paragraphs are spaced as if they were lines in the same paragraph.  Also, the left ends of the lines are indented.

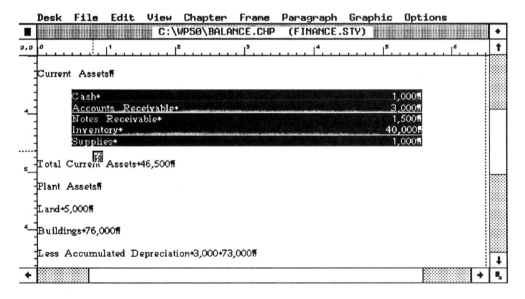

*Figure 3.15   Paragraphs spaced closely.*

The next line in the text, "Total Current Assets," is a column 3 value. To format this paragraph properly, you need to create another tag. Display the side bar again by entering

**[Ctrl/w]**

Select the paragraph.

> **Point** the mouse at "Total"
> **Click**

Create a new tag called **Col 3**.

> **Point** the mouse at Add New Tag
> **Click**

Enter

**Col 3** ⌐

> **Exercise 4:** This paragraph should have a right-aligned tab set at 6.5". Try this on your own. The correct commands can be found under EX-4 at the end of this chapter. Remember that you need to set the paragraph alignment to Left before you can set the tab location.

To complete the column 3 tag, change the spacing so that the line will be indented .75". Another spacing-related change would be to decrease the spacing between the column 2 and column 3 items by about half.

> **Point** the mouse at the Paragraph menu heading
> **Point** the mouse at Spacing
> **Click**

Enter

**[Esc]**
**. 097**
↓ (4 times)
**[Esc]**
**. 75** ↵

The column 3 grand total information is given a unique paragraph format to complement the other paragraph formats already defined.

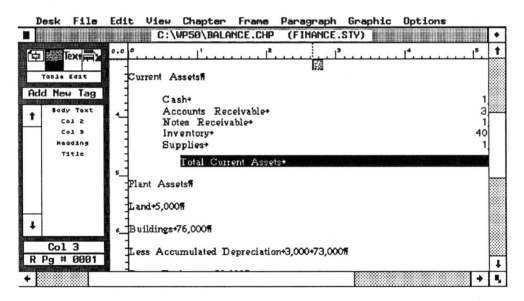

*Figure 3.16   Col 3 tag formats grand total line.*

Now that you have established tags for column 2 and 3 items, you can apply those tags throughout the document. The next Col 2 line is "Land."

---

**Point** the mouse at "Land"
**Click**
**Point** the mouse at Col 2 in the side bar
**Click**

---

## VARIATIONS ON AN EXISTING TAG

The next two items on this financial statement are related, and they need to be treated differently from other items. The numbers 76,000 and 3,000 should be placed in the column 1 position — 4.5" from the column border — to show that one reflects the accumulated depreciation of the other. In accounting, the current value of an asset is often shown by listing the original value of the asset and the amount of depreciation in column 1. The difference between the two values is then placed as a total in column 2. In order to do this, the depreciation line includes a second figure with a second tab.

To format these lines correctly, you must create a new tag that can handle two tab stops when necessary.

Instead of starting over from scratch (i.e. beginning with the Body Text tag) to create this new tag, you can tell Ventura to begin with the settings of another existing tag. In this case, starting with the settings for the Col 2 tag would save you the trouble of setting the Paragraph Alignment and Spacing values, which will be the same for the Col 1, Col 2, and Col 3 tags.

---

**Point** the mouse at "Buildings"
**Click**
**Point** the mouse at Add New Tag
**Click**

---

Enter the name for the tag, but do not enter a return. Name the tag **Col 1**. Enter

**Col 1**

Ventura assumes that you want to begin with the Body Text tag. Change the name of the tag to copy from by entering

↓
**[Esc]**
**Col 2** ⌋

The paragraph has the same format as the Col 2 tag. Your task is to change the tab settings for the new Col 1 tag so that the values will be placed in column 1 of the balance sheet.

---

**Point** the mouse at Paragraph
**Point** the mouse at Tab Settings
**Click**

---

The first tab stop in this tag should appear to the left of the current setting, which is 5.5". Change the setting by reducing the measurement to 4.5". Do not press the Return key after you enter the new value. Enter

**[Esc]**
**04.5**

Recall that in some cases the Col 1 tag will have a second tabbed item to align. This means that you need to set the second tab as a right-aligned tab at 5.5".

To set another tab you must change the number in the **Tab Number** box. That number is increased by clicking on the → symbol and is decreased by clicking on the ← symbol.

To set another tab, you must select the number of that tab.

> **Click** on the → symbol

The number in the Tab Number box changes to 2. When that happens, the values for Tab Type and Tab Location revert back to the default.

> **Exercise 5:** Change the tab to a right-aligned tab at 5.5". Try this on your own. The correct commands can be found under EX-5 at the end of this chapter.

The current paragraph is formatted so that its value falls into the left-most column in the document. The real test of the tag will come when it is applied to the depreciation line, which uses two tabs.

> **Point** the mouse at "Depreciation"
> **Click**
> **Point** the mouse at Col 1
> **Click**

Suppress the side bar so you can see the entire screen. Enter

**[Ctrl/w]**

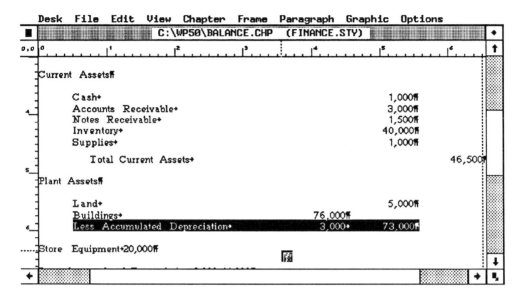

Desk  File  Edit  View  Chapter  Frame  Paragraph  Graphic  Options

C:\WP50\BALANCE.CHP  (FINANCE.STY)

0,0

Current Assets¶

    Cash→                                          1,000¶
    Accounts Receivable→                   3,000¶
    Notes Receivable→                     1,500¶
    Inventory→                             40,000¶
    Supplies→                              1,000¶

       Total Current Assets→                  46,500

Plant Assets¶

    Land→                                     5,000¶
    Buildings→                76,000¶
    Less Accumulated Depreciation→  3,000→    73,000¶

Store Equipment→20,000¶

*Figure 3.17   Col 1 tag aligns two tabs stops.*

Scroll down to display more of the document.

> **Point** at the scroll bar down arrow
> **Click** (3 times)

## TAGGING WITH FUNCTION KEYS

The current document presents a problem caused by the fact that the average screen display—EGA, Hercules, and even VGA—cannot display the full width of the column while the side bar is displayed; however, you cannot select paragraph tags without displaying the side bar display. One solution is to assign the tags to function keys so you do not need to use the side bar to select tags. Enter

**[Ctrl/k]**
↵

> **Point** the mouse at Assign Func. Keys
> **Click**

Enter the names of the tags you want to use with the function keys.

**col 1** ↓
**col 2** ↓
**col 3**

Save the settings by entering

⏎ ⏎

To save the function key assignments as part of this style sheet, you must select the Save box. Note that when this type of dialog box appears, one of the boxes is made with a slightly thicker line than the others. In this case, it is the **Save As** box. The thicker box indicates that the option is the default option. This means that if you press the Return key, the default option will automatically be selected. In this case **Save** is not the default, so you need to use the mouse to select it.

> **Point** the mouse at Save
> **Click**

You can now select paragraphs and use the function keys to select the tags. The next two lines are column 1 items.

> **Point** the mouse at "Store"
> **Click**
> **Point** the mouse at "Depreciation"
> **[Shift/Click]**

Enter

**[F1]**

Set the next five lines as Col 3 items.

---

**Point** the mouse at "Plant"
**Click**
**Point** the mouse at "Investments"
**[Shift/Click]**
**Point** the mouse at "Patents"
**[Shift/Click]**
**Point** the mouse at "Good will"
**[Shift/Click]**
**Point** the mouse at "Assets"
**[Shift/Click]**

---

Enter

**[F3]**

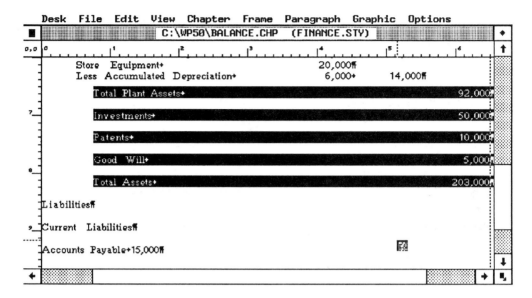

*Figure 3.18 Paragraphs tagged using function keys.*

## MORE SPACING

Note that the spacing between the Col 3 paragraphs is wider than the spacing between the other tagged lines. This happened because when you reduced the spacing for the Col 3 tag, you changed only the Space Above value. When two Col 3 paragraphs occur in a row, Ventura compares the Above and Below values to see which one is greater. In the Col 3 tag, the Below space is at .194", while the Above space has been reduced to .097". Ventura selects the larger value (Below) as the spacing value.

To have the closer spacing of consecutive Col 3 paragraphs, you need to also reduce the Below spacing value.

---

**Point** the mouse at Paragraph
**Point** the mouse at Spacing
**Click**

---

Enter the Below spacing value.

↓
**[Esc]**
**.097** ↵

The spacing between the Col 3 paragraphs is reduced from double-spaced text to one-and-a-half-spaced text.

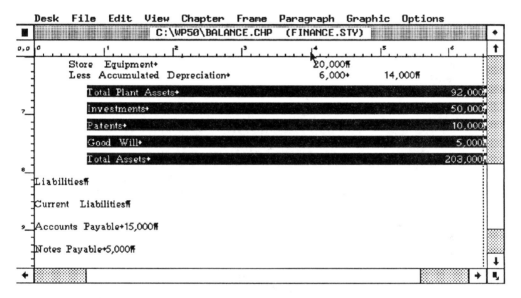

*Figure 3.19    Spacing reduced between Col 3 paragraphs.*

# THE BOTTOM LINE

The line that begins "Total Assets" is a special line on a financial statement. It marks the total for one side of the balance sheet. The value on this line is traditionally written with a double underline.

There are two ways to add the double underline to the text.

**Text Attribute**    This solution is the most obvious because it reflects the logic used in word processing programs. To add a double underline, you would place Ventura in the Text Editing mode, select the characters to be underlined, and choose the double underline setting from the list of text attributes displayed in the side bar.

**Paragraph Attribute**    Another way to create the double underline is to actually treat the underlined number as a separate paragraph from the rest of the text on that line. As two paragraphs, the text would be displayed on the same line by using the side-by-side paragraph technique explained in Chapter 2. The right column paragraph would use a double ruling line below the text to create the double underline.

Which method should be used? Although the first method seems simpler and more direct, the second method, i.e., creating side-by-side paragraphs, is probably the better solution. The reason is that paragraph-oriented solutions provide the greatest flexibility in Ventura because they have two qualities text-oriented changes do not: **reproduction** and **rollback**.

**Reproduction**    When you solve a formatting problem with a paragraph tag, you can reproduce the same format again with a minimum of effort by selecting that tag from the list in the side bar. When you create a change (such as a double underline) with the Text Editing mode, you cannot reproduce the same effect without having to repeat all of the steps you first used to create it; the responsibility for remembering how you achieved the effect is yours, not Ventura's.

**Rollback**

As you have seen, modifications made to a tag after it has been created are automatically applied to all of the paragraphs to which that tag is assigned. The term **roll-back** refers to the ability of tagged paragraphs to update their format according to the latest changes made in their tag's paragraph settings. If you create formats with text editing, you cannot link similar formats in any way; there is no way to automatically adjust all the items except by manually searching though the document and repeating all of the steps needed to create that format each time you use that format.

Thus, while it may seem like more trouble to create a new tag for a simple change like double underlining, in Ventura that solution carries with it additional benefits. As a general rule, paragraph-oriented solutions have the most long-term benefit in Ventura. Text-oriented solutions are usually simpler to perform initially but harder to revise and control later. Paragraph-oriented solutions also offer greater consistency in document formats because the tag automatically reproduces the same settings each time it is used, while text-oriented solutions offer no easy way to be absolutely sure that you have reproduced the same format each time.

The first step in creating a paragraph-oriented solution is to divide the line into two paragraphs. Place Ventura in the Text Editing mode by entering

**[Ctrl/o]**

Position the editing cursor to the right of the final "s" in "Assets."

---

**Point** the mouse to the right of "Assets"
**Click**

---

The cursor is located on the tab symbol. Delete that symbol and replace it with a return by entering

**[Del]** ⏎

You now have two lines — one with the text and the other with the number — appearing consecutively on the page. The next task is to define the numeric paragraph as a side-by-side paragraph. You will need to redisplay the side bar and enter the Paragraph Tagging mode. Enter

**[Ctrl/w]**
**[Ctrl/i]**

Select the paragraph that contains the number 203,000.

> **Point** the mouse at 203,000
> **Click**

Create a new tag called **Bottom Ln**.

> **Point** the mouse at Add New Tag
> **Click**

Enter

**Bottom Ln** ⌐

Note that because the paragraph was formatted as Col 3, Ventura used Col 3, not Body Text, as the tag to copy from when you created Bottom Ln, which means that all of the Col 3 settings are in place.

Following is a list of the changes you need to make to achieve the double-underline format you want.

- **Change Paragraph Alignment.** The proper location for the number is right aligned at 6.5". In this document, that happens to be the location of the right column border. You can place the text at the proper horizontal position by selecting right alignment for the entire paragraph. In cases where the paragraph did not fall on the column edge, you would use the Spacing left and right settings to adjust the position. For example, suppose you wanted this number aligned in column 2, at 5.5". After you select right alignment, set the **In From Right** spacing to 1" to place the text at 5.5". All of the tab effects can be duplicated by paragraph Spacing settings when needed.

- **Change Line Break Setting.** To achieve the correct vertical spacing, you would need to suppress the line break before the paragraph. This is the technique you learned in Chapter 2 for creating the side-by-side paragraphs.

- **Add Ruling Lines Below.** The double underline is created by drawing double ruling lines below the text.

Begin with the Alignment and Break settings.

```
Point the mouse at Paragraph
Point the mouse at Alignment
Click
Point the mouse at Horz. Alignment
Click
Drag to Right
```

Enter

⏎

Note that right alignment caused the text to move out of the document window. Suppress the side bar to widen the document window. Enter

**[Ctrl/w]**

Adjust the vertical location of the text by eliminating the line break before the paragraph.

---

**Point** the mouse at Paragraph
**Point** the mouse at Breaks
**Click**
**Click** on No for Line Break

---

Enter

⏎

The Bottom Ln paragraph is now positioned at the same location it was in when it was positioned by a tab stop. Visually there is no difference.

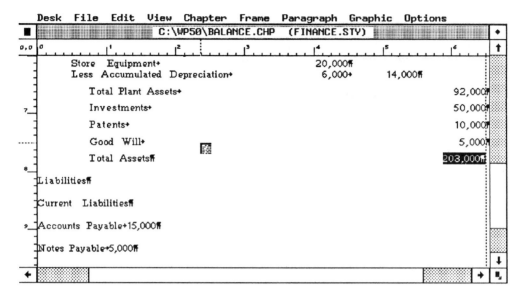

*Figure 3.20    Side-by-side paragraphs emulate tab stops.*

## DOUBLE UNDERLINES

In this case, you have chosen to create the double underline by adding ruling lines below the paragraph text.

---

**Point** the mouse at Paragraph
**Point** the mouse at Ruling Line Below
**Click**

---

In this case, the width setting should be Text so the underline will flow under all of the characters in the paragraph.

---

**Point** the mouse at Width
**Click**
**Drag** to Text

---

To create the actual double underline, you need to fill in the height and spacing characteristics for the ruling lines. The first value, Space Above Rule 1, will produce space between the text and the ruling line. This is usually important for clearing text that contains characters with descenders. In this case, the text will always be numbers, so descenders will not be a problem. Enter a one-point (.014") ruling line.

Enter

↓
**[Esc]**
**.014**

Separate the ruling lines by one point. Enter

**[Esc]**
**.014** ↓
**[Esc]**
**.014** ↵

The underline is drawn below the number. To get a closer look at the double underline, change to the enlarged view mode.

> **Point** the mouse at 203,000

Enter

**[Ctrl/e]**

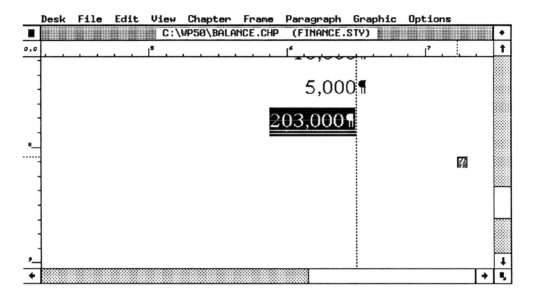

*Figure 3.21   Double ruling lines drawn under text.*

# FORCING A NEW PAGE

You have arrived at the bottom line of the assets section of the balance sheet. To see where you are in terms of the entire page, display the reduced view of the page by entering

**[Ctrl/r]**

Notice that the text does not appear on the reduced display. Instead, Ventura just displays blocks of gray, called **greeked** text, to indicate where the text is located.

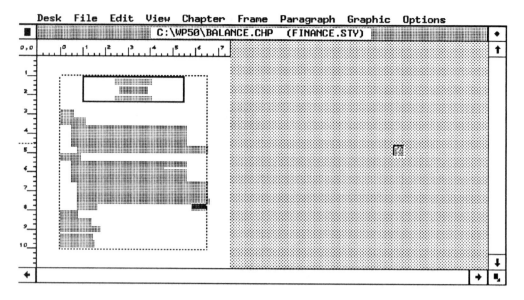

*Figure 3.22    Reduced view displays greeked text.*

The reduced view shows that you have almost filled the first page with the asset section of the document.  It seems logical to begin the "Liability" section of the document on the next page, but because Ventura does not know this, it places the next three lines at the bottom of page 1.

For Ventura to begin the "Liability" section on the next page, you must indicate that a new page should begin following the "Total Assets" line.  Most word processing programs allow you to insert a page break command in the text at the location in which you want to force a new page (e.g., in WordStar a PA command, in WordPerfect [Ctrl/⏎], and in Word [Ctrl/Shift/⏎]), but Ventura approaches page breaks in a different way.  Ventura considers a page break command to be part of the characteristics of a given tag.  This means that you do not insert page breaks directly into the text; you assign page breaks to specific style tags.

In this case, you can modify the Bottom Ln tag to also include a break to start a new page.  Note that the Bottom Ln paragraph is still highlighted.  Display the BREAKS dialog box.

> **Point** the mouse at Paragraph
> **Point** the mouse at Breaks
> **Click**

The dialog box shows the current break settings for the Bottom Ln tag. This time you are not interested in the line break but in the page break settings. The default setting for page break is No. In this case, you want to tell Ventura to start a new page immediately after this paragraph by selecting the After option for Page Break.

> **Click** on After

Enter

⏎

Ventura clears the bottom of the page by placing the next line at the top of page 2, which is not visible at this point.

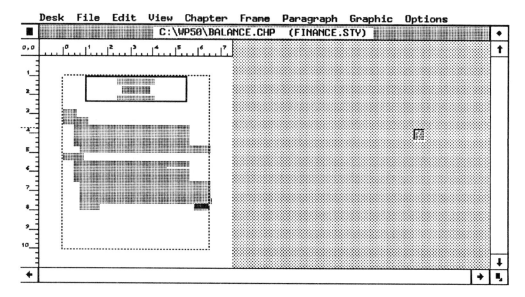

*Figure 3.23    Page break starts next paragraph on new page.*

You can use the PgUp and PgDn keys to move to the previous or next page.  Enter

**[PgDn]**

You can now see the remainder of the text.  Keep in mind that the text has not been tagged and is therefore not properly aligned.  If you display the side bar, you will see the actual page number display.  Enter

**[Ctrl/w]**

Note that the page number is preceded by an "L" to indicate that page 2 is a left page; however, in this example the distinction between right and left pages is not significant.

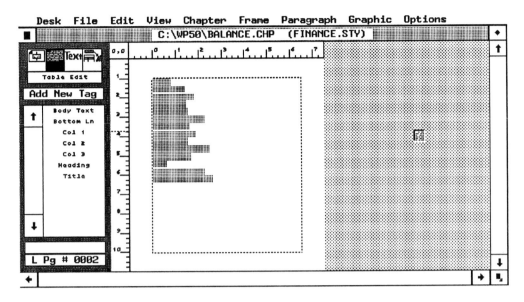

*Figure 3.24    Page 2 of BALANCE.CHP is displayed.*

You can format page 2 very quickly because you have already defined all the necessary tags.  First, place Ventura into the normal view mode.

---

**Point** the mouse at the upper left corner of the text

---

Enter

**[Ctrl/n]**

Now that you know how to tag a paragraph and have a set of tags defined, assign the following tags to the following text items.  Remember to scroll down to see more of the text when necessary.

| Text | Tag As |
|------|--------|
| Liabilities | Heading |
| Accounts Payable | Col 2 |
| Notes Payable | Col 2 |
| Accrued Taxes | Col 2 |
| Total Current Liabilities | Col 3 |
| Mortgages Payable | Col 2 |
| Notes Payable | Col 2 |
| Total Long-term Liabilities | Col 3 |
| Total Liabilities | Col 3 |
| Capital | Heading |
| Walter La Fish | Col 3 |
| Total Liabilities and Capital | Col 3 |

The document window should resemble the following:

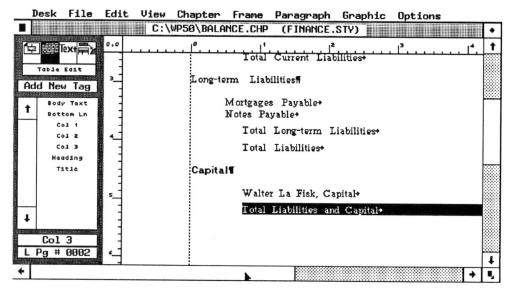

*Figure 3.25   Second page formatted using existing tags.*

To place the double underline under the number 203,000, you need to repeat the procedure by which you divided the line into two paragraphs and assigned the Bottom Ln tag to the number.

To divide the paragraph, change to the Text Editing mode. Enter

**[Ctrl/o]**

Remove the tab and enter a return in its place.

| |
|---|
| **Point** to the right of "Capital"<br>**Click** |

Enter

**[Del]**
⏎

Return to the Paragraph Tagging mode by entering

**[Ctrl/i]**

Tag the number 203,000 as a Bottom Ln paragraph.

| |
|---|
| **Point** the mouse at 203,000<br>**Click**<br>**Point** the mouse at the Bottom Ln<br>**Click** |

The number is now out of the document window. Scroll to the right.

---

**Point** at the scroll bar right arrow
**Click** (3 times)

---

The number is correctly formatted at the page-ending bottom line value.

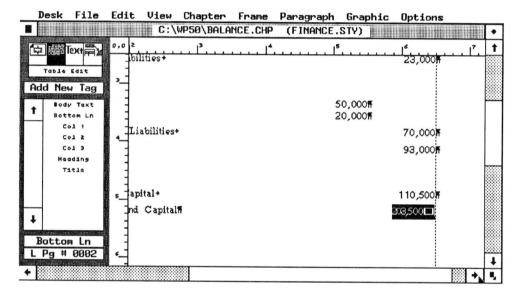

*Figure 3.26    Balance sheet document completed.*

This document demonstrates how you can quickly format a document once you have established the necessary tags. The style sheet you have created can be used with any number of text files that contain similar information. By attaching this style sheet to similar text files, you save time by simply tagging the text with the tags you have already defined. Of course, you can change or add to the tags if you find the situation requires a different format.

As you create more style sheets, you will create a library of formats based on your experiences in creating various documents.

Save the document. Enter

**[Ctrl/s]**

Then, print the document.

```
Point the mouse at File
Point the mouse at To Print
Click
```

To print both pages, enter

⏎

Note that your printer probably printed three pages, with the third page being blank. This resulted from the way the Bottom Ln tag is defined and from the fact that you probably ended the last line of your text with a return when you entered it in the word processing program. The return at the end of the last line causes Ventura to create a new line for the end-of-file marker. Because Bottom Ln forces a new page, the end-of-file marker is moved to the next page — page 3 — causing a blank page to be printed. This is not a major problem. If it occurs, you can correct it by deleting the paragraph end character at the end of the Bottom Ln paragraph. When you have deleted it, the end-of-file symbol (the square) will appear next to the text as it does in Figure 3.26. Be sure to save your changes.

Prepare Ventura for a new document.

```
Point the mouse at File
Point the mouse at New
Click
```

Enter

⏎

# SUMMARY

This chapter discusses two major concepts: the use and structure of tab-aligned text in Ventura and the speed at which a document can be formatted once the basic paragraph tags are created. In this chapter's example document, all of the problems are worked out by creating tags for the first page. Page 2 simply reuses the tags without further modification.

- **Ruling Lines.** Ventura allows you to display special ruler lines that show in real inches, or other selected units of measurement, the location of text and the distances on the page. You can move the end points of the ruler to any horizontal or vertical position on the page to make measurement simpler.

- **Tabs.** Ventura allows you to define up to 16 tab stops as part of a paragraph's style tag. Tabs are measured from the left column margin border of the frame. You can select left, center, right, or decimal alignment for tabs.

- **Page Breaks.** Page breaks in Ventura are assigned as part of a paragraph's style tag. This means that to insert a page break, you must define a special tag that contains the page break setting. Page breaks are selected by using the Breaks option on the Paragraph menu. You can create a break before or after the specified paragraph.

- **Ruling Boxes.** Ventura allows you to draw boxes around paragraphs. Boxes should only be added to paragraphs that you are sure will not be split between pages. The spacing of boxes is the same as the spacing used for Ruling Line Above.

- **Paragraph vs. Text formatting.** Most of the operations performed by adding enhancements from the Text Editing mode can be duplicated by creating specialized paragraph tags. The advantages of using tags to handle even simple formatting are that the formats can be used again by selecting the same tag, and any changes made to that tag's format will roll back through the entire document. Manual text entry formatting depends upon the memory and consistency of the person using the program to ensure the correct formatting each time.

## Answers to Exercises

**EX-1 (see p. 147):** Create Title tag.

| |
|---|
| **Point** the mouse at Add New Tag<br>**Click** |

Enter

**Title** ⌐

**EX-2 (see p. 148):** Set alignment as centered.

| |
|---|
| **Point** the mouse at Paragraph<br>**Point** the mouse at Alignment<br>**Click**<br>**Point** the mouse at Horz. Alignment<br>**Drag** to Center |

Enter

⌐

**EX-3 (see p. 161):** Change alignment to left.

> **Point** the mouse at Paragraph
> **Point** the mouse at Alignment
> **Click**
> **Point** at Horz. Alignment
> **Click**
> **Drag** to Left

Enter

⏎

**EX-4 (see p. 170):** Set right-aligned tab at 6.5"

> **Point** the mouse at Pargraph
> **Point** the mouse at Alignment
> **Click**
> **Point** the mouse at Horz. Alignment
> **Click**
> **Drag** to Left

Then,

> **Point** the mouse at Pargraph
> **Point** the mouse at Tab Setting
> **Click**
> **Point** the mouse at Tab Type
> **Click**
> **Drag** to Right

Enter

**[Esc]**
**06.5** ⏎

**EX-5 (see p. 174):** Change to right-aligned tab at 5.5".

> **Point** the mouse at Tab Type
> **Click**
> **Drag** to Right

Enter

**[Esc]**
**05.5** ⏎

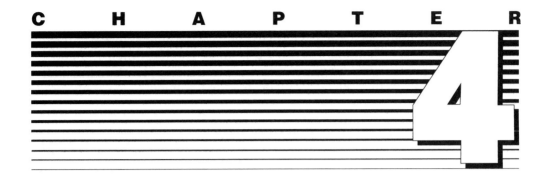

# USING GRAPHICS

**Graphics** refers to nontext characters used to enhance the appearance of a document. In the previous chapters, you used a form of graphics when you added ruling lines and boxes to the paragraphs you were formatting. Ventura has additional graphics features that can be useful in creating documents such as business forms.

Even with the advent of computers, businesses still use a wide variety of paper forms. With Ventura you can create various forms, such as invoices, order forms, and letterheads. Forms can be quickly designed and printed with Ventura. They can be revised and updated even faster. The only limit is your imagination.

In this chapter, you will learn some of the basic techniques available in Ventura for creating standard forms and using graphics. The example in this chapter will be an invoice form, but the principles discussed can be applied to almost any type of form you might want to create.

In this example, you will create a document directly in Ventura. The amount of text that appears on a form is minimal, so it will be just as easy to enter the text directly into the Ventura document.

The first step is to load the DEFAULT.STY style sheet so that you can begin constructing the tags you need from scratch. You will recall that Ventura automatically assumes you want to work with the last style sheet file used when you load the program. For example, at the end of the last chapter the final style sheet used was FINANCE.STY. Change to DEFAULT.STY.

---

**Point** the mouse at File
**Point** the mouse at Load Diff. Style
**Click**

---

You can now select DEFAULT.STY from the selector window or simply type in the name. If you prefer to use point and click mouse operations, feel free to substitute those actions for keyboard entries when appropriate. Enter

**default** ⏎

Create a new style sheet called INVOICE.STY.

> **Point** the mouse at File
> **Point** the mouse at Save as New Style
> **Click**

Enter the name of the new style sheet.

**invoice** ⏎

Place Ventura in reduced view mode by entering

**[Ctrl/r]**

You are now ready to begin creating the form.

# USING RULER MEASUREMENTS

Because Ventura is so visually oriented, the tendency is to rely on your eye for making placement decisions. The accuracy of this type of placement will vary from individual to individual, depending upon a person's acuity and artistic sense.

Ventura provides rulers to help you more accurately judge alignment. In Chapter 3, you learned how to use the Options menu to turn on the ruler display. If your ruler lines do not appear at the top and left edges of the document window, turn the rulers on by doing the following:

> **Point** the mouse at Options
> **Point** the mouse at Show Rulers
> **Click**

In Chapter 3, you also adjusted the horizontal position of the ruler. Because the document you are about to create requires vertical as well as horizontal measurements, you should move the vertical ruler down 1" so that it begins measuring from the top of the column instead of from the top of the page.

Display the SET RULER dialog box.

| |
|---|
| **Point** the mouse at Options<br>**Point** the mouse at Set Ruler<br>**Click** |

↓
**[Esc]**
**01** ⏎

Ventura has shifted the ruler line measurements so that 0" marks the edge of the column borders rather than the edge of the page. By changing the rulers, you eliminate the need to mentally add an inch each time you try to calculate a location.

## CREATING A LETTERHEAD

A good place to begin is to create a letterhead for the company name and address at the top of the form. You may even want to create a company logo, using Ventura's graphics features.

Place Ventura into the Text Editing mode. Enter

**[Ctrl/o]**

| |
|---|
| **Point** the mouse at the upper left corner<br>**Click** |

Switch to the normal display mode so you can see the text as you enter it. Enter

**[Ctrl/n]**

Enter the company name and address into the document:

**La Fish Enterprises [Ctrl/⏎]**
**1250 Walnut Blvd. [Ctrl/⏎]**
**Suite 1000 [Ctrl/⏎]**
**Pine Creek, CA 94596**

To format this paragraph, you must create a tag. Place Ventura in the Paragraph Tagging mode by entering

**[Ctrl/i]**

> **Point** the mouse at "La Fish"
> **Click**

Note that Ventura highlights all the lines because the line-end characters create a single paragraph with several short lines. Using line ends in place of paragraph ends makes it easy to format a series of related short lines. You will want to change the font and alignment of this group, so you should create a new tag.

> **Point** the mouse at Add New tag
> **Click**

Enter

**ltrhead ⏎**

**Exercise 1:**     Change the font of the ltrhead tag to Swiss, 14-point
bold and the alignment to center. Try this on your
own. The correct commands can be found under EX-1
at the end of this chapter.

The screen display should resemble the following:

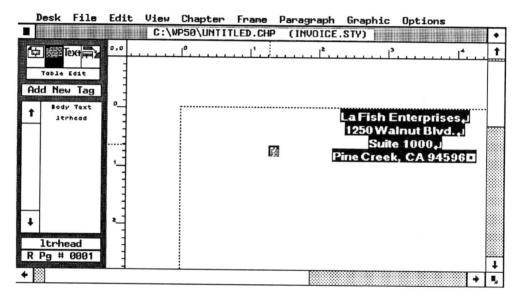

*Figure 4.1     Heading text centered on page.*

## ADDING GRAPHICS

The text you have just entered creates a letterhead, but you might want to enhance the letterhead with graphics. To add graphics to a document, you must
enter the Graphic Drawing mode. Enter

**[Ctrl/p]**

The side bar changes from the text entry options to the graphics options. These
options consist of six icons — the graphic selector (arrow) icon and five icons that
represent the types of graphics you can add to your document.

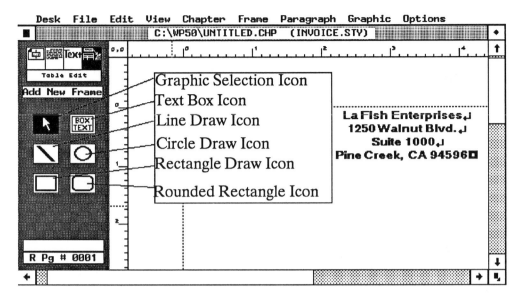

*Figure 4.2    Side bar displays graphics options.*

Suppose you want to draw a rectangle with rounded edges around the company name and address.  First, scroll to the right so the text is more centered in the window.

---

**Point** at the scroll bar right arrow  (2 times)
**Click**

---

Next, you need to select the drawing tool you want to use.

---

**Point** the mouse at the rounded rectangle icon
**Click**

---

The rounded rectangle icon is highlighted, and the shape of the mouse cursor changes to indicate that the rounded rectangle is the selected drawing tool. Items are drawn by pointing at the location in which you want to place the upper left corner of the graphic and then dragging the mouse to where you want the lower right corner to be. As you drag the mouse, the graphic will be enlarged or reduced, depending on the direction in which you drag. Note that you can continuously change the size of the graphic until you decide to release the mouse. At that point, the graphic is inserted into the document.

Begin drawing by pointing the mouse above and to the left of the first letter in the company name. If you look at the ruler lines, you should be at approximately 0" vertical and 2" horizontal. Note that the mouse cursor appears as a rounded corner.

> **Point** at 0" vertical, 2" horizontal
> **Hold down** the mouse button

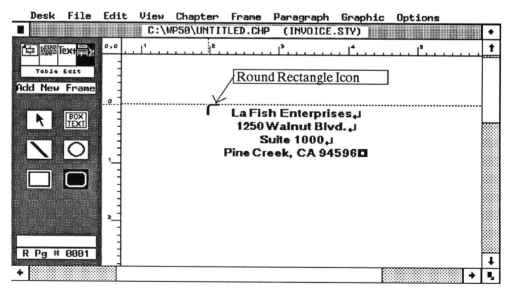

*Figure 4.3    Rounded rectangle drawing cursor positioned.*

As you drag the mouse, an outline will indicate the shape you are drawing. Drag the outline so that it surrounds the entire company name and address. The position should be approximately 1" vertical and 4.5" horizontal.

---

**Drag** the mouse to 1" vertical, 4.5" horizontal

---

When you release the mouse, Ventura draws the rounded rectangle.

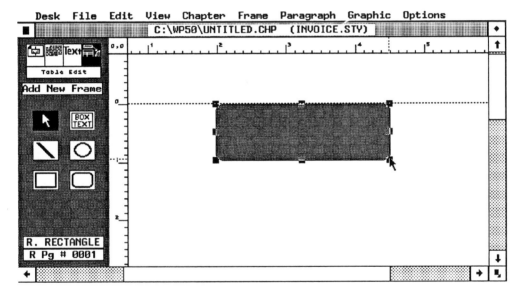

*Figure 4.4     Rounded rectangle drawn over company name and address.*

You might be surprised to see that the rectangle has obscured the text. This does not mean that the text has been erased. It is still there, but it is temporarily hidden by the graphic you have just drawn.

Save the invoice you have begun to create as a Ventura chapter by entering

**[Ctrl/s]**

The ITEM SELECTOR dialog box will appear. Enter

**invoice⏎**

Note that Ventura automatically adds a CHP extension to the filename you just entered.

## Line and Fill Attributes

When you create a graphic, there are two categories of settings that affect the display. These options are located on the Options menu.

**Fill Attributes**    The fill attributes control how the space enclosed by the graphic appears. You can select the background color and pattern and whether the attribute will be transparent or opaque. The FILL ATTRIBUTES dialog box can be displayed by entering [Ctrl/F].

**Line Attributes**    You can change the width of the line that is drawn to create the circle or rectangle with this option. It is also possible to remove the line by selecting None. If the object is a straight line, you can add arrows to the ends. The LINE ATTRIBUTES dialog box can be displayed by entering [Ctrl/L].

In the current example, the fill attributes of the rounded rectangle prevent the text from showing through the graphic. To allow the text to appear inside the rounded rectangle, you must change the fill attributes. Enter

**[Ctrl/F]**

Ventura displays the FILL ATTRIBUTES dialog box.

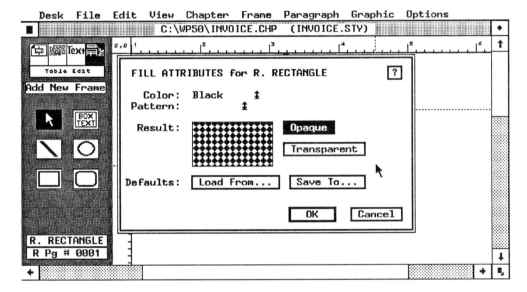

*Figure 4.5    FILL ATTRIBUTES dialog box.*

The two settings in this box are Color and Pattern. You can also choose to have the interior of the object be transparent or opaque with regard to objects underneath it. In this case, you want to allow the text to show through the box.

> **Point** the mouse at Transparent
> **Click**

In addition, if you are planning to allow text to show through the box, you will probably want to change the pattern to a light gray so that the text will be easy to read. A background that is too dark or complicated will interfere with the text. Ventura has seven gray tones in addition to the options for hollow or solid color. The gray tones increase in density as the number increases (i.e., 1 is the lightest shade, and 7 is the darkest shade). In this case, select shade 2.

---

**Point** the mouse at Pattern
**Click**
**Drag** to 2

---

Save the modifications to the rectangle by entering

⏎

The text now shows through the rectangle.

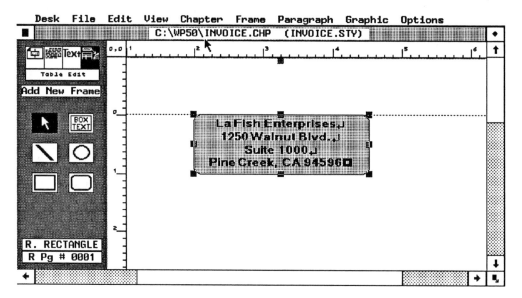

*Figure 4.6    Transparent rectangle allows text to show through.*

You can also adjust the thickness of the line that outlines the rectangle. Enter

**[Ctrl/L]**

Ventura displays the LINE ATTRIBUTES dialog box.

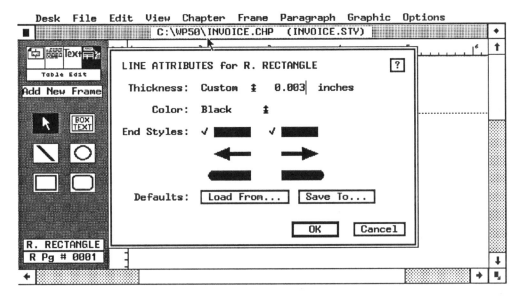

*Figure 4.7    LINE ATTRIBUTES dialog box.*

Note that the current unit of measurement for the thickness setting is in inches. Change the unit of measurement to fractional points.

**Point** the mouse at inches
**Click**  (3 times)

Change the thickness of the line to three points. Enter

**[Esc]**
03 ⏎

The line around the rectangle is thickened to three points.

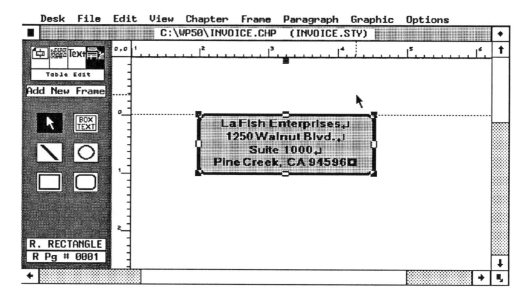

*Figure 4.8     Rectangle outline thickened.*

In the previous dialog box you were asked to change the unit of measurement from inches to fractional points. Your own personal preference will decide the correct unit of measurement for a particular task; however, thinking in terms of points rather than inches has some advantage when you are working with very small items such as ruling lines or small text characters. It is always easier to deal with whole numbers rather than large decimal numbers. Recall that a point is approximately 0.01389". When you are thinking about adjustments to line height, the idea of one, two, or three points as line thickness may be easier to deal with than .014", .028", and .042". On the other hand, when you are dealing with larger measurements such as margins, column indents, or page sizes, measuring in inches is probably easier. Thinking about 1.5" margins is probably a lot clearer than thinking about 108-point margins.

Unless you are a professional typographer and have dealt with points as a unit of measurement for some time, you will probably find that using points for small measurements and inches for large measurements is the best way to deal with units of measure.

## USING BOXED TEXT

If you have been working through this book sequentially, up to this point all the text you have formatted with Ventura has been paragraph-oriented text that was formatted in lines between margins. This is the way word processing programs work with text; however, Ventura has the ability to place text at any location on the page. One method for placing text at specific locations is called boxed text.

**Boxed text** is text that is typed into a small box, or mini-frame, that can be moved to any location on the screen. The boxed text frame can be positioned anywhere on the page. Boxed text can be thought of as the Ventura equivalent of Post-it notes that are saved with the final document. The box around the text also provides automatic ruling lines around the text, which can be used to create fill-in forms in which ruling lines are needed around all of the text items.

Boxed text is created in Ventura's Graphic Drawing mode. This technique combines Ventura's graphic drawing capabilities with the paragraph-oriented text methods you have used in the first three chapters. The invoice form you are about to create will consist of a number of small text boxes. Each box will contain the name of some data item that you want to fill in. For example, one box should be laid out for the date, another for the P.O. number, another for the company name, and so on. To begin, you will create a box for the date.

The date box should begin at the left column guide, about 1.5" from the top. This is the kind of situation in which the ruler lines come in handy. As you move the mouse, the line in the ruler will keep track of your location.

Scroll to the left.

| |
|---|
| **Click** on the scroll bar left arrow (2 times) |

Select box text from the side bar display.

> **Point** the mouse at the box text icon
> **Click**

Text boxes are created in the same way as other graphic items, such as the rounded rectangle you created previously, by pointing at the upper left position of the box and then dragging the mouse to the lower left corner.

To draw the first text box on the page, point the mouse at the left column guide about 1.5" down the page, as shown in Figure 4.9.

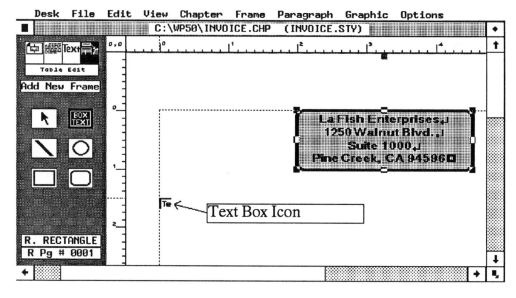

*Figure 4.9    Mouse pointed at starting position for box.*

To create the text box, drag the mouse. In this case, you want to create a box .5" high and 2" wide, which means you must drag the mouse down to the position 2" vertical and 2" horizontal.

**Drag** the mouse to 2" vertical, 2" horizontal

Ventura draws a box on the page. An end-of-file symbol appears in the box.

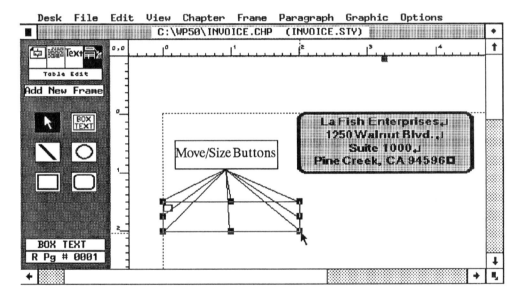

*Figure 4.10    Text box drawn on page.*

On the border of the box, Ventura displays eight small boxes called buttons. When the buttons are visible, the graphic on which they are visible is the currently selected graphic. (To avoid confusing references to these buttons with references to the mouse button, the buttons surrounding a selected graphic will be referred to as **selection buttons**.) Selecting a graphic has about the same meaning as highlighting text. It indicates that the commands that you issue will affect that graphic and not any other graphic that has been entered in the same document.

## Editing and Formatting Box Text

Once you have created a text box, you can use the Text Editing mode to enter text into the box. Enter

**[Ctrl/o]**

Note that in Text Editing mode, the box's selection buttons disappear. Graphic commands cannot be used in the Text Editing mode, so the buttons have no function and are removed from the screen display. The Text Editing mode functions the same way inside of a text box as it does when you are editing text in the master frame.

To activate the Text Editing mode inside the text box, click the mouse anywhere inside the box.

---

**Point** the mouse inside the text box
**Click**

---

The text cursor appears beside the end-of-file symbol. Enter

**DATE:**

Your screen should resemble the following:

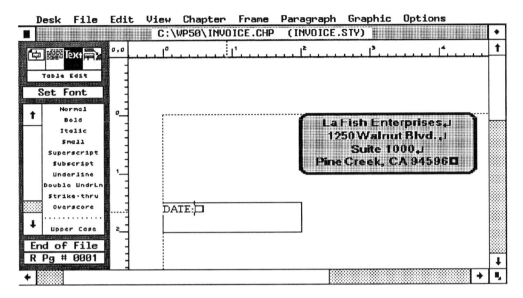

*Figure 4.11    Text entered inside text box.*

Now that you have entered text into your box, you may want to select format options such as font, spacing, etc. for the text inside of the text box. For those types of changes, you can use the Paragraph Tagging mode. Change Ventura to the Paragraph Tagging mode by entering

**[Ctrl/i]**

| |
|---|
| **Point** the mouse at "DATE:" |
| **Click** |

Examine the box above the page number. It displays **Z_BOXTEXT**. Ventura automatically tags all boxed text as Z_BOXTEXT. You might wonder where this tag came from because your side bar list shows only Body Text and ltrhead as its tags. Ventura keeps a special set of tags reserved for features such as boxed text, page headers and footers, and footnotes. These tags are automatically included in every style sheet but they are not normally displayed in the side bar list. Ventura calls these tags **generated tags** because they are automatically created when you implement a special feature that requires a tag. Ventura will display the generated tags along with your user-defined tags if you request that option from the Options menu.

---

**Point** the mouse at Options
**Point** the mouse at Set Preferences
**Click**

---

This dialog box contains a number of options that affect the way Ventura operates.

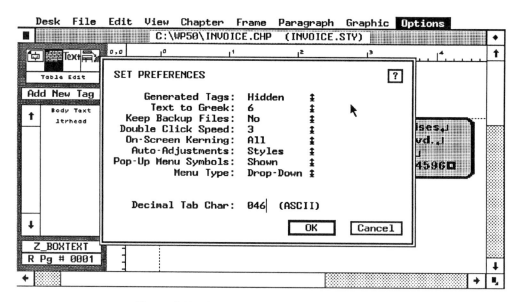

*Figure 4.12   SET PREFERENCES dialog box.*

The first option in this dialog box is the status of the generated tags. The default setting is **Hidden**. Change it to **Shown.**

> **Point** the mouse at Generated Tags
> **Click**
> **Drag** to Shown

Enter

⏎

The name **Z_BOXTEXT** now appears in the side bar listing of tags. The next step is to select the font you want to use for the boxed text. Select Swiss, 14-point so that the text in the boxes will match the text in the letterhead.

> **Point** the mouse at Paragraph
> **Point** the mouse at Font
> **Click**
> **Point** the mouse at Swiss
> **Click**
> **Point** the mouse at 14
> **Click**

Enter

⏎

The text is formatted for that font. Changing the Z_BOXTEXT tag will affect all the text entered in text boxes. This means that when you create the next box, the text will automatically be formatted as Swiss, 14-point. If you want to change only this one box and leave the other boxes as Swiss, 14-point, you can create a new tag instead of modifying Z_BOXTEXT. On the other hand, you can also tag the text within a box with any one of the style tags, such as ltrhead, that you created on your current style sheet if you wanted that format inside the box.

One problem remains. You have probably noticed that the top of the text is aligned with the top line of the box. The text would look much better if it were centered vertically between the top and the bottom lines of the box. This problem can be solved by using the Spacing option on the Paragraph menu.

> **Point** the mouse at Paragraph
> **Point** the mouse at Spacing
> **Click**

In the center of the box you will see the **Add in Above** option. This option has two settings: Always and When Not at Column Top. The currently selected setting is When Not at Column Top. This setting tells Ventura not to add space above a line if it is the first line in a column. This setting makes sense when you are working with text in the master frame because you will usually want the first paragraph on the page to be aligned flush with the top column guide on the page.

Ventura considers the first line in a text box as the top of a column or page. In this case, you do want the Above space added to the column.

> **Point** the mouse at Always
> **Click**

Now Ventura will add the space above the text, which will separate the text from the line at the top of the box. Ventura does not allow you to create margins for boxed text; you must handle spacing problems from the Paragraph menu. But one question remains.

How much space should be placed above the text?  In Ventura, there are two ways to handle a problem like this.  Most people will simply use trial and error until they arrive at something they think looks correct.  While there is nothing wrong with trial and error, taking a moment to calculate some values will help you save time and create more consistent formats.

In this case, the two key values are the height of the text box — .5" — and the height of the characters — 14 points.  14-point text is about .2" in height.  This means that there is about .3" inches of blank space to be divided above and below the text. Half of .3" is .15", so a good guess as to the correct height would be .15".  Place the text cursor on the Above line.

---

**Point** the mouse at .227 on the Above line
**Click**

---

Enter

**[Esc]**
**.15** ⏎

The text is approximately centered between the top and the bottom of the box.

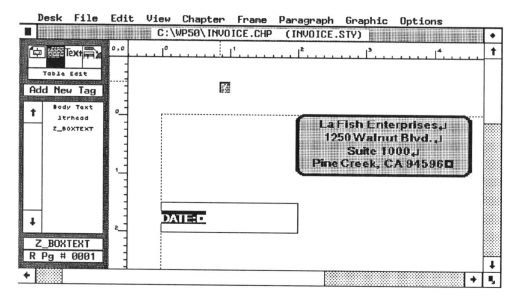

*Figure 4.13    Text formatted to fit text box.*

That may seem like a lot of work for just one box, but because of the way Ventura uses style settings, you have actually set up the way you will format all the boxes on this form.

## Making Copies

The next task is to create a box for the P.O. number. Ventura allows you to copy text, frames, or graphics, which can be a useful shortcut when you want to create a slight modification of an existing item. With Ventura, you can make copies by using the [Shift/Del] key combination and the Ins (Insert) key.

- **[Shift/Del]** copies the highlighted text, frame, or graphic into the computer's memory.

- **[Ins]** places the text, frame, or graphic in the computer's memory into the document.

To make a copy of the box, you must first highlight the box. The box is a graphic item, so you must switch Ventura back into Graphic Drawing mode. Enter

**[Ctrl/p]**

In Graphic Drawing mode, while the graphic selection (arrow) icon is highlighted, you can select (i.e., highlight) a graphic object by pointing at any part of the object and clicking the mouse. One simple way is to point at the text in the box.

> **Point** the mouse at "DATE:"
> **Click**

Buttons are displayed on the box, indicating that you have selected that graphic object. To copy this frame into the memory, enter

**[Shift/Del]**

Note that there is nothing on the screen that indicates that you have performed this action. You must mentally keep track of what has been copied.

You are now ready to insert a copy of the box into the text; however, before you do this there is something you will need to consider. Your goal will be to place the new box next to the existing box and then repeat that process throughout the entire form, but placing objects on the screen in correct alignment is not as easy as you might think. When you want to align objects exactly, you will often find the mouse very sensitive to slight movements, which makes it difficult to get an exact alignment.

In Ventura, you can control the sensitivity of the mouse by creating an invisible grid that will control how far an object will move each time it is dragged.

For example, it might be useful to move objects such as text boxes in increments of 1/4" or 1/2". This would make it simple to properly align items because Ventura would not allow you to move an odd amount, such as 7/32".

Movement of graphics is controlled from the **Graphic** menu.

| **Point** the mouse at Graphic |

Ventura displays the Graphic menu.

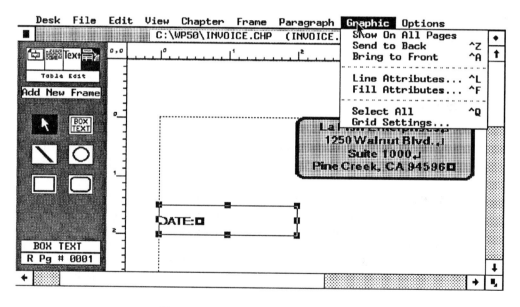

*Figure 4.14   Graphic menu displayed.*

In this case, you are concerned with the Grid Settings.

---

**Point** the mouse at Grid Settings
**Click**

---

The GRID SETTINGS dialog box appears.

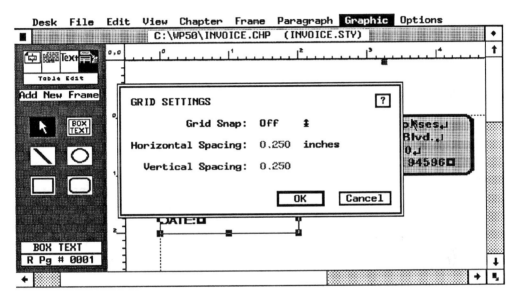

*Figure 4.15    GRID SETTINGS dialog box.*

The first option is **Grid Snap**. Grid Snap is a useful feature because it causes graphic objects to move only in some evenly spaced increment. This helps you align objects correctly. The dialog box also allows you to specify the width and height of each increment of movement. In this case, set the grid snap to 1/2" in both directions. Turn on the grid.

> **Point** the mouse at Grid Snap
> **Click**
> **Drag** to On

Enter the values for the horizontal and vertical movements.

**[Esc]**
.5 ↓
**[Esc]**
.5 ↵

Note that the grid does not appear on the screen. It will, however, affect the way an object moves when it is dragged around the page.

## Inserting Graphics

Even though it has been a few moments since you copied the box into memory, Ventura retains a copy of the object until you copy another one or quit the program. This means that you could copy a graphic from one document to another by loading a new chapter before you insert the object. In this case, you want to place the copy onto the current page. Enter

**[Ins]**

The screen clears for a moment and then redraws itself. If you examine the screen, you will see that it appears to be exactly as it was before, but that appearance is deceiving. There are really two boxes on the screen. Ventura places the copy of the graphic in the same location as the original. What you see on the screen is the copy you have just inserted. The original box can't be seen because the copy is on top of it. When you move the copy, you will see the original box beneath it.

To move a graphic box, you must drag the object by first pointing anywhere inside the box or circle. The cursor will change to a four-directional arrow. This symbol indicates that the object will move as you move the mouse. Remember to hold the button down until you have moved the graphic into the correct position.

> **Point** the mouse at the box
> **Hold down** the mouse button

The cursor changes shape to a four-directional arrow. This icon tells you that you can move the box by dragging the mouse.

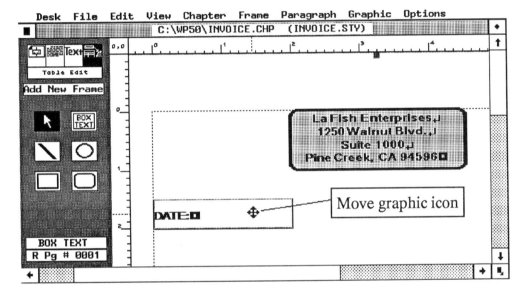

*Figure 4.16   Mouse icon changes to four-directional arrow.*

Now that you have the graphic selected for movement, drag the mouse to the right. Remember to keep holding down the mouse button. As you move the mouse, you will notice that the box does not move smoothly. Instead, it jumps .5" to the right (see Figure 4.17) as a result of the grid settings you selected. You can easily move the box .5", 1", 1.5", etc. because the grid will not allow you to stop at locations in between. Keep holding down the mouse button.

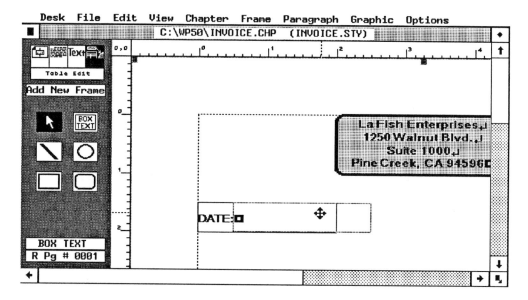

*Figure 4.17   Text box moved .5" to the right.*

Keep moving the mouse to the right until you have positioned the boxes side by side. Then release the mouse button.

---

**Drag** the mouse until boxes are side by side
**Release** the mouse button

---

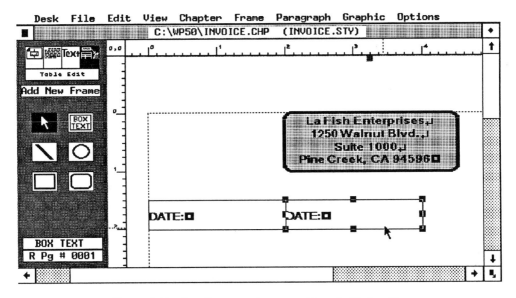

*Figure 4.18   Duplicate text boxes positioned side by side.*

Notice that the grid setting helps you maintain the alignment without much effort while you are dragging an object. If you had not set the grid, it would be much more difficult and tedious, if not impossible, to make exact alignments. The grid also forces you to place objects that are uniformly spaced on the page.

Change the text to read "P.O. Number:" in the box. First, return to the Text Editing mode. Enter

**[Ctrl/o]**

---

**Point** to the right of "DATE:"
**Click.**

---

Delete the word "DATE:" by using the Backspace key and entering "P.O. Number:" in its place. Enter

**[Backspace]** (5 times)
**P.O. Number:**

## Changing Shapes

The DATE: and P.O. Number: boxes are exactly the same size; however, you should leave more room for the P.O. number to be entered. You could do this by changing the spacing or size of the text box. Ventura allows you to change the size and shape of a box after you have placed it in the document.

Before you do this, it might be helpful to scroll to the right.

---

**Point** at the scroll bar right arrow
**Click** (2 times)

---

To change the shape of the box, activate the Graphic Drawing mode by entering

**[Ctrl/p]**

Select the P.O. Number: box.

---

**Point** the mouse at P.O.
**Click**

---

Selection buttons appear on the P.O. Number: box. Selection buttons are the key to changing the shape and size of a graphic. They allow you to expand or contract the box. To use a selection button, point the mouse cursor at the selection button, and press and hold down the mouse button. The cursor will change to a hand with a pointing finger. This icon tells you that you have entered the sizing mode. Note that the different selection buttons surrounding the box allow you to change its size by stretching or contracting it in different directions. The buttons in the corners of the box will allow you to move those corners horizontally or vertically, or both ways at the same time. The buttons that appear in the center of the lines allow for movement in one direction only. The buttons on the horizontal lines will only move vertically, and the buttons on the vertical lines will move only horizontally.

In this case, you want to choose the selection button in the upper right corner of the text box.

---

**Point** the mouse at the upper right selection button
**Hold down** the mouse button

---

The mouse cursor will change to a hand with a pointing finger.

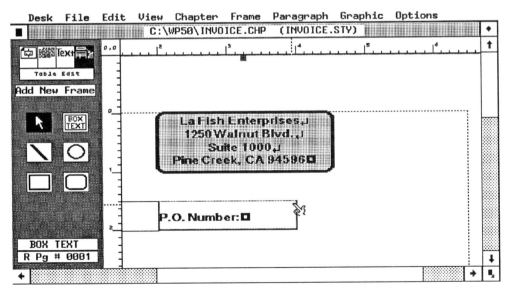

*Figure 4.19   Pointing finger icon indicates that sizing mode is active.*

Move the mouse to the right until you reach the 5" mark on the ruler. As you do, the box stretches in that direction, 1/2" at a time.

> **Drag** the mouse to the 5" mark
> **Release** the mouse button

You have expanded the size of the box.

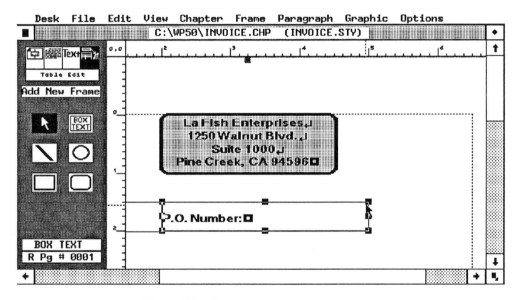

*Figure 4.20    Text box expanded by dragging.*

## More Boxes

Now that you have the basic idea of how to create boxes, you are ready to move a bit faster. As you begin to fill out the form with boxes, it might be easier to work in the reduced display mode. Enter

**[Ctrl/r]**

You are about to draw several additional text boxes. You may have noticed that as soon as you release the mouse button after drawing an object, Ventura automatically shifts into the graphic selection mode. There are times when you will want to remain in the same drawing mode (i.e., boxes, lines, etc.) so you can create several items without having to reselect the drawing tool you want to continue using. You can achieve multiple graphic selection by holding down the Shift key while you drag the mouse. This procedure will be referred to as [**Shift/Drag**].

The next box will be for the company name. It will begin at the lower left corner of the DATE box and stretch across the entire page.

> **Point** the mouse at Box Text
> **Click**

Using the same method as before, press and hold down the mouse button; dragging the mouse, draw a .5"-high box across the entire column. The box is shown in Figure 4.21.

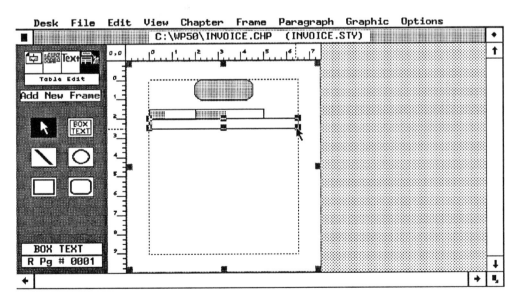

*Figure 4.21    Frame-width text box added to document.*

Select the box text icon again.

**Point** the mouse at the box text icon
**Click**

Draw another box with the upper left corner at 2.5" down on the column guide, stretching from 0" to 4" across and from 2.5" to 3.5" down (i.e., so it is 4" wide and 1" high). This box will hold the address and should appear as shown in Figure 4.22.

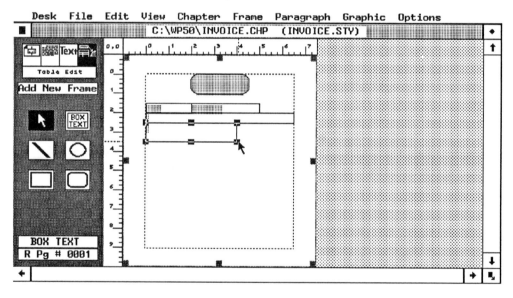

*Figure 4.22   Heading box drawn on page.*

Now that you have created the boxes, you will want to edit them so they contain the proper headings. Change the display mode to normal, and enter Text Editing mode.

---

**Point** the mouse at "DATE:"
**Click**

---

Enter

**[Ctrl/n]**
**[Ctrl/o]**

Enter the titles "COMPANY:" and "ADDRESS:" into the boxes, respectively. The document should resemble Figure 4.23.

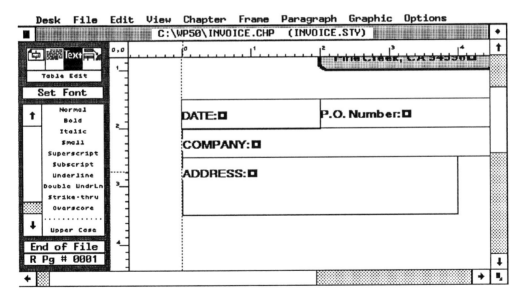

*Figure 4.23   Additional boxes labeled.*

## ADDING GRAPHIC LINES

You have completed the top portion of the invoice form. Before you go on to complete the bottom section, you may want to add a graphic that helps distinguish the top section from the bottom section. Ventura allows you to draw straight lines. Change the display mode to reduced. Enter

**[Ctrl/r]**

Place Ventura into the Graphic Drawing mode by entering

**[Ctrl/p]**

To draw a line, select line draw — the \ (line draw) icon — from the graphics icons shown on the side bar display.

> **Point** the mouse at the line draw icon
> **Click**

Then,

> **Point** the mouse at the left column guide

The cursor now appears as a pencil icon. Line drawing is performed by dragging the mouse.

> **Point** the mouse at the left column guide, about 4" down
> **Drag** across to the right column guide

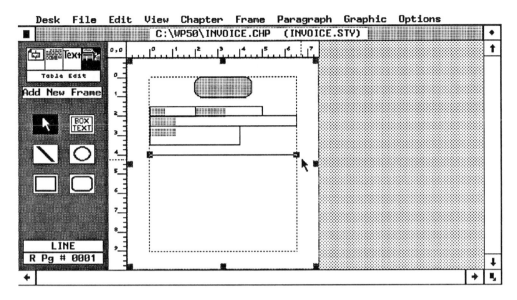

*Figure 4.24    Line drawn across columns.*

Change the thickness of this line by using the LINE ATTRIBUTES dialog box. Enter

**[Ctrl/L]**

The menu reveals that the line thickness is currently set at .24 points. Increase the thickness to 9 points. Enter

**[Esc]**
**09** ⌐

## DRAWING SMALLER BOXES

The next section of the invoice will consist of a series of smaller boxes. These boxes will contain the items or services purchased. These boxes do not need to be as large as the boxes you have been drawing.

**Exercise 2:** To keep the math simple, make the boxes .25" high. The best way to control this measurement is to change the vertical grid setting to .25". Try this on your own. The correct commands can be found at the end of this chapter under EX-2.

The next task is to create four small boxes on each line. There will be boxes for the description, price, quantity, and total cost of the items. Select the box text icon from the side bar.

Following is a table that shows the staring point, the upper left corner, and the ending point of four new text boxes. Draw the text boxes on the current document. All of the boxes are .25" in height. Note that if you [Shift/Drag], Ventura will remain in the text box mode instead of switching to the graphic selection mode after each drawing.

| **Upper Left** | **Lower Right** |
| --- | --- |
| 5" vertical, 0" horizontal | 5.25" vertical, 3" horizontal |
| 5" vertical, 3" horizontal | 5.25" vertical, 4.5" horizontal |
| 5" vertical, 4.5" horizontal | 5.25" vertical, 4.5" horizontal |
| 5" vertical, 5.5" horizontal | 5.25" vertical, 6.5" horizontal. |

When you have finished drawing, you should have four .25"-high boxes with widths of 3", 1.5", 1," and 1", respectively, as shown in Figure 4.5.

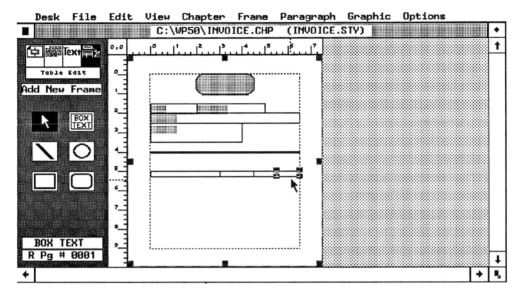

*Figure 4.25    Four boxes drawn side by side.*

## COPYING MULTIPLE GRAPHICS

The boxes that you have just created will eventually contain the column headings "DESCRIPTION," "QUANTITY," "PRICE," and "COST."  You will enter these headings later.  For now, you want to make a number of copies of the boxes as they are, without text.  The idea is to create a grid of boxes that will serve as the items section of the invoice form.

Ventura allows you to select more than one graphic object at a time in the same way that you can select more than one paragraph at a time for paragraph tagging operations.  This also means that once you have selected the group of graphics you can copy, move, expand, or contract all of the selected items at the same time.

The first step in performing this type of operation is to select all the objects at one time.  Begin by selecting the left-most 1/4" box.

---

**Point** the mouse at the left-most box
**Click**

---

241

You now want to add to the selection the next box to the right. You can do so by using the [Shift/Click] method.

---

**Point** at the next box to the right
**[Shift/Click]**

---

Now the selection buttons appear on both boxes, indicating that you have two boxes selected. Expand the selection to include the third box on the line.

---

**Point** at the next box to the right
**[Shift/Click]**

---

Repeat the process for the last box on the line.

---

**Point** at the next box to the right
**[Shift/Click]**

---

All four boxes are part of the same selection. Any operation performed now will affect all four boxes.

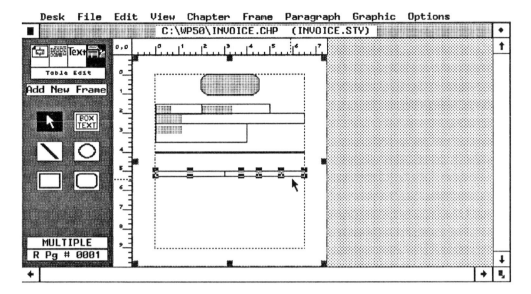

*Figure 4.26   Four text boxes selected at once.*

Now that you have the boxes selected, you can place a copy of them into memory by entering

**[Shift/Del]**

With a copy of the four boxes in memory, you can duplicate them.  Insert a copy into the document by entering

**[Ins]**

Remember that you can't see both sets of boxes because the copy you just inserted is positioned directly on top of the orginal.  You need to drag the copy down to its proper position, one line below the original set of boxes, but where should you point to move a multiple selection of boxes?

There is only one way to make a mistake. Do not point at any of the selection buttons. Pointing at a graphic's selection button tells Ventura that you want to change the shape of that box, not change its location.

You can point at the space inside any of the boxes. Ventura treats all the boxes selected as a single graphic so it doesn't really matter which one you point at. All of the boxes will move together.

> **Point** the mouse inside any box
> **Drag** down .25"

You now have two lines of identical text boxes.

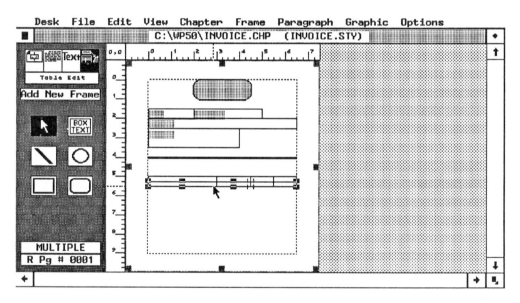

*Figure 4.27   Multiple selection of boxes copied and positioned.*

To make another line of boxes, insert another copy. Remember that once an object or group of objects has been placed into memory, you can make as many duplicates as you like. Enter

**[Ins]**

The selection buttons move back to the original location. This is because the new copy is always inserted on top of the original. Drag this copy into place, below the two lines of boxes.

Repeat the process two more times. This will give you five lines of boxes, as shown in Figure 4.28.

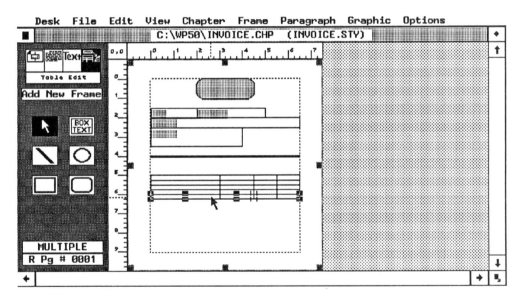

*Figure 4.28    Five lines of duplicate boxes create a grid-like pattern.*

Notice that the effect of placing the boxes together creates a grid-like pattern of columns and rows. When the document is printed, you will not be able to tell that it was created by placing boxes next to each other. The lines from each box will overlap, forming a single grid pattern.

## MOVING FASTER

Adding boxes doesn't take much effort, but you can get the job done even faster. Now that you have made more than one line of boxes, you can select several lines as a group. Copy that group into memory and insert two, three, or more lines at a time. As an example, extend the selection to include five rows of boxes.

You can create one large selection by using [Shift/Click] to select all 20 boxes, i.e., five rows of four boxes. The boxes are pretty small in the reduced mode, so it might be easier for you to select in the normal display mode. Before you change modes, point at the left column guide on the current line.

---

**Point** the mouse at the upper left text box

---

Change modes by entering

**[Ctrl/n]**

Select the first box, the one in the upper left corner of the grid.

---

**Point** the mouse at the upper left box
**Click**

---

Use the [Shift/Click] technique to select the four text boxes below the selected box. Note that as you select each box, the selection buttons move to outline the expanded selection. When you have selected all five boxes in the left column, the selection buttons will resemble those shown in Figure 4.29.

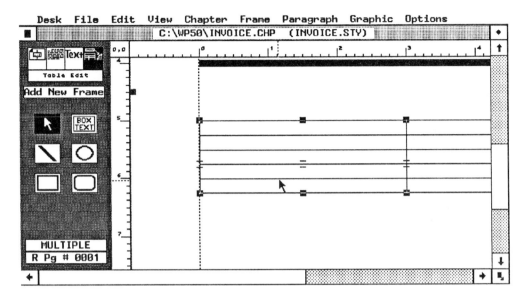

*Figure 4.29   Multiple selection of five boxes.*

Enlarge the selection by using [Shift/Click] to include all of the boxes in the second column.

When you have added those boxes, scroll to the right.

> **Point** at the scroll bar right arrow
> **Click**  (3 times)

[Shift/Click] to select the remaining ten boxes.  The completed selection should look like the selection in Figure 4.30.

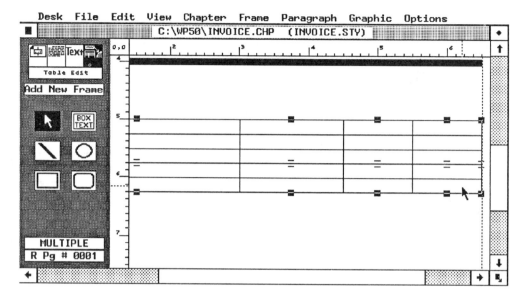

*Figure 4.30    Twenty text boxes selected at one time.*

You can now place a copy of all 20 boxes into memory by entering

**[Shift/Del]**

Return to the reduced mode by entering

**[Ctrl/r]**

Now insert a copy of the 20-box graphic by entering

**[Ins]**

Position the copied graphic by dragging it below the original grid.

---

**Drag** to 6.5" vertical

---

When you are done, the screen should resemble Figure 4.31.

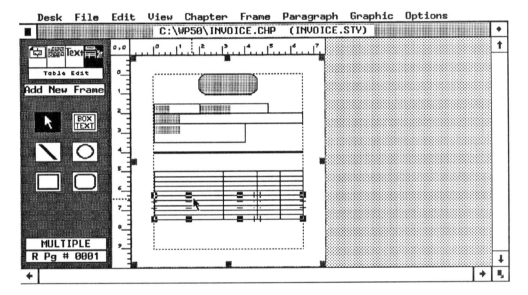

*Figure 4.31   Duplicate graphic positioned on page.*

## HEADING BOXES

You have now created a grid of .25" boxes. However, the first row of boxes was meant to be for column headings. Recall that the character font used for the text boxes was designed for boxes that were .5" in height. You have two options. You can create a new tag that uses a smaller point size so that the characters will fit into a .25" box, or you can expand the top row of boxes to .5". There is space between the top of the box grid and the address section at the top of the document, so you have room to expand the top row of boxes.

Use the [Shift/Click] method to select the four boxes on the top row of the grid. Note that in the reduced view mode it can be tricky to select small items such as the text boxes. In selecting the top row of boxes, point the tip of the mouse cursor at the top line of the box rather then at the center or bottom line. Pointing at the top will help you select the correct row even in the reduced view mode.

When you have selected the four boxes, you can expand the height of the boxes to .5" by dragging any of the selection buttons on the top line of the selection upward .25".

> **Drag** top selection button upward .25"

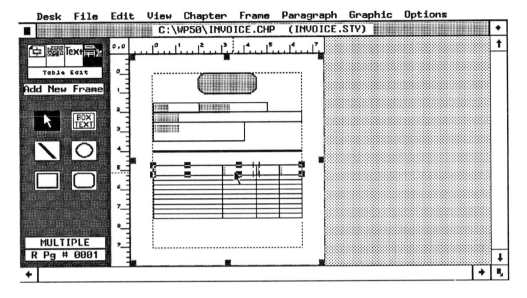

*Figure 4.32   Top row expanded to .5" height.*

## Box Backgrounds

The .5" boxes will hold the headings for the columns.  There is another attribute of boxed text that you can take advantage of to make the headings stand out from the other boxes.

Ventura allows you to select a background color and/or pattern for each box.  Because most printers can only print in black, the colors consist of a variety of gray tones.  You can change the fill attribute of text boxes as well as rectangles.  The fill attributes can be applied to a multiple selection as well as to one item at a time.

Change the fill attribute of the current selection by entering

**[Ctrl/f]**

Ventura displays the FILL ATTRIBUTES dialog box for the text box. The default values for the text box are different from the ones for rectangles. The text box is set as a solid white box that is transparent for the object underneath it. In this case, you need to make two changes. The color should be changed to black and the pattern to a gray tone.

```
Point the mouse at Color
Click
Drag to Black
```

Then,

```
Point the mouse at Pattern
Click
Drag to 1
```

Enter

⌐

The boxes are now shaded.

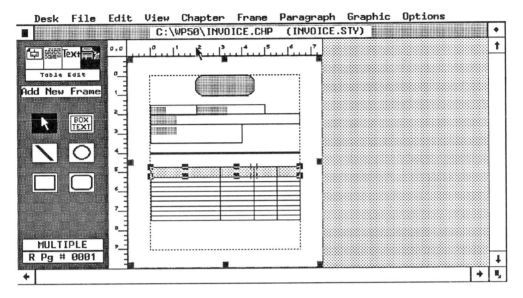

*Figure 4.33   Shaded boxes displayed.*

## Entering Headings

Now that the top row of boxes has been set up for headings, you need to enter the text into the boxes. This is best done in the normal display mode, where the text is readable.

---

**Point** the mouse at the left shaded box

---

Enter

**[Ctrl/n]**

Place Ventura into the Text Editing mode by entering

**[Ctrl/o]**

Enter the headings **DESCRIPTION**, **PRICE**, **QUANTITY**, and **COST**, respectively, into the four boxes. You will need to scroll to the right to enter all four headings.

When you are done, the screen should resemble Figure 4.34.

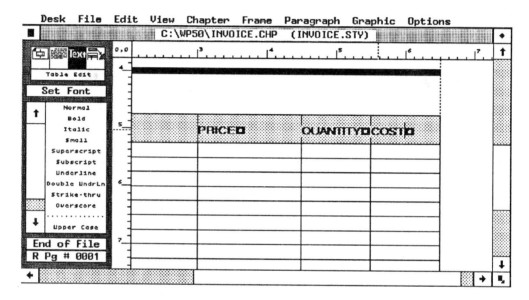

*Figure 4.34    Text entered into heading boxes.*

## SUPERIMPOSING TEXT

The final item that must be added to this form is the place in which the total amount due is listed. This item is important, so you will want to make good use of Ventura's facilities for making it stand out. Scroll the document window to the lower right corner of the page. One way to do this is to switch to the reduced view mode, point at the area on the page you want to enlarge, and change back to the normal mode. Remember that when you are in reduced mode, Ventura uses the mouse location as a guide for which section of the page to enlarge when you change to the normal mode. The same relationship exists when switching between normal and enlarged view modes. Enter

**[Ctrl/r]**

---
**Point** at lower right corner of the column guides

---

Enter

**[Ctrl/n]**

Suppose that you wanted to create a rounded rectangle that contained the text "Amount Due." The text box is always a rectangle with right angles. The rounded rectangle is a graphic item with no text. What is the solution?

The solution is to use both a text box and a rounded rectangle to create the type of graphic you want to use. This technique uses a text box to superimpose text over other graphics.

Begin by creating a rounded rectangle. Select the rounded rectangle icon.

---
**Point** the mouse at the rounded rectangle icon
**Click**

---

The rectangle's upper left corner should be 8" vertical and 5" horizontal. Drag the rectangle to the lower right corner of the column guides, 9" vertical and 6.5" horizontal. The rectangle should resemble the one in Figure 4.35.

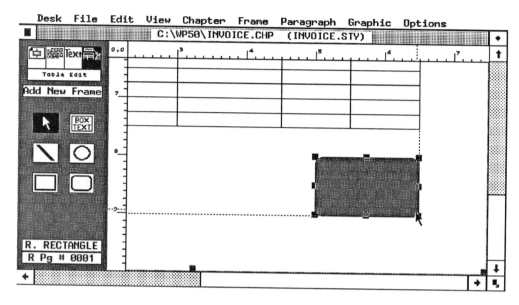

*Figure 4.35    Rounded rectangle drawn in lower right corner.*

To insert text into that rectangle, you must create a text box that will contain that text and then place that box directly over the rectangle.  Select the box text icon.

---

**Point** the mouse at the box text icon
**Click**

---

Draw a text box over the same area in which you have drawn the rounded rectangle.  The screen should resemble Figure 4.36.

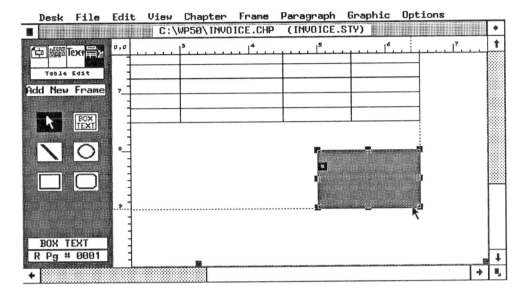

*Figure 4.36    Text box superimposed over rounded rectangle.*

To prevent the superimposed text box from interfering with the display of the rounded rectangle, you must set the line attributes to None so that the outline of the text box will be invisible.  Only the text you enter will appear superimposed on the rounded rectangle.  Enter

**[Ctrl/L]**

To eliminate the lines of the text box, select None from the list of thickness options.

---

**Point** the mouse at Thickness
**Click**
**Drag** to None

---

Then enter

↵

The outline of the text box is removed. Change to the Text Editing mode in order to enter the text. Enter

**[Ctrl/o]**

Activate the text cursor.

| |
|---|
| **Point** the mouse inside the text box |

Enter

**Amount Due:**

As you type, the shaded background appears to be changed to white. This is only a temporary distortion. To see the correct display, force Ventura to rewrite the screen display by entering

**[Esc]**

The text is superimposed over the rounded rectangle.

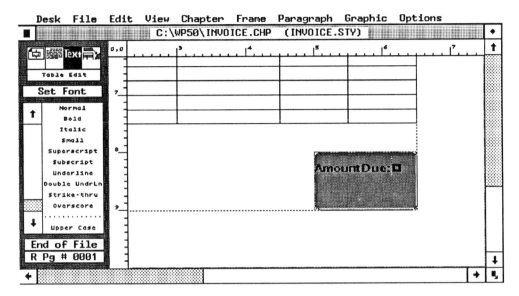

*Figure 4.37   Text displayed over rounded rectangle.*

You can place another rectangle on top of the current display to create an area of white within the shaded rectangle so that someone could enter a number without being concerned that it would not be legibly written over the shading. Return to the Graphic Display mode. Enter

**[Ctrl/p]**

---

**Point** the mouse at the rounded rectangle icon
**Click**

---

Draw a rectangle below the "Amount Due:" label, as shown in Figure 4.38.

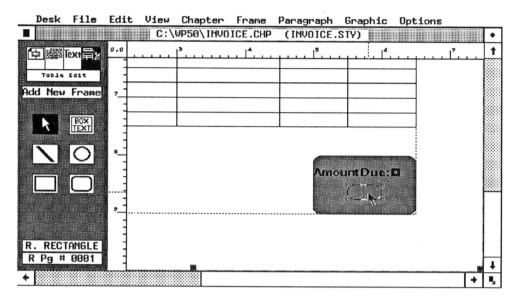

*Figure 4.38    Rectangle drawn inside rounded rectangle.*

**Exercise 3:**    To create white space inside the shaded rectangle, you must change the settings of the smaller rectangle to have no line and to fill the center with opaque, solid white. Turn off the outline. Try this on your own. The correct commands can be found under EX-3 at the end of this chapter.

Change the fill attributes to solid, white, and opaque. Enter

**[Ctrl/f]**

---

**Point** the mouse at Color
**Click**
**Drag** to White
**Point** the mouse at Pattern
**Click**
**Drag** to Solid

---

Enter

⏎

The small rectangle creates a white area inside of the larger rectangle.

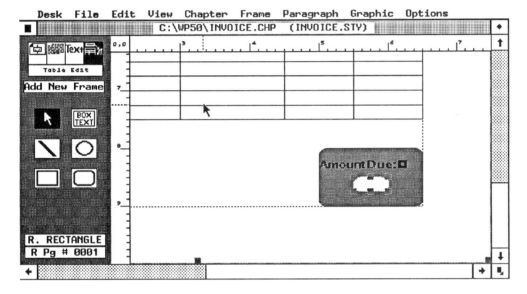

*Figure 4.39    White rectangle superimposed on shaded rectangle.*

The final graphic on the page is the result of combining three different graphs, each superimposed on the other. While Ventura's graphics are limited compared to full-powered graphics packages, they are adequate for creating many of the effects you would need to enhance a standard document. By combining the simple graphic elements in different ways, you can create a surprising variety of images.

Now print the document.

> **Point** the mouse at File
> **Point** the mouse at Print
> **Click**

Enter

⏎

Save the document by entering

**[Ctrl/s]**

Display a new chapter so that you are ready to start a new document.

> **Point** the mouse at File
> **Point** the mouse at New
> **Click**

Enter

⏎

# SUMMARY

- **Rulers.** Ventura can display rulers that mark off the page display with vertical and horizontal measurements. When you move the mouse cursor, Ventura displays a line in both rulers to show you the cursor's position. You can select the measurement format — inches, centimeters or picas — and the starting location of the rulers. Changing the starting location allows you to compensate for any margins on the page, so, for example, you don't need to add an inch to all your calculations to compensate for a 1" margin.

- **Graphics.** Ventura's Graphic Drawing mode allows you to add rectangles, circles, ovals, lines, and text boxes to your documents.

- **Text Boxes.** Text boxes are mini-frames. They allow you to place text at any location on the page. The box's size defines its margins.

- **Graphic Selection.** Graphic "selection" is roughly equivalent to highlighting text in the Text Editing mode or tagging paragraphs in the Paragraph Tagging mode. When a graphic item is selected, small black squares are displayed on its border. These squares are called "buttons," and are referred to as "selection buttons" in this book. Selection buttons are used to change the size and shape of graphic objects. Selected graphics can be deleted, copied, or moved on the page. You can select more than one graphic at a time by using the [Shift/Click] method.

- **Dragging Graphics.** You can change the position of a selected graphic by using the "drag" method. To drag an object, point the mouse cursor at any place in the object except at one of the buttons. Hold down the mouse button. The object enters a drag mode. Moving the mouse cursor will cause the object to move on the page.

- **Copying Graphics.** You can copy a selected graphic or graphics into memory by using the [Shift/Del] key combination. Entering [Ins] places a copy of the object in memory onto the page. You can then use the "dragging" method to move the graphic.

- **Changing Size.** The size and shape of graphics can be altered by pointing the mouse cursor at one of the graphic object's selection buttons. Hold down the mouse button and move the mouse cursor (this is called "dragging"). The graphic will stretch in the direction of the movement.

- **Grid Spacing**. To make creating, dragging, and changing graphics more consistent, Ventura allows you to select size increments for movements and changes. The horizontal and vertical increments cause the graphic to change or move in jumps rather than in smooth movements. Setting a grid can make it simple to align graphics consistently on a page.

- **Line Attributes.** Graphic lines can be displayed with a variety of thicknesses. [Ctrl/l] displays the LINE ATTRIBUTE dialog box.

- **Fill Attributes.** Graphic boxes, ovals, circles, and text boxes can have white, gray, or black backgrounds. [Ctrl/f] displays the FILL AT-TRIBUTE dialog box.

- **Generated Tags.** Ventura automatically generates special style tags when you select special features such as headers, footers, footnotes, and boxed text. Generated tags are used to format incidental text that is stored in footnotes, heads, and boxed text. Ventura normally does not display the names of these tags in the side bar display. You can choose to display these tags by changing the setting on the Set Preferences menu.

## Answers to Exercises

**EX-1 (see p. 206):** Change the font to Swiss, 14-point bold and the alignment to Center.

> **Point** the mouse at Paragraph
> **Point** the mouse at Font
> **Click**
> **Point** the mouse at Swiss
> **Click**
> **Point** at 14
> **Click**

(Note that the Swiss, 14-point font is automatically bold.)

Enter

↵

> **Point** the mouse at Paragraph
> **Point** the mouse at Alignment
> **Click**
> **Point** the mouse at Horz. Alignment
> **Click**
> **Drag** to Center

Enter

⏎

**EX-2 (see p. 240):** Change the vertical grid setting to .25".

> **Point** the mouse at Graphic
> **Point** the mouse at Grid Settings
> **Click**

Enter

↓
**[Esc]**
**.25** ⏎

**EX-3 (see p. 260):** Create white space inside the shaded rectangle.

Enter

**[Ctrl/L]**

> **Point** the mouse at Thickness
> **Click**
> **Drag** to None

Enter

↵

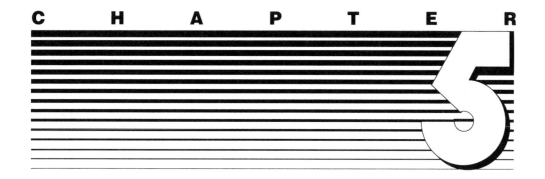

# MULTIPLE-FRAME DOCUMENTS

In the first four chapters, you explored many Ventura features. Each chapter has built upon the concepts of the previous chapter and has added a layer of complexity to the document layout process.

In this chapter, you will take one of the most significant steps in learning how to use Ventura. You will learn the how and why of using more than one frame in a single document.

In Chapter 4, you saw that boxed text would allow you to place information at specific locations on a page. Boxed text freed you from the need to enter text into the master frame. Instead, you pasted the boxes wherever you wanted on the page.

However, boxed text is limited in its scope. Ventura supplies other techniques that allow you to create additional frames on the page. Each frame is capable of all of the operations that can be performed on the master frame. For example, you can load text into a frame from a text file. If you create multiple frames on the same page, you can load text from several files and combine them into a single document.

In this chapter, the goal will be to create an advertisement layout. The layout will require you to load information from several separate files and place them all on the same page. Some of the files will be text. The others are graphics files that contain images and pictures.

## PREPARING THE FILES

The first step in putting together a project like this is to prepare the files — text, and pictures — that you will want to use in the document.

The document will be a direct mail flyer advertising a computer called the PXL6000. Below is the text of a document called **PXL6000.WP** that was entered using WordPerfect. Prepare the file as shown. Note that the arrows mark the location of hard returns, i.e., the ends of paragraphs.

If you are thinking about upgrading your computer system why not consider today's best buy the PXL-6000 computer.␛

This machine provides the power user will all the horsepower they can use assembled in a state-of-the-art cube shaped computer that fits just as well under an airline seat as it does on you desk.␛

With all this power the PXL-6000 is still easy to use and runs all of your favorite software.␛

The PXL-6000 provides more standard features than any other computer in its class made in the U.S.A.␛

Worried about price? The PXL-6000 is surprisingly affordable. We will beat advertized price plus if you act before December 31st we will throw in a set of wine glasses perfect for holiday entertaining.

*Figure 5.1    PXL6000.WP document.*

The PXL6000.WP document contains a general description of the PXL6000 computer and reasons why you should purchase it.

Create this document, and save it with the filename PXL6000.WP. (Be sure to use an appropriate extension if you aren't using WordPerfect to create the document.)

The next figure shows a second document. This document is called **FEATURES.WP** and contains a list of the main features of the PXL6000 computer.

For only $3799 you get: ↙
4 Megabytes of fast (80 ns) internal memory ↙
Four speed(8 to 16 MHz), software selectable, 80286 processor ↙
Clock/calendar built-in ↙
One 1.2 megabyte floppy disk ↙
One 360 kilobyte floppy disk ↙
100% VGA compatible graphics adapter, 256 colors, 640 by 480 resolution ↙
40 megabyte hard disk (28 ms) ↙
102 character keyboard with 12 function keys ↙
1 parallel printer port ↙2 serial communications ports ↙
14" VGA compatible color monitor ↙
MS-DOS version 3.3 ↙
1200 baud internal modem add $600 ↙
80 megabyte hard disk add $400

*Figure 5.2    FEATURES.WP document.*

You should create this document and save it with the filename **FEATURES.WP**. (Be sure to use an appropriate extension if you aren't using WordPerfect to create the document.)

## GRAPHICS FILES

Ventura can combine high-resolution images along with text. The images can come from a number of sources, such as specialized drawing and painting programs or special devices called **scanners** that convert pictures or drawings on paper to computer-based images.

Most graphics and scanner programs are compatible with Ventura. Ventura can even read images created on a Macintosh computer; however, note that you need special programs and/or devices to connect IBM PCs or compatibles and Macintosh computers in order to transfer the files because the disks used in PCs and Macintosh computers are not compatible.

- **Graphics Programs.** The IBM PC has available a large number of graphics programs that can create images that can be imported into Ventura. Ventura can read graph files created with Lotus 1-2-3, drawings prepared with PC Paintbrush and GEM Draw, and picture files (PIC extension) created with Lotus 1-2-3 or compatible programs.

- **Scanned Images.** Image scanners are available that will create a bit-mapped computer image from any paper image that you can put through a scanner. Small scanners (those that can capture images no wider than 4") can be purchased for less than $400. Full-page scanners begin at about $1500.

# DIRECTORIES

Before you begin working with Ventura, you need to have some graphics files to work with. Ventura supplies three such files on the *Examples* disk, which is usually disk #4. You will need to locate this disk and copy the graphics files from it onto your hard disk.

Keeping track of files when you are creating a document that consists of several files, including text and graphics, can be a problem. One way to better organize this type of operation is to create a DOS disk directory and place all the files you want to work with in that directory. If you are familiar with DOS concepts, you probably know what directories are and how to create and use them. If you are not familiar with DOS, you can simply follow the instructions included in this book. Unfortunately, it is beyond the scope of this book to offer a complete explanation of DOS commands.

You should begin at the operating system level. The DOS prompt, usually **C:\**, will be displayed. If your prompt shows a different directory, e.g., **C:\WP50**, do not be concerned. The procedure that follows will work as long as you are located anywhere on the C drive.

The first step is to create a new directory that you will use to hold all of the files that are used in creating this document. The directory will be called **FLYERS** because you will use this directory to hold files used for creating advertising flyers. Note that in the DOS commands that follow, equal signs are used instead of spaces. If you are not familiar with DOS, it is sometimes easier to enter a visible character instead of looking for the correct number of spaces between words. DOS allows you to enter an equal sign ( = ) or a comma (,) in place of spaces. Enter

**md = c:\flyers** ⏎

The two text files, PXL6000.WP and FEATURES.WP, are probably stored in the same directory as your word processor, e.g. c:\WP50. Copy those files to the new directory that you created. Enter

**copy = c:\wp50\pxl6000.wp = c:\flyers** ⏎

DOS confirms the operation by displaying the message **1 File(s) copied**. Copy the other text file to the same directory by entering

**copy = c:\wp50\features.wp = c:\flyers** ⏎

The next step is to copy the three graphics files from the *Examples* disk into the same directory.

Place the *Examples* floppy disk into drive A. Enter

**copy = a:*.gem = c:\flyers** ⏎

This time two files, **NOZZLE.GEM** and **COLUMBIA.GEM,** are copied. Enter another copy command to get the third graphics file:

**copy = a:*.img = c:\flyers** ⏎

The file **CHANEL.IMG** is copied into the directory.

You can check to see that all five files have been placed in the correct directory by entering

**dir = c:\flyers** ⏎

DOS will list the five files copied to that directory.

```
C:\>dir=c:\flyers

Volume in drive C is Rob Krumm
Directory of  C:\FLYERS

             .          <DIR>      11-15-88   1:08p
             ..         <DIR>      11-15-88   1:08p
        PXL6000  WP        1262    11-15-88  12:16p
        FEATURES WP         845    11-15-88  12:16p
        NOZZLE   GEM      20360     8-27-86   9:45a
        COLUMBIA GEM      13602     8-27-86   9:42a
        CHANEL   IMG      37599     1-01-86   2:29p
             7 File(s)    2193408 bytes free

C:\>
```

*Figure 5.3    Files copied to new directory.*

You can now load Ventura in the usual manner and begin to work on this new document.

## CREATING A NEW STYLE SHEET

If you have been following the lessons in this book, the style sheet INVOICE.STY created in Chapter 4 was automatically loaded when you started Ventura.

In this case, the first step will be to create a new style sheet for the new document. You will also want to be sure to place this new style sheet file in the same directory as the other files you have just copied.  To begin, load the DEFAULT.STY style sheet.

---

**Point** the mouse at File
**Point** the mouse at Load Diff. Style
**Click**
**Point** the mouse at DEFAULT.STY
**Double Click**

---

Now save a copy of this style sheet under a new name in a new directory.  Call the style sheet **ADD**, for "advertising flyers."

> **Point** the mouse at File
> **Point** the mouse at Save As New Style
> **Click**

Before you enter the name of the style sheet, you will want to activate the new directory, **FLYERS**. To display a list of directories, use the black button in the upper left corner of the file list box.

> **Click** on the directory button

The file list box will display a list of directories that includes the FLYERS directory.

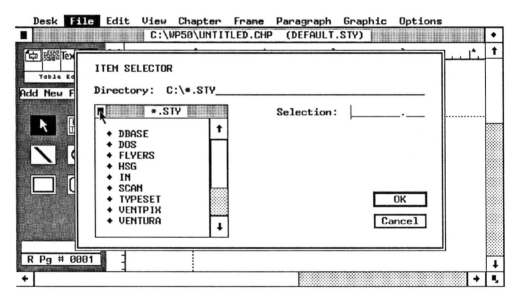

*Figure 5.4    New FLYERS directory appears in item selector display.*

Select the new directory.

> **Point** the mouse at FLYERS
> **Click**

You can now create the new style sheet by entering the name of the style sheet. Enter

**add** ⏎

You have now created the style sheet file for this document and placed it in the newly created FLYERS directory.

## ADDING A FRAME

In this document, you will need to create a number of frames. Multiple-frame documents have several advantages. Primarily, they allow you to treat different parts of the text as independent items. Each frame can have a different set of margins and columns. You can quickly change the arrangement of a page by changing the location of one or more frames. This is much quicker and easier than cutting and pasting text. When you move or copy text, you do not move the margins and other settings along with the text. The text conforms to the margins and settings of its new location. When you move a frame, the text and settings for that frame are unchanged. Only the frame's location on the page is altered. Place Ventura into the reduced view mode by entering

**[Ctrl/r]**

The first frame you create will contain the letterhead address block. Place Ventura into the Frame Setting mode. Enter

**[Ctrl/u]**

The master frame is selected. You can tell that a frame is selected because Ventura displays selection buttons on the frame. Recall that Ventura displays buttons on graphic objects to indicate their selection. The frame that is selected is the master, or underlying, frame that Ventura automatically creates for each document.

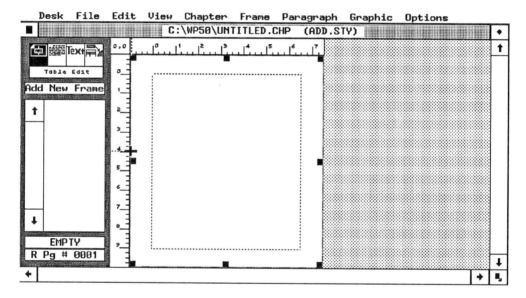

*Figure 5.5    Buttons indicate active frame.*

Ventura always has at least one frame in every document — the master frame. Up to this point, all of your work has taken place in the master frame. But that is going to change. You will create additional frames. There are four reasons why you need to use additional frames:

- Each frame can hold text from only one document source. In this document, you will want to combine text from several files.

- Frames can have individual settings for margins and columns. This allows you to combine different layout styles on the same page.

- When you create graphics, the graphics are attached to a frame. If you attach a graphic to the master frame, it will repeat on all pages. If you create another frame, the graphic will appear only on the page with that particular frame.

- You can quickly move frames to new locations without having to reformat the text inside the frame. You can also size frames to accommodate smaller or larger text files.

Note that there is only one master frame. All other frames are treated as additional frames. You will learn the difference between the master frame and the additional frame in the following discussions.

When the frame mode is active, the words **Add New Frame** appear above the side bar. The list box in the side bar lists the names of the files that are being used in this document.

The first part of this document will be a company letterhead at the top of the page. Instead of directly entering that text into the master frame, you will place that text into a new, separate frame. If you place the letterhead information in a separate frame, it will not be affected by operations you perform later, such as creating multiple columns. To create a new frame,

---

**Point** the mouse at Add New Frame
**Click**

---

The Add New Frame box is highlighted.

---

**Point** at the upper left corner of the column guides

---

You will notice that the cursor is now a right angle with the letters "FR" inside. This is the frame cursor.

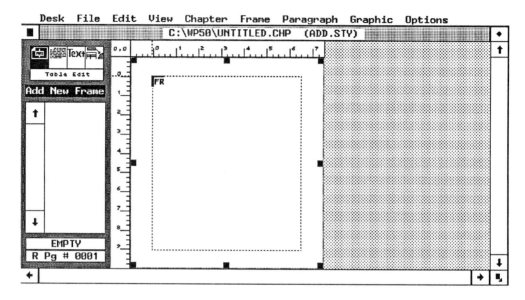

*Figure 5.6    Draw new frame cursor.*

You use the same basic technique to draw frames as to create boxed text.

- Point the mouse cursor at the location in which you want the upper left corner of the frame to be placed.

- Drag the mouse to the position in which the lower right corner of the frame should be located. Ventura draws the frame as you move.

As with boxed text, Ventura provides a means of getting the right size frame without having to move the mouse to the exact location; however, the way Ventura treats frame alignment is a bit different from the way it treats graphics. Ventura assumes that frames will contain text or images that are integrated into text. Instead of using a spacing grid to help with alignment, Ventura uses two settings on the Options menu that affect frame placement.

> **Point** the mouse at Options

In the third section of the menu, you will see two settings, **Turn Column Snap Off** and **Turn Line Snap Off**. The **Off** tells you that these features are currently active. The features are called **Snap** because they cause Ventura to align your frames at specific locations in the document.

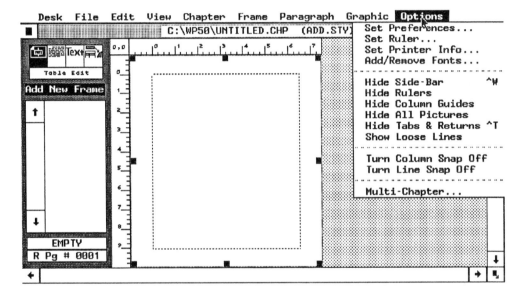

*Figure 5.7    Options menu.*

**Column Snap**

The column snap aligns the left or right edge of a frame on the nearest column guide if you draw the box within .1" of that column guide. This means that if the cursor is within .1" of a column guide, Ventura snaps the frame edge to the column guide. This feature makes it possible to draw a frame that is exactly equal to the current column width without having to drag the frame to the exact location.

**Line Snap**     The line snap causes the bottom and top of the frame to align to the next text line. The amount of space between line snaps is not always the same. The size is determined by the amount of inter-line spacing entered for the Body Text tag. The default value is about .19" for 12-point Dutch text. The reason Ventura associates frame placement with inter-line spacing is to make sure that frames are not drawn at sizes that overlap part of a line of text. This is usually the best way to size frames because it simplifies integration of frames with text in the master frame.

Both snaps are currently on, so your frame will snap when you draw it. To exit the menu without changing the setting,

---

**Point** the mouse at a blank area
**Click**

---

Now you are ready to draw the new frame. The frame should be as wide as the column guides and about 1.5" high.

---

**Point** at the upper left column guide corner
**Drag** to 1.5" vertical, 6.5" horizontal

---

You will now have a box at the top of the screen. This is your new frame. Note that Ventura has displayed the selection button on this frame to indicate that it is the active frame. The selection buttons that were on the master frame have been removed because it is no longer the active frame.

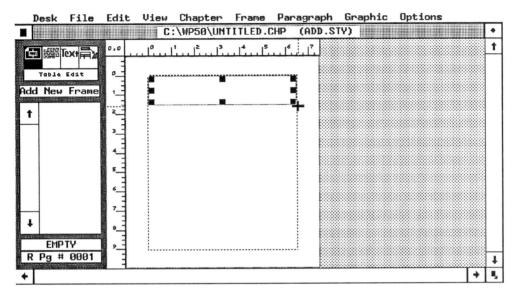

*Figure 5.8     Frame drawn at top of page.*

## SELECTING FRAMES

Because you have more than one frame on the page, you need to know how to select the frame you want to work with. You can select a frame by pointing the mouse cursor anywhere inside that frame and clicking the mouse button. Select the master frame.

---

**Point** the mouse anywhere in the right margin
**Click**

---

The button appears on the master frame. Now, reselect the new frame.

---

**Point** the mouse anywhere inside the new frame
**Click**

---

The new frame is selected.

## ADDING TEXT

Now that you have created a new frame, you can enter the name and address of the company in one of two ways:

- Enter the text mode and manually enter text directly into the frame.

- Load the text from a text file stored on the disk.

In this case, you have not prepared any text file for the name and address, so you will need to enter them directly into the frame.

Activate the Text Editing mode by entering

**[Ctrl/o]**

---

**Point** the mouse inside the new frame
**Click**

---

This positions the text cursor for text entry into the new frame. To make text entry simpler, change from reduced to normal mode by entering

**[Ctrl/n]**

Enter the address and phone information:

**The Crummy Computer Company [Ctrl/⏎]**
**1242B Partridge Avenue [Ctrl/⏎]**
**Wilmington, Delaware 20300 [Ctrl/⏎**
**210-777-3000**

The next step is to format the text by creating appropriate paragraph style tags. Change to the Paragraph Tagging mode by entering

**[Ctrl/i]**

You cannot create or modify a paragraph tag unless you have selected at least one paragraph.

---

**Point** the mouse at "Wilmington"
**Click**
**Point** the mouse at Add New Tag
**Click**

---

Enter the name of the new tag.

**address** ⏎

## VERTICAL ALIGNMENT

In previous chapters you dealt with the concept of horizontal alignment. This option allowed you to align text with the left side, right side, or center of the master frame. You could also select justified text in which the right and left ends of text lines entered would be aligned flush with the right and left frame edges, respectively.

Ventura also allows vertical alignment within a frame. Vertical alignment refers to the placement of a paragraph at the top, bottom, or middle of a page. This option is used when there is only a single line or paragraph of text in the frame. In previous documents you created, the master frame contained several paragraphs, but in the current document, you have a new frame with only a single paragraph of text.

Suppose you want Ventura to align that paragraph so there is the same amount of space above and below the text within the new frame. You could achieve that effect by selecting Middle as your vertical alignment option.

> **Point** the mouse at Paragraph
> **Point** the mouse at Alignment
> **Click**

Note that the second option in this dialog box is called **Vert. Alignment**.

> **Point** the mouse at Vert. Alignment
> **Click**
> **Drag** to Middle

You will want to center the text horizontally as well.

> **Point** the mouse at Horz. Alignment
> **Click**
> **Drag** to Center

Enter

↵

The paragraph is now centered vertically and horizontally within the current frame. Note that in the Paragraph Tagging mode, the frame outlines do not appear. To see more clearly that the text is aligned in the center vertically as well as horizontally, change to the Frame Setting mode. Enter

**[Ctrl/u]**

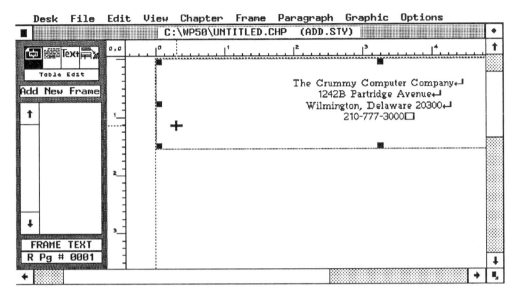

*Figure 5.9    Vertical alignment centers paragraph vertically.*

Keep in mind that vertical alignment is a specialized tool that works best for centering a single line or paragraph within a small frame. If you select vertical centering in a multiple-paragraph document, only the first paragraph will appear on the current page.

The vertical alignment feature can also be used to align text with the bottom edge of the frame as well as the top and middle of the frame.

## FRAME OPERATIONS

Now that you have established a separate frame for the address block, you can use the commands from the Frame menu to enhance the display. To use the Frame menu commands, you must be in the Frame Setting mode. Enter

**[Ctrl/u]**

Ventura now displays the frame border lines. The selection buttons on the frame border serve the same purpose on a frame as they do on a graphics item. You can use them to enlarge or contract the size of the frame. Also, as previously mentioned, they also indicate which frame is currently selected.

The box over the page number reads **FRAME TEXT**. Ventura stores text entered into additional frames in a file with a **CAP** extension. The CAP file is assigned the same name that you assign to the chapter file. The text in the CAP file is always stored in standard ASCII format.

To make the address section of the document stand out from the rest of the document, you might want to enclose that frame with a lined box.

> **Point** the mouse at Frame

Ventura displays the **Frame** menu.

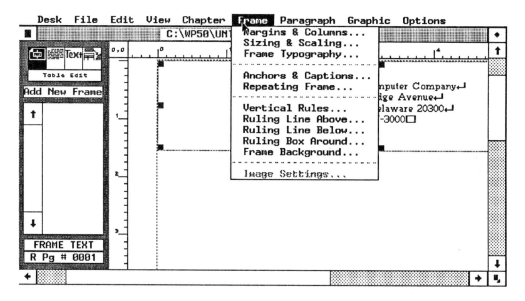

*Figure 5.10    Frame menu displayed.*

In this case, you want to add a box around the frame.

> **Point** the mouse at Ruling Box Around
> **Click**

Ventura displays the **RULING BOX AROUND** dialog box. This menu has the same set of options as the Paragraph menu's RULING BOX AROUND dialog box. The selections you make have essentially the same meanings as in the paragraph dialog box. The only difference is that the box will be drawn around the entire frame instead of around a particular paragraph. The first setting allows you to select the width of the ruling box. When you select the width, you will notice that several options are listed but that all options except Frame are grayed, indicating that they are not available. Select the Frame width.

> **Point** the mouse at Width
> **Click** and **hold down** the mouse button
> **Drag** to Frame

The bottom part of the display is now active. Here you can enter the specifications for the line you want to place around the frame. In fact, you can define up to three lines at one time, just as you can for a paragraph ruling box. In this case, create a double-line box by entering

↓
**[Esc]**
.042 ↓
**[Esc]**
.028 ↓
**[Esc]**
.014 ⏎

The double-line ruling box is drawn around the frame.

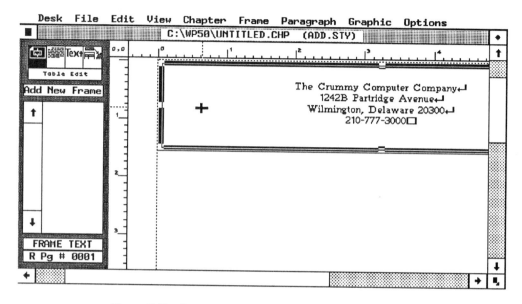

*Figure 5.11   Double-line ruling box drawn around frame.*

## SIZING FRAMES BY NUMBERS

The simplest way to size a frame is the mouse-dragging method you have just used; however, it is possible to adjust the size of a frame after you have drawn the frame. The adjustment can be made by entering size values rather than dragging with the mouse. The advantage of this method is that you can create a frame of an exact width and height.

Suppose that below the letterhead frame you wanted to create a frame that contained a headline for the page. The first step would be to create a frame to hold the headline. In this case, you have decided that the frame should have a specific height and width, e.g., 1" high and 6.5" wide.

You can begin by drawing a frame of any size at any position on the page.

> **Point** the mouse at Add New Frame
> **Click**

Draw a frame about 1" square below the lower left corner of the previous frame. The frame should resemble the one shown in Figure 5.12.

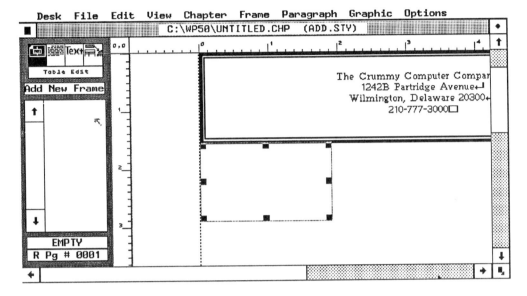

*Figure 5.12    Small frame added to document.*

The exact size of the frame you created is not important. The size of the frame can be adjusted from the Frame menu, using the Sizing & Scaling option.

---

**Point** the mouse at Frame
**Point** the mouse at Sizing & Scaling
**Click**

---

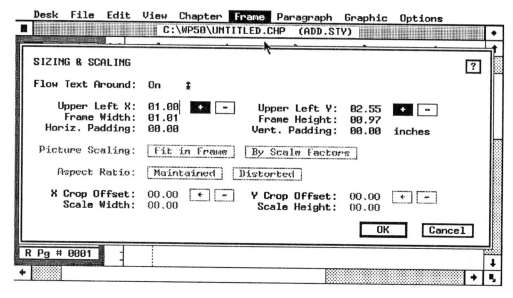

*Figure 5.13    SIZING & SCALING dialog box.*

The SIZING & SCALING dialog box displays an exact numerical description of the frame you have just created. Because dragging is an imprecise method of sizing, your values will probably differ from those shown in Figure 5.13.

The location of the frame is determined by two values: **Upper Left X** and **Upper Left Y**. These values indicate the position of the upper left corner of the frame.

The Upper Left X value refers to the horizontal position, and the Upper Left Y value refers to the vertical position. Figure 5.13 shows that the current frame is located 1" from the left edge of the page and 2.55" down from the top of the page (again, your values may differ from the ones in Figure 5.13).

The size of the frame itself is shown in the Frame Width and Frame Height values. The frame in this example is currently .97" high and 1.01" wide.

What is important about these values is that you can revise them by entering other values. The frame that you are working with will adjust its location and size on the page according to the values you enter.

In this case, you want the frame to be 6.5" wide and 1" high. You also want to place the upper left corner of the frame at 1" horizontal and 2.75" vertical. Enter those values into the dialog box.

[Esc]
01 ↓
[Esc]
02.75 ↓
[Esc]
06.5 ↓
[Esc]
01 ↵

The frame now appears at the specified location and its size is adjusted to fit the size specifications.

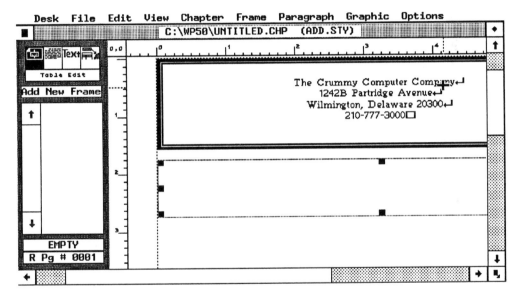

*Figure 5.14   Frame altered by entering values.*

Now that the frame has been positioned and sized correctly, the next task is to add the headline text to the frame.  Enter the Text Editing mode.

**[Ctrl/o]**

> **Point** the mouse inside the frame
> **Click**

Enter the headline text.

**How much power can you fit into a 1.5 foot cube?**

## WHITE-ON-BLACK LETTERING

Because the headline of a flyer is supposed to attract some attention, you will want to make the text stand out from the rest of the document. One way to do that is to reverse the coloring by placing white letters on a black background. It is important to note that many of the popular laser printers such as the HP LaserJet will not be able to print white letters on a black background even though Ventura will display those colors on the screen. Postscript printers, however, can print this effect.

The first step is to create a new style tag for the headline. The primary feature of this tag will be white lettering instead of black.

Place Ventura in the Paragraph Tagging mode by entering

**[Ctrl/i]**

> **Point** the mouse at "How"
> **Click**
> **Point** the mouse at Add New Tag
> **Click**

Enter the name of the new tag:

**Reverse** ↵

The process of getting white characters on a black background is fairly straightforward when you are working with small frames such as the current frame. You must change the color of the font to white and then change the frame background color to black. This is the reverse of the default colors, black text on a white background. First, change the text to white.

---

**Point** the mouse at Paragraph
**Point** the mouse at Font
**Click**

---

Change the color of the font by selecting White from the list of colors.

---

**Point** the mouse at White
**Click**

---

In addition, change the size and typeface of the font to a larger and bolder font that will stand out more clearly against the background.

---

**Point** the mouse at Swiss
**Click**
**Point** the mouse at 18
**Click**

---

Enter

↵

The text seems to disappear, and only an empty box remains on the screen because the text now has the same color attribute as the background of the frame — white — so it blends in with the background. The way to solve this problem is to change the frame's background color to black or gray. Place Ventura into the Frame Setting mode by entering

**[Ctrl/u]**

Change the background color of the frame to black.

---

**Point** the mouse at Frame
**Point** the mouse at Frame Background
**Click**

---

The **FRAME BACKGROUND** dialog box appears. This box has the same settings as the Graphic menu's FILL ATTRIBUTES dialog box — Color and Pattern. Note that the frame's color is already set to black. However, it is the pattern setting — Hollow — that causes the frame to appear as white. Changing the pattern to Solid will change the interior of the frame to solid black and cause the white text to appear in contrast.

---

**Point** the mouse at Pattern
**Click**
**Drag** to Solid

---

Enter

↵

You can now see the white letters against the black background.

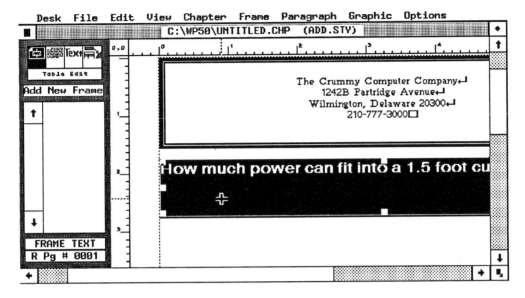

*Figure 5.15    White text on black background.*

This headline would look better if it were placed at the center of the frame.  The Vertical Alignment and Horizontal Alignment settings on the Paragraph Alignment menu will achieve this effect.  Place Ventura in the Paragraph Tagging mode by entering

**[Ctrl/i]**

Select the paragraph within the frame.

---

**Point** the mouse at "How much"
**Click**

---

Note that on the black background the highlight is now white instead of black.

**Exercise 1:** Use the Paragraph menu's ALIGNMENT dialog box to select vertical and horizontal centering. Try this on your own. The correct commands can be found under EX-1 at the end of this chapter.

The text is now centered within the frame.

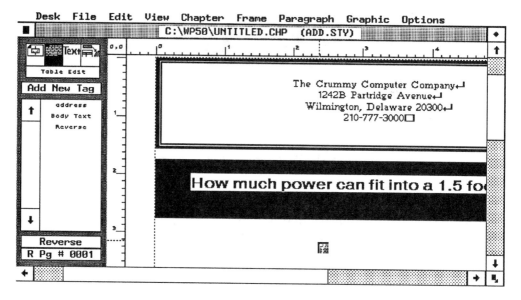

*Figure 5.16    Reversed text centered in the frame.*

## WHITE RULING LINES

The frame background color, which is now set to black, fills the entire frame width and height. The effect of the black background might be better if the edges of the frame were indented by about .25".

One method for indenting the frame's edges would be to place a ruling box around it, as you did for the address frame. The difference in this case is that the color of the ruling box would need to be white rather than black. This technique would cause the outside of the frame to appear as a white area, making the black background look as if it had been indented. Place Ventura in the Frame Setting mode by entering

**[Ctrl/u]**

Display the RULING BOX AROUND dialog box.

---

**Point** the mouse at Frame
**Point** the mouse at Ruling Box Around
**Click**

---

**Exercise 2:**  Change the color of the ruling line to white, and select Frame as the width.  Try this on your own.  The correct commands can be found under EX-2 at the end of this chapter.

Enter a .25" height for the ruling line.

↓
**[Esc]**
**.25** ⌐」

The black background is indented from the frame edges by .25".

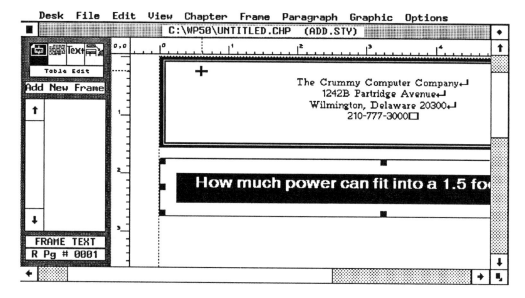

*Figure 5.17   Frame background indented with white ruling line.*

# FILLING A FRAME WITH TEXT

Now you can fill the remainder of the page with specific information about the PXL6000 computer and the graphics. That information has already been entered into text and graphics files. In a multiple-frame page layout, each file that you want to place on a page will require a separate frame. The first file you will want to place on the page is the PXL6000.WP file. Place Ventura in the reduced view mode by entering

**[Ctrl/r]**

Draw a new frame on the page. Don't worry about the size and location. You will adjust that by using the Sizing & Scaling options later.

**Point** the mouse at Add New Frame
**Click**
**Draw** a new frame anywhere on the page

In normal circumstances, you would attempt to draw the box at the exact location and with whatever dimensions you want, but in this case, you will enter exact values given in this book into the SIZING & SCALING dialog box. That way, you can be sure that the frame has been drawn exactly like the frames in this book's figures. Display the SIZING & SCALING dialog box.

---

**Point** the mouse at Frame
**Point** the mouse at Sizing & Scaling
**Click**

---

Enter the following values. They will position and size your frame to match the figures in this book.

**[Esc]**
**01** ↓
**[Esc]**
**03.72** ↓
**[Esc]**
**06.5** ↓
**[Esc]**
**02.53** ↵

The screen should display a new frame like the one in Figure 5.18.

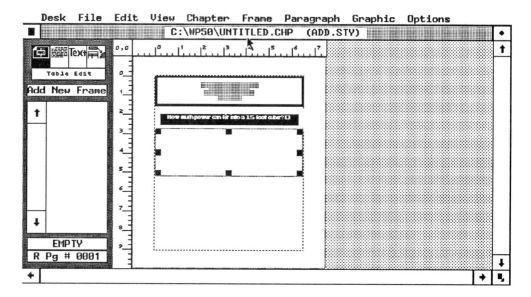

*Figure 5.18    Frame located and sized from dialog box settings.*

## LOADING A TEXT FILE INTO A FRAME

Because you have already entered the text into a word processing document, you can load the file into the frame by using the File menu.

> **Point** the mouse at File

The Load Text/Picture option is used to load text or graphics from other programs compatible with Ventura.

> **Point** the mouse at Load Text/Picture
> **Click**

The LOAD TEXT/PICTURE dialog box appears. The file type should be set for Text, and the text format set for your word processor — WordPerfect 5.0 in this example. Although you only need one of two text files at this moment, you can load both files at the same time and save yourself from having to go through this procedure again. Change the # of files option to **Several.**

---

**Point** the mouse at Several
**Click**

---

Enter

⏎

Recall that in this case you will want to change the active directory to the FLYERS directory so that all the files — text and graphics — used for this document will be in one location. Change to the FLYERS directory.

---

**Click** on the change directory button
**Click** on FLYERS

---

The text files **PXL6000.WP** and **FEATURES.WP** are displayed in the item selector box. Load both files.

---

**Point** the mouse at PXL6000.WP
**Double Click**
**Point** the mouse at FEATURES.WP
**Double Click**

---

Ventura loads the text but does not return to the text display. Because you selected Several, the file selector display will remain on the screen until you specifically exit the file loading mode. Enter

↵

Note that the side bar displays the names of the two files you just loaded. However, none of the text appears inside the frame because Ventura cannot be sure which of the files you loaded should be used in the selected frame. Ventura waits for you indicate which file you want inserted into the selected frame. You can do this by clicking on the name of the file, which appears in the list box on the side bar display. First, make sure that you have selected the correct frame.

> **Point** the mouse at the empty frame
> **Click**

Now select the file to be inserted into that frame.

> **Point** the mouse at PXL6000.WP
> **Click**

Ventura flows the text into the frame. In the reduced view mode, the text appears as greeked text. Save the file as a chapter by entering

[Ctrl/s]

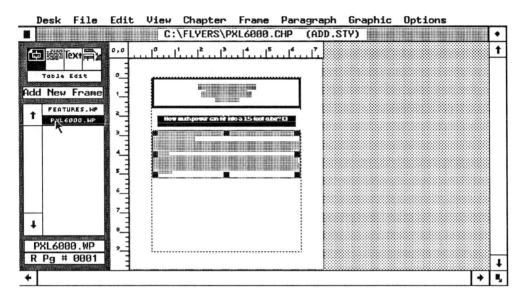

*Figure 5.19    Reduced view of text inserted into new frame.*

To get a better view of the text, change Ventura's display mode to normal view.

---

**Point** at the upper left corner of the frame

---

Enter

**[Ctrl/n]**

The text, which is formatted as Body Text, is displayed inside the frame.

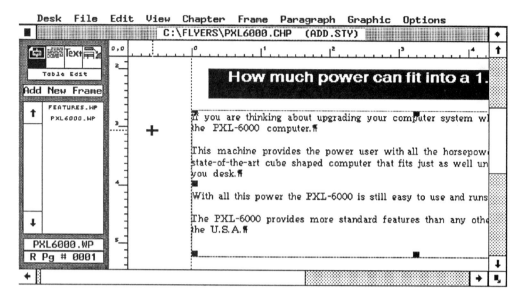

*Figure 5.20   Normal view of text inside a new frame.*

# COLUMNS

One of the major advantages of using multiple frames is that each frame can be structured with a specific set of margins and columns. Each frame's settings are independent of any other frame in the document. The new frame that you have just created has a single column of text and no margins. These are the default settings when you create a new frame. The text flows from the left edge of the frame to the right edge without interruption and is formatted as Body Text.

Frame columns are used to create newspaper-like columns in a frame. This type of column layout is different from the side-by-side columns you created in earlier chapters. In those chapters, you used a paragraph tag to create paragraphs that appeared to line up in columns. Frame columns divide the entire frame into a series of columns and the text automatically flows into those columns. Frame columns are used when you want all or almost all of the text in the frame to be column oriented. Paragraph columns are used when only a few of the paragraphs in the document will actually be column oriented.

In this case, you want all of the text in the frame to be organized into columns. While frame is still selected, display the **MARGINS & COLUMNS** dialog box.

> **Point** the mouse at Frame
> **Point** the mouse at Margins & Columns
> **Click**

The MARGINS & COLUMNS dialog box appears. The top row in the box lists the number of columns for the selected frame. Ventura allows you to divide a frame into a total of eight columns. In this case, you want three columns.

> **Point** the mouse at 3
> **Click**

When you select more than one column, Ventura automatically calculates the width of each column by evenly dividing the frame width among the columns. You can see the values for each column by looking in the Widths column. The columns are assumed to be all the same size, in this case 2.17".

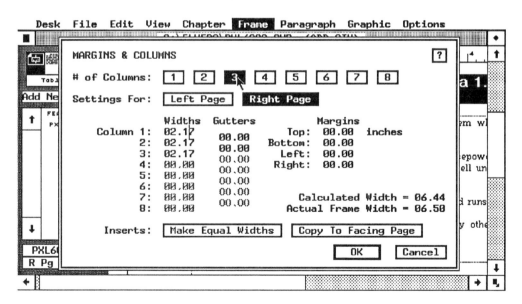

*Figure 5.21   Three-column layout selected.*

Next to the Widths column, Ventura displays the Gutters column. A **gutter** is space between columns. When you have three columns, you also have two potential gutter settings. Gutter settings help you place space between the line endings of one column and the line beginnings of the column to its right.

Ventura does not automatically insert gutter space. If you do not specify gutter spacing, the text in the columns will be directly adjacent. This is especially true when the text alignment is set for Justified.

The gutter spacing between columns 1 and 2 is set on line 2. Create .1" column gutters by entering

↓ (3 times)
**[Esc]**
**.1** ↓
**[Esc]**
**.1**

Before you leave this dialog box, you might also want to consider whether you need to create any margins for the frame itself. In this case, you will leave the margins at zero, at least for the time being, but many times you will want to enter margins. Exit the dialog box by entering

↵

The frame displays the text in three columns. Note that in the normal display mode you can only see the first two columns. Scroll to the right.

---

**Point** at the scroll bar right arrow
**Click** (2 times)

---

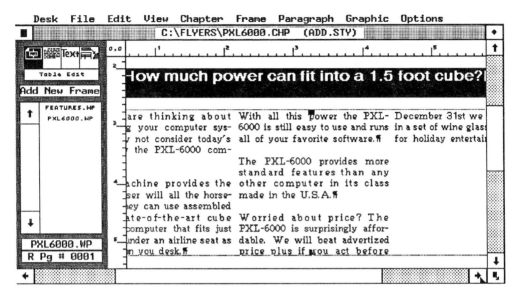

*Figure 5.22    Text formatted in three columns within frame.*

# VERTICAL LINES

Now that you have divided text into columns, you have the option of adding vertical lines between the columns. These lines run up and down in the gutter space between the text columns. Vertical lines are set as a quality of the frame. This means that when vertical ruling lines are added to a frame, Ventura automatically inserts the lines between the columns. If you change the number of columns specified for that frame, Ventura will increase or decrease the number of vertical ruling lines according to the number of columns. Vertical ruling lines will also lengthen automatically if you change the length of the frame.

To add vertical lines to this frame:

---

**Point** the mouse at Frame
**Point** the mouse at Vertical Rules
**Click**

---

Ventura displays the **VERTICAL RULES** dialog box.

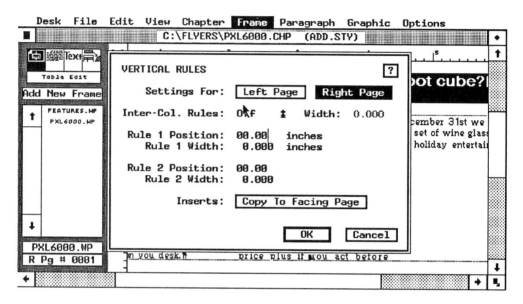

*Figure 5.23   VERTICAL RULES dialog box.*

Ventura allows you to create two types of vertical lines within a frame. The first are called **Inter-Col. Rules**. These are lines automatically positioned between columns. The other ruling lines, **Rule 1** and **Rule 2**, allow you to choose the exact location of the ruling line. These vertical lines can be placed at any horizontal position on the page and are measured from the left edge of the page, not from the left edge of the frame. For example, if you specified 4.25" as the position, Ventura would draw a line down the middle of the page within the frame. Ventura will not check to see whether that position is empty or filled with text when it draws the line. Use this option only when you want to manually control the exact location of a vertical line. Rule 2 functions the same way and allows you to specify the location of a second vertical line.

In this case, choose the Inter-Col(umn) rules.

> **Point** the mouse at Inter-Col. Rules
> **Click**
> **Drag** to On

Ventura automatically enters a line width of .003". To accept this width, enter

↵

Ventura adds vertical rules between the columns.

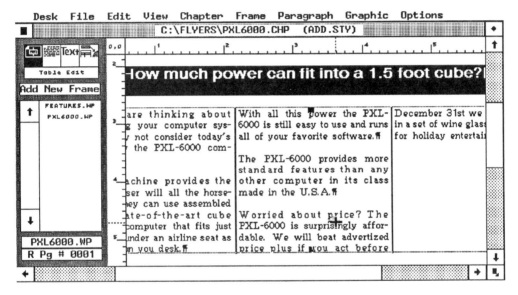

*Figure 5.24    Vertical rules added between columns.*

## EMPHASIZED PARAGRAPHS

When text is arranged in columns, special effects are often used to add emphasis to various parts of the text. In this example, you will add two frequently used special effects to the text in this frame.

- **Big First Letter.** This effect (more traditionally known as a dropped capital) is most often used with the first paragraph in a section or chapter. The first letter of the first word is printed in a much larger type size than the rest of the text. This effect dates back to the middle ages when large first letters were used to embellish handwritten manuscripts.

- **Lifts.** The term "lift" refers to a part of the text that is printed in enlarged, bold print and marked off from the other paragraphs by ruling lines. This effect is often used in magazines to display paragraphs of special interest, which can be spotted quickly on a page.

## Creating a Big First Letter

Begin with the **big first letter** effect. Zoom in on the first paragraph of the frame.

| |
|---|
| **Point** at the first paragraph |

Enter

**[Ctrl/e]**

Scroll the display back to the left so that you can completely see the text in the first column.

| |
|---|
| **Point** at the scroll bar left arrow<br>**Click** |

The first letter in the text is the letter "I" in the word "If." The big first letter effect is implemented through a paragraph tag. Enter the Paragraph Tagging mode.

**[Ctrl/i]**

| |
|---|
| **Point** the mouse at "If"<br>**Click** |

You will need to create a new tag for this effect.

---
**Point** the mouse at Add New Tag
**Click**

---

Enter the name of the new tag.

**Big Letter** ⏎

To create the special effect, select Special Effects from the Paragraph menu.

---
**Point** the mouse at Paragraph
**Point** the mouse at Special Effects
**Click**

---

Ventura displays the SPECIAL EFFECTS dialog box.

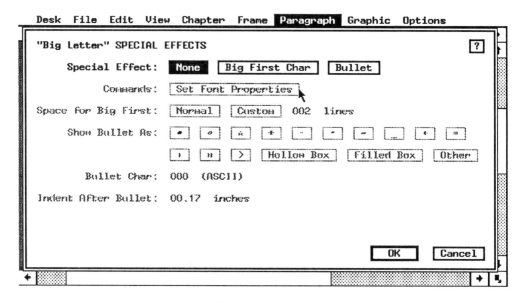

*Figure 5.25   SPECIAL EFFECTS dialog box.*

To create the big first letter effect, select that option.

---

**Point** the mouse at Big First Char.
**Click**

---

The next step is to select a font for the big first letter.

---

**Point** the mouse at Set Font Properties
**Click**

---

The FONTS dialog box appears. The idea of the big first letter format is to select a font for the first letter of the paragraph that is larger than the base font for that tag. In this case, the base font size is 12 points. A 24-point font would be twice that size. Select a 24-point bold font.

> **Point** the mouse at 24
> **Click**

(Note that 24-point fonts are automatically bold in Ventura.) Complete the tag by entering

┘ ( 2 times)

The first letter of the paragraph is expanded to 24-points while all of the other characters remain in the 12-point base font.

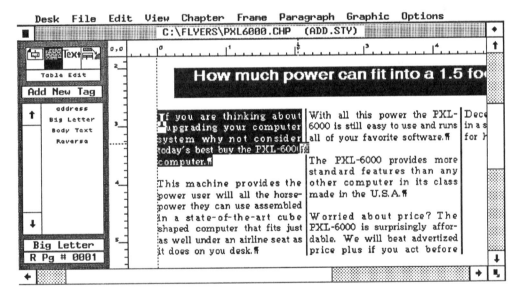

*Figure 5.26    The big first letter effect added to lead paragraph.*

## Creating a Lift

A **lift** is a paragraph that stands out from the rest of the text because it is in a different font and is marked off by ruling lines. Lifts are commonly used in magazines to draw the reader's attention to an article by emphasizing a particular quotation from the text.

In this case, you want the reader to notice the paragraph that contains the phrase "made in the U.S.A."

Select that paragraph.

> **Point** the mouse at "made in the U.S.A."
> **Click**

Create a new tag called **Lift**.

> **Point** the mouse at Add New Tag
> **Click**

Enter

**Lift** ⏎

To create a lift, you need to make three changes in the paragraph's format.

- Change the text font to a larger and bolder font.

- Add a ruling line above the text.

- Add a ruling line below the text.

Begin with step #1, changing the font.

```
Point the mouse at Paragraph
Point the mouse at Font
Click
```

Select a Swiss, 14-point, bold font.

```
Point the mouse at Swiss
Click
Point the mouse at 14
Click
```

(Note that Ventura automatically makes the Swiss 14-point font bold.) Next, add the ruling lines.

```
Point the mouse at Paragraph
Point the mouse at Ruling Line Above
Click
```

In this case, you want to select the Column width option so Ventura will draw the line across the column in which the paragraph appears.

```
Point the mouse at Width
Click
Drag to Column
```

Enter a three-point ruling line (i.e., .042"):

↓
**[Esc]**
**.042** ⏎

**Exercise 3:**    You need to duplicate the previous operation except that this time you want the ruling line to appear below the paragraph. Try this on your own. The correct commands can be found under EX-3 at the end of this chapter.

The paragraph is formatted as a lift paragraph.

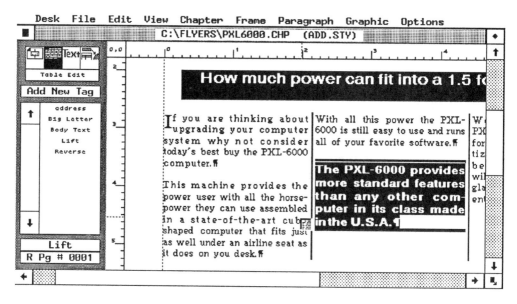

*Figure 5.27    Lift paragraph formatted.*

# COLUMN BALANCE

When Ventura places text into columns, it normally fills up each column before starting the next. The last column in the layout may be only partially filled with text, while the others are full columns. Ventura includes a setting that will automatically attempt to evenly distribute the text into all of the columns so that no one column is very much shorter than the others.

This setting is found in the **FRAME TYPOGRAPHY SETTINGS** dialog box, which is accessed from the Frame menu.

> **Point** the mouse at Frame
> **Point** the mouse at Frame Typography
> **Click**

Ventura displays the FRAME TYPOGRAPHY SETTINGS dialog box.

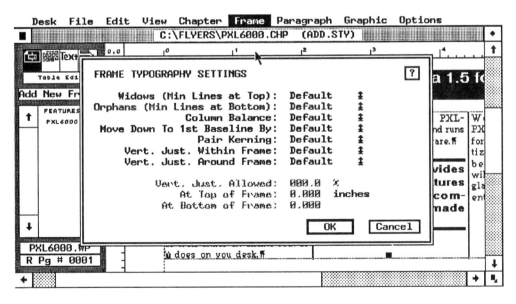

*Figure 5.28   FRAME TYPOGRAPHY SETTINGS dialog box.*

This dialog box is used to modify frame-level settings. The settings in this dialog box refer to how text will be treated within a given frame. In this case, you are interested in the **Column Balance** setting, which has a default setting of Off. To have Ventura automatically balance the text in the columns, turn the setting On.

> **Point** the mouse at Column Balance
> **Click**
> **Drag** to On

Enter

↵

The text in all three columns is now about the same length.

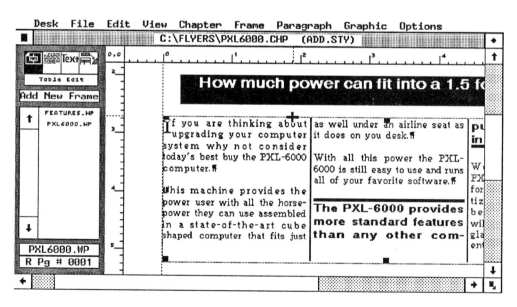

*Figure 5.29    Column text is balanced.*

Note that Ventura lists three options for this setting: On, Off, and Default. The default setting indicates that Ventura uses a hierarchical system of setting typographic attributes. The Chapter, Frame, and Paragraph menus each have an option for typographical settings. When the Default option is selected, Ventura uses the setting on the previous level. For example, in the Frame menu, any options that show a Default setting will use the values entered in the CHAPTER TYPOGRAPHY SETTINGS dialog box.

## ADDING ANOTHER FRAME

There is one more text file to be added to the document: **FEATURES.WP.** Place Ventura into the reduced view mode by entering

**[Ctrl/r]**

You need to create a new frame for the text.

---

**Point** the mouse at Add New Frame
**Click**

---

Below the last frame, draw a frame that covers the bottom part of the page. Don't worry about the exact dimensions of the frame. You will use the SIZING & SCALING dialog box settings to make sure they are the same as those used in this book.

---

**Draw** a frame

---

Enter the correct location and size values for this frame.

> **Point** the mouse at Frame
> **Point** the mouse at Sizing & Scaling
> **Click**

Enter the following values.

**[Esc]**
**01** ↓
**[Esc]**
**06.24** ↓
**[Esc]**
**06.5** ↓
**[Esc]**
**03.88** ↵

The frame should resemble the one in Figure 5.30.

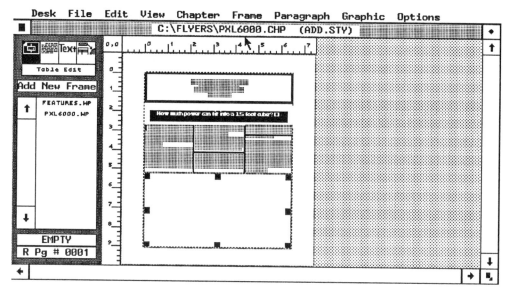

*Figure 5.30    Frame drawn in bottom portion of page.*

In this frame, you want to place the text entered in the document FEA-TURES.WP. That document is currently listed in the side bar display. Selecting that filename will place that text into the frame.

---

**Point** the mouse at FEATURES.WP
**Click**

---

The text appears in the frame as greeked text. Return to the normal display mode.

---

**Point** at the upper left corner of the new frame

---

Enter

[**Ctrl/n**]

## BULLET TAGS

The next task is to create a new paragraph format for the text in the FEA-TURES.WP file. Remember that the text in this file is not organized into text paragraphs but is really a list of product features. Such lists are referred to as **bullet** lists. Ventura has a special format for bullet text, and you can combine that feature with the font and spacing of your choice.

To create a bullet format for this text, begin by placing Ventura into the Paragraph Tagging mode. Enter

[**Ctrl/i**]

---

**Point** the mouse at "Megabytes"
**Click**

---

Before you make any formatting changes, you must create a new tag.

---

**Point** the mouse at Add New Tag
**Click**

---

Enter the name of the new tag:

**Bullet** ⏎

To create a bullet, you can select the bullet format from the SPECIAL EFFECTS dialog box.

---

**Point** the mouse at Paragraph
**Point** the mouse at Special Effects
**Click**

---

The SPECIAL EFFECTS dialog box appears. This time you want to select the Bullet effect.

---

**Point** the mouse at Bullet
**Click**

---

When you select Bullet, you then have the option of choosing the bullet character you want. The bullet character is a character that is printed at the beginning of every bullet paragraph. The default value for Bullet is a large black dot. You can select any of the other characters shown on the menu or select another character that is not on the list by entering the ASCII code number for that character. The actual printed character for that ASCII code will differ from font to font. Ventura also has selections for hollow or filled squares. The hollow square is useful when you want to create a check box such as those printed on forms in which you select items you want by checking the boxes next to them.

In this case, select the long dash, the seventh character on the line, as the bullet character.

| |
|---|
| **Point** the mouse at the long dash<br>**Click** |

The last setting in the dialog box is **Indent After Bullet**. The indent value is used to indent the text of the paragraph following the bullet. The default value is .25". Accept that value and the others that you have just set by entering

↵

A long dash appears in front of the paragraph as the bullet character.

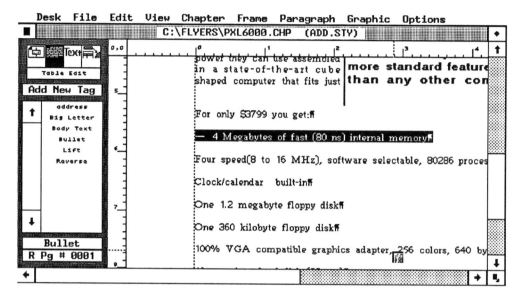

*Figure 5.31   Long dash bullet character.*

Tag the other lines in the frame as bullets by using the [Shift/Click] method. (Remember to hold the Shift key down until you have made all your selections.)

---

**Point** the mouse at "Four Speed"
**[Shift/Click]**
**Point** the mouse at "Clock/calendar"
**[Shift/Click]**
**Point** the mouse at "360"
**[Shift/Click]**
**Point** the mouse at "VGA"
**[Shift/Click]**

---

Select the Bullet tag.

---

**Point** the mouse at the Bullet tag
**Click**

---

**Exercise 4:** Scroll and tag the next three paragraphs as Bullet. Try this on your own. The correct commands can be found under EX-4 at the end of this chapter.

Your screen should resemble Figure 5.32.

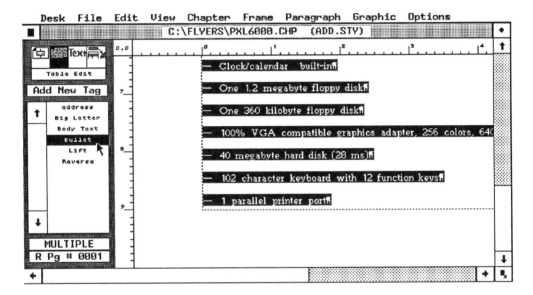

*Figure 5.32   Lines formatted as bullet list.*

## INCREASING TEXT WITH COLUMNS

In creating the bullets inside the new frame, you have run into a problem. You have reached the bottom of the frame, which is also the bottom of the page, without having displayed all of the text from the FEATURES.WP document in the frame. You can tell that you have not reached the end of the text because the end-of-file symbol is not visible.

One advantage of a column layout is that dividing the frame into columns can increase the amount of text you can fit into a frame. This is generally true when the text contains a number of paragraphs that are too short to stretch across the entire frame width.

You can make more efficient use of this frame by creating columns. In this case, create a four-column layout for this frame. Begin by changing to the Frame Setting mode by entering

**[Ctrl/u]**

Create a four-column layout for this frame.

```
Point the mouse at Frame
Point the mouse at Columns & Margins
Click
```

Select four columns.

```
Point the mouse at 4
Click
```

Ventura automatically divides the frame into four even columns. Enter the values for the column gutters at .25".

↓ (4 times)
**[Esc]**
.25 ↓
**[Esc]**
.25 ↓
**[Esc]**
.25 ↵

The text is aligned into four columns. Note that with the column layout, the rest of the text from the FEATURES.WP file appears in the frame.

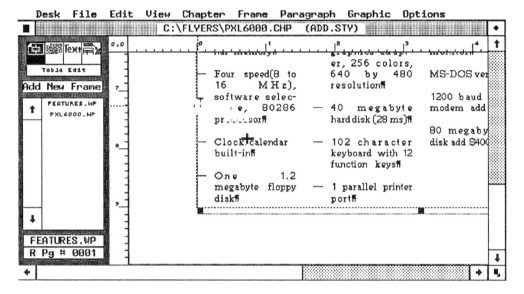

*Figure 5.33    Frame divided into four columns.*

**Exercise 5:**    To tag the remaining paragraphs as Bullet, scroll to the right and upward. Try this on your own. The correct commands can be found under EX-5 at the end of this chapter.

If you examine some of the bullet paragraphs carefully, you will notice that they contain large gaps between words. This is caused by the Justified alignment setting. When lines are wrapped into narrow columns, their appearance can be improved by removing justification.

---

**Point** the mouse at Paragraph
**Point** the mouse at Alignment
**Click**
**Point** the mouse at Horz. Alignment
**Click**

---

Enter

⏎

The justification is removed from the bullet paragraphs.

The final step in formatting this text is to format the first paragraph in the frame, the one that contains the price of the computer, as a bullet paragraph but with a larger font and a larger bullet.

---

**Point** the mouse at "$3799"
**Click**

---

Create a new tag.

---

**Point** the mouse at Add New Tag
**Click**

---

The new tag will be called **Big Bullet**. Instead of copying the tag from Body Text, copy the tag from Bullet. That will allow you to start with the same settings as the Bullet tag. Enter

**Big Bullet** ↓
**[Esc]**
**Bullet** ⏎

Change the font of the **Big Bullet** tag to Swiss, 18-point bold.

**Point** the mouse at Paragraph
**Point** the mouse at Font
**Click**
**Point** the mouse at Swiss
**Click**
**Point** the mouse at 18
**Click**

(Note that in Ventura Swiss, 18-point text is automatically bold.) Change the bullet character from a dash to a filled box.

**Point** the mouse at Paragraph
**Point** the mouse at Special Effects
**Click**
**Point** the mouse at Filled Box
**Click**

Enter

⏎

The document window should resemble the one in Figure 5.34.

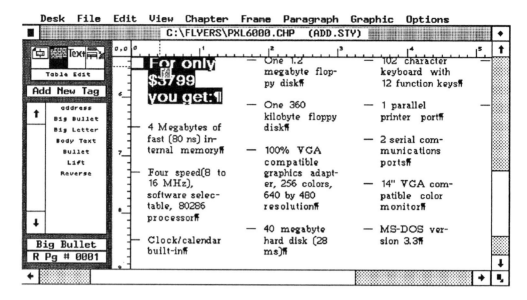

*Figure 5.34    Big Bullet paragraph added to frame.*

## ALIGNMENT AND COLUMNS

When you select a multiple-column layout for a frame, all of the text is automatically wrapped into the columns. If you look at the Big Bullet paragraph, it appears somewhat cramped wrapped in the narrow column. There is a way to allow this one paragraph to flow across the columns instead of being restricted to the narrow column width.

Ventura recognizes two possible ways to wrap lines of text within a frame: column width or frame width. In the documents you created previously, each frame consisted of a single column that was identical in width to the frame. It would have made no practical difference which width was used for alignment purposes, but in a multiple-column layout the difference is significant. If a paragraph tag is set for frame width, then the column borders are ignored, and the text is formatted between the edges of the frame.

In this case, it might improve the overall appearance of the text in the frame to allow the Big Bullet paragraph to be aligned across the entire frame width. Keep in mind that when you change the alignment width of a tag, only those paragraphs with that tag will be affected. The other paragraphs in the frame will continue to be aligned in columns. In most cases, the frame width paragraphs should be the first ones in the text. Setting a paragraph in the middle of a column to frame width will usually cause it to overlap other column width paragraphs. Display the Paragraph menu's ALIGNMENT dialog box.

```
Point the mouse at Paragraph
Point the mouse at Alignment
Click
```

The sixth item on the menu is **Overall Width**. This item allows you to choose between column-wide and frame-wide alignment. The default setting is **Column-Wide**. Change it to **Frame-Wide**.

```
Point the mouse at Overall-Width
Click
Drag to Frame-Wide
```

While the ALIGNMENT dialog box is still displayed, you can also center the paragraph horizontally in the frame.

```
Point the mouse at Horz. Alignment
Click
Drag to Center
```

Complete the alignment settings by entering

↵

The paragraph is centered above the four columns. Note that Ventura has placed all the columns somewhat lower in the frame to accommodate the centered heading.

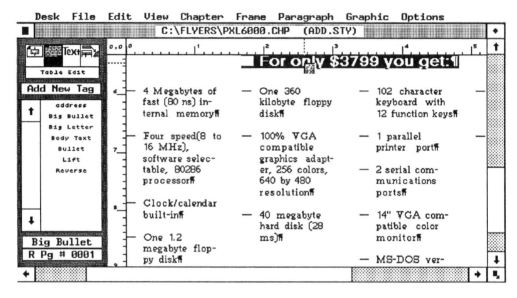

*Figure 5.35   Paragraph aligned on frame width.*

## GRAPHIC IMAGES

You have now placed and formatted the text portion of the document. Three graphic images still need to be placed on the page. Graphics are handled much like text files. Each graphic must be placed in its own frame. The size and the location of the frame determine the size and location of the image on the page.

The first image will be the COLUMBIA.GEM file. This is a drawing of the space shuttle, and it will be used as part of the letterhead — as a company logo. Place Ventura in the reduced display mode by entering

**[Ctrl/r]**

Activate the Frame Setting mode by entering

**[Ctrl/u]**

Draw a new frame in the upper left corner of the screen. The frame should overlap the left portion of the letterhead frame. Don't worry about the exact size. You can enter the exact dimension in the SIZING & SCALING dialog box.

---

**Point** the mouse at Add New Frame
**Click**
**Draw** a new frame in the upper left corner of the document

---

As discussed previously, the normal procedure would be to size and locate the frame by sight; however, you can make sure that your frame is in the same location and is the same size as the frames in this book by entering the following values in the SIZING & SCALING dialog box.

---

**Point** the mouse at Frame
**Point** the mouse at Sizing & Scaling
**Click**

---

Enter

**[Esc]**
**01 ↓**
**[Esc]**
**01 ↓**
**[Esc]**
**01.88 ↓**
**[Esc]**
**1.55 ↵**

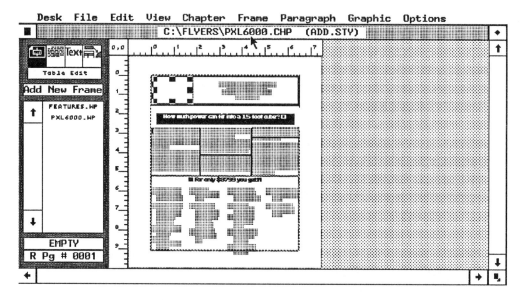

*Figure 5.36 New frame added in upper left corner.*

You can now add the image to the new frame. Return to the normal display mode.

---

**Point** the mouse at the upper left corner of the frame

---

Enter

**[Ctrl/n]**

Graphics are loaded from the same menu option as text files.

---

**Point** the mouse at File
**Point** the mouse at Load Text/Picture
**Click**

---

Ventura allows you to load two types of graphic images.

**Line-Art**     Line-art refers to graphics that were created with programs that produce vector graphic images. A **vector** graphic image file consists of mathematical descriptions of lines and patterns that create an image. Suppose an image contains a straight line. The vector, or line-art, method stores values that indicate the starting and ending points and the line thickness. Any program that reads this file will use these values to reconstruct the line based on the values that describe it. Many popular graphics programs use this system, including GEM DRAW, Lotus Freelance, and Harvard Business Graphics. Note that many of these graphics programs use their own fonts to format text within the line-art graphic. When these images are imported into Ventura, the fonts must be converted to fonts currently available in Ventura, which may cause some misalignment of text and graphics. Be sure to test the results of this conversion process if your line-art graphic includes text.

**Image**     Image files differ from line-art in that they do not contain a mathematical description; rather, they contain an actual image of the picture. This image is made up of black and white dots and consists of a series of binary values that indicate where on the image the black dots and white dots should appear. This type of image is called a **bit-mapped** image. Scanners, for example, create bit-mapped images of the pictures they scan. Image files contain a facsimile of an image — not mathematical descriptions as in line art — so they tend to lose definition if they are expanded or stretched to fit a new frame.

In this case, the COLUMBIA.GEM file is a line-art graphic. Select the Line-Art option.

---

**Point** the mouse at Line-Art
**Click**

---

When Line-Art is selected, the bottom of the dialog box changes to display the types of line-art files that Ventura can work with. Keep in mind that many different products will use the same standard formats, so don't be immediately alarmed if the name of your graphics program does not appear on this menu. For example, Pixie and Harvard Graphics both convert files to the CGM format, which means that images from those programs can be used with Ventura.

The default setting is GEM. Because the COLUMBIA.GEM file is a GEM format file, you can leave that option selected.

Select **Several** as your # of Files option so you can load both the COLUMBIA.GEM and NOZZLE.GEM files at the same time.

---

**Point** the mouse at Several
**Click**

---

Display the ITEM SELECTOR dialog box by entering

⏎

The ITEM SELECTOR dialog box may appear empty because it has defaulted to the TYPESET directory. Recall that you copied the images into the FLYERS directory. Select the FLYERS directory.

---

**Click** on the black directory button
**Click** on FLYERS

---

The names of the two GEM files are displayed. Load the files into the current chapter.

> **Point** the mouse at COLUMBIA.GEM
> **Double Click**
> **Point** the mouse at NOZZLE.GEM
> **Double Click**

Enter

↵

The names of the GEM files appear in the list box in the side bar display along with the names of the text files.

To insert the COLUMBIA.GEM file into the new frame, select it from the side bar display.

> **Point** the mouse at COLUMBIA.GEM
> **Click**

The image is filled into the new frame. Ventura automatically scales the image to fit into the frame.

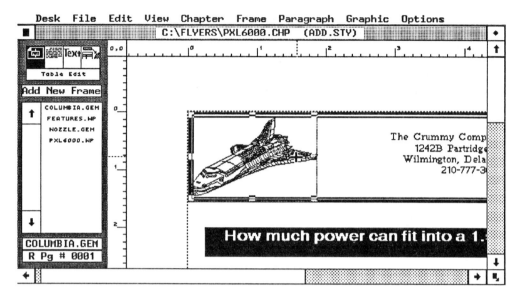

*Figure 5.37    COLUMBIA.GEM added to frame.*

## THE FLOW-AROUND FEATURE

When you added the frame that now holds the COLUMBIA.GEM graphic, Ventura automatically adjusted the text in the other fames to make room for the new frame. This feature is called **flow-around**. It causes the text in existing frames to flow around new frames that are added to the document. In most cases, this is exactly what you want to happen because Ventura automatically avoids overlapping of frames.

Note that this is exactly the opposite of the way Ventura treats graphics, such as text boxes, added in the Graphic Drawing mode. Those items are automatically superimposed on frames and their contents.

However, in the case of the COLUMBIA.GEM graphic, the frame was drawn over space that was already blank. Ventura moved the text to the right to make room for the drawing anyway, based on the flow-around frame principle. This means that the text is no longer centered on the page. In this case, you want to turn off the flow-around feature so that the placement of the COLUMBIA.GEM graphic will not affect text placement in that frame. In a sense, you want Ventura to treat the image as if it were created in Ventura's Graphic Drawing mode, which allows it to be superimposed on other frames.

The flow-around setting is located in the SIZING & SCALING dialog box.

> **Point** the mouse at Frame
> **Point** the mouse at Sizing & Scaling
> **Click**

Change the Flow Text Around setting to Off.

> **Point** the mouse at Flow Text Around
> **Click**
> **Drag** to Off

Enter

↵

The text moves back to the alignment it had before you added the image.

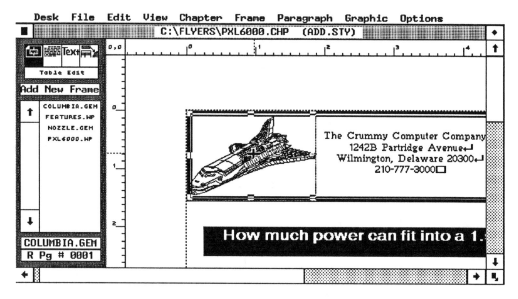

*Figure 5.38    Flow-around setting turned off.*

# MARGINS WITH IMAGES

You may have noticed that the nose of the COLUMBIA.GEM graphic overlaps the ruling lines that surround the frame over which it is superimposed. You can avoid this type of overlap by adding margins to the image frame. The margins reduce the image area within the frame but do not change the frame size or location.

> **Point** the mouse at Frame
> **Point** the mouse at Margins & Columns
> **Click**

In this case, you want to create left and bottom margins that prevent the picture from overlapping the ruling lines. The ruling lines are .084" thick. Note that you could obtain that value by selecting the frame with the ruling lines and displaying the RULING BOX AROUND dialog box. At the bottom of each dialog box is the Overall Height setting that adds up all the rules and spaces.

Create the margins by entering the values for the margins in the dialog box.

↓  (2 times)
**[Esc]**
**.09** ↓
**[Esc]**
**.09** ⌐

The graphic is redrawn with the new margins so that it does not overlap the ruling lines.

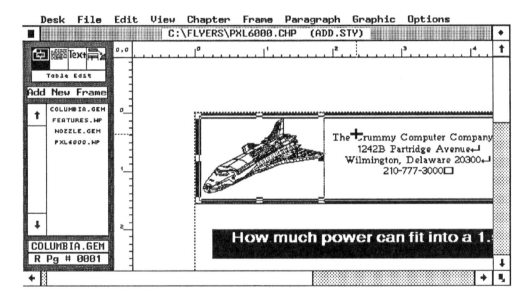

*Figure 5.39   Margins used to avoid overlapping graphics.*

## COPYING A FRAME

The next image to be placed on the page is the NOZZLE.GEM drawing. You will place this drawing on the right side of the address information. Instead of creating a new frame from scratch, you can copy the current frame and then drag the copied frame to a new location.

Place a copy of the current frame in memory by entering

**[Shift/Del]**

Paste a copy of the frame onto the page by entering

**[Ins]**

Change the view to the reduced mode by entering

**[Ctrl/r]**

Drag the frame to the right edge of the address frame.

| |
|---|
| **Point** the mouse inside the COLUMBIA.GEM frame<br>**Drag** to the right edge of the page |

You now have two copies of the COLUMBIA.GEM graphic. Change the image inside the frame to the NOZZLE.GEM graphic.

| |
|---|
| **Point** the mouse at the filename NOZZLE.GEM<br>**Click** |

The NOZZLE.GEM drawing is placed inside the frame. The address is now flanked by images on the left and the right.

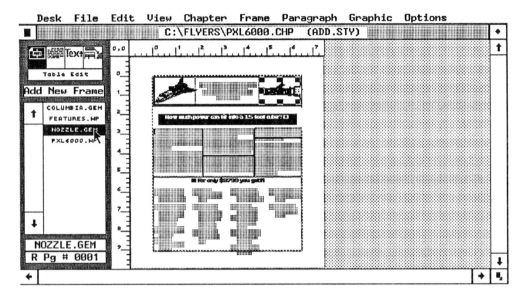

*Figure 5.40   NOZZLE.GEM image added to document.*

# IMAGES AND TEXT

The final image to be placed on this page will need to take advantage of the flow-around feature because it will be placed in the center of a frame that contains text.

The new frame will be placed in the bottom (bullet) frame. In this case, you can draw the frame anywhere and adjust the size and location with the SIZING & SCALING dialog box settings.

---

**Point** the mouse at Add New Frame
**Click**
**Draw** a new frame anywhere in the bullet frame

---

Adjust the frame by using the SIZING & SCALING dialog box.

> **Point** the mouse at Frame
> **Point** the mouse at Sizing & Scaling
> **Click**

Enter

**[Esc]**
**02.65 ↓**
**[Esc]**
**07.6 ↓**
**[Esc]**
**01.55 ↓**
**[Esc]**
**02 ⏎**

The new frame will appear inside the bullet frame. Ventura will automatically flow the text around the frame so that no overlap will take place between the information in the two frames.

Change to the normal view.

> **Point** the mouse at the upper left corner of the new frame

Enter

**[Ctrl/n]**

The file that will be used to fill this frame is a bit-mapped image file—CHANEL.IMG.

---

**Point** the mouse at File
**Point** the mouse at Load Text/Picture
**Click**

---

Select Image as the file type.

---

**Point** the mouse at Image
**Click**

---

Ventura displays four format options for images. The default setting is for GEM IMG files. This is the correct format for the image you want to load. Enter

⏎

> **Exercise 6:** The default directory for IMG selection is TYPESET. Change to the FLYERS directory and load the CHANEL.IMG file. Try this on your own. The correct commands can be found under EX-6 at the end of this chapter .

The image is loaded into the frame. This image is typical of the kind of graphic produced when a scanner is used to capture the image of a photograph. In this case, it is a photograph of a woman. Note that the image displayed on the screen will appear somewhat broken up. This is caused by the difference in the resolution of the screen display and the resolution of the scanned image. When the page is printed, the image will appear with the full resolution of the printer, which should produce a much clearer image.

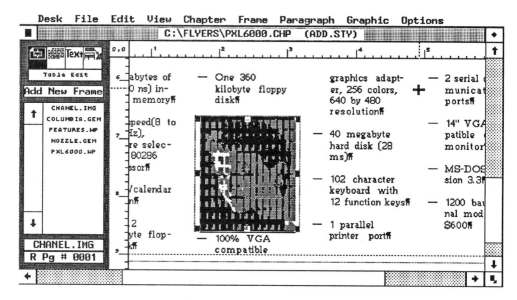

*Figure 5.41   Image file loaded into a frame.*

Ventura automatically attempts to place the image into the frame by making the best fit possible. However, you can change the way the image is displayed by enlarging, reducing, or cropping the image. You can also add captions to the frame.

Suppose you want to enlarge the image within the frame. This operation is carried out from the SIZING & SCALING dialog box.

**Point** the mouse at Frame
**Point** the mouse at Sizing & Scaling
**Click**

You will note that when the frame contains an image or picture, the settings in the bottom portion of the box become available. These settings control the way the image is sized and scaled within the frame.

**Picture Scaling**  This option can be set for Fit to Frame or Scale by Factors. **Fit to Frame** tells Ventura to use the current shape of the frame as a guide to how the picture should be scaled. When selected, this option results in the calculation of a scale that will permit the entire image to appear in the frame. If the image is a different shape from the frame into which it is placed, this technique may result in blank area inside the frame. **Scale by Factors** allows you to select the area of the overall picture to display in the frame. This process is called **cropping**, a term borrowed from the field of photography where parts of an image are truncated to better fit a specific space.

**Aspect Ratio**  The **aspect ratio** is the relative weight assigned to the width and the height factors used to scale the picture. Ventura has two options: **Maintained** tells Ventura to maintain the original values for height-to-width ratio, even if the image is cropped. **Distorted** allows you to enter your own values for the height and width scaling. Because you can control the width and height factors separately, you can pull, push, stretch, or compress the image the way you want.

As an example, you might want to change the aspect ratio of the image so it will be stretched sideways to fill the empty space on the sides.

To make these changes, you must first select the Scale by Factors and Distorted options from the SIZING & SCALING dialog box.

---

**Point** the mouse at Scale by Factors
**Click**
**Point** the mouse at Distorted
**Click**

---

You can now gain access to the settings at the bottom of the screen that control the image size and scale. The Scale Width setting is 1.51", and the height is 2.13". These values indicate that the original scale of the image was approximately 1.5" by 2", meaning that the image is slightly taller than it is wide. Because you have selected Scale by Factors and Distorted as options, Ventura will now display the image in its original form, regardless of the shape of the frame that contains it. Enter

⏎

The image is enlarged within the frame. Note that part of the image is no longer visible within the frame.

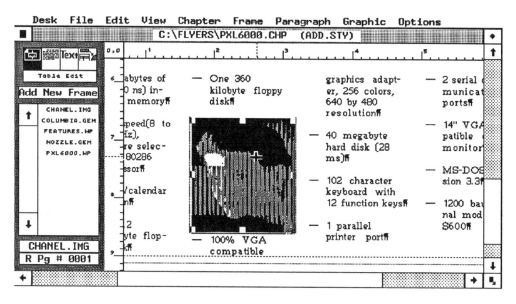

*Figure 5.42   Image expanded inside of frame.*

# DISTORTING THE IMAGE

Ventura allows you to distort the height and width ratio of the picture. Display the SIZING & SCALING dialog box.

---

**Point** the mouse at Frame
**Point** the mouse at Sizing & Scaling
**Click**

---

You can now enter values of your own for the width and height ratios of the image. For example, if you changed height to 4", the image would be doubled in height. This would create a distorted image. If you also expand the width in the same ratio (1.5" doubled equals 3"), you would maintain the basic structure of the image while enlarging it. Enter the following scaling values.

↓ ( 8 times)
**[Esc]**
**03** ↓
**[Esc]**
**04.24** ⏎

The image is enlarged to double its previous size. Note that because the frame size has not changed, only the upper left corner of the image appears in the frame.

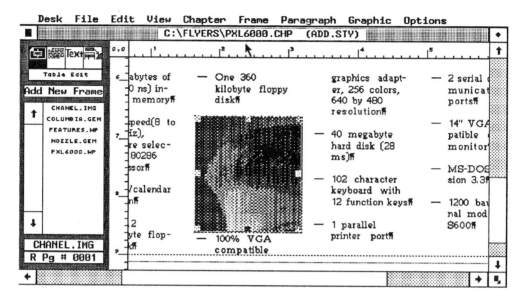

*Figure 5.43   Image enlarged with scaling factors.*

# CROPPING WITH THE MOUSE

When an image is scaled so that only part of it can be seen in the frame, you can perform cropping by using the mouse in combination with the Alt key [Alt/Drag]. **Cropping** is a term borrowed from photography. It refers to the selection of part of a photograph for display. In photography, cropping involves cutting the picture so that you remove the unwanted areas, leaving only the image you want. In Ventura, the cropping process is much more dynamic. Unlike photography, in which cropping mistakes destroy the picture, in Ventura cropping can always be revised without harming the image.

> **Point** the mouse inside the graphic frame
> **Hold down** the Alt key
> **Press** and **hold down** the mouse button

The mouse cursor will change to a hand icon (Figure 5.44). The hand icon will remain as long as you continue to hold down both the mouse button and the Alt key. This technique will be referred to as **[Alt/Drag]**.

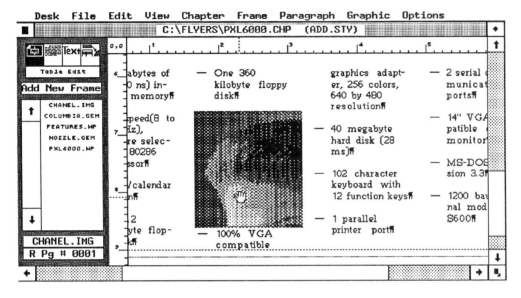

*Figure 5.44    Hand icon indicates image cropping mode.*

**[Alt/Drag]**

As you drag, the image will move within the frame.  You can drag the image in any direction.  Continue dragging until you have displayed most of the woman's face, as shown in Figure 5.45.  Then release the Alt key and the mouse button.

You can also perform cropping by entering exact measurements.  Display the SIZING & SCALING dialog box.

**Point** the mouse at Frame
**Point** the mouse at Sizing & Scaling
**Click**

If you examine the value for Y Crop Offset, you will see that it has changed from 0.00 to some value, probably .42" and 1.48". The Y Crop Offset value indicates the amount of space the image has been cropped upward or downward. The + or - indicates whether the crop has been upward or downward, respectively. The X Crop value indicates any cropping to the left or right. This value is the number of inches that the image has been cropped. You can enter specific values for the X and Y cropping you want. These values will move the image within the frame in the same way as the [Alt/Drag] method. Enter

↓ (6 times)
**[Esc]**
**.5** ↓
**[Esc]**
**01.5** ⏎

The image is adjusted to the new cropping position.

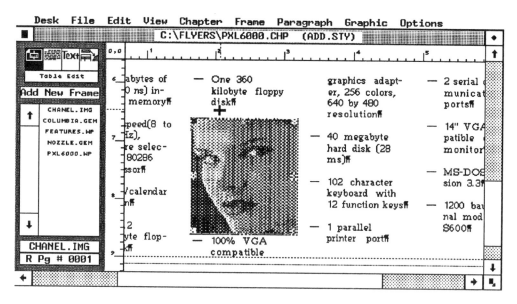

*Figure 5.45    Cropped image displayed in frame.*

# CAPTIONS

Ventura allows you to add captions to the frames by using the ANCHORS & CAPTIONS dialog box, which is accessed from the Frame menu.

---

**Point** the mouse at Frame
**Point** the mouse at Anchors & Captions
**Click**

---

This dialog box allows you to attach a caption to the frame.

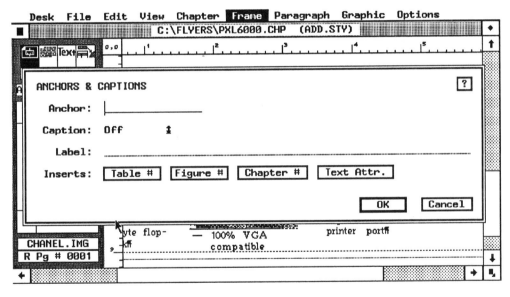

*Figure 5.46   ANCHORS & CAPTIONS dialog box.*

To add a caption to a frame, you need to select the location of the frame from the Caption setting. You can select above, below, left, or right for the caption. In this case, use the most frequently used setting—Below.

---

**Point** the mouse at Caption
**Click**
**Drag** to Below

---

The text cursor in the dialog box moves to the Label line. Here, you enter the text of the caption. In addition to text, you can insert special symbols that will tell Ventura to automatically enter the current table number, figure number, or chapter number. For example, entering [F#] onto the label line would cause Ventura to automatically number each figure consecutively in the chapter. In this case, enter some text. No figure numbers are needed. Enter

**I just love my PCX-6000!** ⌐

Ventura adds a small box below the picture and places the text of the caption in that box. The caption is automatically formatted with a generated tag called Z_LABEL CAP. This tag uses the same font as Body Text but is set for center alignment.

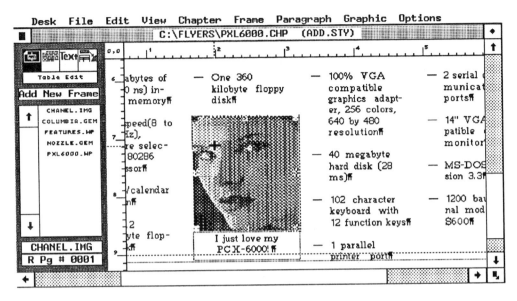

*Figure 5.47    Caption added to picture.*

You can change the font and other format attributes of the caption text by creating or using a different tag for it.

To see the final document you have created, return to the reduced view mode. Enter

**[Ctrl/r]**

This document is really the result of several different files inserted into a number of different frames on a single page.

The use of multiple frames allows you to create different formats at different positions on the page. Each frame's layout is independent of the other frames; however, when frames are layered in the same position, Ventura will flow the text of the underlying frame around the new frame.

You can now print your document.

---

**Point** the mouse at File
**Point** the mouse at To Print
**Click**
**Point** the mouse at OK
**Click**

---

Save the chapter by entering

**[Ctrl/s]**

Clear Ventura of the chapter.

---

**Point** the mouse at File
**Point** the mouse at New
**Click**

---

# SUMMARY

In this chapter, you learned how complex layouts including several text files, images, and columns can be placed into the same document. With Ventura, you can coordinate and organize data from many sources into a single document.

- **Multiple Frames.** Ventura allows you to add as many frames as you want to a document. Ventura always creates a master frame. All other frames are created by using the Add New Frame option available in the Frame Setting mode. Multiple-frame documents allow you to combine picture files and text from several documents to create a single Ventura document.

- **Pictures.** Ventura is compatible with a variety of programs that produce graphic or picture files. The most common examples are Lotus 1-2-3 graph files with PIC extensions.

- **Drawing Frames.** When Add New Frame is selected, you can draw a frame on the displayed page. The mouse cursor changes to a special symbol to indicate you are in the frame drawing mode. Frames can be any size, up to a full page. Frame drawing is aided by line and column snap. Frame drawing is not affected by grid settings. Grid settings affect only graphics in the Graphic Drawing mode.

- **Sizing Frames.** The size of frames can be specified by numeric values if you use the SIZING & SCALING dialog box, which is accessed from the Frame menu.

- **Reverse Lettering.** You can achieve white-on-black printing by changing the font color to white and the frame background to black.

- **Columns.** A frame can be divided into a number of text columns. You can select the number of columns by using the MARGINS & COLUMNS dialog box, which is accessed from the Frame menu. Ventura allows you to specify a gutter between columns. The gutter separates the text formatted into the columns.

- **Vertical Lines.** Ventura can automatically draw vertical lines between columns in a frame. The Vertical Rules option on the Frame menu allows you select inter-column lines. You can also specify one or two vertical lines to be drawn at a specific horizontal position within a frame.

- **Special Effects.** Ventura can create two special effects for paragraph formats. The first is a Big First Char. option that allows you to select a large font and point size for the first letter in a paragraph. The second is a Bullet option. The Bullet option automatically indents a paragraph and places a character (e.g., a black dot) in front of each paragraph.

- **Column or Frame Alignment.** In multiple-column frames, Ventura allows you to decide if a paragraph format should be aligned on the column width or the width of the entire frame. For example, paragraphs centered on the frame width appear centered over all the columns. Paragraphs centered by column width will appear centered within the column in which they are located.

- **Flow-Around.** When a frame is inserted on top of an existing frame, the text in the bottom frame will flow around the frame placed on top. This option allows frames to be layered on top of each other.

- **Scaling Pictures.** When picture files from other applications are imported into a Ventura document, you can control the size, scale, and cropping of the picture. Ventura attempts to maintain the original width-to-height ratio of the drawing. You can choose to select a new ratio to better fit the picture to the frame you have drawn for it. If a picture is enlarged so that only a portion can be displayed in the frame, Ventura permits you to crop the picture to expose the portion you want. You can perform cropping with the mouse by using the [Alt/Drag] technique or by entering values in the SIZING & SCALING dialog box.

- **Captions.** The ANCHORS & CAPTIONS dialog box allows you to add captions to frames.

## Answers to Exercises

**EX-1 (see p. 296):**  Select vertical and horizontal centering.

> **Point** the mouse at Paragraph
> **Point** the mouse at Alignment
> **Click**
> **Point** the mouse at Horz. Alignment
> **Click**
> **Drag** to Center
> **Point** the mouse at Vert. Alignment
> **Click**
> **Drag** to Middle

**EX-2 (see p. 297):**  Change the color of the ruling line to white.

> **Point** the mouse at Width
> **Click**
> **Drag** to Frame
> **Point** the mouse at Color
> **Click**
> **Drag** to White

**EX-3 (see p. 316):**  Create a ruling line below the paragraph.

> **Point** the mouse at Paragraph
> **Point** the mouse at Ruling Line Below
> **Click**
> **Point** the mouse at Width
> **Click**
> **Drag** to Column

Enter


↓
**[Esc]**
**.042** ⏎


**EX-4 (see p. 325):** Scroll downward, and tag the next three paragraphs as Bullet.

**EX-4 (see p. 325):**

> **Point** at the scroll bar down arrow
> **Click** (2 times)

Then,

> **Point** the mouse at "40 Megabyte"
> **[Shift/Click]**
> **Point** the mouse at "102 character"
> **[Shift/Click]**
> **Point** the mouse at "parallel"
> **[Shift/Click]**
> **Point** the mouse at the Bullet tag
> **Click**

**EX-5 (see p. 327):** Scroll right and upward, and tag remaining paragraphs as Bullet.

**EX-5 (see p. 327):**

> **Point** at the scroll bar right arrow
> **Click**
> **Point** at the scroll bar up arrow
> **Click**

Enter

**[Ctrl/i]**

---

**Point** the mouse at "serial"
**[Shift/Click]**
**Point** the mouse at "VGA"
**[Shift/Click]**
**Point** the mouse at "MS-DOS"
**[Shift/Click]**
**Point** the mouse at "1200 Baud"
**[Shift/Click]**
**Point** the mouse at "80 megabyte"
**[Shift/Click]**
**Point** the mouse at the Bullet tag
**Click**

---

**EX-6 (see p. 345):** (see p. 345) Change to the FLYERS directory, and load the CHANEL.IMG file.

---

**Click** on the black directory button
**Click** on FLYERS
**Point** the mouse at CHANEL.IMG
**Double Click**

---

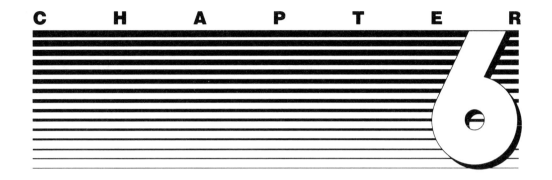

# MULTIPLE-PAGE LAYOUTS

All of the Ventura documents you have prepared so far have been single-page layouts. In business, this is the most common use for programs such as Ventura. But Ventura also has the power to format multiple-page documents from letters, to reports to entire books such as this one.

Multiple-page documents combine many of the features and techniques already discussed in previous chapters in which you created the various types of single-page layouts. In addition, multiple-page documents include features such as page headers and footers, page numbering, tables of contents, and indexes.

Multiple-page documents are different from single-page documents in a broader respect as well. Unlike the small documents you have worked with up to now, a multiple-page document usually consists of one large text file that is perhaps supported by small files containing charts, tables, or illustrations.

In creating large documents, it is highly recommended that you use a different strategic approach from the one you used with the small documents discussed in earlier chapters. In those documents, the text for the document was prepared in your word processor, but no attempt was made to format the paragraphs until the text had been loaded into a Ventura frame. You then used paragraph tagging to differentiate the styles of different paragraphs. While large documents can be handled in the same way, Ventura provides a more efficient way of tagging paragraphs, which is important when you are working with a large number of paragraphs.

The key to this technique is to insert codes Ventura will recognize into the text of the document as you type it in your word processor. Ventura normally recognizes simple formatting such as bold and underlined text in compatible word processor files. For example, if you use the Bold command ([F6] in WordPerfect) or the Underline command ([F8] in WordPerfect), Ventura will recognize those text attributes and create the equivalent effect when the file is loaded into Ventura. Bold text requires that the selected font have a boldface font available. If only a normal typeface is available, Ventura will display all the text as normal; however, the bold code will remain in the document. If you change the font to one that does have bold, the bold format will then appear.

However, formatting codes that affect margins, font styles, point size, or other sophisticated attributes implemented in your word processor will not automatically be translated into Ventura when the file is loaded, which is unfortunate because in large documents the best time to add many of these attributes to the text is as it is being prepared. Word processors generally work much more quickly than does Ventura when it comes to entering and editing text. However, Ventura does provide a way to enter formatting instructions into the text of your document. These instructions follow a special format that Ventura will recognize and convert into Ventura format features. These codes are entered as part of the regular text of the document. To learn how these codes are entered, first load your word processing program.

## TEXT FORMATTING CODES

To understand how Ventura treats text file codes, you can begin by loading the file — FEATURES.WP — you prepared for Chapter 5. Load your word processor (the assumption in this book is that you are using WordPerfect 5.0). Then retrieve the text of FEATURES.WP by entering

**[Shift/F10]**
**c:\flyers\features.wp** ⏎

When you load the document, you will see that Ventura has altered the document to include special text codes that indicate the formatting tags used for each paragraph.

```
@BIG BULLET = For only $3799 you get:
@BULLET = 4 Megabytes of fast (80 ns) internal memory
@BULLET = Four speed(8 to 16 MHz), software selectable, 80286
processor
@BULLET = Clock/calendar built-in
@BULLET = One 1.2 megabyte floppy disk
@BULLET = One 360 kilobyte floppy disk
@BULLET = 100% VGA compatible graphics adapter, 256 colors, 640 by
480 resolution
@BULLET = 40 megabyte hard disk (28 ms)
@BULLET = 102 character keyboard with 12 function keys
@BULLET = 1 parallel printer port
@BULLET = 2 serial communications ports
@BULLET = 14" VGA compatible color monitor
@BULLET = MS-DOS version 3.3
@BULLET = 1200 baud internal modem add $600
@BULLET = 80 megabyte hard disk add $400




C:\FLYERS\FEATURES.WP                    Doc 1 Pg 1 Ln 1" Pos 1"
```

*Figure 6.1    Text document with formatting tags.*

Ventura uses a special format to assign formatting tags to paragraphs. The @ sign must be the first character in the paragraph. It is followed by the name of the style tag, a space, an = sign, and another space, followed by the text of the paragraph. In this case, there are two types of paragraph formatting codes inserted into the document, @BIG BULLET and @BULLET. Note that any paragraph without a tag would be formatted as body text.

You can see that while you were tagging paragraphs in Ventura, Ventura was modifying your text file to include the text codes that correspond to formatting tags assigned in Ventura. There are several important implications in the relationship between Ventura and the text files it uses.

- Whenever a file is loaded into a Ventura chapter, the text of the file is modified to reflect editing changes and styling formats applied to the paragraphs. This means that your original document will not be the same after it has been loaded into Ventura. In addition to adding Ventura formats, all non-converted word processing formats, such as margin changes, will be eliminated from the text file.

- If you want to preserve your text file in its original word processor format, including margin and pitch settings, you should make a copy of the file before you import it into Ventura.

- You can add or change Ventura formats and style tags by typing the appropriate text codes into your word processor document. This means that you can style a document you are creating or revise the tags in a document previously loaded into Ventura, which enables you to use features such as search and replace to quickly change style tags in a large document.

- If you do not enter a style tag code at the beginning of a paragraph, Ventura will assign the Body Text style to that paragraph.

In addition to style tags, you can insert text formatting codes that control Ventura features such as font and point size, footnotes, and index entries. Codes that control individual features such as these use angle brackets ( < > ). For example, if you wanted to change the point size of one word from the standard style tag, you would enter

**This is < P014 > 14 Point < P225 > text.**

The < P014 > tells Ventura to change the point size to 14. The < P225 > instructs Ventura to return to the normal point size for that style tag.

The fact that Ventura interprets the < > and @ signs as text codes means that if you want to include those characters as part of your text rather than use them as formatting codes, you must perform an extra step. The @ is only a problem if you want it to appear as the first character in a paragraph, which is often the case if you write about technical topics (such as computer software) in which @ is often used as part of a computer command or function. In those cases, entering @@ at the beginning of the paragraph will cause the @ symbol to appear as text. Ventura will know that the text is not a tag code. Your Ventura document will show only a single @. The < > (angle brackets) will be considered as part of a code wherever they appear. If you want to include them in you text, e.g., < return >, you can enclose the angle brackets themselves inside a pair of angle brackets (e.g., < < return > > entered in your word processing program will appear as < return > in Ventura). You can avoid this problem by using [ ] or {} brackets, which Ventura will treat as text characters not codes, but do this only if you want the [ ] or {} brackets to appear in your document.

Many of Ventura's formatting codes can be manually inserted into the text of a document. Following is a table that summarizes the text codes. Note that *nnn* stands for a three-digit number from 000 to 999. Ellipses (...) stand for the text or number you will enter to complete the code.

| Code | Function |
| --- | --- |
| <$B0> | Draw hollow box |
| <$B1> | Draw filled box |
| <J*nnn*> | Jump text from baseline |
| <B%*n*> | Begin manual kerning |
| <B> | Bold |
| <C*nnn*> | Color |
| <=> | Double underline |
| <I> | Italics |
| <R> | Line break |
| <M> | Medium weight typeface |
| <O> | Overscore |
| <P*nnn*> | Point size |
| <D> | Resume normal text |
| <S> | Small text |
| <X> | Strikethrough text |
| <V> | Subscript |
| <^> | Superscript |
| <F*nnn*> | Font number |
| <U> | Underline |
| <N> | Non-breaking space |
| <$F...> | Footnote |
| <$E...> | Fractions |
| <$I...> | Index entry |
| <$R...> | Page number code |
| <$&...> | Frame anchor |

You can make good use of text codes when you prepare a large document. By entering the style tags directly into your text, you preformat the document with the style codes you want. This means that you don't have to go through a long document and highlight and format each word you want to have a special format. You can use codes to pre-assign paragraph tags as well, which can save you time and effort because it will generally take more time to tag each paragraph in Ventura than it will to enter the codes in your word processor (use of these codes will be discussed in the next section). As indicated in the summary of text codes, you can also add codes for font changes, footnotes, frame anchors, and index entries.

Another benefit of this system is that you can use the codes to add text features that your word processor or text editor does not directly support. For example, in Ventura the [Ctrl/◄┘] command inserts a line break. WordPerfect does not have a command to create line breaks; however, by ending a line with the code < R >, you can achieve a line break when the document is loaded into Ventura.

## CREATING A TAGGED TEXT FILE

Now that you have an idea of how Ventura treats text files, you can put the concept to practical use in the document you need to prepare. Begin with a new document. If you are using WordPerfect, enter the Exit command to clear the text window:

**[F7]**
**n**
**n**

The document you are about to prepare is a report on the world's smallest country, Andorra. Instead of just entering the text, you will also insert paragraph tags and text formatting commands. When Ventura loads the text files, these codes will have the same effect on the document as text you format by highlighting it and using Ventura menus and dialog boxes.

You could enter the names of paragraph tags you used in one of the style sheet files you created in earlier chapters, but you are not limited to that approach. You can also begin a document and make up paragraph tag names that haven't been previously used in any document.

When Ventura finds an unknown paragraph tag in the text, it automatically creates a tag and places the name of the tag into the side bar. Of course, Ventura does not know what characteristics you want to assign to the tag, so Ventura simply assigns the new tags the same format settings as the Body Text style.

You still need to create the settings that distinguish one paragraph style from another, but the important fact is that all of the paragraphs that should be formatted a particular way are already tagged. If you highlight any one paragraph that has been assigned that particular tag, you only need to enter that tag's settings once. Ventura will automatically update all the paragraphs that have the same tag throughout the entire document. One of Ventura's greatest features is this ability to automatically update all paragraphs that are assigned the same tag.

For example, in the report you are about to create, you will enter a number of topic headings. If you tag each topic heading with a specific tag, e.g., @SUB HEAD, Ventura will automatically format all @SUB HEAD lines as soon as you define the fonts and settings for any one of the paragraphs.

To begin, you will want to enter the major heading for the report. Be sure to enter a space before and after the = sign in the example that follows. Enter

**@MAJOR HEAD = THE WORLD'S SMALLEST NATION** ⏎

The next line will be the first subheading in the document. Enter

**@SUB HEAD = ABOUT ANDORRA** ⏎

The next paragraph will be normal body text. This means that no tag codes are required. Note that the codes <I> and <D> are included to italicize the word "Andorra." Enter

**In a world of powers and super-powers that fight to be the largest and most powerful nations, somebody has to be at the bottom of the ladder. That nation is the tiny mountain land of <I>Andorra<D>.** ⏎

Add another body text paragraph.

**The nation of Andorra is officially called the Valleys of Andorra. The nation is located in the heart of the Pyrenees Mountains between the better known nations of France and Spain. Andorra marks the beginning of the Iberian peninsula.** ⅃

The document should resemble the one in Figure 6.2:

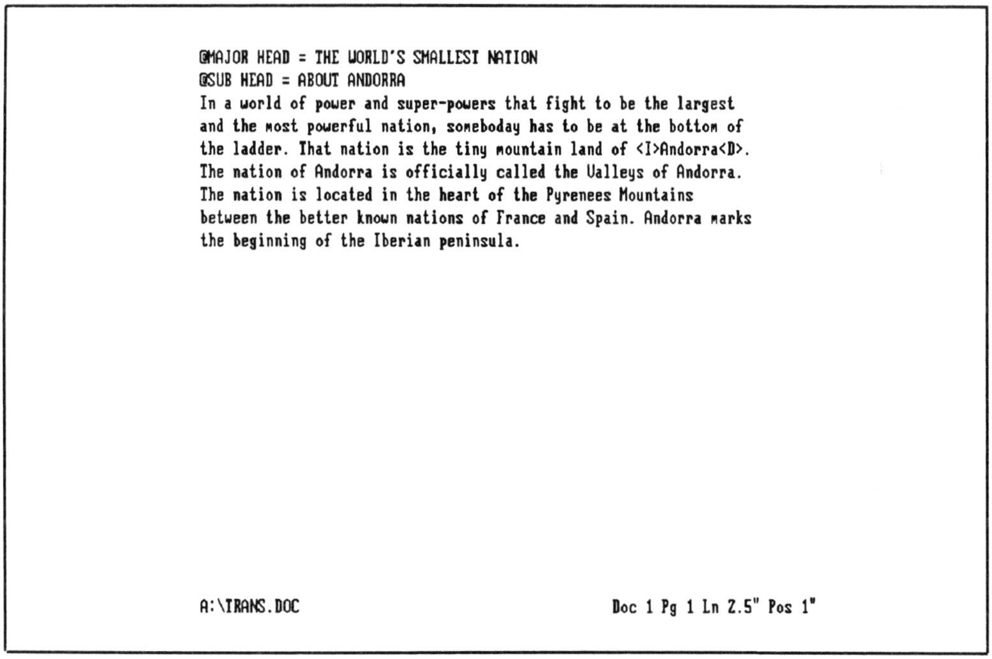

```
@MAJOR HEAD = THE WORLD'S SMALLEST NATION
@SUB HEAD = ABOUT ANDORRA
In a world of power and super-powers that fight to be the largest
and the most powerful nation, someboday has to be at the bottom of
the ladder. That nation is the tiny mountain land of <I>Andorra<D>.
The nation of Andorra is officially called the Valleys of Andorra.
The nation is located in the heart of the Pyrenees Mountains
between the better known nations of France and Spain. Andorra marks
the beginning of the Iberian peninsula.




A:\TRANS.DOC                         Doc 1 Pg 1 Ln 2.5" Pos 1"
```

*Figure 6.2    Text document created with formatting tags.*

## ADDING FOOTNOTES

Ventura supports footnotes in the text of the document. You can create footnotes in Ventura, but by far the best method is to enter footnotes directly into the word processing text file. Enter the next section heading in the document, but do not enter ⏎ at the end of the line.

@SUB HEAD = VITAL STATISTICS

Suppose that you needed to footnote the information in this section. To create a footnote, you type a special code into the text of that footnote. The coded footnote is placed into the text document at the position in the text where you want the footnote reference number or symbol to be placed. Ventura will automatically number of the footnotes and place the footnote text at the bottom of the appropriate page. Footnotes are created by entering <$Fxxxxxxx> where xxxxxxxx is the text of the footnote. Enter

<$FWorld Almanac, Enterprise Associates, 1985> ⏎

The text entered into the code will appear as a footnote on the bottom of the page. A reference number for the footnote will be displayed in the location in which you placed the codes. Ventura will automatically generate the correct numbering sequence.

The next item on the list is a topic heading. Enter

@TOPIC = POPULATION ⏎

Enter the following paragraph, but do not enter ⏎ at the end:

The 35,000 people of Andorra live on 188 square miles of land. That is a population density of about 180.85 people per square mile. The United States has an average population of about 65 people per square mile, the Soviet Union 30 people per square mile, and China 278 people per square mile.

# ANCHORING FRAMES

Suppose you want to use Lotus 1-2-3 to create a graph that compares population densities among the countries mentioned in the text you just entered. In single-page layouts, the position of frames is determined visually; however, in multiple-page documents, the position of frames within the text is determined by the logic of the text. For example, the graph of population densities should follow the paragraph about population. Ventura allows you to insert **anchors** into the text. Anchors are markers that indicate where frames should be positioned in the text. Anchors are important in large documents because they can be used to rearrange frames automatically, based on the position of the text in the document. This helps maintain the correct layout even when the text is altered.

An anchor is a special code that contains the name of the frame. As with the names of the paragraph tags, it is not necessary to have created the frame ahead of time. You can simply anticipate that you will eventually create such a frame and that it should be located at this position in the text. Ventura will not attempt to anchor frames when a text file is loaded. A separate command called **Re-Anchor frames**, which is accessed from the Chapter menu, is used to position frames in a document. The frame anchoring system allows you to create long documents with illustrations, charts, and tables without having to manually position each item on the correct page. Enter

**< $&pop density[V] >**

The [V] tells Ventura that the frame should be placed below the anchor. If you had entered [^], Ventura would have positioned the frame above the anchor in the text. If you used a [-], Ventura would position the frame immediately following the anchor. This type of location could place the frame in the middle of a paragraph. If the brackets are not entered, the frame will be placed on the same page as the anchor but at the same vertical and horizontal location in which the frame was originally placed when it was created.

## ENTERING INDEX REFERENCES

Index references can also be added directly to the text of your document. These references do not appear in the text of your document but can be used to generate an index of topics. Ventura uses the location of the index items to determine the page numbers for the index items. As with footnotes, you can also enter index codes in Ventura, using the Ventura menu options; however, it is usually easier and faster to enter the index items in your word processor. (For table of contents items, however, you need not enter special codes because Ventura uses paragraph tags to distinguish table of contents entry items. The @SUB HEAD tag could be used to insert all the subheading items into the table of contents.)

For example, suppose you want to generate an index for this report. You can insert codes into the text that will create index references. Keep in mind that you are not required to generate an index just because you enter index codes. Entering the codes simply gives you that option in case you later decide to produce the index.

Suppose you want to create an index entry for population density. The code symbol for an index entry is **$I**. A simple index entry would resemble the following:

**< $Ipopulation density >**

Ventura also allows you to create major headings and subheadings for an index. For example, if you had several entries for population, you could enter "population" as the main heading and the particular topic as a subheading. A semicolon is used to separate the major heading from the subheading, for example,

**< $Ipopulation;density >**
**< $Ipopulation;totals >**

The result would be an index entry such as the following:

> Population
>    density, 2
>    totals, 3

Ventura permits you to add a **sort order key** to index entries. A sort order key is used to determine the placement of an entry if you do not want Ventura to sort strictly according to alphabetical order. For example, an index entry might read "The Second World War"; however, you might want the item to appear under "S" for Second or "W" for War. You can insert a sort order for either the major entry or the subentry, for example,

**< $IThe Second World War[War] >**

In this case, create an simple entry for population density. Enter

**< $Ipopulation;density > ⌐**

Begin entering the next paragraph.

**@TOPIC = ETHNIC GROUPS ⌐**
**Andorra is populated by three major ethnic groupings. Despite Andorra's long history these groups live rather separate lives. The majority of Andorrans are Spanish while the native Andorran population is a minority of about**

## Creating Fractions

After the word "about" you want to enter a fraction to indicate one third of the population is native Andorran. Ventura will create a correctly sized fraction if you enter the numbers with a special code. The < $E > code tells Ventura to format the text as a fraction. Enter

**< $E1/3 >. ⌐**

# COMPLETING THE EXAMPLE DOCUMENT

You now know how to create special text codes that will save you time in formatting a document in Ventura. The complete report on Andorra follows. Enter the rest of the text. The ⏎ symbol indicates where a return should be entered. When you have completed the text, save it as **ANDORRA.WP** in the \WP50 directory (or use an appropriate extension and subdirectory if you are using another word processor); then exit your word processing program.

---

@MAJOR HEAD = THE WORLD'S SMALLEST NATION ⏎
@SUB HEAD = ABOUT ANDORRA⏎
In a world of power and super-powers that fight to be the largest
and the most powerful nation, somebody has to be at the bottom of
the ladder. That nation is the tiny mountain land of <I>Andorra<D>. ⏎
The nation of Andorra is officially called the Valleys of Andorra.
The nation is located in the heart of the Pyrenees Mountains
between the better known nations of France and Spain. Andorra marks
the beginning of the Iberian peninsula. ⏎
@SUB HEAD =VITAL STATISTICS<**$FWorld Almanac, Enterprise
Associates, 1985>**⏎
@TOPIC = POPULATION⏎
The 35,000 people of Andorra live on 188 square miles of land.
That is a population density of about 180.85 people per square
mile. The United States has an average population of about 65
people per square mile, the Soviet Union 30 people per square mile,
and China 278 people per square mile.<**$&pop
density[V]>**<**$Ipopulation;density>** ⏎
@TOPIC = ETHNIC GROUPS ⏎
Andorra is populated by three major ethnic groupings. Despite
Andorra's long history these groups live rather separate lives. The
majority of Andorrans are Spanish while the native Andorran
population is a minority of about <**$E1/3>.**<**$&ethnic[V]>**<**$Iethnic
groups>** ⏎
@SUB HEAD =HEALTH RATES ⏎
Andorra has an annual birth rate of 16.5 per thousand. The death
rate is 5.0 per thousand annually. The population shows a natural
increase rate of 1.2%. ⏎
@SUB HEAD =COMMUNICATIONS IN ANDORRA ⏎
Andorra has rather limited communication in comparison to its
neighbor to the north, France. Andorra has about 10,000 telephones
currently installed, 6,000 radios and some 3,000 televisions sets
of which there is one big screen set located in the capital city,
Andorra la Vella.<**$&communications[V]>** ⏎

*continued...*

```
@SUB HEAD =GOVERNMENT ⏎
@TOPIC = HEAD OF STATE ⏎
```
Andorra is ruled by two princes. One is usually the head of state
in France and the other is the Bishop of Urgel in Spain. This joint
sovereignty has been in effect since 1278. The current co-princes
are Francois Miterrand, President of France, and the current Roman
Catholic Bishop of Urgel, Spain , Joan Marti y Alanis. ⏎
```
@TOPIC = DIVISIONS ⏎
```
Andorra is divided in seven parishes. ⏎
```
@TOPIC = HEAD OF GOVERNMENT ⏎
```
Andorra is ruled by a local governor who is appointed by the local
council. The current head is Syndic Estanislao Sangra Font, elected
in January of 1971. ⏎
```
@SUB HEAD = ECONOMICS ⏎
@TOPIC = INDUSTRY ⏎
```
The main economic activity is tourism and some goat herding. Sheep
were introduced from Spain in 1856 but migrated back over the
Pyrenees to the warmer climate of Spain. ⏎
```
@TOPIC = LABOR ⏎
```
Some 20% of the population is engaged in agricultural activities.
The remainder of the population is employed in government services.
The mainstay of the economy is tourism. Andorra is a major ski
resort for southern France. Unfortunately the Spanish don't ski.
Andorra is a duty free country that attracts some 7 million
tourists a year. ⏎
```
@TOPIC = CURRENCY ⏎
```
Andorrans use two types of currency: ⏎
```
@LIST = The French franc. ⏎
@ LIST = The Spanish peseta. ⏎
```

*Figure 6.3    Completed text document ANDORRA.WP*

## Spreadsheet Data

In addition to the text entered into the file **ANDORRA.WP**, your report will include two other types of data: spreadsheet tables and graphics. While it is possible to perform this type of integration with a number of different spreadsheet programs, the example shown in this chapter will use Lotus 1-2-3 Release 2.01 because it is currently an extremely popular spreadsheet program. It is necessary to assume that you know spreadsheet program operations to the extent that you can create the spreadsheet shown in Figure 6.4 and can create the charts shown in Figures 6.5, 6.6, and 6.7.

Note that the spreadsheet contains information in column C that is used to select patterns for the pie charts. The values in column C should used as the B range for the pie charts. If you are using Release 1 of 1-2-3, these values will have no effect on the charts.

Figure 6.4 shows a 1-2-3 spreadsheet that contains statistical data about Andorra. If you have 1-2-3, Quattro, VP-Planner, or another 1-2-3-compatible program, create this spreadheet. Note that column A is set to a width of 14, and the global format is set to comma with zero decimal places.

You can use this data to create graphs. Below are three graphs created from this data. If you have 1-2-3, you can create these graphs for use in your report. Remember to use the / G(raph) S(ave) command to create the PIC files needed for Ventura. You will need to create three charts, COMM.PIC, ETHNIC.PIC and POPDEN.PIC (see Figures 6.5, 6.6, and 6.7).

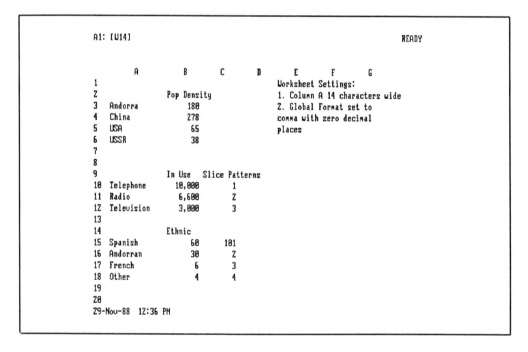

*Figure 6.4    Lotus 1-2-3 spreadsheet.*

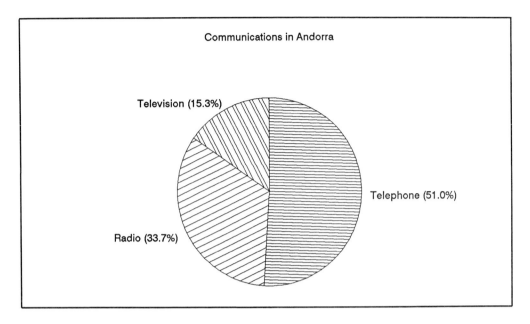

*Figure 6.5    COMM.PIC chart.*

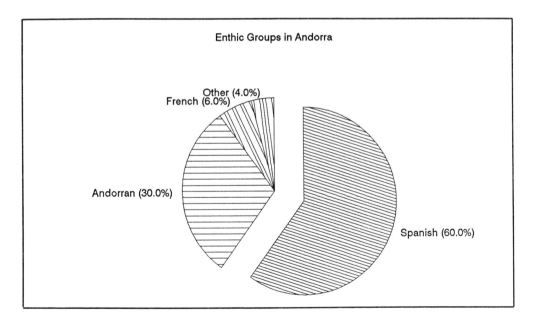

*Figure 6.6    ETHNIC.PIC chart.*

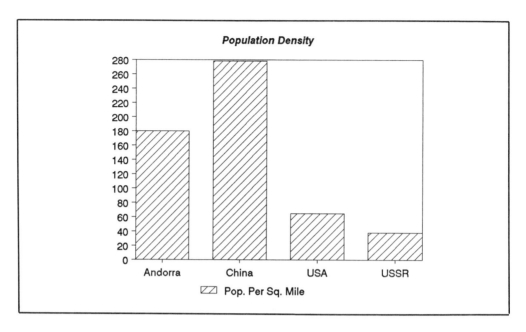

*Figure 6.7    POPDEN.PIC chart.*

## Transferring Text from Lotus 1-2-3

In addition to chart information, you may want to include some of the numeric data used to create the charts as part of the Ventura document. From 1-2-3 data, you can also create text files that can be loaded into Ventura frames as document files. For example, suppose you wanted to insert the text of one of the statistical tables into your Ventura report. 1-2-3 files are not compatible with Ventura, but you can create text files that Ventura can load in the same way that it loads word processing files.

To create a text file with 1-2-3, you use the / P(rint) F(ile) command. For example, in cells A9 through B12 of the worksheet, you have entered a table of communications information. To create a text file with that data, enter

**/pf**
**comm** ⏎
**r**
**a9.b12** ⏎
**oouq**
**gq**

You have created a text file called **COMM.PRN**. The Option Other Unformatted command was used during the Print File to eliminate any margins or page breaks that 1-2-3 would normally insert into the text file. Ventura will create its own margins and page breaks, so you want to eliminate any 1-2-3 formatting. Lotus 1-2-3 automatically attaches the PRN extension to the text file.

You now have all the text and graphic files you need to create the Andorra report:

1.  ANDORRA.WP, created in WordPerfect (or whichever word processing program you use).

2.  POPDEN.PIC, COMM.PIC, and ETHNIC.PIC created with 1-2-3.

3.  COMM.PRN, a 1-2-3 text file.

You can now exit 1-2-3 and load Ventura in the normal manner.

## FORMATTING EMBEDDED TAGS

In the previous chapters, the text files you loaded into Ventura were unformatted, i.e., they did not contain special codes that would be interpreted by Ventura when the text file was loaded. In this example, you entered tag and formatting codes into the document before loading it into Ventura, but you do not currently have any style sheets designed to work with those tags. Fortunately, Ventura will automatically integrate any paragraph tag names it finds into the current style sheet. To help you distinguish between tags that were part of the original style sheet and the ones added because of the text document, Ventura displays the names of the new tags in uppercase letters, which is why it is best to enter tag names in lowercase or mixed case when you create them manually in Ventura; this makes it easier to distinguish between the existing tags and the new tags.

You should now load the DEFAULT.STY style sheet so you can begin with a clean style sheet.

---

**Point** the mouse at File
**Point** the mouse at Load Diff. Style
**Click**

---

The item selector display probably shows the FLYERS directory. Change the directory setting from the keyboard rather than with the mouse. Enter

↑
**[Esc]**
**\typeset\*.sty** ⏎
**default** ⏎

The default style sheet is loaded into the current chapter.

You are now ready to load the text of the ANDORRA.WP file into the master frame of this Ventura document. Note how Ventura automatically displays in the side bar the names of the style tags you entered into the text of the document just as if you had created each tag in Ventura.

> **Point** the mouse at File
> **Point** the mouse at Load Text/Picture
> **Click**
> **Point** the mouse at Text
> **Click**

Enter

⏎

Note that the FLYERS directory, the last directory from which you loaded text files appears in the selector box. Change the directory to your word processing directory. Enter

↑
**[Esc]**
**\wp50\*.wp** ⏎

A list of your word processor files is displayed beginning with ANDORRA.WP. Load that text file.

```
Point the mouse at ANDORRA.WP
Double Click
```

The filename appears in the side bar display. Remember that Ventura won't load the text into the frame until you tell it to.

```
Point the mouse at ANDORRA.WP
Click
```

The text is inserted into the master frame. Save the file as a chapter file. Enter

**[Crtl/S]**

Change to the Paragraph Tagging mode by entering

**[Ctrl/i]**

The side bar display shows in uppercase the names of the style tags you entered into your document. Only Body Text, which was part of the default style sheet, appears in mixed case.

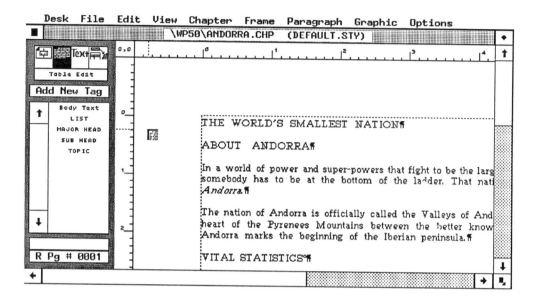

*Figure 6.8    Embedded codes create tags listed in uppercase letters.*

Your task is now much simpler than if you had loaded an unformatted document. You need only define the settings for each tag, and the style will flow through the entire document because each paragraph is already assigned its correct style tag. In this sense, the document you created was preformatted. To begin defining the document's paragraph tag settings, you will want to change to the normal display mode. Enter

**[Ctrl/n]**

## HEADING STYLES

You are now ready to begin the process of defining styles for the tags that were entered in the text file. To begin, you will want to assign style settings to the heading tags you have inserted into the document. At this point, all the text looks the same. When Ventura encountered undefined tag names in the text, it automatically created tags and assigned them the same settings as the Body Text tag.

Before you begin to differentiate the styles, create a new style sheet file.

> **Point** the mouse at File
> **Point** the mouse at Save as New Style
> **Click**

Enter the name of the new style sheet.

**report** ⏎

Define the major heading of the report.

> **Point** the mouse at "WORLD'S"
> **Click**

This highlights the first paragraph. Note that the name MAJOR HEAD appears in the box above the page number. When you modify a tag, the first choice on the Paragraph menu is Font. In this case, you will want to use a large typeface.

> **Exercise 1:** Set the font for this paragraph to Swiss, 24-point bold. Try this on your own. The correct commands can be found under EX-1 at the end of this chapter.

The major heading stands out because of its new font.

## Spacing for Major Headings

While changing the font helps make headings stand out, it is not the only tool available for creating a more dramatic layout. A major heading, such as the title of a chapter in a book, can include spacing settings that will increase its effect.

In this case, you might want to place several inches of blank space above the heading so that it will begin about 1/3 of the way down the page. This type of spacing is often used on title pages of books and reports.

> **Point** the mouse at Paragraph
> **Point** the mouse at Spacing
> **Click**

Enter a new value for the space above the paragraph.

**[Esc]**
**2.5** ↵

The heading appears in exactly the same place it was in before you entered the new value. Recall the special Add in Above setting in the SPACING dialog box. Return to the SPACING dialog box. Whenever you want to return to the last dialog box that you used, you can use a keyboard shortcut. The [Ctrl/x] command will display the last dialog box. Enter

**[Ctrl/x]**

In the center of the dialog box, you will see the Add in Above setting. The currently selected option is When Not at Column Top. This setting is used to avoid placing blank space at the top of a page, but in this case you want the space to be placed above the heading.

> **Point** the mouse at Always
> **Click**

Enter

↵

With this change, the spacing is inserted above the major heading (see Figure 6.9).

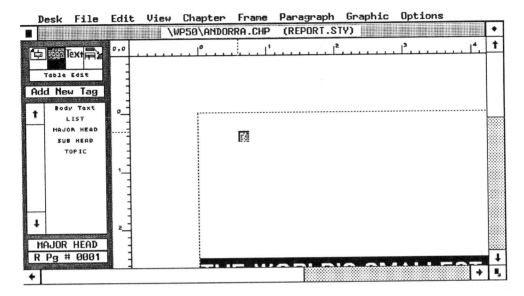

*Figure 6.9    Space added above heading.*

To see more of the text, scroll down.

> **Point** at the scroll bar down arrow
> **Click**  (6 times)

## Ruling Lines

You can also make a heading stand out by adding a ruling line below the title.

> **Point** the mouse at Paragraph
> **Point** the mouse at Ruling Line Below
> **Click**

Select a frame-wide line.

---

**Point** the mouse at Width
**Click**
**Drag** to Frame

---

Next, enter the thickness of the line.

↓
**[Esc]**
**.1** ⌐

The line is drawn beneath the text.

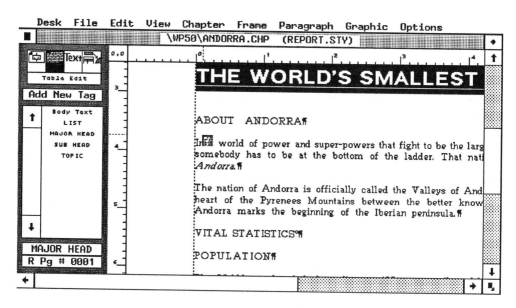

*Figure 6.10    Ruling line added to heading.*

## Subheadings

Now that you have created the major heading for the report, you will want to set the style for the subheadings.

In setting the style for the subheadings, consider their function. In this document, the subheadings mark off specific sections, which means that you will want the subheadings to be easily identified by people who are skimming through your report.

To make your subheadings easy to identify, use a variation on the concept of ruling lines. In this case, the ruling line will be manipulated so it appears as a shaded background for the text.

Because all of the subheading paragraphs are already tagged, any change that you make to one SUB HEAD paragraph tag will ripple though all the subheadings in the document. Highlight the first subheading.

---

**Point** the mouse at "ABOUT"
**Click**

---

**Exercise 2:**   If you intend to shade the background, you will want
to choose a font that will stand out against a gray
background. In this case, select Swiss, 18-point bold.
Try this on your own. The correct commands can
be found under EX-2 at the end of this chapter.

The subheading's typeface is changed. The text "VITAL STATISTICS" is also changed because it was also assigned the SUB HEAD tag. When you define a format for any one of the tags, all of the other paragraphs assigned that same tag will be updated to reflect the style definition.

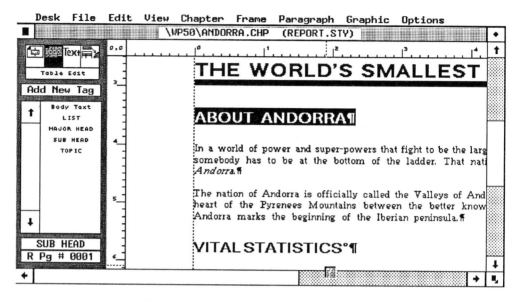

*Figure 6.11   Font for subheadings changed.*

## Gray Backgrounds

Changing the background of a specific paragraph tag is a bit tricky. In Chapter 5, you changed the background color of a small frame to solid black and displayed white text on top of it. It is also possible to use black letters but change the background to a gray pattern.

However, in this case you cannot use the same method as was used in Chapter 5, where you changed the background color of an entire frame, because you only want to change the background of specific paragraphs, i.e., those tagged as SUB HEAD.

The answer to this problem may seem odd when you first see it implemented. Ventura uses its ruling line feature to effect the background change.

Recall that when you set a ruling line, Ventura allows you to enter the amount of space to be left between the ruling line and the text. In most cases, you enter a positive value for this distance. A **positive** value is one that adds space to the text, but Ventura will accept a negative value. When spacing is entered as **negative**, it is subtracted from the normal spacing text, causing the ruling line to overlap the text. The result is that the text prints over the ruling line, making it appear as if there is a shaded background.

To create this effect, use the Rule Lining Above option.

---

**Point** the mouse at Paragraph
**Point** the mouse at Ruling Line Above
**Click**

---

First set the width to frame-wide lines.

---

**Point** the mouse at Width
**Click**
**Drag** to Frame

---

Next select the pattern. The default value is Solid. The pattern determines the shading of the line. You can select a number value for the shading where 1 is the lightest gray and 7 is the darkest. Solid produces a solid black line.

---

**Point** the mouse at Pattern
**Click**
**Drag** to 2

---

Next, you need to consider the height of the line. In this case, you want to enter a line that will cover the text. Remember that you selected an 18-point font for the subheadings.

You can figure out how high 18-point text is in inches by remembering that there are 72 points to an inch. This means that 18-point text is 18/72" (or 1/4") high, so to cover the text your line should be at least 1/4" high. You might choose to make the line larger than the text. This would create a gray background above or below the text itself. In this example, the gray will be the same height as the text. Enter

↓
**[Esc].25**

The next step is the tricky one. At this point, the 1/4" gray line would appear just above the text. To force Ventura to overlap the line and the text, you must subtract space from the layout by entering a value for the Space Below Rule 3 setting.

Remember that the overall rule can contain several line and spacing values. Ventura assumes that the ruling lines should begin at the top of the first line in the paragraph. The Space Below Rule 3 setting affects the placement of all of the other ruling lines. If you enter a negative value for Space Below Rule 3, Ventura will start the ruling line below the top of the first line of the paragraph. If you enter a negative value equal to the overall height of the ruling lines, Ventura will overlap the text and ruling line.

In this case, the value will be .25", which will create a gray line the same height as the typeface.

↓ (5 times)
**[Esc] .25**

The next step is the crucial one for the effect you are trying to achieve. You must change the setting to negative space. The negative setting will cause the ruling line and the text to overlap. If you set the positive and negative spacing values both at .25", the overlap will be 100%. Note the two boxes, plus (+) and minus (-), next to the Space Below Rule 3 setting.

**Point** the mouse at -
**Click**

Complete the entry by pressing

↵

The subheadings now appear against a gray background.

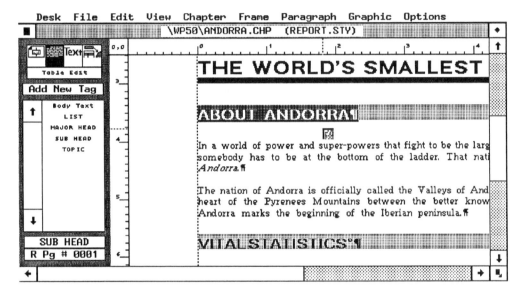

*Figure 6.12    Shaded backgrounds added to all subheadings.*

The change you made to this subheading will affect all paragraphs tagged as SUB HEAD.

## MOVING BETWEEN PAGES

The text in the ANDORRA.WP file was too large to fit onto a single page. Ventura will automatically generate as many pages as needed for the document file loaded into the master frame. Keep in mind that when you load text into frames other than the master frame, pages will not be automatically generated. You will learn more about this in Chapter 8.

The [PgUp] and [PgDn] keys can be used to move to the previous and next pages, respectively, in a document. Display the second page of the document by entering

**[PgDn]**

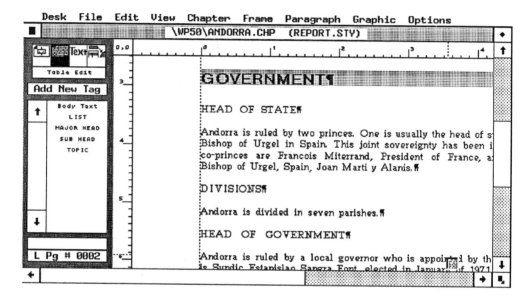

*Figure 6.13   Page 2 displayed.*

Note that the subheading on page 2 is formatted with the same specifications as the subheadings on page one. In multiple-page documents, you can use the following keys to change pages:

| Key | Result |
| --- | --- |
| **[Home]** | first page in chapter |
| **[End]** | last page in chapter |
| **[PgDn]** | next page |
| **[PgUp]** | previous page |

You can also move to specific pages by using the **Goto** command. Enter

**[Ctrl/g]**

The screen displays the GO TO PAGE dialog box.

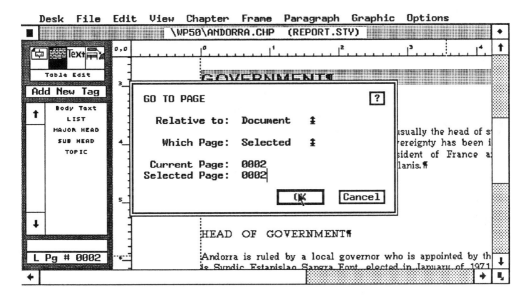

*Figure 6.14   GO TO PAGE dialog box.*

To move to a selected page, enter the number of the page.

Enter

**1** ⏎

Page 1 is now displayed.

## CHANGING MARGINS

The pages you have been looking at are using the default margins, 1" for the top, bottom, left, and right margins. In a report or book format, you might want to increase the margins, making the lines a bit shorter. To change the margins, place Ventura into the Frame Setting mode. Enter

**[Ctrl/u]**

The master frame should still be selected. Remember, selection is indicated by the appearance of the frame buttons. If the master frame is not selected, select it by pointing the mouse anywhere in the frame and clicking.

Next, display the MARGINS & COLUMNS dialog box.

> **Point** the mouse at Frame
> **Point** the mouse at Margins & Columns
> **Click**

Enter

↓ (3 times)
**[Esc]**
**01.25** ↓
**[Esc]**
**01.25** ↵

The frame margins narrow the width of the text. You can confirm this change by looking at the ruler line to see where the column guide is now positioned.

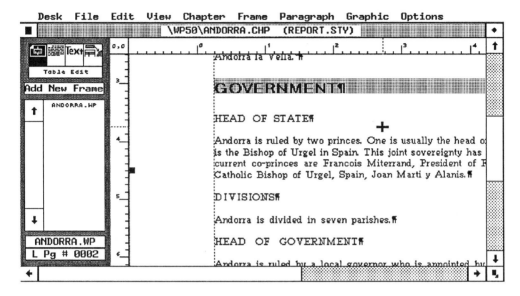

*Figure 6.15   Master frame margins changed.*

## TOPIC HEADINGS

The next step in formatting this document is to define the type of format you want to use for the TOPIC headings in the text. Place Ventura into the Paragraph Tagging mode. Enter

**[Ctrl/i]**

Move to page 2 by entering

**[PgDn]**

Below the subheading "GOVERNMENT," the topic heading "HEAD OF STATE" appears. Select that paragraph.

> **Point** the mouse at "HEAD OF STATE"
> **Click**

Note that the name of the tag appears in the side bar display just above the page number. This confirms that you have selected a TOPIC paragraph.

> **Exercise 3:** Select the font for the TOPIC tag. In this case, choose Swiss, 14-point bold. This will make the TOPIC headings smaller than the subheadings but larger than the text. Try this on your own. The correct commands can be found under EX-3 at the end of this chapter.

Note that when you make this change, other paragraphs already tagged as TOPIC automatically show the new font.

Add a ruling line below the TOPIC headings.

> **Point** the mouse at Paragraph
> **Point** the mouse at Ruling Line Below
> **Click**

In this case, you want to limit the ruling line to the width of the text. This gives you the same effect as underlining because the line will extend only as far as the text.

> **Point** the mouse at Width
> **Click**
> **Drag** to Text

When drawing a line beneath the text, you will want to add some space to separate the ruling line from the text.  Enter

**[Esc]**
**.028** ↓
**[Esc]**
**.014** ⏎

All of the TOPIC paragraphs are underlined.  The subheading and topic headings are all formatted because they were already tagged in the word processing text file you created before loading Ventura.

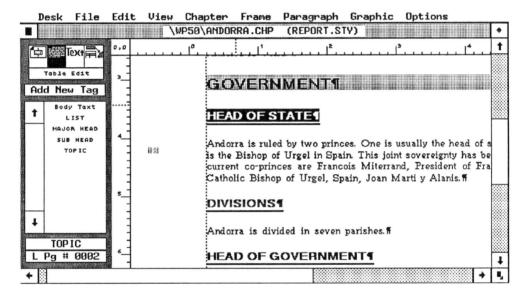

*Figure 6.16    Ruling lines added to TOPIC paragraphs.*

## HEADERS AND FOOTERS

In documents such as this, you will usually want to add page headers and/or footers. The headers are used to designate information about the chapter, including chapter number and page numbers. Return to page 1 by entering

**[PgUp]**

Place Ventura into the reduced display mode by entering

**[Ctrl/r]**

Ventura allows you to add simple headers and/or footers by using the Headers & Footers option on the Chapter menu.

> **Point** the mouse at Chapter
> **Point** the mouse at Headers & Footers
> **Click**

The **HEADERS & FOOTERS** dialog box is displayed.

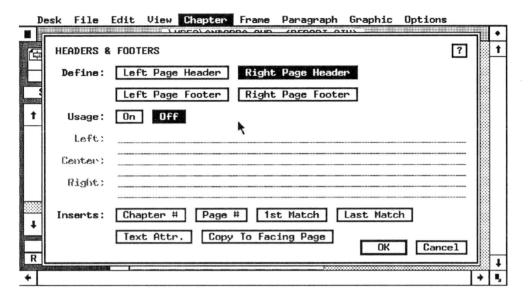

*Figure 6.17  HEADERS & FOOTERS dialog box.*

Ventura allows you to define separate headers and footers for left and right pages. The left-page and right-page distinction is important when you intend to reproduce your document by printing on both sides of the paper. In this chapter the assumption is made that you intend to have both left and right pages.

The first step in defining a header is to turn the header or footer on. The Right Page Header setting is currently selected.

---

**Point** the mouse at On
**Click**

---

The lines labeled Left, Center, and Right appear as solid lines, indicating that they are now open for entry.

A page header or footer can contain any text characters and some special items:

**Chapter #**      Inserts the current chapter number into the header.
Symbol: **[C#]**

**Page #**      Inserts the current page number into the header.
Symbol: **[P#]**

**1st Match**      This option allows you to insert the text from a tagged paragraph into the header or footer. For example, suppose that you wanted the text of the first subheading on the page to be inserted into the header for that page. The symbol [<sub head] placed into the header would cause Ventura to insert the text from the first SUB HEAD paragraph on that page into the header. The advantage of this type of header is that its contents will change as the subheadings on its pages change. Note that this option should be used only with style tags that are applied to short-line paragraphs such as headings.

**Last Match**      This option operates the same as the 1st Match option except that it selects the last match on the page for the header text.

**Text Attr.**      This option provides an optional method of inserting text codes into a header or footer. Ventura will normally apply the same font to all of the header text. If you want to vary the characters within a header, you can insert the standard text formatting codes discussed at the beginning of this chapter into the header text to change fonts or add characteristics such as italics or bold.

You can combine several of the options to create a single header. Suppose you wanted to print the current major heading and the current subheading as a page header. The major heading would be normal but the subheading would be in italics.

Begin by inserting the code for the major heading.

> **Point** the mouse at 1st Match
> **Click**

When you select 1st Match, Ventura inserts a sample symbol, **[<tag name]**, where *tag name* should be replaced by the name of the tag you want. The symbol as it is inserted will not function correctly. Edit the symbol by removing *tag name* and inserting the actual name of the tag. Enter

←
**[Backspace]** (8 times)
**major head** →

You can enter text characters as well as symbols. Add a colon and a space by entering

**:**
**[Space bar]**

The rest of the header should appear in italics. Enter the symbol for italics.

**<I>**

Next enter the symbol for inserting the subheading. You might find it easier to directly enter the exact symbol you want rather than insert and edit the default symbol. Enter

**[<sub head]**

Enter a code that will set the text back to normal.

**<D>**

The header specification is shown in Figure 6.18.

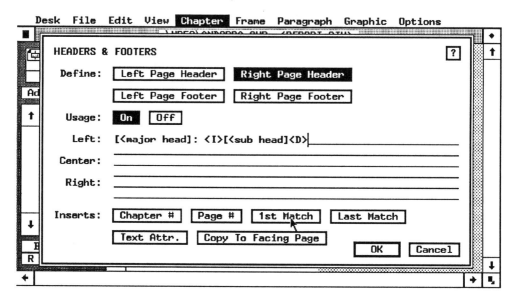

*Figure 6.18   Header specification containing special symbols.*

Complete the entry by pressing

↵

The reduced view shows the page header as a bar of greeked text at the top of the page.  Return to the normal view mode.

Point at the upper left corner of the page

**[Ctrl/n]**

The text of the header reflects the current text of the major headings and sub-headings.  Note that the subheading text is italicized.

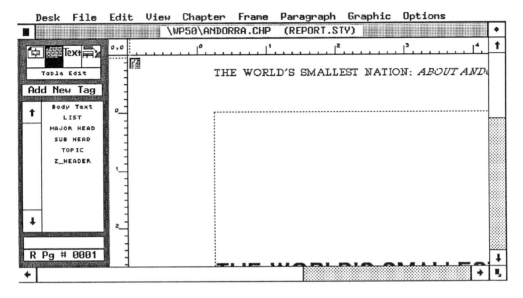

*Figure 6.19    Header appears at the top of the page.*

The side bar list displays a new tag, **Z_HEADER**. Ventura automatically generated this tag when you created the header. This tag is automatically assigned to the page header text and can be used to format the page header. Place a ruling line under the page header.

---

**Point** the mouse at "WORLD'S"
**Click**
**Point** the mouse at Paragraph
**Point** the mouse at Ruling Line Below
**Click**

---

Add a one-point ruling line.

---

**Point** the mouse at Width
**Click**
**Drag** to Frame

---

Enter

↓
**[Esc]**
**.014** ↵

Copy the header to the left pages.

---

**Point** the mouse at Chapter
**Point** the mouse at Headers & Footers
**Click**

---

To copy the header to the left pages, click on the **Copy to Facing Page** box.

---

**Point** the mouse at Copy to Facing Page
**Click**

---

Enter

↵

Display page 2, a left page, by entering

**[PgDn]**

The header also appears on this page, but it is aligned with the right side of the page. Usually you will want left page headers to appear on the left edge of the page and right page headers to appear on the right edge of the page so that when the document is reproduced the header text will be aligned with the outer edge of the paper.

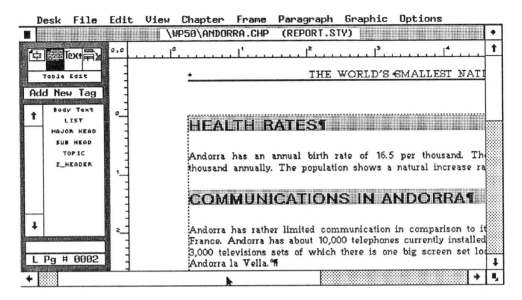

*Figure 6.20   Header copied to left page.*

## Footers and Page Numbers

In addition to page headers, footers are often added to pages in order to implement page numbering.  Scroll to the bottom of the page.

---

**Point** at the scroll bar down arrow
**Click**  (8 times)

---

Return to page 1 by entering

**[PgUp]**

To add a page footer to the document, display the HEADERS & FOOTERS dialog box again.

---

**Point** the mouse at Chapter
**Point** the mouse at Headers & Footers
**Click**

---

Turn on the right page footer.

---

**Point** the mouse at Right Page Footer
**Click**
**Point** the mouse at On
**Click**

---

Page numbers are often center aligned. Place the text cursor on the center line by entering

↓ (2 times)

In this case, you will want to create a chapter/page number footer, e.g., Chapter 1−1. Begin by entering

**Chapter**
**[Space bar]**

To insert the chapter number, select the Chapter # box.

---

**Point** at Chapter #
**Click**

---

The chapter number symbol — [C#] — is inserted into the footer.

## Special Characters

If you have used MS-DOS computers in the past, you may know that the computer can often display or print more characters and symbols than appear on the keyboard. This is also the case in Ventura. Ventura fonts usually contain more characters than you see on your keyboard. A full list of the characters contained in the Ventura fonts can be found in Appendix E of the Ventura documentation. Each character is assigned a decimal number value. If you find a character that you want to insert into your text, but you do not have a key on your keyboard that corresponds to that key, you can insert that character into your text by holding down the [Alt] key and typing that character's number value on the numeric keypad. Note that you cannot use the number keys on the top keyboard row — only use those on the numeric keypad.

Entering special characters in headers and footers is a bit different from entering them in regular text. In this case you need to use a text code technique. For example, character 197 is an extended dash ( — ). In typesetting this dash is called an **em dash**. The term "em dash" refers to the width of the letter M in the current font. The widest letter in a standard font is the letter M. An em dash is as wide as the letter "M," which is wider than the standard hyphen (-) entered from the keyboard.

Suppose you want to place an em dash between the chapter number and the page number. You must enter the code symbol < 197>. The 197 is the ASCII decimal number of that character in the font. Enter

**< 197> [P#]**

The copyright symbol is character 189. Add it to the page footer by entering

**< 189>**

Copy the footer to the left pages.

> **Point** the mouse at Copy to Facing Page
> **Click**

Accept these header and footer entries by entering

↵

The footer appears at the bottom of the page. Note the insertion of the special characters based on the decimal codes entered into the footer.

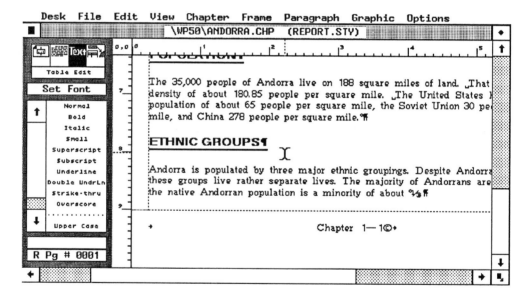

*Figure 6.21 Footer created with chapter and page numbers.*

Move to the next page by entering

**[PgDn]**

The page number updates to page 2. Return to page 1 by entering

**[PgUp]**

## Numbering Options

When you select chapter or page numbers, Ventura automatically inserts standard Arabic numerals that correspond to the actual numbers of the pages. The style and value of numbers displayed for chapter and page numbers can be altered by using the **Update Counters** option on the **Chapter** menu. In this example, you will want to change the style of the chapter numbers to uppercase Roman numerals.

---

**Point** the mouse at Chapter
**Point** the mouse at Update Counters
**Click**

---

Ventura displays the UPDATE COUNTERS dialog box.

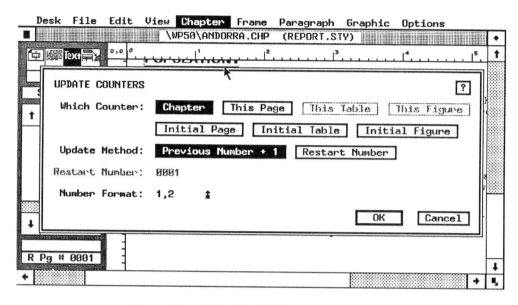

*Figure 6.22 UPDATE COUNTERS dialog box.*

The menu consists of three related options. The first option allows you to select which counter you want to work with. Ventura maintains four independent counters for chapter, page, figure, and table numbers. Figure and table numbers are generated when you add captions to additional frames. They are not available when you are working with the master frame. It is important to note that page, figure, and table numbers have an **Initial** option as well as a **This** option. The This option changes the numbering on the current page, figure, or table. The Initial option changes the page, figure, or table sequence from the beginning of the chapter.

The update method is set to **Previous Number +1**, which means that the page numbers are consecutive with the first page in the chapter—page 1. This option also relates to multiple-file operations (i.e., when several chapters are printed as a unit), which are discussed in Chapter 7. Previous Number +1 allows multiple-chapter output to be numbered consecutively. The **Restart Number** option allows you to enter a specific value to use as the base number for the numbering sequence.

The **Numeric format** option allows you to select among Arabic numbers, Roman Numerals (upper- and lowercase), and alphabetical letters (upper- and lowercase) as numbering sequences.

To change the chapter number from Arabic to Roman numerals, select the uppercase Roman Numeral from the Number format list.

> **Point** the mouse at Number Format
> **Click**
> **Drag** to I, II

Change the initial page number to 101.

> **Click** on Initial Page
> **Click** on Restart Number

The text cursor is positioned on the restart number line. Enter

**[Esc]**
**0101** ↵

The number sequence and format shown in the page footer are adjusted to the new counter specifications.

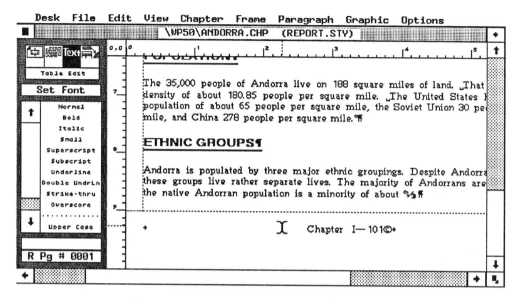

*Figure 6.23   Chapter and page counters updated.*

## Suppressing Headers and Footers

In multiple-page documents, it is not unusual to want to display headers or footers on some pages and not on others. For example, in this document, headers are used to display page numbers; however, it is customary to suppress page numbers on the first page of a chapter, so Ventura allows you to designate which pages should display headers or footers. The Chapter menu contains options for turning the header or footer on or off on the current page.

> **Point** the mouse at Chapter
> **Point** the mouse at Turn Header Off
> **Click**

Check the results by switching to the reduced view mode. Enter

**[Ctrl/r]**

The header no longer appears at the top of the page.  Enter

**[PgDn]**

Page 2 does show both a header and a footer.  Return to page 1 by entering

**[PgUp]**

Place Ventura in the normal view mode so that you can see the bottom of the first page.

| |
|---|
| **Point** at the lower left corner of the frame |

Enter

**[Ctrl/n]**

## FOOTNOTES

Recall that you created footnote text in the document ANDORRA.WP.  That text has not appeared in the document so far.  Ventura's default setting is to suppress footnote text entered into the document.  Footnote text can be displayed using the Footnote Settings option on the Chapter menu to activate Ventura footnote features.

| |
|---|
| **Point** the mouse at Chapter<br>**Point** the mouse at Footnote Settings<br>**Click** |

The footnote setting dialog box lists the options that allow you to control the style and sequence of the footnotes in the current chapter.

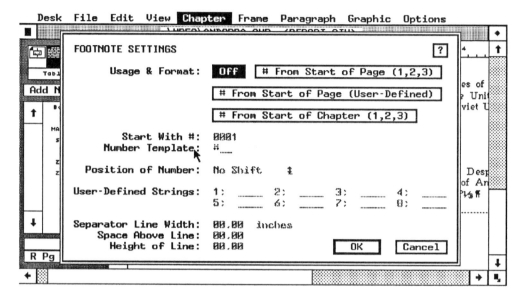

*Figure 6.24   FOOTNOTE SETTINGS dialog box.*

The first section of the menu deals with the general format used to create footnotes. The default setting is **Off**. The other three settings display footnotes at the bottom of each page that contains a footnote code. The three settings differ in the way that the footnotes are referenced in the text.

The first option, **# From Start of Page (1,2,3)**, places reference numbers on the page for each footnote. The numbering begins at 1 on each page. The second option, **# From Start of Page (User Defined)**, creates footnote references out of symbols rather than numbers. The default value is *. This means that the first footnote on the page will be *, the second **, and so on. You can enter other symbols, such as + or #, if you want. The final choice, **# From Start of Chapter (1,2,3)**, numbers the footnotes consecutively from the beginning of the chapter.

---

**Point** the mouse at # From Start of Chapter (1,2,3)
**Click**

---

The next section allows you to select the starting number for the footnotes and a template for the footnote reference. The default value is 1. Use this option to continue footnote numbering from the end of a previous chapter. In that way you can make your footnotes consecutive through an entire document. The # indicates that the number itself will be used as the footnote reference. You can add characters to the template to create references with additional characters. For example, a template of (#) would create footnote references such as (1), (2), (3), etc. If you want superscript or subscript references, you can select them with the **Position of Number** option.

---

> **Point** the mouse at Position of Number
> **Click**
> **Drag** to Superscript

---

The bottom of the display allows you to create a ruling line that will separate the text from the footnotes. To create a line, enter

↓ (2 times)
**[Esc] 06.5**
↵ (2 times)
**[Esc] .02** ↵

The footnote text is inserted at the bottom of the page.

**417**

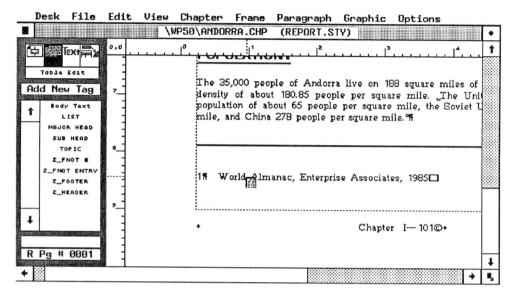

*Figure 6.25    Footnote text displayed at the bottom of the page.*

The footnote reference number has automatically been numbered as 1. Although you cannot see it at this moment, a footnote reference number has been inserted into the document at the point in the text where you entered the <$F> code.

If you look at the list of tags in the side bar, two additional generated tags have been added:

- Z_FNOT #.  Controls the format of the footnote.

- Z_FNOT ENTRY.  Controls the format of the footnote text.

**Exercise 4:**    Footnote text is usually printed in a smaller point size than the body text, so use the paragraph tagging method to change the font of the footnote text to Dutch, 8-point. Try this on your own.  The correct commands can be found under EX-4 at the end of the chapter.

# HEADER, FOOTER, AND FOOTNOTE FRAMES

When page-oriented text such as headers, footers, and footnotes are added to a chapter, Ventura automatically generates frames into which these items are placed. These frames are not like frames that you would draw in that their position on the page is fixed (i.e., cannot be moved), which makes sense because the placement of headers, footers, and footnotes is logically related to the structure of the page; however, there are some attributes of these special frames that you can control, such as the margins, ruling lines, and frame background. Suppose you want to reduce the amount of margin space in the footnote frame.

Begin by activating the Frame Setting mode. Enter

**[Ctrl/u]**

Select the footnote frame by clicking inside that frame.

---

**Point** the mouse at "World Almanac"
**Click**

---

If you examine the box above the page number in the side bar display, you will see the name **FOOTNOTE** displayed as the selected frame.

---

**Point** the mouse at Frame
**Point** the mouse at Margins & Columns
**Click**

---

The MARGINS AND COLUMNS dialog box reveals that Ventura automatically creates 1/4" margins at the top and bottom of the footnote frame. Eliminate these margins by entering

↓
**[Esc]**
↓
**[Esc]**
⏎

The amount of vertical space used by the footnote frame is reduced by .5", which leaves more room for text on the page.

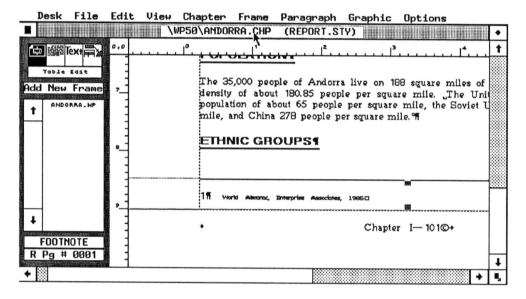

*Figure 6.26   Footnote frame with top and bottom margins removed.*

This principle can also be applied to the frames that hold the page headers and footers if necessary.

## Keep Together

The reduction of the footnote frame's margins caused Ventura to end the page with the TOPIC paragraph "ETHNIC GROUPS." The appearance of the document might be improved if a heading always appeared on the same page as the first paragraph of text under that heading.

Ventura provides a special setting in the **BREAKS** dialog box that will prevent the topic heading from appearing by itself at the bottom of a page. Change to the Paragraph Tagging mode by entering

**[Ctrl/i]**

Select one of the topic paragraphs.

> **Point** the mouse at "ETHNIC GROUPS"
> **Click**

Display the BREAKS dialog box.

> **Point** the mouse at Paragraph
> **Point** the mouse at Breaks
> **Click**

The last option in the dialog box is the **Keep with Next** option. When this option is turned on, the current paragraph tag, TOPIC, will not appear on a page unless these is room to display part of the following paragraph.

> **Point** the mouse at Yes next to Keep with Next
> **Click**

Enter

↵

The isolated heading is moved to the beginning of the next page.

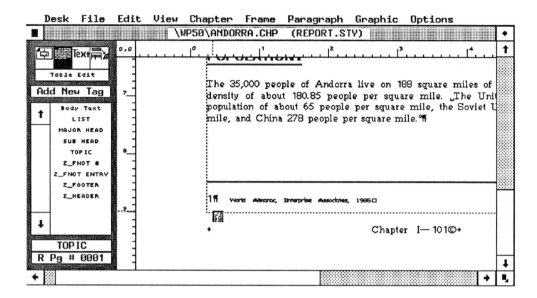

*Figure 6.27 Topic heading moved to next page.*

## PARAGRAPH NUMBERING

Ventura can also generate paragraph numbers, which means that you can create outline headings automatically. Ventura uses the tag names to locate the paragraphs that should be numbered in a document. For example, suppose that you wanted to number the MAJOR, SUB, and TOPIC headings in the current chapter. The option to create these paragraph numbers is Auto-Numbering, which is found on the Chapter menu.

> **Point** the mouse at Chapter
> **Point** the mouse at Auto-Numbering
> **Click**

Ventura displays the **AUTO-NUMBERING** dialog box.

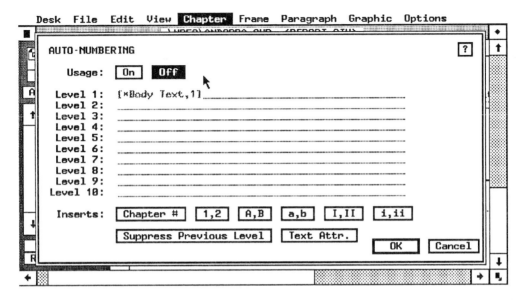

*Figure 6.28   AUTO-NUMBERING dialog box.*

You can specify up to ten levels of numbering. In this example, there are only two levels.

---

**Point** the mouse at On
**Click**

---

This turns Auto-Numbering on and allows you to enter tag names on the level lines. Ventura places a Body Text tag on the first level. Clear that tag by entering

[Esc]

To create a numbering sequence, select one of the numbering styles from the bottom of the menu. In this example, you will label the subheadings as A, B, C, etc. and the topics as 1, 2 3, etc. Begin with the subheadings.

**Point** the mouse at A,B
**Click**

Ventura inserts a code — [*tag name,A] — onto the Level 1 line. As with the header and footer codes, you must manually replace *tag name* with the name of an existing style tag. The "A" indicates the style of numbering selected. Enter

← (3 times)
[Backspace] (8 times)
sub head ↓

As with the header symbols, you might find it simpler to directly enter the codes once you understand the pattern. To create numbers for the subheadings, enter

[*sub head,1] ↓

Enter the code for the topic headings.

[*topic,1] [-]

The [-] code added following [*topic,1] is used to suppress the previous numbering level. Without this code, the numbering for subheadings would be A1, A2, A3 where the A is the value of the previous (i.e., subheading) numbering level. With it, the first numbering level is suppressed, and only the second level (i.e., topic) numbers are printed.

The dialog box should resemble the one in Figure 6.29.

**424**

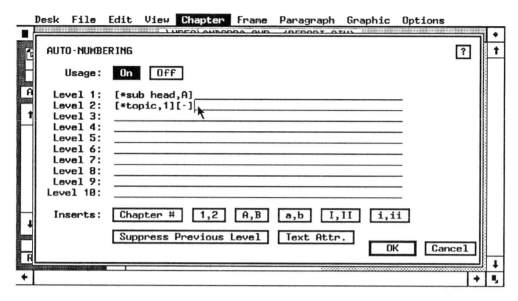

*Figure 6.29   Auto-Numbering specifications.*

Complete the menu by entering

↵

Ventura automatically goes through the document and numbers the paragraphs. Two new style tags are automatically generated, Z_SEC1 for level 1 numbers and Z_SEC2 for level 2 numbers.

Instead of placing the numbers on the same line as the subheading and topic text, Ventura inserted the numbers as paragraphs in front of the subheadings and topic headings.  Instead of the following,

A.   ABOUT ANDORRA

the result was something like the following:

A.

ABOUT ANDORRA

However, Ventura can create the look you want. You must modify the format of the paragraphs that you want to number.

You need to change two characteristics. First, indent the heading paragraph to make room for the paragraph number on the left. Then, remove the line break before the heading. This will cause the line to print on the same line as the previous paragraph. The result will look like a single line of text combining the paragraph number with the heading that needs to be numbered.

The subheading "VITAL STATISTICS" should be visible in the document window. Select that paragraph.

> **Point** the mouse at "VITAL STATISTICS"
> **Click**

Change the spacing to create a .25" indent.

> **Point** the mouse at Paragraph
> **Point** the mouse at Spacing
> **Click**

↓ (4 times)
**[Esc]**
.25 ⏎

Next, suppress the line break before the paragraph.

**Point** the mouse at Paragraph
**Point** the mouse at Breaks
**Click**
**Click** on No next to Line Break

Enter

⤶

**Exercise 5:** Repeat the process for the topic headings. Try this on your own. The correct commands can be found under EX-5 at the end of this chapter.

The numbers now appear next to the headings.

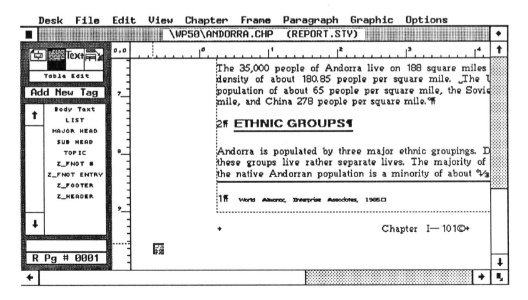

*Figure 6.30   Auto-numbers placed beside heading text.*

You may have noticed that the auto-numbers are formatted with the same font as Body Text. The numbering might look better in the same font as the heading text.

> **Point** the mouse at 2
> **Click**

The tag name **Z_SEC2** will appear above the page number in the side bar display. Ventura automatically generates tags Z_SEC1, Z_SEC2, etc. when auto-numbers are created. Change the font of the Z_SEC2 tag.

> **Point** the mouse at Paragraph
> **Point** the mouse at Font
> **Click**
> **Point** the mouse at Swiss
> **Click**

Enter

⏎

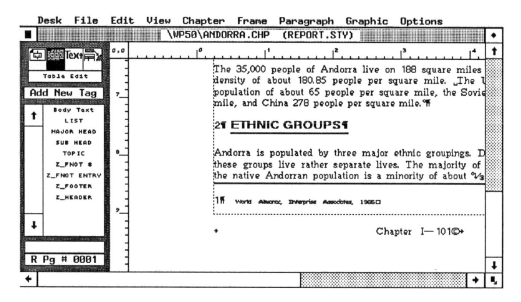

*Figure 6.31   Same font set for number and heading*

Note that because the topic paragraphs are set to be kept on the same page as the paragraphs that follow them (i.e., they use the Keep with Next option), you should set the Z_SEC2 tag the same way so that the number will always appear on the same page as the topic heading.

---

**Point** the mouse at Paragraph
**Point** the mouse at Breaks
**Click**
**Click** on Yes next to Keep with Next

---

Enter

⏎

## ADDING PICTURES AND TABLES

Next, you will want to add the information stored in other files to the document.

Four files should be added:

- three graphs, **POPDEN.PIC**, **COMM.PIC**, and **ETHNIC.PIC**

- a table of values, **COMM.PRN**

In the previous chapters, you needed to carefully plot the position of each frame as it was inserted, but that is not the case here. Remember that you created anchors for the three graphs in the text of the document. These anchors can be used to automatically position frames such as the ones that will contain the graphs. Using anchors requires a different strategy for adding frames to a document.

For example, instead of trying to position frames manually, you can simply enter all the frames at the end of the document. Then, let Ventura automatically place the frames at the proper place in the text, based on the position of the frame anchors.

To implement this technique, move to the end of the document. Enter

**[End]**

Place Ventura in the reduced view mode. Enter

**[Ctrl/r]**

To create a new frame, place Ventura in the Frame Setting mode. Enter

**[Ctrl/u]**

> **Point** the mouse at Add New Frame
> **Click**

At the bottom of the page, draw a frame that is as wide as the master frame and about 2.25" high, as shown in Figure 6.32. Don't worry about the exact height of the frame; that information will be entered later in the SIZING & SCALING dialog box.

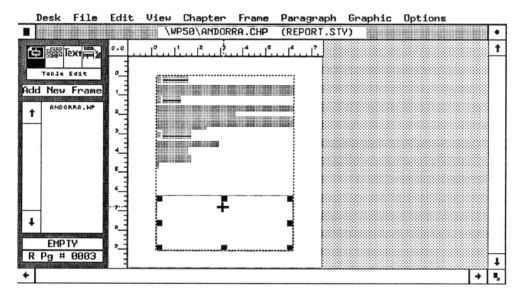

*Figure 6.32    Frame added to last page of document.*

To make the size of the frame more exact, use the SIZING & SCALING dialog box.

> **Point** the mouse at Frame
> **Point** the mouse at Sizing & Scaling
> **Click**

The Frame Width and Frame Height settings control the size of the frame. The width should be exactly 6" because of the column snap feature, but the height will vary. In this case, set the height to exactly 2.25". Enter

↓ (3 times)
**[Esc]**
**02.25** ⏎

## Anchor Names and Captions

Now that you have created a frame, you must perform the following steps:

1. Give the frame an anchor name so Ventura will know where in the text the frame should be positioned.

2. Create a caption for the frame if you want.

3. Load the picture or text file into the frame.

You can perform these operations in almost any order. In this case, begin with the first step listed above, creating a frame anchor name.

The anchor name of the frame should be the exact same name that you used when you inserted location anchors into the document. You may not remember exactly what the anchor names were; however, there is a trick to getting Ventura to display the anchor names. The trick is to tell Ventura to anchor all the frames in the text. This won't accomplish much at the moment because you haven't created the frame anchor names, but what it will do is cause Ventura to display each of the anchor names for which there is not yet an anchor, reminding you of the names you entered.

---

**Point** the mouse at Chapter
**Point** the mouse at Re-Anchor Frames
**Click**

---

Ventura displays a box on the screen. In this case, you want to check all the anchors.

```
Point the mouse at All Pages
Click
```

Ventura encounters the first anchor and displays its name.

You can see that this display shows you the name of the anchor, **pop density**, and asks you to decide upon an action. You don't want to change anything, so use the **Ignore** option.

```
Point the mouse at Ignore
Click
```

The next anchor name, **ethnic**, appears.

```
Point the mouse at Ignore
Click
```

The last anchor name, **communications**, is displayed.

```
Point the mouse at Ignore
Click
```

You have now been able to review your anchor names. Your next task is to assign the anchor name to a frame. Begin with the pop density anchor. First, reselect the new frame.

---

**Point** the mouse at the new frame
**Click**

---

Display the ANCHORS & CAPTIONS dialog box.

---

**Point** the mouse at Frame
**Point** the mouse at Anchors & Captions
**Click**

---

The ANCHORS & CAPTIONS dialog box appears.

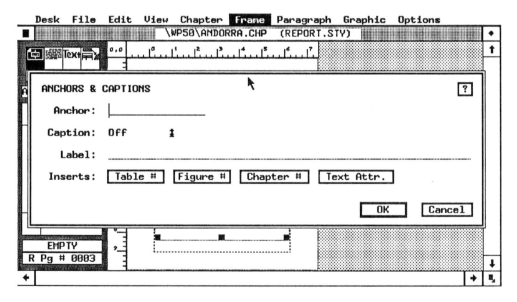

*Figure 6.33   ANCHORS & CAPTIONS dialog box.*

This menu has two purposes. You can create an anchor name and/or a caption for a frame. In this example, you will do both. Begin by entering the anchor name of the frame. The frame anchor will serve to associate this frame with the anchor code — [$&pop density,[V] — you entered into the text of the document. Enter

**pop density**

You also want to create a caption for the frame. A caption can contain any type of text and special codes for table, figure, and chapter numbers. Ventura keeps counters for tables and figures as well as for pages and chapters. This means that you can create a caption that will automatically number the figures in the chapter.

First select the location of the caption.

---

**Point** the mouse at Caption
**Click**
**Drag** to Below

---

Now enter the text of the caption. The code [F#] tells Ventura to insert a figure number into the caption. Note that clicking on the figure number would also insert the code into the caption. Enter

**Figure [F#]**

Complete the menu by entering

↵

To see the effect of the caption, change to the normal view mode.

**Point** at the upper left corner of the new frame

Enter

**[Ctrl/n]**

Ventura has automatically added a small frame, 1/2" high, below the new frame. The caption "Figure 1" appears in the frame. This is the caption frame that was automatically generated by Ventura when you chose to place a caption on the frame. The frame and its caption will move together when the frame's location is changed.

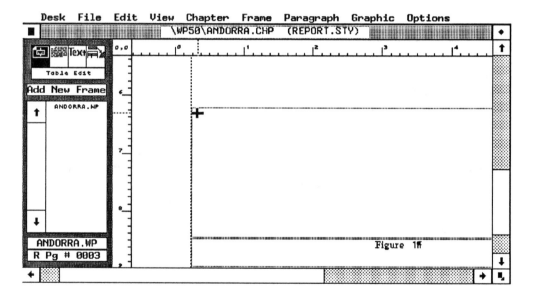

*Figure 6.34   Caption added to new frame.*

Also note that when the first caption is created, Ventura automatically creates a new tag, Z_CAPTION, that controls the format of frame captions. Changes to the font, spacing, or other characteristics of the Z_CAPTION tag would change the format of all frame captions. Keep in mind that the size of the caption frame will not automatically adjust to changes in the caption's point size or spacing. Adjustments to the size of the caption frame must be made in the Frame Setting mode on a frame-by-frame basis.

When a frame is used to insert a chart into the document, the appearance can be improved by drawing a box around the frame. The Frame menu contains an option to add a ruling box around a frame.

---

**Point** the mouse at Frame
**Point** the mouse at Ruling Box Around
**Click**

---

The dialog box displayed is the same as the one used when you place a box around a paragraph. Create a box with a one-point, .007", line around the frame. The box should be indented .05" from the edge of the frame.

---

**Point** the mouse at Width
**Click**
**Drag** to Frame

---

Enter

[Esc]
.05 ↓
[Esc]
.007 ↵

After you have added the frame box, there is another factor to consider — the frame margins. Keep in mind that adding a ruling box or line to a frame does not automatically create margins within the frame. If you loaded an image or line-art that filled the frame right to the frame edges, the ruling lines would print on top of the image. In this case, you might want to add a margin, e.g., .1", so that any graphic inserted into the frame would not come in contact with the frame box.

---

**Point** the mouse at Frame
**Point** the mouse at Margins & Columns
**Click**

---

Enter

↓
**[Esc]**
**.1** ↓
**[Esc]**
**.1** ↓
**[Esc]**
**.1** ↓
**[Esc]**
**.1** ↵

Before you complete the operation by loading the picture into the frame, copy the frame into memory. The other two graphs will fit into the exact same frame. All you will need to do is change the anchor name. By copying this frame into memory now, you can recall a copy when you want to add the next two graphs. Copy the frame into memory by entering

**[Shift/Del]**

The next step is to load the graph file.

> **Point** the mouse at File
> **Point** the mouse at Load Text/Picture
> **Click**

This time, you want to load line-art data.

> **Point** the mouse at Line-Art
> **Click**

Select Lotus .PIC as the file format.

> **Point** the mouse at Lotus .PIC
> **Click**

Then,

> **Point** the mouse at Several
> **Click**

Enter

↵

Enter the name of the directory you want load the files from; in this example, the directory is assumed to be \123. Enter

↑
**[Esc]**
**\123\\*.pic** ⏎

Load the three picture files you need.

---

**Point** the mouse at COMM.PIC
**Double Click**
**Point** the mouse at ETHNIC.PIC
**Double Click**
**Point** the mouse at POPDEN.PIC
**Double Click**

---

Enter

⏎

The three pictures are added to the list of files in the side bar display. Insert the POPDEN.PIC graph into this frame.

---

**Point** the mouse at POPDEN.PIC
**Click**

---

The graph is displayed in the frame.

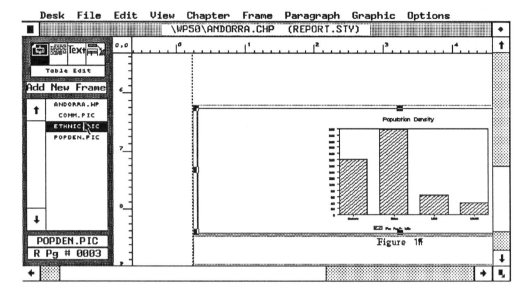

*Figure 6.35    Graph inserted into frame.*

You can now save some effort by retrieving a copy of the frame from memory. Enter

**[Ins]**

The new frame is placed on top of the previous frame.  Because the frames are transparent, the POP DENSITY frame shows through.  This makes it appear as if there is only one frame on the page.  However, if you look at the side bar, you will see **EMPTY** in the box above the page number. This indicates that the selected frame is an empty one.  Normally, you would want to move the frames so that they would not overlap, but in this case it is just as easy to complete the loading and then let Ventura automatically reposition the frames.

Enter the anchor name of the frame.

> **Point** the mouse at Frame
> **Point** the mouse at Anchors & Captions
> **Click**

Enter

**ethnic** ⏎

Load the graph into this frame.

> **Point** the mouse at ETHNIC.PIC
> **Click**

The process needs to be repeated for one more picture. Insert another empty frame. Enter

**[Ins]**

> **Point** the mouse at Frame
> **Point** the mouse at Anchors & Captions
> **Click**

Enter

**communications** ⏎

> **Point** the mouse at COMM.PIC
> **Click**

All three images are superimposed on one another.

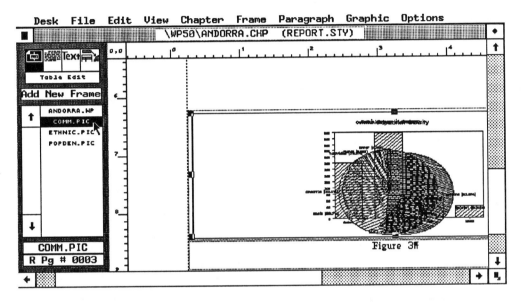

*Figure 6.36   Graphic frames created by copying.*

## Re-Anchoring Frames

You have now set the stage for Ventura to automatically rearrange the frames. The Chapter menu contains a command called **Re-Anchor Frames** that can be used to place the frames according to the location of the anchor codes in the text.

> **Point** the mouse at Chapter
> **Point** the mouse at Re-Anchor Frames
> **Click**

The default option, **This Page**, re-anchors only those frames that have codes on the current page. The **All Pages** option tells Ventura to evaluate the entire chapter and make sure that all frames with anchor names are positioned relative to the anchor codes. In this case, you want to choose All Pages.

> **Point** the mouse at All Pages
> **Click**

Ventura distributes the frames to the text locations in which the anchors have been entered. To see the results of re-anchoring, change to the reduced view mode by entering

**[Ctrl/r]**

The communications pie chart has been repositioned to the top of page 3.

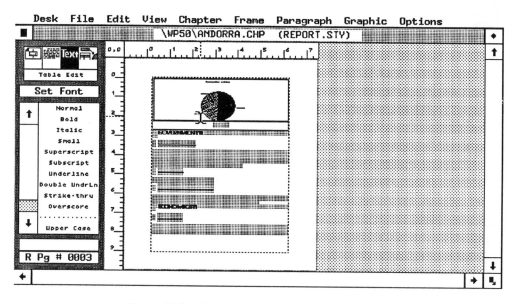

*Figure 6.37 Frame repositioned by re-anchoring.*

Move to page 2 by entering

**[PgUp]**

Page 2 shows the location of the other two charts. When you re-anchor frames, Ventura will move frames to different pages in order to correctly place the frames relative to the text anchors.

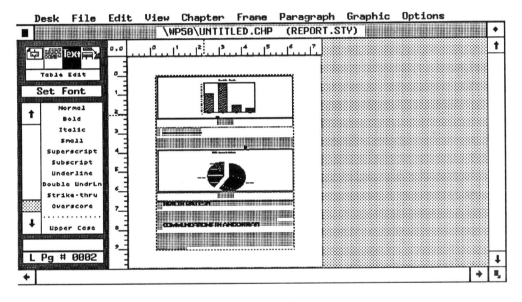

*Figure 6.38    Two charts placed on a different page by re-anchoring.*

The system of frame anchors allows you to assemble a complex document with a minimum of manual frame manipulation. By planning ahead, you can assemble a document that is composed of a large number of frames without having to manually adjust each frame on the page. This is a clear example of how you can improve the operation of a program by taking advantage of automatic commands rather than manually carrying out each individual operation.

## Adding a New Anchor and Frame

The three anchored frames were easily positioned because you had already inserted the frame anchors into the document as you created it.

However, one frame remains to be added that is not yet either loaded or anchored. While it is preferable to place all the anchors into the text before it is loaded, you can add anchors at any time by using the Edit menu. The frame that needs to be added is the table of values imported from 1-2-3 in the form of a text file. The table shows the raw data used to create the communications graph.

Move to page 3 by entering

**[Ctrl/g]**
**3** ⏎

Change to the normal view mode.

> **Point** at the upper left corner of the master frame

Enter

**[Ctrl/n]**

The table should be inserted before the "E. GOVERNMENT" subheading and the chart. This means that the anchor should be placed before the "E."

Anchors are inserted in the Text Editing mode. Change to the Text Editing mode by entering

**[Ctrl/o]**

> **Point** the mouse at "G" in "GOVERNMENT"
> **Click**

To add the anchor to the text, you will want to position the cursor before the "G" in "GOVERNMENT." You cannot edit the paragraph label, "E.," because that text is automatically generated by Ventura. The text cursor should be in front of the letter "G." Use the ← key to move the text cursor to the beginning of the line, which is where you will insert the anchor.

> **Point** the mouse at Edit
> **Point** the mouse at Insert Special Item
> **Click**

Ventura displays the Special Item box. Note that the box that appears in Figure 6.39 shows the list of special items available in the Professional Extension version of Ventura. If you are using the normal Ventura 2.0 version, your list will include the following special items:

| | |
|---|---|
| **Box Char** | F1 |
| **Footnote** | F2 |
| **Index Entry** | F3 |
| **Fraction** | F4 |
| **Frame Anchor** | F5 |

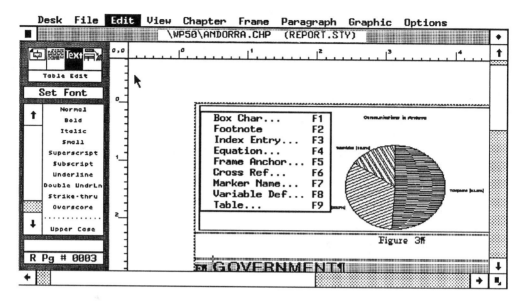

*Figure 6.39   Special Item box, Professional Extension edition.*

To insert a frame anchor code into the text, enter

**[F5]**

Ventura displays a dialog box for creating a frame anchor.

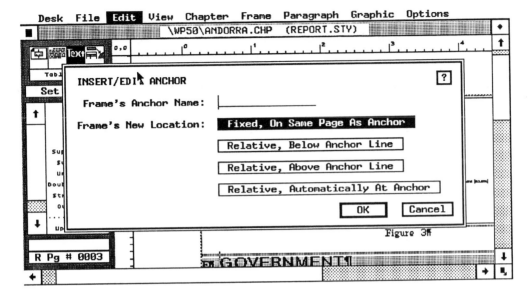

*Figure 6.40    INSERT/EDIT ANCHOR dialog box.*

In this case, you want the frame to be positioned above the anchor location. The Fixed option makes sure that the frame always appears at the same vertical position on the page. For example, if you placed a frame in the middle of the page, when it was re-anchored, it would be placed in the middle of whichever page contained the text anchor. The position of the anchor on the page — top or bottom — would not affect the vertical placement of the frame. Enter the name of the anchor:

**comm table**

> **Point** the mouse at Relative, Above Anchor Line
> **Click**

Enter

↵

Ventura displays a small circle in the text whenever a frame anchor or other special item has been inserted. Note that because of the shaded background, the circle may be hard to see. If you look very closely, you should see it.

With the anchor inserted, you can go back to the last page of the document to load the frame. The Re-Anchoring command will take care of the actual placement of the frame. Enter

**[Ctrl/r]**

Return to the Frame Setting mode. Enter

**[Ctrl/u]**

Insert another copy of the empty frame. Remember that the frame is still in memory. It will remain in memory until you delete another frame or exit Ventura. This makes it possible to copy a frame from one document to another by copying a frame into memory, loading a different chapter, and then inserting the frame into that chapter. Enter

**[Ins]**

Note that the newly inserted frame is automatically selected. Give this frame an anchor name.

**Point** the mouse at Frame
**Point** the mouse at Anchors & Captions
**Click**

Enter

**comm table ↓**

Because this frame is a table, not a figure, you will want to change the caption. Enter

**[Esc]**
**Table [T#]** ⏎

Now you need to load the text file into that frame.

> **Point** the mouse at File
> **Point** the mouse at Load Text/Picture
> **Click**
> **Point** the mouse at Text
> **Click**

The format of a Lotus text file is closest to WordStar. The ASCII setting expects to encounter two return characters at the end of each line. If the text file has only one, as does a Lotus PRN file, the WordStar format is the one you should use.

> **Point** the mouse at WordStar US
> **Click**

Enter

⏎

The item selector attempts to find files with a WS extension in a directory called WS. In this case, that is not what you are looking for. The file you want to load is a 1-2-3 file with a PRN extension. Enter

↑
**[Esc]**
**\123\\*.prn** ⌐

The selector box displays the PRN files.

---

**Point** the mouse at COMM.PRN
**Double Click**

---

The text is loaded into the new frame. To examine the text more closely,

---

**Point** the mouse at the upper left corner of the COMM.PRN frame.

---

Enter

**[Ctrl/n]**

The screen displays the text. You can see that the information is not properly aligned in columns. Also, note that a special symbol appears between the text items. These symbols mark the location of "hard" space characters. The hard space characters and misaligned columns are related.

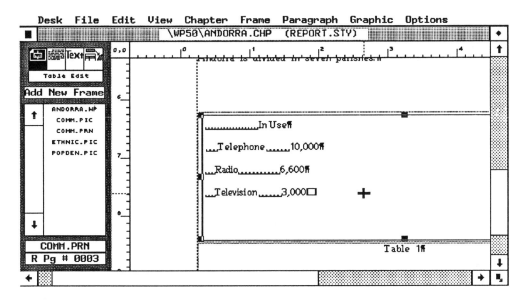

*Figure 6.41    Text from Lotus PRN file inserted into frame.*

Both are a result of how Lotus 1-2-3 and most text-oriented IBM PC programs handle spacing. In these programs, all printed text is treated as **monospaced text**. Monospaced text is text in which the same amount of space is taken up by all of the characters printed. This means that a **W**, which is a wide character, will occupy the same width of space as an **l**, which is a narrow character. The advantage of this system is that getting text to align in columns is a simple matter of counting the number of characters. If there is a gap on a line, it can be filled with blank spaces because in a monospaced font a space requires the same amount of room as any other character.

Ventura uses a much more complicated system in which each character in each font is assigned a specific width. Spacing in Ventura is more than just a count of the number of characters; it matters which characters are actually entered, i.e. wide ones or narrow ones. These fonts are called **proportionally spaced fonts** because space is assigned in proportion to the physical width of each character.

The file produced by 1-2-3 does not take into account this difference in formatting. The columns do not align properly in Ventura for this reason.

There are two possible solutions:

1.   The simplest solution is to format the text with a monospaced font such as Courier 10-point. However, this solution only applies to users who have such a font available on their system. The Courier typeface creates printing that looks as if it was typed on a typewriter. This solution usually requires you to create a tag for formatting the table text.

2.   Edit the text. This means that you must manually remove the spaces between items and replace them with [Tab] characters. The tabs can then be aligned using Ventura's tab alignment features. While this solution takes longer, it has the benefit of allowing you to print the table with proportionally spaced fonts. If you have a large file, you might want to edit it in your word processor.

In this case, use the Courier method, i.e., change to a monospaced font. Place Ventura in the Paragraph Tagging mode by entering

**[Ctrl/i]**

> **Point** the mouse at "In Use"
> **Click**

Create a new tag.

> **Point** the mouse at Add New Tag
> **Click**

Enter

**spreadsheet** ⏎

Select the Courier typeface for the spreadsheet tag.

```
Point the mouse at Paragraph
Point the mouse at Font
Click
Point the mouse at Courier
Click
```

Enter

↵

The spreadsheet paragraph is formatted with the monospaced Courier typeface. Use the [Shift-Click] method to tag the other three lines of the spreadsheet.

```
Point the mouse at "Telephone"
[Shift/Click]
Point the mouse at "Radio"
[Shift/Click]
Point the mouse at "Television"
[Shift/Click]
Point the mouse at spreadsheet in the side bar
Click
```

The text now appears to line up in columns just as it did when it was entered into the 1-2-3 spreadsheet.

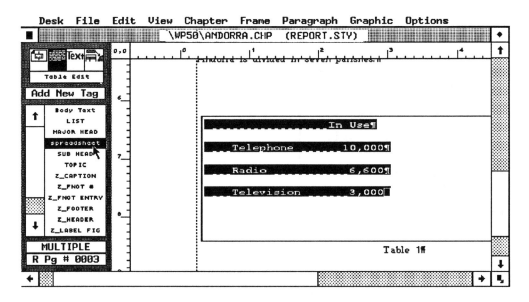

*Figure 6.42    Nonproportionally spaced text aligned in columns.*

**Exercise 6:**    The text in the table frame is squeezed into the upper right corner of the frame.  You might want to position the text more toward the center of the column.  Create a 1.5" indent by modifying the paragraph tag.  Try this on your own.  The correct commands can be found at the end of the chapter under EX-6.

To place the frame in its proper position according to the text anchors, use the Re-Anchor frames command.

---

**Point** the mouse at Chapter
**Point** the mouse at Re-Anchor Frames
**Click**
**Point** the mouse at All Pages
**Click**

---

Save the completed document. Enter

**[Ctrl/s]**

You can now print the document if you want to see your work. In the next chapter, you will learn how to create the table of contents and index from this document.

## SUMMARY

- **Text Files**. Ventura alters the text of text files loaded into frames. Ventura inserts text codes that indicate style tags, font changes, text attributes, index entries, and footnotes. Conversely, adding text codes to document files will cause Ventura to automatically tag and format text. This means that you can designate Ventura style tags as you create a text file.

- **Text Formatting Codes**. Ventura style tags are entered into text files by using the following formats:

| Code | Function |
|---|---|
| <$B0> | Draw hollow box |
| <$B1> | Draw filled box |
| <Jnnn> | Jump text from baseline |
| <B%n> | Begin manual kerning |
| <B> | Bold |
| <Cnnn> | Color |
| <=> | Double underline |
| <I> | Italics |
| <R> | Line break |
| <M> | Medium weight typeface |
| <O> | Overscore |
| <Pnnn> | Point size |
| <D> | Resume normal text |
| <S> | Small text |
| <X> | Strikethrough text |
| <V> | Subscript |

*continued...*

| Code | Function |
|------|----------|
| <^> | Superscript |
| <F*nnn*> | Font number |
| <U> | Underline |
| <N> | Nonbreaking space |
| <$F...> | Footnote |
| <$E...> | Fractions |
| <$I...> | Index entry |
| <$R...> | Page number code |
| <$&...> | Frame anchor |
| <*nnn*> | Special font character by number |

- **Frame Anchors**. Frame anchors are used to position frames at specific locations within a document. By inserting frame anchors into the document, you can have Ventura automatically position the frames within a document by using the Re-Anchor Frames command. A frame anchor is inserted into the text by entering

  **<$&anchor name[^] >** (places frame above anchor)

  **<$&anchor name[V] >** (places frame below anchor)

- **Gray Backgrounds**. You can create the effect of printing text on a gray or black background for individual paragraph tags by using a special form of the Ruling Line Above command. The ruling line is set for a height that covers or exceeds the height of the typeface. For example, for 18-point type, set the line at a height of 18/72", or .25". The background effect is achieved by setting the Space Below Rule 3 option to a negative value equal to or in excess of ruling line height. This causes the text of the paragraph and the ruling line to overlap, producing the background effect.

- **Headers and Footers**. Ventura allows you to create page headers and footers. You can define separate headers and footers for the left and right pages. The header or footer will appear on all pages unless you use the Page menu to turn off the header or footer on specific pages.

  In addition to text, headers and footers can include page and chapter numbers. The starting page and chapter numbers can be controlled from the Page menu. The default value for both is 1.

Text enhancements can be added to headers and footers by using text codes. For example, <P014> sets the text to 14-point type.

Headers and footers can also include text from the document. You can specify a tag name, usually a heading of some kind, that will be inserted into the header or footer on that page. If no text with the specified tag appears on that page, you can tell Ventura to use the last previous or next occurrence of that tag name.

- **Footnote Settings**. Footnotes will not appear in the text unless the footnote settings are turned on. You can select the numbering style, sequence, and normal, super-, or subscript footnote references. You can also create a line to separate footnotes from the rest of the text.

- **Paragraph Numbering**. Ventura can automatically generate a paragraph numbering sequence in the text, based on tag names. Each tag is assigned a numbering level and sequence style. The paragraph numbers are separate paragraphs from the text of the tagged paragraphs they number. This means that they will appear on the line above the tagged text, not on the same line. To place the numbers on the same lines as the tagged text, you must alter the tagged text by indenting the paragraph and suppressing the line break before the paragraph.

- **Frame Anchor Names**. Frames added to the main document can be assigned anchor names. These names are meant to match up with anchors placed into the text. The Re-Anchor frames command will reorganize the document, placing each frame above or below the anchors in the text. This system allows you to associate illustrations with text while you edit your document.

- **Captions**. Frames can also have captions. A caption can be any text that you want to appear above, below, to the right, or to the left of a specific frame. Ventura will also consecutively number the captions. Ventura uses two caption counters: one for figures and the other for tables.

## Answers to Exercises

**EX-1 (see p. 385):**  Set the MAJOR HEAD font to Swiss, 24-point bold.

> **Point** the mouse at Paragraph
> **Point** the mouse at Font
> **Click**
> **Point** the mouse at Swiss
> **Click**
> **Point** the mouse at 24
> **Click**

Enter

⏎

**EX-2 (see p. 389):**  Select Swiss, 18-point bold as the SUB HEAD font.

> **Point** the mouse at Paragraph
> **Point** the mouse at Font
> **Click**
> **Point** the mouse at Swiss
> **Click**
> **Point** the mouse a 18
> **Click**

Enter

⏎

**EX-3 (see p. 398):** Select Swiss, 14-point bold as the TOPIC font.

> **Point** the mouse at Paragraph
> **Point** the mouse at Font
> **Click**
> **Point** the mouse at Swiss
> **Click**
> **Point** the mouse a 14
> **Click**

Enter

↵

**EX-4 (see p. 418):** Change the font of the footnote text to Dutch, 8-point.

> **Point** the mouse at "World Almanac"
> **Click**

Then,

> **Point** the mouse at Paragraph
> **Point** the mouse at Font
> **Click**
> **Point** the mouse at 8
> **Click**

Enter

↵

**EX-5 (see p. 427):** Indent the topic paragraph to make room for the paragraph number on the left. Then, remove the line break before the heading.

**Point** the mouse at "POPULATION"
**Click**

Then,

**Point** the mouse at Paragraph
**Point** the mouse at Spacing
**Click**

Enter

↓ (4 times)
**[Esc]**
.25 ⏎

**Point** the mouse at Paragraph
**Point** the mouse at Breaks
**Click**
**Click** on No next to Line Break

Enter

⏎

**EX-6: (see p. 456)**  Create a 1.5" indent by modifying the paragraph tag.

(see p. 456)

---

**Point** the mouse at Paragraph
**Point** the mouse at Spacing
**Click**

---

Enter

↓ (4 times)
**[Esc]**
**01.5 ⏎**

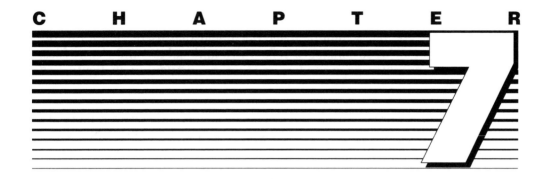

C H A P T E R

# 7

# MULTIPLE-DOCUMENT OPERATIONS

In Chapter 6, you created a multiple-page document that used Ventura to organize a layout that included a major text file with additional text and picture files. Ventura created footnotes, page headers and footers, and paragraph, figure, and table numbers.

All of these features were implemented in a single document; however, there are operations that can only be performed using Ventura multiple-chapter commands. The term **multiple-chapter** is a bit misleading. Many of the operations that fall under the heading of multi-chapter operations can apply to a single document or chapter. For example, the ANDORRA chapter contains table of contents and index items. You can generate an index for that one document or combine other documents with that one to create a multiple-chapter table of contents or index.

Perhaps a better name for the operations that Ventura calls multiple-chapter would be **reference tasks**. Regardless of the name used, multiple-chapter operations have some important things in common. First, they are performed on chapter files that have been saved. You cannot perform any of these operations on a document that you are working on but have not saved. All the multiple-chapter operations are conducted automatically. You do not have explicit manual control over what takes place. For example, when Ventura generates an index, it does so automatically based on the codes inserted into the files you are indexing. You do not see the text of the documents or the generated index. The index is stored directly on disk in the form of a text file that must then be loaded into a chapter to be viewed. Multiple-chapter operations can be performed only on full chapters. You cannot index part of a chapter.

In this chapter, you will use the ANDORRA document prepared in Chapter 6 to generate an index and table of contents and to perform other multiple-chapter tasks. To begin this chapter, load Ventura in the usual manner.

## THE PUBLICATION FILE

All multiple-chapter, or reference, operations begin with a publication file. Publication files group related chapters together so that operations such as indexing and table of contents generation can "know" which files compose the entire document. As mentioned before, a publication file can contain only a single chapter if that is all you need to work with.

The first step is to select Multi-Chapter operations from the Options menu.

> **Point** the mouse at Options
> **Point** the mouse at Multi-Chapter
> **Click**

Ventura displays the **MULTI-CHAPTER OPERATIONS** dialog box.

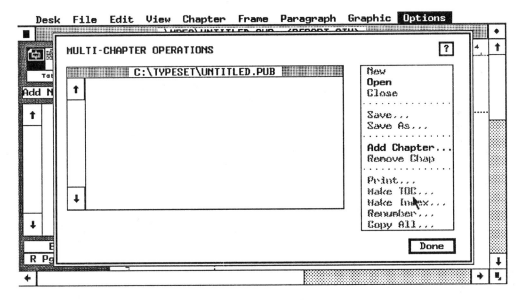

*Figure 7.1    MULTI-CHAPTER OPERATIONS dialog box.*

In the center of the menu box is a file selector box. Because Multi-Chapter operations work on entire files, the selector box is the focus of your operations. On the right side of the box is a list of command options. Only two are currently available:

- **Open**. This option is used to open an existing publication file, but you can also use this option to create a new publication file. Ventura uses the file extension PUB for publication files.

- **Add Chapter**. This option allows you to add a chapter to the current publication file. The current screen display shows the temporary name assigned by Ventura—**UNTITLED.PUB**—as the name of the publication file.

In this case, you will begin to create a new publication file by adding a chapter.

---

**Point** the mouse at Add Chapter
**Click**

---

Ventura overlays the MULTI-CHAPTER OPERATIONS dialog box with an ITEM SELECTOR dialog box. You can use the display to locate the chapters you want to add to the publication file. Ventura displays the directory in which the last chapter file was saved. If your word processor is WordPerfect and you have been following along in this book, you have been saving files in the \WP50 directory because that is where you have been loading your master text files from.

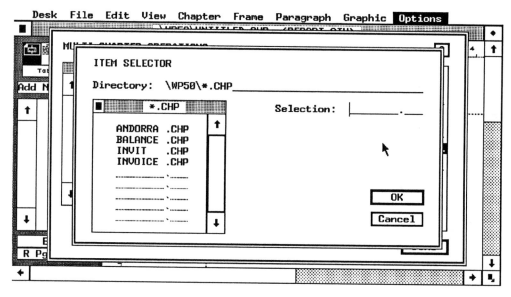

*Figure 7.2    ITEM SELECTOR dialog box used to add chapters to a publication file.*

Select the ANDORRA.CHP chapter.

---

**Point** the mouse at ANDORRA.CHP
**Double Click**

---

The chapter you selected is then entered into the multi-chapter display. For chapters in a publication file, Ventura displays both the drive and directory name as well as the chapter name because you can have chapters that are stored in different directories or drives as part of the same publication file.

Currently the publication file is called UNTITLED. To create a publication file for the chapter, use the Save command.

---

**Point** the mouse at Save
**Click**

---

Enter the name of the publication file. Ventura will default to the last directory used to save a publication file. If you have never created a publication file, that directory will be the **\TYPESET** directory. Create a publication file called ANDRPT (Andorra Report). Enter

**andrpt** ⏎

You have now established the name of this publication file, which appears in the title bar of the chapter list box.

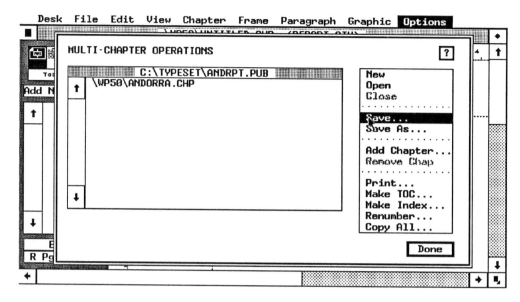

*Figure 7.3    Publication filename assigned.*

## Adding a Chapter

You can add new chapters to the publication file in the same way that you added the first one.

---

**Point** the mouse at Add Chapter
**Click**

---

Add the invoice chapter.

---

**Point** the mouse at INVOICE.CHP
**Double Click**

---

You now have two chapters in the publication file. The order in which the files are listed is significant for the table of contents operation because Ventura assumes that the order of the chapters in the publication file list is the order in which the chapters will appear in the final document.

Ventura always places the new file at the bottom of the list. If this order is not correct, you can change the order of the files by dragging the names to new locations. In this example, INVOICE.CHP follows ANDORRA.CHP because you loaded it after you loaded the Andorra file. Suppose the order of the files should be reversed. You can use the drag method to change their position.

> **Point** and the mouse at ANDORRA.CHP
> **Click**
> **Drag** below INVOICE.CHP

A hand appears, indicating that you have activated the drag mode, and a dotted line box (which represents the selected chapter, ANDORRA.CHP) moves down as you drag the mouse. When you release the button, Ventura rearranges the chapters in the list, placing the selected chapter at the position it was dragged to and moving the other chapters to compensate for the change in order.

## Removing a Chapter

You can also remove a chapter from a publication. First highlight the name of the file you want to remove.

> **Point** the mouse at INVOICE.CHP
> **Click**
> **Point** the mouse at Remove Chapter
> **Click**

The name of the chapter is removed from the publication file list. Remember that using this method you cannot delete a chapter from the disk; you can only delete its name from the list of chapters in the publication file.

## Opening a Chapter File

One of the options in the multi-chapter display is **Open**. It is important to understand that Open in this case has a very different meaning from the Open option you select from the File menu. In multiple-chapter operations, Open is used to display a list of all the files — text, pictures, style sheets, etc. — that are used by the chapter file. This feature is useful because it is sometimes difficult to sort out which files belong to chapters.

To see the list for ANDORRA, make sure that the ANDORRA.CHP file is highlighted.

> **Point** the mouse at ANDORRA.CHP
> **Click**

When a selected chapter is opened, Ventura displays a list of all of the files — text, graphics, and style sheets — that are used in that chapter.

> **Point** the mouse at Open
> **Click**

Ventura displays a box warning you that you are about to lose some data if you don't use the Save command. This box refers to the changes you made when you added and then removed INVOICE.CHP.

> **Point** the mouse at Save
> **Click**

Ventura lists the files that are used by ANDORRA.CHP.

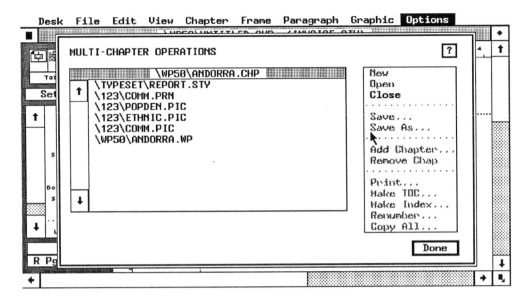

*Figure 7.4    Open chapter option lists supporting files.*

You can see that there are six files from three different directories. The Open mutli-chapter list command is a handy way to see a list of the files used in a given chapter. To return to the publication display, select the Close command.

> **Point** the mouse at Close
> **Click**

# GENERATING A TABLE OF CONTENTS

Ventura can produce a table of contents from the chapter or chapters listed in the publication file. In this example, there is only one file. You can create a table of contents for this one chapter, or you could add other chapters. Ventura produces the table of contents by searching each chapter for specific paragraph style tags. The text from those tags is copied into a table of contents file. As mentioned previously, the text in the table of contents file reflects the order in which the tagged text appears in the chapter and the order in which the chapters are listed in the publication file.

To create a table of contents, select the **Make TOC** option.

---

**Point** the mouse at Make TOC
**Click**

---

Ventura displays the GENERATE TABLE OF CONTENTS dialog box.

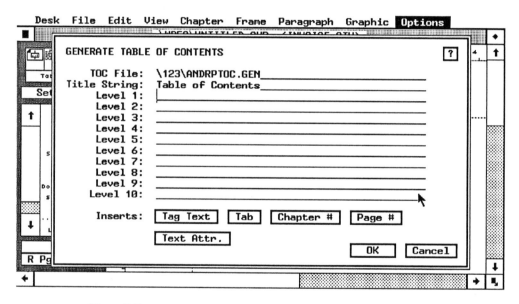

*Figure 7.5* *GENERATE TABLE OF CONTENTS dialog box.*

The dialog box consists of three types of entries.

The first line—**TOC file**—contains the name of the text file that Ventura will create. This file will contain the text copied from the chapter files. Ventura automatically creates a name for this file. It takes the first five characters of the publication file (in this case, ANDRP) and adds TOC and an extension of .GEN (generated text). In this case, that makes ANDRPTOC.GEN the suggested name of the file. However, you might have noticed that the directory for the text file is assumed to be \123. If this is not the directory you want the text stored in, then you can change the filename and its directory.

In this case, you might want to tell Ventura to place the table of contents text file into the same directory as the WordPerfect text files you have been using. The generated text files are always ASCII format files with two returns at the end of each line. You can edit these files with word processors that work with ASCII text files. WordPerfect uses the [Ctrl/F5] command to load and save ASCII format files. To change the directory, enter

↑ (2 times)
**[Esc]**
**c:\wp50\andrptoc.gen**
↓

The next item on the menu — **Title String** — is the text of the title that will be inserted at the beginning of the table of contents. The default text is Table of Contents. This text is not very crucial because it can be edited later.

Change the title to **Contents**. Enter

**[Esc]**
**Contents** ↓

The next ten lines are very significant. They will contain the information that tells Ventura what information to take from the multi-chapter file and place into the table of contents text file. Ventura allows you to specify up to ten levels for the table of contents. In practice, most users will never use more than three or four levels. Many publishers like to keep tables of contents to two or three levels.

A typical table of contents sets the first level as chapter headings, the second as subheadings, and the third as any topic headings that fall under the subheadings.

Begin with the chapter heading level. Enter

**Chapter**
**[Space bar]**

You probably want to insert the chapter number next.

> **Point** the mouse at Chapter #
> **Click**

Separate the chapter number from the chapter heading with a tab.

> **Point** the mouse at Tab
> **Click**

The next item on the line will tell Ventura what text should be used as the chapter heading. Ventura selects text based on the style tag used for a particular paragraph. In this example, the MAJOR HEAD tag was used for the main chapter title. To insert a tag name, select the **Tag Text** box.

> **Point** the mouse at Tag Text box
> **Click**

Ventura inserts the symbol [*tag name] on the line. Remember that this symbol cannot be left as it is. You must change the words *tag name* to the name of an actual tag used in the document. Enter

> ←
> **[Backspace]** (8 times)
> **major head**

The final step is to add the page number on which the major heading is found.

Enter

$\rightarrow$

Insert a tab between the heading text and the page number.

| **Point** the mouse at Tab |
|---|
| **Click** |

Now insert the code for the page number.

| **Point** the mouse at Page # |
|---|
| **Click** |

The dialog box should resemble the one in Figure 7.6.

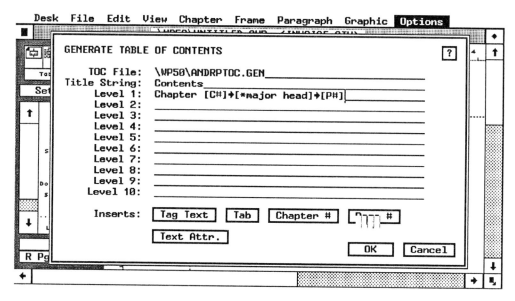

*Figure 7.6    Table of contents level item specified.*

Now you are ready to create the next level of the table of contents.  Enter

↓

The second-level heading usually consists of the text of the subheading.  You can enter the name of the text tag manually; you do not need to use the Tag Text box. Enter

**[*sub head]**

Add the page number.

```
Point the mouse at Tab
Click
Point the mouse at Page #
Click
```

The third level and final entry will be the TOPIC tags. Enter the name of the tag used for third-level headings.

↓
**[*topic]**

Add the page number codes.

```
Point the mouse at Tab
Click
Point the mouse at Page #
Click
```

The specifications are complete and should resemble Figure 7.7.

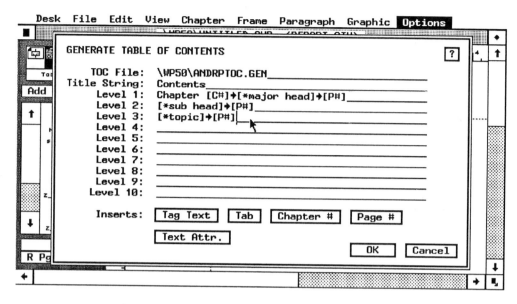

*Figure 7.7    Table of contents set up for three levels.*

You are now ready to generate a table of contents file. Keep in mind that once you create a table of contents specification for a publication file, Ventura will store the setup so that you can use it over again. You only need to set up a specification from scratch when you start a new publication file. This means that as you add, remove, or rearrange chapters in the publications file, you can simply run the same table of contents specifications to get an updated table of contents.

To begin the generation process, select OK.

> **Point** the mouse at OK
> **Click**

Ventura displays a box on the screen that shows the files it is loading and working with. When this process is complete, the ANDRPTOC.GEN file is written to disk. This file contains the table of contents text. It is not really a finished table of contents. In order to get the final product, you will need to load that text file into a Ventura chapter and format the text so it looks like a real table of contents. The table of contents operation you have just carried out simply creates a text file with the proper headings and page numbers.

Note that if you edit or revise the chapters included in the table of contents, you will probably change the location of some of the headings. Ventura is not designed to automatically update the table of contents file, so whenever you make changes you must generate the table of contents again to make sure that your page numbers are accurate. For this reason, table of contents generation should be the last operation in the document creation process.

## GENERATING AN INDEX

Generating an index is much the same as generating a table of contents; however, indexes are not sensitive to the order of the chapters because the index is listed alphabetically.

Like table of contents generation, index generation produces a text file with the index entries and their page numbers. This text file still needs to be loaded into a Ventura chapter file and formatted before you can print out an index.

To begin the index process, select **Make Index** from the MULTI-CHAPTER OPERATIONS dialog box, which is accessed from the Options menu.

---

**Point** the mouse at Options
**Point** at Multi-Chapter
**Click**
**Point** at Make Index
**Click**

---

Ventura displays the GENERATE INDEX dialog box.

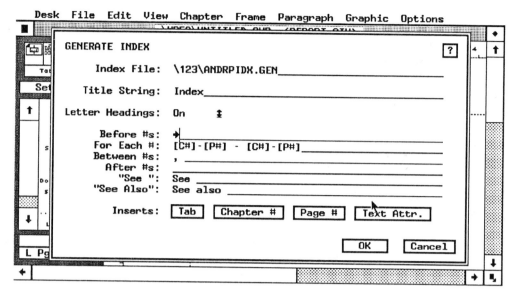

*Figure 7.8    GENERATE INDEX dialog box.*

In some ways, indexes are less complicated than tables of contents. One reason is that Ventura already knows where to find the index text. Unlike in tables of contents, where entries are drawn by tag name, the index text was entered into special index codes that do not appear in the text of the document. Ventura automatically knows that index generation is aimed at finding those specific items.

Ventura displays a default setup for the index file. This is a frequently used index format, so you may want to simply accept the default.

Before you do, it is important to look at the settings to know what they mean. The top line shows the name of the index text file. Note the drive and directory location to see if they are the ones you want. In this case, you will want to change the location to put the file in your \WP50 directory. Enter

↑ (2 times)
[Esc]
\wp50\andrpidx.gen
↓

The title for the index is entered as **Index**. In this case, you can leave the title as is. Enter

↓

Next is the **Letter Headings** option. When on, which is the default value, this setting creates alphabetical headings — A, B, C, etc. — in the index. If you are concerned about the length of the index, as is the case when printing a large manuscript, you may want to save space by turning the Letter Headings off.

The next section is a series of specifications that define the format of the index entries. The index entries for this document consist of four main parts.

- **Before #s**. This line specifies the character that should be inserted between the index entry text and the page number for that index item. The default value is a tab. For example, if the index entry text on page five was "ethnic groups," the index entry would be written as **Ethnic groups** [Tab] **5**. The actual amount of space between the text and the number would be controlled by the tab settings used for the paragraph tag. One reason to use a tab is to have an index in which the page numbers are aligned in a vertical column.

- **For Each #**. This option specifies the format in which the page number of the index item should be written. The default setting is chapter number, hyphen, page number — [C#] - [P#] — (e.g., 1-5).

- **Between #s**. This option specifies the characters that will be used to separate page number references when the same index item appears on adjacent pages. The default is to insert a comma and a space (e.g., Ethnic groups 1-5, 2-7, 5-22).

- **After #s**. This option is used to insert text following the last page reference. Typically this option is used to enter text attribute codes that reset the text from font or point size changes made in any of the other three index specifications.

One of the most common variations to the default setting is to change the **Before** **#s** to a comma and a space. This would cause the reference page numbers to appear right after the index entry text instead of being tab aligned. In that case, the page numbers would not align in a vertical column but would flow to the left or right depending on the length of the index item text. Enter

**[Backspace]**
, (comma)
**[Space bar]**
↓

The next item determines the type of page numbering used. The default is to use both chapter and page numbers (e.g., 1-10). In this case, use only the page numbers. Enter

**[Esc]**
**[P#]-[P#]**

You can leave the rest of the default specifications are they are. The index setup should resemble Figure 7.9.

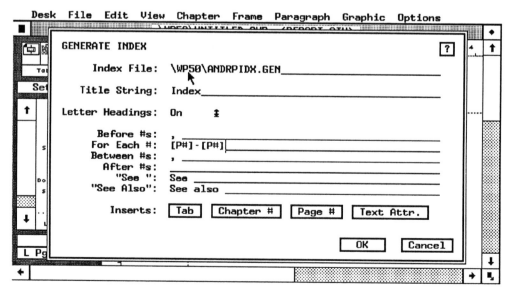

*Figure 7.9    Index generation setup.*

To generate the index, select OK.

> **Point** the mouse at OK
> **Click**

You have created two new text files, ANDRPTOC.GEN (the table of contents), and ANDRPIDX.GEN (the index). You can now exit the MULTI-CHAPTER OPERATIONS dialog box.

> **Point** the mouse at Done
> **Click**

Ventura displays a message box to determine if you want to save the changes you have made. The changes refer to the new specifications for table of contents and index generation. Save those specifications so they will be available if you ever need to generate the table of contents or index again.

> **Point** the mouse at Save
> **Click**

Keep in mind that generating the index and table of contents is only part of the job of creating an index and table of contents for the document. The next step will be to load the text files you have just generated and create the correct paragraph and chapter formats in which you want them displayed.

## FORMATTING THE TABLE OF CONTENTS

The previous section of this chapter showed you how to generate text files that contain the base information for the table of contents and the index. Those files contain text but are not formatted Ventura chapters; they are not ready to be printed. To get the table of contents and index to print, you must create Ventura documents from the text files.

The only difference between normal text files and the ones created when a table of contents or index is generated is that Ventura automatically tags the paragraphs of generated files with special generated tags.

To format the table of contents, all you need to do is define the paragraph format of the tags that have already been entered into the text.

Begin by loading the table of contents text file into the current document.

---

**Point** the mouse at File
**Point** the mouse at Load Text/Picture
**Click**

---

The menu box appears. Remember that the text file was created automatically by Ventura, which means you should use the **generated** format.

---

**Point** the mouse at Generated
**Click**

---

Enter

⏎

Ventura displays the file selector box. Ventura may not suggest the correct directory. You can use the cursor to change the selector display or manually enter the
selector specification. In this case, because you know the location and the names
of the files needed, make a manual entry.

↑
[Esc]
\wp50\*.gen ↵

Ventura displays the two files that you have just created through multi-chapter
operations.

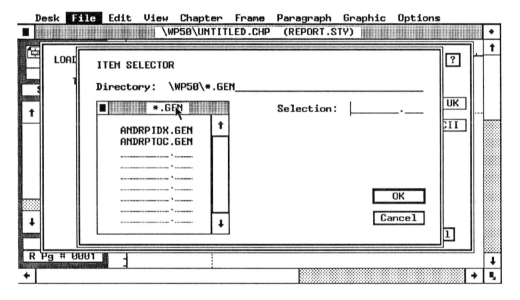

*Figure 7.10    Generated text files listed in selector box.*

Load the text of the table of contents.

**Point** the mouse at ANDRPTOC.GEN
**Double Click**

Then,

---

**Point** at the master frame
**Click**
**Point** at ANDRPTOC.GEN in the side bar
**Click**

---

Ventura loads the text of the table of contents into the document window. Headings are frequently entered in all uppercase letters. When the table of contents is compiled, Ventura extracts the text exactly as it is entered into the document. This means that all items in the table of contents may be in uppercase. If you want to change the text, you can use the Capitalize option in the Text Entry mode to change the all uppercase text to mixed case without having to re-enter any text.

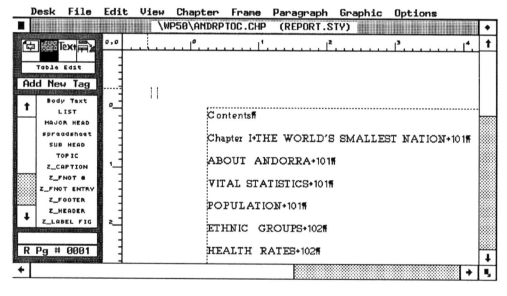

*Figure 7.11   Table of contents text loaded into master frame.*

Note that the auto-numbers are not included in the table of contents because they are really separate paragraphs from the headings they label. If you want to include the auto-numbers in the table of contents, you can generate numbers in this document by using the Auto-Number feature again, this time entering the table of contents tag names.

The top line of the text is the title of the table of contents. Place Ventura in the Paragraph Tagging mode. Enter

**[Ctrl/i]**

Highlight the first line of the text.

```
Point the mouse at "Contents"
Click
```

**Exercise 1:** The box above the page number shows the name of this tag as Z_TOC TITLE (table of contents title). This tag was automatically generated during the table of contents generation. The text was determined by the heading entered in the GENERATE TABLE OF CONTENTS dialog box. Change this title tag to create a centered title in Swiss 24-point bold. Try this on your own. The correct commands can be found under EX-1 at the end of this chapter.

**Exercise 2:** Center the text horizontally as well. Try this on your own. The correct commands can be found under EX-2 at the end of this chapter.

## Formatting Levels

The next step is to format the first level of the table of contents, the chapter heading.

---

**Point** the mouse at Chapter
**Click**

---

The box on top of the page number shows the name of the tag, **Z_TOC LVL 1**. Ventura creates a separate tag for each level in the table of contents, Z_TOC LVL 2, Z_TOC LVL 3, etc. Change the font to Swiss, 14-point bold.

---

**Point** the mouse at Paragraph
**Point** the mouse at Font
**Click**
**Point** the mouse at Swiss
**Click**
**Point** the mouse at 14
**Click**

---

Enter

↵

Next, create the tab stops that will align the text on that line. Recall that Ventura sets the default alignment of new tags to justified.

**Exercise 3:** First change the alignment to left. Try this on your own. The correct commands can be found under EX-3 at the end of this chapter.

> **Point** the mouse at Paragraph
> **Point** the mouse at Tab Settings
> **Click**

The first tab should be set at 1.5". Enter

**[Esc]**
**01.5**

The second tab on the line should be set as a right-aligned tab at 5.5". Right-aligned tabs will align whole numbers correctly.

> **Point** the mouse at the → icon
> **Click**
> **Point** the mouse at Tab Type
> **Click**
> **Drag** to Right

Enter

**[Esc]**
**05.5**
⏎

The first line is now formatted correctly although you cannot see the right end of the line. Scroll to the right.

> **Click** on the scroll bar right arrow (2 times)

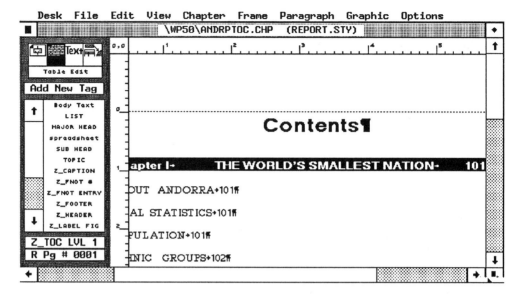

*Figure 7.12   First-level TOC heading formatted.*

## Tabs with Leaders

There are two more levels to format for the table of contents.  Select a paragraph that is a second-level TOC item.

---

**Point** the mouse at "ABOUT ANDORRA"
**Click**

---

The paragraph is tagged as **Z_TOC LVL 2**.  For the second-level paragraph tag, you want to perform the following steps:

1.    Change the alignment from justified to left.

2.    Create an indent of 1.5", matching the tab used on the first level.

3.    Create a tab at 5.5" for the page number.

```
Point the mouse at Paragraph
Point the mouse at Alignment
Click
```

Select left alignment.

```
Point the mouse at Horz. Alignment
Click
Drag to Left
```

You can use the In/Outdent Width setting to alter the alignment of the TOC items. Note that the In/Outdent Width can be used in this case because all the second-level paragraphs have the same number of lines – one. Enter

**[Esc]**
**01.5**
⏎

Not only did the line you highlighted change, but all the subheadings in the table of contents changed because they all share the same paragraph style tag, **Z_TOC LVL 2**, which was inserted into the text file while the table of contents was generated. This saves you a lot of time in formatting the Table of Contents.

Create the tab for the page number. In this case, you will want to create a dot leader between the text and the page number.

```
Point the mouse at Paragraph
Point the mouse at Tab Settings
Click
Point the mouse at Tab Type
Click
Drag to Right
```

To create the dot leader, select **Tab Shown as**. This setting controls how the space between tab stops will be displayed. You can change the space between tabs from an open space (blank) to a line of dots. The characters that fill the space are called tab **leaders**. The default leader is a period, ASCII character 46. This type of leader is frequently used in tables of contents.

---

**Point** the mouse at Tabs Shown as
**Click**
**Drag** to Leader Char

---

Enter the value for the page number tab.

**[Esc]**
**05.5** ⏎

The second-level headings are formatted.

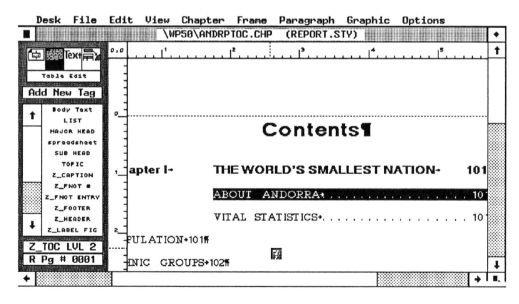

*Figure 7.13    Second-level heading uses dot leaders with tab.*

## Swapping Tags

The third-level headings should be formatted exactly like the second-level headings except that their indent should be set at 1.75" (.25" farther to the right) so the headings will appear in proper outline format.

The obvious way to achieve this result is to modify the setting used for the **Z_TOC LVL 3** tag in the same way that you did the **Z_TOC LVL 2** tag; however, this approach would require you to manually enter many of the same commands you used for **Z_TOC LVL 2**. When Ventura creates generated tags, the format of the tags is copied from the current **Body Text** tag.

As you may recall from working through previous chapters, there is a shortcut that allows you to copy the settings used in one tag into another tag. If you copy the **Z_TOC LVL 2** into the **Z_TOC LVL 3** tag, you can simply change the indent from 1.5" to 1.75".

While Ventura does not provide a specific command to accomplish this task, you can use some of the existing commands to effect the change you have in mind. The process involves the following steps:

1. **Add New Tag**. The new tag will be copied from the tag you want to duplicate. For example, you could create a new tag called **Temp**. The Temp tag can be copied from Z_TOC LVL 2, which will give Temp the same format characteristics as Z_TOC LVL 2.

2. **Remove Tag**. The second step is to remove the **Z_TOC LVL 3** tag from the document. Because every paragraph must have a tag, Ventura will ask you the name of the tag to substitute for the tag you are deleting. In this example, you would delete Z_TOC LVL 3 and replace it with Temp. In effect, you are replacing all the Z_TOC LVL 3 tags with Temp tags. The Temp tag will carry with it the formatting you wanted to copy from Z_TOC LVL 2.

3. **Rename Tag**. This step is optional. Rename **Temp** to Z_TOC LVL 3. While this step would have no effect on the formatting, it would return the document to the original tag names used in the generated text file.

The first step is to create the **Temp** tag. You don't want to apply the tag to any paragraph just yet, so deselect all paragraphs by clicking on a blank area of the document, such as the top margin area.

---

**Click** on the top margin area

---

No paragraphs are currently selected. Note that you can still add a new tag even when no paragraphs are selected.

---

**Point** the mouse at Add New Tag
**Click**

---

Enter the name of the tag you want to create, Temp, and the tag it should be copied from Z_TOC LVL 2. Enter

**Temp ↓**
**[Esc]**
**z_toc lvl 2 ⏎**

To delete or rename tags, you must first save the chapter file. Enter

**[Ctrl/s]**

You can remove and rename tags in the UPDATE TAG LIST dialog box. Enter

**[Ctrl/k]**

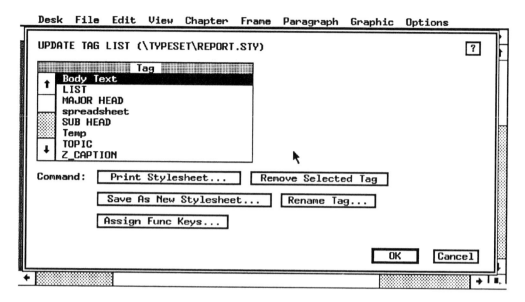

*Figure 7.14   UPDATE TAG LIST dialog box.*

The first task is to remove the Z_TOC LVL 3 tag from the style sheet and substitute the Temp tag for it.

The names of the tags appear in the selector box. You will need to scroll the list down to see the name of the tag you want to remove.

---

**Click** on the ↓ icon   (11 times)
**Point** the mouse at Z_TOC LVL 3
**Click**

---

After selecting Z_TOC LVL 3, you can choose the operation you want to carry out — in this case, Remove Selected Tag.

---

**Point** the mouse at Remove Selected Tag
**Click**

---

Ventura displays another dialog box. This box allows you to enter the name of the tag with which you want the selected tag to be replaced. The default tag name entered is Body Text. Change that name to **Temp**.

↓
**[Esc]**
**Temp** ↵

To see the effect of the swap, return to the document window by entering

↵

Ventura displays a message box that asks if you want the changes you have just made in the style sheet to be saved as part of the existing style sheet or if you want them stored as part of another style sheet. If you select Save, the changes will affect the current style sheet, which is what you want to do.

> **Point** the mouse at Save
> **Click**

Note that all of the second- and third-level headings have the same format. You can now make the one change you want to differentiate the third-level headings from the second-level headings.

> **Point** the mouse at Population
> **Click**
> **Point** the mouse at Paragraph
> **Point** the mouse at Alignment
> **Click**

Enter

**[Esc]**
**01.75** ⮠

The table of contents is formatted with three levels.

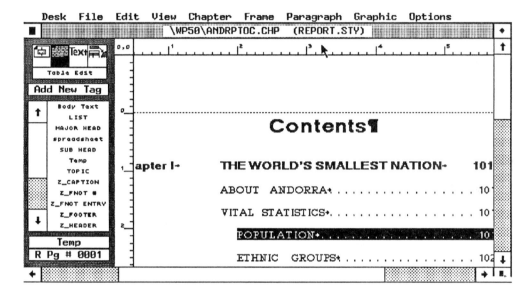

*Figure 7.15   Table of contents formatted with three levels of headings.*

The last step, which is optional, is to change the name of the Temp tag back to the original third-level tag name, Z_TOC LVL 3.  Enter

**[Ctrl/s]**
**[Ctrl/k]**

Because the Temp tag was selected in the document window, it is also automatically selected when you display the UPDATE TAG LIST dialog box.

Change the name back to the original.

---

**Point** the mouse at Rename Tag
**Click**

---

Enter

↓
**Z̄_TOC LVL 3** ⅃

---

**Point** the mouse at Save
**Click**

---

When Ventura returns you to the document window, the tag name is changed to Z_TOC LVL 3. You have changed the format without having to go through all of the formatting steps. The benefit of this strategy increases as the complexity of your style tags increases.

The table of contents is ready for printing.

---

**Point** the mouse at File
**Point** the mouse at To Print
**Click**

---

Enter

⅃

When you have printed the text, you can clear the document window for formatting the index. Enter

**[Ctrl/s]**

---

**Point** the mouse at File
**Point** the mouse at New
**Click**

---

# FORMATTING THE INDEX

The next task is to load the index text generated by the multi-chapter operations and format the document. Load the text of the index.

---

**Point** the mouse at File
**Point** the mouse at Load Text/Picture
**Click**

---

Enter

↵

---

**Point** the mouse at ANDRPIDX.GEN
**Double Click**

---

Ventura loads the file but does not display it yet.

---

**Point** the mouse at ANDRPIDX.GEN in the side bar display
**Click**

---

Scroll to the left.

---

**Click** on scroll bar left arrow

---

The index text appears in the document frame.

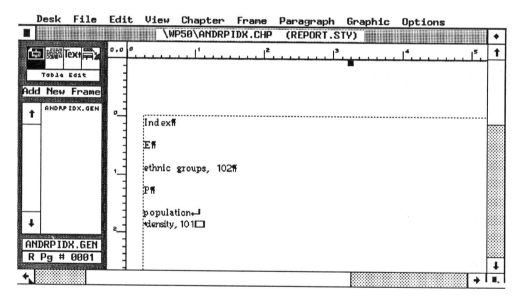

*Figure 7.16   Index text loaded into document.*

The index in this example is very small. Index generation creates only three format tags:

**Z_INDEX TITLE**        tag for the index title
**Z_INDEX LTR**        tag for the letter headings
**Z_INDEX MAIN**     tag for the index text

In most cases, you will find that the default layout is adequate. The most common change made to index text is formatting it as two-column text to save space.

In this case, you will make two formatting changes to the index. You will change the letter headings to a larger, bold typeface, and you will indent the index subheadings. Place Ventura in the Paragraph Tagging mode by entering

**[Ctrl/i]**

---

**Point** the mouse at "E"
**Click**

---

The tag name appears in the side bar as Z_INDEX LTR. Change the font to 14-point text.

---

**Point** the mouse at Paragraph
**Point** the mouse at Font
**Click**
**Point** the mouse at 14
**Click**

---

The index generation process added tabs to the subheadings, but they are not in effect because the alignment of generated tags is automatically set to justified.

Select the index entry paragraph.

---

**Point** the mouse at "ethnic"
**Click**

---

Change the alignment to left.

---

**Point** the mouse at Paragraph
**Point** the mouse at Alignment
**Click**
**Point** the mouse at Horz. Alignment
**Click**
**Drag** to Left

---

Enter

↵

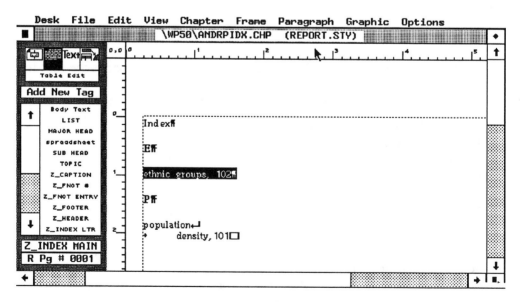

*Figure 7.17   Index tags formatted.*

Save the index file by entering.

**[Ctrl/s]**

You have now created the table of contents and index chapter files for your multiple-chapter ANDORRA document.

## ADDING TABLE AND INDEX FILES

The final step in this process is to add the newly created index and table of contents files to the publication file, which will enable you to print the document, table of contents, and index as a single unit. Display the MULTI-CHAPTER OPERATIONS dialog box.

> **Point** the mouse at Options
> **Point** the mouse at Multi-Chapter
> **Click**

The ANDRPAPH publication file is displayed. Add the table of contents file to the publication file.

> **Point** the mouse at Add Chapter
> **Click**

The ITEM SELECTOR dialog box displays the list of chapters, including the table of contents and the index chapters for the ANDORRA document. Add the table of contents chapter.

> **Point** the mouse at ANDRPTOC.CHP
> **Double Click**

The file is added to the publication list. As discussed previously, Ventura adds new files to the bottom of the list. In this case, you will want to place the table of contents file at the top of the list because it should be printed before the chapter.

You can change the position of the file by dragging it up. (Dragging refers to pointing and holding down the mouse button while you move the mouse.)

---

**Point** the mouse at ANDRPTOC.CHP
**Drag** it to the top of the list

---

Now add the index file.

---

**Point** the mouse at ANDRPIDX.CHP
**Double Click**

---

All three related chapters are in the same publication file.

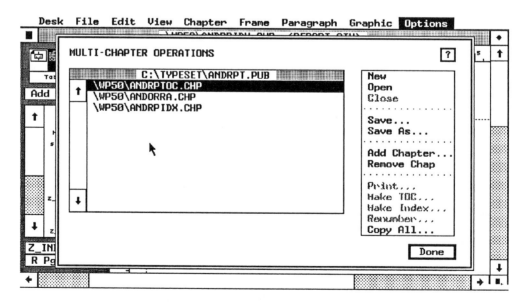

*Figure 7.18    Three chapters contained in a publication file.*

Save the modified file by entering

↵

> **Point** the mouse at Save
> **Click**

## PRINTING A PUBLICATION FILE

Once you have created and saved a publication file, you can use the Multi-Chapter Print command to print all of the chapters in the publication file.

Note that the Print option is not available while any of the chapter files are highlighted. To prepare for printing, you must deselect the chapters by pointing at a blank area in the dialog box and clicking.

> **Click** on a blank area in the dialog box

Print the chapter.

> **Point** the mouse at Print
> **Click**

The PRINT dialog box appears. Enter

↵

When the printing is complete, you are returned to the MULTI-CHAPTER OPERATIONS dialog box.

Return to the document window.

---

> **Point** the mouse at Done
> **Click**

---

## MOVING A CHAPTER

The multiple-page ANDORRA document illustrates how many different computer files can go into making up a single printed document. This Ventura feature is very different from the way most word processing programs operate. A word processing document is usually stored in a single computer file. A file can easily be transferred or copied, using DOS commands or, in the case of most word processing programs, using the built-in Copy command. For example, in Word-Perfect, a file can be copied using [F5] 8.

However, Ventura chapters and publication files consist of many different computer files. In order to copy the entire set of files needed to complete a printed document, you need to keep track of all the computer files. Even with simple documents, such as the ANDORRA document, this is quite a task.

Ventura has a command in the MULTI-CHAPTER OPERATIONS dialog box that helps you copy all the files that belong to a single publication.

The best way to work with these groups of files is to take advantage of the DOS concept of a directory. You can create a new DOS directory and copy all of the files that make up a document into that directory. There are two reasons why this is a good idea.

1.	When all the files related to a given publication are placed into a directory, it is easy to copy or move all the files. You also reduce the danger of deleting a necessary file because all relevant files will be grouped together.

2.	You can use the DOS BACKUP command to back up all the files in a directory.

When you created the flyer in Chapter 5, you created a directory and copied the files *before* you created the chapter. You might assume that you can simply use DOS to accomplish the same thing *after* you have created a chapter; however, once a chapter has been created, moving files to a new directory or disk becomes more complicated.

Recall that when you use the Open command in the MULTI-CHAPTER OPERATIONS dialog box, the files listed as part of the selected chapter include the drive and directory of each file. If you want to move a chapter, you must also give Ventura an opportunity to update the list of files that chapter contains to match their new locations. If you use DOS alone, the chapter file will still look for the files in their original location when the chapter is opened.

For example, suppose you want to move the files that make up the ANDRPT publication file to a new directory. The first step is to create a DOS directory for the files. You can create a directory outside Ventura, using the DOS command **CD**, but Ventura also allows you to create a directory from its menus.

---

**Point** the mouse at File
**Point** the mouse at DOS File Ops
**Click**

---

Ventura displays the DOS FILE OPERATIONS dialog box.

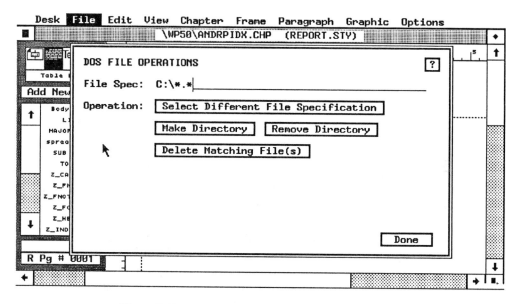

*Figure 7.19   DOS FILE OPERATIONS dialog box.*

To create a new directory, enter the name of that directory on the File Spec line.

**[Esc]**
**c:\report**

Then,

---

**Point** the mouse at Make Directory
**Click**

---

Ventura creates a new directory on disk.  Exit the dialog box.

---

**Point** the mouse at Done
**Click**

---

You can now use the MULTI-CHAPTER OPERATIONS dialog box to have Ventura copy all the related files to the new directory.

**Point** the mouse at Options
**Point** the mouse at Multi-Chapter
**Click**

The last option on this menu is **Copy All**.

**Point** the mouse at Copy All
**Click**

Ventura displays the COPY ALL dialog box.

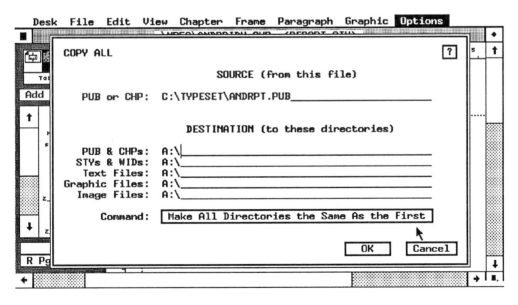

*Figure 7.20    COPY ALL dialog box.*

This dialog box displays a list of the types of files used by Ventura and the directory to which these files will be copied. Each line in the dialog box controls the location of a special group of files.

- **PUB & CHP**. This line sets the directory for all chapter and publication files.

- **STYs & WIDs**. This line sets the directory for the style sheet and width table files. A width table file holds information about the spacing used for the fonts. The width table is created when you install Ventura. The default width table is called OUTPUT.WID. Ventura also creates one width table for each printer you install. For example, if you install Ventura for an HP LaserJet and a postscript printer, Ventura creates two width tables, HPLJPLUS.WID and POSTSCPT.WID. If you want to add new fonts to the Ventura printing system, you will need to create width table files. Adding fonts to your Ventura system is discussed in Appendix A.

- **Text Files**.

- **Graphics Files** (line-art).

- **Image Files**.

In most cases, you will want to copy all of the files to the same directory. For example, to transfer a chapter to a floppy disk, you would want to enter **A:\** as the directory on all of the lines. Note that Ventura assumes all the files can fit onto the destination disk. If Ventura runs out of room while copying files, a message is displayed, and the command terminates. Enter the name of the directory to which you want to copy these files.

**c:\report**

You can change the directories or accept the layout. Ventura provides a shortcut to changing the directory. If you enter the new directory in the first line, PUB & CHPs, you can use the **Make All Directories the Same as the First** option to copy that directory name onto the other file specification lines.

> **Point** the mouse at Make All Directories the Same As the First
> **Click**

Begin the copying process.

> **Point** the mouse at OK
> **Click**

Ventura copies all the files until it reaches the style sheet, REPORT.STY.

> **Point** the mouse at Done
> **Click**

Clear the document window.

> **Point** the mouse at File
> **Point** the mouse at New
> **Click**

## PRINTING OUT A STYLE SHEET

The information contained in a document's style sheet can be converted into a text file. Note that Ventura does not provide a direct means of printing a style sheet. The Print Style Sheet command operates like the Multi-Chapter Make TOC and Make Index commands in that it creates a text file, which can then be loaded into a chapter, formatted, and printed.

Suppose you want to print information about the current style sheet. This option is found on the UPDATE TAG LIST dialog box. Enter

**[Ctrl/k]**

Create the style sheet information file by using the Print Style Sheet option.

---

**Point** the mouse at Print Style Sheet
**Click**

---

Ventura displays the ITEM SELECTOR dialog box to allow you to enter a name for the text file about to be generated. Enter

**report.sty.** ⏎

Ventura generates the style sheet data and then returns to the UPDATE TAG LIST dialog box. Return to the document window. Enter

⏎

If you want to inspect or print the information generated about the style sheet, you must load the text file into the current master frame.

---

**Point** the mouse at File
**Point** the mouse at Load Text/Picture
**Click**

---

Enter

↵

Select the new file, REPORTSY.GEN.

---

**Point** the mouse at REPORTSY.GEN
**Double Click**

---

Load the text into the master frame.

---

**Point** the mouse at REPORTSY.GEN
**Click**

---

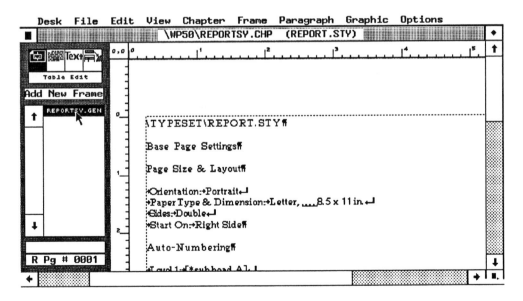

*Figure 7.21   Style sheet information file.*

Note that the information about the style sheet can be quite lengthy. The REPORT.STY information is about 16 pages long. The text also contains a number of new tags that use tab stops for formatting. You can print the document as is or format the style tags for a more professional look. Also note that style sheet information files are standard DOS text files that can be printed with any word processor or text editor that prints DOS text files.

Save the style sheet document. Enter

**[Ctrl/s]**

Exit Ventura.

---

**Point** the mouse at File
**Point** the mouse at Quit
**Click**

---

## SUMMARY

- **Publication Files**. Ventura allows you to create a publication file that can be used in organizational and reference tasks that involve one or more chapter files. Ventura uses the PUB extension to indicate a publication file. Publication files allow you to create tables of contents and indexes. Chapters can be added to and removed from the publication file at any time. You can create a publication file with only one chapter if you want.

- **Table of Contents**. Ventura will generate a table of contents from a publication file. Ventura selects the headings by searching for specified style tags used in the chapters in the publication file. The table of contents is ordered according to the order of the chapters listed in the publication file. The table of contents generated by Ventura is a text file. It is not ready to print. To be printed, the text file must be loaded and formatted and saved as a chapter file. Ventura automatically tags each heading with a generated style tag.

- **Indexes**. Indexes are produced in the same way as table of contents files. The index text is drawn from the data stored in the index codes that are inserted in the text files that make up the publication file. Index entries are alphabetized. If you want, Ventura will insert letter headings into the index. Like table of contents files, the index output file is a text file that cannot be printed unless it is loaded and saved as a chapter file.

- **Copying Files**. Ventura allows you to copy all the files related to all the chapters in a publication file. The Copy All option on the Multi-Chapter menu is used for this purpose. The main reason for using this command is to isolate all the necessary files for a publication in a unique disk directory for copying or backup purposes.

- **Printing Style Sheet Information**. Ventura does not directly print style sheet information; however, it can create a text file with style sheet data, which can then be loaded, saved as a Ventura chapter file, formatted, and printed.

## Answers to Exercises

**EX-1 (see p. 489):** Change the Z_TOC TITLE tag to Swiss, 24-point bold with center alignment.

```
Point the mouse at Paragraph
Point the mouse at Font
Click
Point the mouse at Swiss
Click
Point the mouse at 24
Click
```

Then,

```
Point the mouse at Paragraph
Click
Point the mouse at Alignment
Click
Drag to Left
```

Enter

⏎

**EX-2 (see p. 489):** Center the text horizontally as well.

> **Point** the mouse at Paragraph
> **Point** the mouse at Alignment
> **Click**
> **Point** the mouse at Horz. Alignment
> **Click**
> **Drag** to Center

Enter

⏎

**EX-3 (see p. 490):** Change the alignment to left.

> **Point** the mouse at Paragraph
> **Point** the mouse at Alignment
> **Click**
> **Point** the mouse at Horz.  Alignment
> **Click**
> **Drag** to Left

Enter

⏎

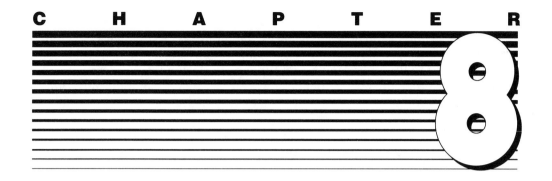

# NEWSLETTERS

The newsletter is one of the documents most commonly associated with desktop publishing programs like Ventura. A newsletter requires techniques similar to those used in the multiple-frame and multiple-page documents you created in Chapters 5 and 6. Like those documents, newsletters use multiple frames to combine text from several document files into a single printed output.

In most of the Ventura documents you have worked on so far, you have created the master frame that contained the main text file, and you used other frames to insert text or graphics. A newsletter is by definition a document that combines individual articles into a single layout. When you create a newsletter, each article is stored in a text file. Each file is then placed into a frame, but the master frame remains empty of text. The master frame's function in a newsletter is to create a column framework into which the text of the articles can flow.

In this chapter, you will learn the details of newsletter creation by combining three articles into a single newsletter. The three sample articles, shown in Figures 8.1, 8.2, and 8.3, will be used as the text of the articles for the newsletter. The three files contain about 950 words. If you want to avoid entering the text, you can substitute text you have already created and format it to roughly the same length as the sample files.

The first step in newsletter creation is to create the text for the articles. As in the rest of this book, the assumption is made that you are using WordPerfect 5.0 as your word processing program. Note that the ⏎ symbols in the figures indicate where paragraphs end.

Create the document shown in Figure 8.1 (300 words). Save it as **JAVELIN.WP**.

@HEADLINE = JAVELIN PLUS ⏎

Javelin Plus adds database operations to the existing Javelin package. Javelin is a program designed for building financial models but it differs from standard spreadsheet programs in a number of significant respects. ⏎

@SUB HEAD = DIFFERENT THAN SPREADSHEETS⏎

The most important difference between Javelin and spreadsheets like 1-2-3, Supercalc, and MultiPlan is that data is stored in time series blocks, not spreadsheet cells. A time series block is a list of dates with corresponding values. The entire block is assigned a variable name. ⏎

For example, suppose you have income and expense figures for four quarters. The data is not assigned row and column locations as is the case in a standard spreadsheet. Instead, data is related by virtue of the time period for which it is entered.⏎

@SUB HEAD = TIME SERIES ANALYSIS ⏎

The advantage of this is that you can carry out a series of calculations by relating one time series to another. A good example would be the calculation of the net income for each quarter. In Javelin this done by writing a formula using the variable names. Example: net = income-expenses. ⏎

@SUB HEAD = DATE CORRESPONDENCE ⏎

You don't have to worry about copying formulas into the corresponding cells. Because each value is related to a specific period of time, Javelin can figure out which numbers should be subtracted; it then creates a new table called NET with the results of the calculation.⏎

Javelin can also display the relationship between variables as a diagram. ⏎

Javelin has always had as strong database flavor. Each time series block can be viewed as a simple two-field database. ⏎

Since all the variables have the same time periods, then all the variables have a field in common that can be used to relate each to a corresponding item: a sort of mini-relational database.

*Figure 8.1    JAVELIN.WP text.*

Create the document shown in Figure 8.2 (400 words).  Save it as **OS2.WP**.

---

@HEADLINE = WHAT WILL OS/2 MEAN TO YOU?⏎
It is now more than 6 months since OS/2 was officially announced. The "new" operating system is still little more than a name to everyone except a handful of developers. Of course, the lack of actual software has not seemed to deter a lot of people from praising and damning the yet-to-appear product. ⏎
@SUB HEAD = WHAT OS/2 OFFERS⏎
I don't know anymore than any other average computer user what OS/2 will be like and how the computing world will react to it. ⏎
One point made in the computer press is that most of the features that OS/2 is supposed to offer already can be implemented by existing software and hardware. ⏎
Programs like DeskQview offer multitasking and many applications that can already use extended memory and graphics interfaces (like Windows and Gem) are already available.⏎
OS/2 is important, not so much because it will implement new ideas, but rather that it will create a standard way of implementing the type of features that have slowly been creeping into the IBM PC world over the past five years.⏎
@SUB HEAD = OS/2 OFFERS GRAPHIC INTERFACE⏎
While multitasking and memory expansion get the most attention, I believe the graphics interface is the feature that will most immediately affect the user. ⏎
Microsoft believes the PC world should look more like the Mac world. In fact, the PC world has had software like this for some time.⏎
Digital Research's GEM Desktop and Windows from Microsoft show how you might implement a graphic interface on a PC. ⏎
The Ventura desktop publishing program uses a form of GEM as its basic operating environment. ⏎
@SUB HEAD = LASER PRINTER SUPPORT⏎
But it is programs like Ventura and GEM that illustrate exactly why OS/2 is significant. Today, most programs on the PC use the built-in set of 254 characters to display all the information on the screen.⏎
This system is fast and simple but it lacks the flexibility to show on the screen many of the effects implemented by today's sophisticated printers.⏎
As printer technology moves forward, the PC's display ability has remained almost at a standstill. ⏎
One reason is if you want to create a display in which there is a close correspondence between the printed page, with its font changes and high resolution graphics, and the screen display, where will you get the characters?

*Figure 8.2    OS2.WP text.*

Create the document shown in Figure 8.3 (250 words).  Save it as **PLANNER.WP**.

---

@HEADLINE = VP PLANNER PLUS ↵
When Paperback Software released VP Planner a little more than a year ago, the program made headlines even in the non-computer press, not because of its functional parts but because it embroiled Paperback in a legal fight with the giant of the spreadsheet companies, Lotus Development Corporation. ↵
@SUB HEAD = COPYRIGHT DISPUTE↵
Lotus claimed that VP Planner had copied the look and feel of their 1-2-3 program, which they considered a violation of their copyrights. ↵
The controversy probably helped bring VP Planner to the attention of a lot of people who might not have otherwise thought about the program.↵
@SUB HEAD = CREATIVITY DISCOURAGED? ↵
It also raised a lot of questions concerning what copyrights mean in the computer industry, how innovation and creativity can be encouraged, and what role can be played by software standards. ↵
VP Planner is really two products. ↵
One is a spreadsheet that accepts Lotus 1-2-3 commands and macros. ↵
@SUB HEAD = DATABASE IMPROVED↵
The other program is a database. In VP Planner Plus, the integration of the two programs has been greatly improved and the functional aspects of the database module built up substantially. ↵
VP Planner Plus remains a program with a dual character.↵
On the one hand it is a fully functional spreadsheet that performs keystroke for keystroke like 1-2-3. On the other hand VP PLanner Plus provides two types of structured database files that can be used by themselves or integrated into spreadsheets.

---

*Figure 8.3    PLANNER.WP text.*

When you have finished creating the text files, load Ventura in the usual manner.

## MASTER FRAME LAYOUT

When you begin to create a newsletter, the role played by the master frame will be very different from its role in previous documents. When you create a newsletter, the assumption is made that each page will be divided into a series of frames, each of which will contain all or part of a document file. In newsletters or newspapers, the front page is usually divided among several articles.

Because several articles begin on the same page, there will probably not be enough room to display all of the text. This means that you will have to create a second, third, fourth page, etc., adding more frames until all of the text from all of the articles has been positioned.

As mentioned previously, in this type of document, the master frame is used not to hold the text of the articles but to serve as a framework into which the text frames are pasted. Having a master frame helps you make sure frames are placed on the page properly so there are no gaps or overlaps between the frames that contain the actual text.

The column- and line-snap features make it easy to create frames that fit correctly within the master frame without gaps or overlapping. The first decision you need to make in formatting a newsletter is how many vertical columns will the text be divided into. For example, if you will be using a 12-point font (the default value) for Body Text, you can reasonably print two or three columns of text on one page. If you want to use a smaller point size, e.g., 10-point text, you would use four or five columns. You could also increase the number of columns by changing the page orientation to landscape rather than portrait. This option can be found in the Chapter menu under the **Page Size & Layout** option.

**Exercise 1:** Because the number of columns in the master frame and the page size and orientation are all part of the style sheet settings, you should create a new style sheet for the newsletter. Remember that creating a new style sheet requires you to load the default style sheet. Try this on your own. The correct commands can be found under EX-1 at the end of this chapter.

Now that you have created a new style sheet for the newsletter settings, you can make the decision as to the number of columns you want to lay out. In this case, you will divide the page into six columns.

That seems to contradict what was said about using only two or three columns on a portrait-oriented page; however, the number of columns you lay out on the master frame is only a guide for the number of columns to use for text formatting. Suppose you intend to divide the 6.5" master frame into three text columns that are 2.17" wide (6.5" divided by 3 = approximately 2.17"). When you draw a frame, you have three width choices:

| Columns | Width |
|---------|-------|
| 1 | 2.17" |
| 2 | 4.33" |
| 3 | 6.50" |

By dividing the master frame into six columns, you can lay out frames in a greater variety of widths while still maintaining 2.17" as the minimum width.

| Columns | Width |
|---------|-------|
| 2 | 2.17" |
| 3 | 3.25" |
| 4 | 4.33" |
| 5 | 5.40" |
| 6 | 6.50" |

You can improve the appearance of the newsletter by varying the width of the frames that contain the articles. By creating more columns in the master frame, you allow for greater variety. Activate the Frame Setting mode by entering

**[Ctrl/u]**

To create the column, use the Margins & Columns option on the Frame menu.

---

**Point** the mouse at Frame
**Point** the mouse at Margins & Columns
**Click**

---

To create six columns, select the number 6.

> **Point** the mouse at 6
> **Click**

Ventura assumes, correctly in this case, that you want the columns evenly spaced; 6.5" divided by 6 equals a column width of approximately 1.08" for each column. Return to the document window by entering

⏎

View the page in the reduced mode by entering

**[Ctrl/r]**

The frame is divided into six columns by the column guide lines.

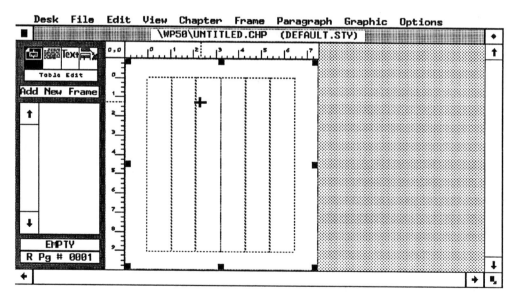

*Figure 8.4    Page divided into six vertical columns.*

# ROTATED TEXT

The first item to place on any newsletter is the **masthead** or **logo** for the newsletter. The masthead is used to identify the newsletter by name and also includes information such as issue, date, and number.

Usually the masthead is placed at the top of the newsletter, but there are other creative variations to this setup. One way to vary the appearance of the masthead is to take advantage of Ventura's ability to display rotated text. Ventura can display text rotated by 90, 180, or 270 degrees.

This means that it is possible to print the masthead of the newsletter rotated 90 degrees down the left side of the page.

The first step is to create a frame into which the masthead can be inserted. Activate the Frame Drawing mode.

---

> **Point** the mouse at Add New Frame
> **Click**

---

Draw a long, narrow frame from the upper left corner of the master frame to the lower right corner of the first column, as shown in Figure 8.5.

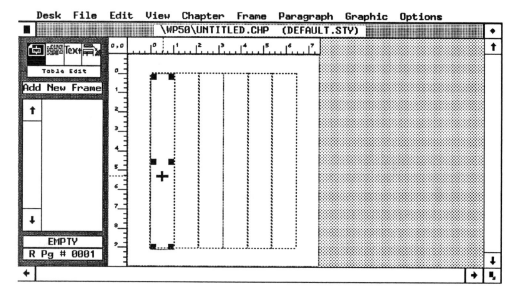

*Figure 8.5    Frame drawn down the left side of the page.*

Place Ventura in the Text Entry mode.

**[Ctrl/o]**

> **Point** inside the new frame
> **Click**

You can now enter text into the frame.  Because you are in the reduced mode, you may want to turn off the greeking so you can see the text, however small, as you enter it.  Because of the operations you are going to perform, i.e., rotating text, it is best to maintain a full page view instead of using the normal view.  Turn off the greeking by using the Options menu.

> **Point** the mouse at Options
> **Point** the mouse at Set Preferences
> **Click**

Then,

> **Point** the mouse at Text to Greek
> **Click**
> **Drag** to None

Enter

↵

To begin entering text, you must click on the end-of-file marker, the square box just inside the upper left corner of the frame.

> **Point** the mouse at end-of-file marker
> **Click**

If you have clicked in the right place, the words **End of File** will appear just above the page number beneath the side bar.  Enter

**Future Technology Tid Bits [Ctrl/↵]**
**Volume 5 [Tab]**
**Number 12 [Tab]**
**May 1, 1989**

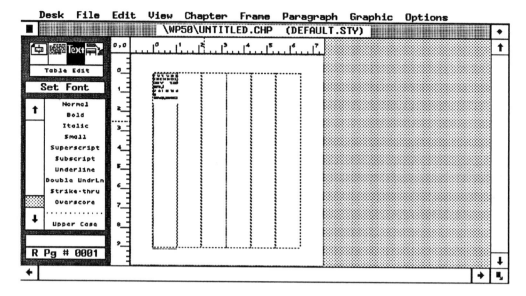

*Figure 8.6    Text entered into narrow frame.*

The text you have typed doesn't seem to do very much for the appearance of the newsletter, but you can radically change the appearance of the text by using Ventura paragraph format commands. Place Ventura in the Paragraph Tagging mode. Enter

**[Ctrl/i]**

Select the text you have entered.

**Point** the mouse at the text
**Click**

Create a new tag.

> **Point** the mouse at Add New Tag
> **Click**

Enter

**masthead** ⏎

First, change the font to Swiss, 24-point bold.

> **Point** the mouse at Paragraph
> **Point** the mouse at Font
> **Click**
> **Point** the mouse at Swiss
> **Click**
> **Point** the mouse at 24
> **Click**

Enter

⏎

The text is enlarged but is still jumbled into the narrow, 1.08" column.

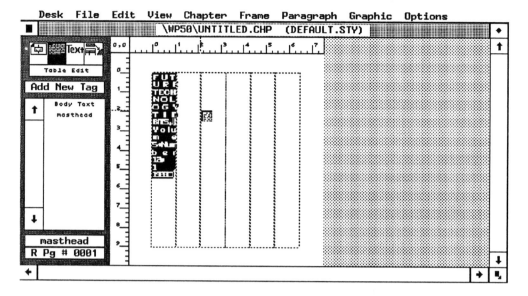

*Figure 8.7     Swiss 24-point text in narrow column.*

However, the goal of this layout is to rotate the direction of the text 90 degrees. Text rotation is achieved by using the Paragraph menu's ALIGNMENT dialog box.

> **Point** the mouse at Paragraph
> **Point** the mouse at ALIGNMENT
> **Click**

The third option in the dialog box is **Text Rotation.** This option has three settings — 90, 180, and 270 degrees — in addition to the default, which is no rotation. In this case, you want to rotate the text 90 degrees.

> **Point** the mouse at Text Rotation
> **Click**
> **Drag** to 90

Enter

⏎

The text is rotated 90 degrees and is printed sideways down the left column on the page.

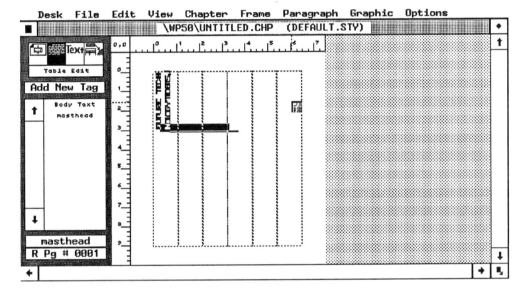

*Figure 8.8     Text rotated 90 degrees.*

However, the masthead is not aligned as you might have hoped. The text seems to be pushed into the upper part of the frame, which does not allow enough room to display the full length of the text. To see why the text is positioned as it is and how that position can be changed, you need to return to the Paragraph menu's ALIGNMENT dialog box. Recall that [Ctrl/x] causes Ventura to redisplay that last dialog box you used. Enter

**[Ctrl/x]**

The key to the location of the rotated text is found in the last line in the dialog box, **Maximum Rotated Height.** This setting is important for managing blocks of rotated text within documents that contain normal text. The setting limits the amount of vertical space used by a paragraph that is set for rotated text. The default value is 3". This means that when the text is rotated, it will print a line 3" in height from the beginning of the paragraph. If all of the text cannot fit on the first line, this setting creates a second line of text to the right of the first, and so on, until all of the text has been wrapped. In a sense, this setting performs a similar function to a right margin except that because the text is rotated 90 degrees, it is actually a top margin that happens to run along the right side of the page.

However, in this example, you have created an entire column, 10" in height, for the rotated text. To allow the text to flow into the entire height of the column, you must increase the maximum height from the default of 3" to the height of the column, which is 10". Enter

↓ (2 times)
**10** ↵

The text is now allowed to fill as much of the 10" column as it can, which means that both lines have enough room to display their full contents.

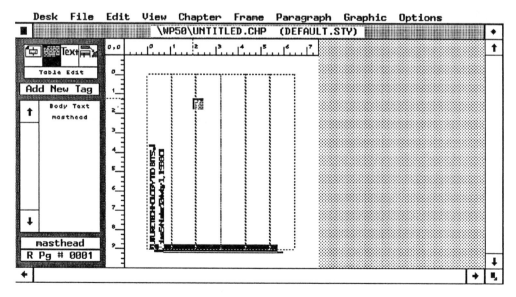

*Figure 8.9    Maximum rotated height increased.*

It is now clear the lines of text are not long enough to fill the entire column. It might look better if the text were centered between the top and the bottom margins. To make this adjustment, you would use the Horz. (horizontal) Alignment setting. This may seem odd until you realize that when you rotate the text 90 degrees, the horizontal and vertical axes are switched. Return to the ALIGNMENT dialog box by entering

**[Ctrl/x]**

Change the horizontal alignment to center.

```
Point the mouse at Horz. Alignment
Click
Drag to Center
```

Enter

↵

The text is now centered between the top and bottom margins.

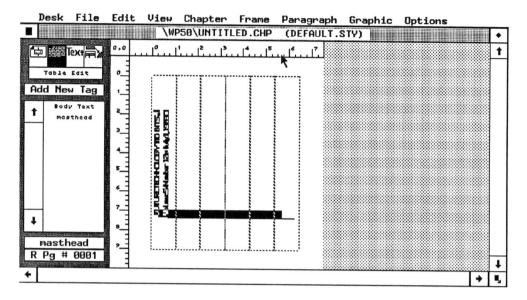

*Figure 8.10   Rotated text is centered between top and bottom margins.*

Recall that tabs were entered to separate items on the second line of the mast-head.  For those tabs to operate, you must set the correct tab locations just as if the text was being printed horizontally.  Set tab 1 at 2.5" and tab 2 at 5".

> **Point** the mouse at Paragraph
> **Point** the mouse at Tab Settings
> **Click**

Enter

**[Esc]**
**02.5**

Move to tab 2.

> **Point** the mouse at the → icon
> **Click**

Enter

**[Esc]**
05 ⏎

The text on line two of the masthead is separated by tab alignment.

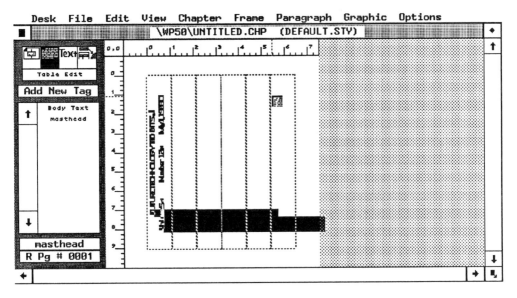

*Figure 8.11   Tab stops align rotated text.*

Note the highlight across the bottom of the page. Ventura highlights an area that represents the shape of the text if it were not rotated 90 degrees. The paragraph highlight is not rotated to match the paragraph text.

To complete the masthead, you can enhance the frame by drawing a ruling line around it and filling the frame with a shaded background. Begin with a frame ruling box. Turn on the Frame Setting mode by entering

**[Ctrl/u]**

Select the Frame menu's Ruling Box Around option.

```
Point the mouse at Frame
Point the mouse at Ruling Box Around
Click
```

Set the width to Frame-Width.

```
Point the mouse at Width
Click
Drag to Frame
```

Enter the thickness of the line.

↓
**[Esc]**
**.1**

In this case, create a broken or dashed line instead of a solid line.

```
Point the mouse at Dashes
Click
Drag to On
```

The model in the upper left corner of the dialog box shows the pattern of dashes that will be used to draw the ruling box. You can control the pattern of dashes by the Dash Width and Dash Spacing options. The default value is dashes that are .03" wide and separated by .03" of space. You can change the dash pattern by changing these values. Enter

↓ (7 times)
**[Esc]**
.05 ↓
.01 ↵

Ventura draws a ruling box consisting of a dashed line around the frame. Note that in the reduced mode, the resolution does not allow Ventura to display the dashed line clearly.

Complete the masthead by shading the frame background.

---

**Point** the mouse at Frame
**Point** the mouse at Frame Background
**Click**
**Point** the mouse at Pattern
**Click**
**Drag** to 2

---

Enter

↵

The completed masthead appears in Figure 8.12.

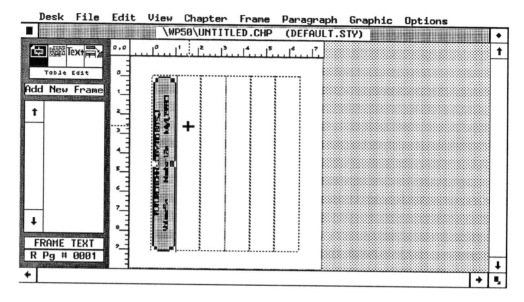

*Figure 8.12    Completed masthead rotated 90 degrees.*

## ADDING AN ARTICLE

The next step in the layout of the newsletter is to lay out the frames that will be used to contain the text of the articles. In this example, there are three articles. There are a number of ways to combine the frames on a page. For example, you might put two articles at the top of the page and one at the bottom, or perhaps the other way around.

In this case, you will begin by placing a frame at the top of the page. This will be the **lead article** in the newsletter because of its prominent position on the page. Place Ventura in the Frame Setting mode.

> **Point** the mouse at Add New Frame
> **Click**

Draw a frame with the upper left corner next to the masthead. The width should include the rest of the column, and the height should be about 4.5" as shown in Figure 8.13.

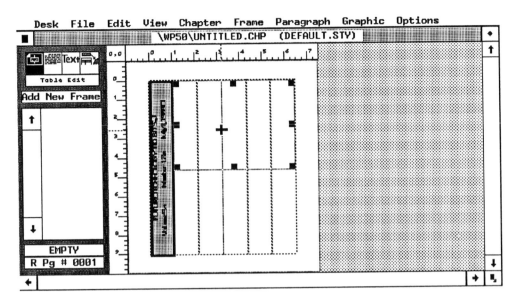

*Figure 8.13    Frame drawn for the lead article.*

Next, load the text files.

> **Point** the mouse at File
> **Point** the mouse at Load Text/Picture
> **Click**

Select the correct format for your word processor. In this example, WordPerfect 5.0 will be used.

> **Point** the mouse at WordPerfect 5
> **Click**

Select the Several option so you can load all three article files at once.

> **Point** the mouse at Several
> **Click**

Enter

↵

Select the three files you prepared for the newsletter.

> **Point** the mouse at JAVELIN.WP
> **Double Click**
> **Point** the mouse at OS2.WP
> **Double Click**
> **Point** the mouse at PLANNER.WP
> **Double Click**

Enter

↵

The lead article will be the OS/2 article. Select the new frame to receive the text, and then select OS2.WP from the side bar list.

> **Point** the mouse at the new frame
> **Click**
> **Point** the mouse at OS2.WP in the side bar display
> **Click**

The text of the OS/2 article fills the new frame. Note that the text is formatted in a single column with a width equal to the frame width. Keep in mind that the column setup you created was for the master frame only. Its purpose was to guide you in drawing the article frames. Once you have drawn the frame, you can determine the number of columns you want in each frame independently of the columns in the master frame or any of the other articles. Create two text columns within this frame.

> **Point** the mouse at Frame
> **Point** the mouse at Margins & Columns
> **Click**

Create two columns.

> **Point** the mouse at 2
> **Click**

Create a gutter between the columns by entering

↓ (2 times)
**[Esc]**
**.1**

Considering the location of the article, you will probably want to create margins on the left and the bottom to separate the text in this frame from the masthead (on the left) and the other articles that will be placed below it. Enter

↓ (2 times)
**[Esc]**
**.1** ↓
**[esc]**
**.1** ↵

The text is now formatted in two columns within the frame at the top of the page.

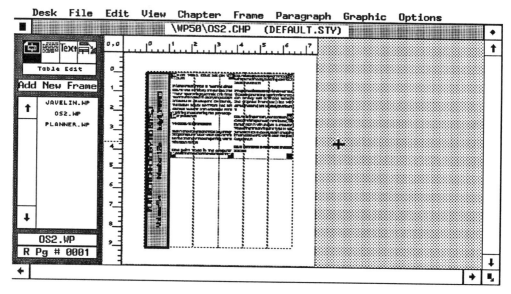

*Figure 8.14   Top article divided into two columns.*

## FORMATTING AN ARTICLE

With the text of the article inserted into the frame, you can now format the text. In this example, formatting consists of setting the style for the heading tags, HEADLINE and SUB HEAD, that will be used in the articles. Begin with the HEADLINE format. It will probably be easier to work in the normal display mode.

| |
|---|
| **Point** at the upper left corner of the OS2 frame |

Enter

**[Ctrl/n]**

Activate the Paragraph Tagging mode.  Enter

**[Ctrl/i]**

Select the headline paragraph.

> **Point** the mouse at "WHAT WILL"
> **Click**

Note that this paragraph is already tagged as HEADLINE because of the paragraph tag codes entered along with the text.  This saves you the time and effort of tagging the paragraphs after they have been loaded into Ventura.

**Exercise 2:**    Change the font of this paragraph to Swiss 18-point, bold.  Try this on your own.  The correct commands can be found under EX-2 at the end of this chapter.

## Column vs. Frame Width

The current headline text for the OS/2 article is formatted so that it fits into one of the columns within the frame as shown in Figure 8.15.

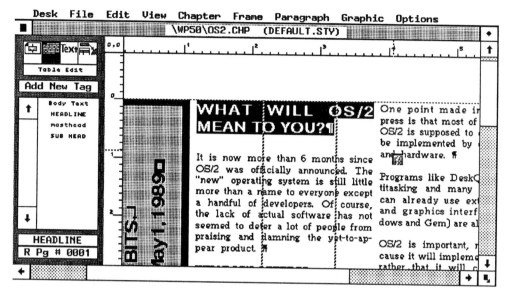

*Figure 8.15   Headline text wrapped in column.*

However, headlines often span across all the columns in an article. This effect can be achieved by altering the alignment characteristics of the tag to use the frame width rather than the column width as the factor that determines where the lines of text will be wrapped. Ventura's default setting for alignment width is Column-Width. For this example, change this tag to Frame-Width.

> **Point** the mouse at Paragraph
> **Point** the mouse at Alignment
> **Click**

The Overall Width setting controls line width.

> **Point** the mouse at Overall Width
> **Click**
> **Drag** to Frame-Wide

Enter

↵

The headline now flows across the top of the frame. Paragraphs formatted with frame width are formatted independently of any columns established within the frame. Note that you would probably only use this option for the first paragraph or paragraphs in a frame because a frame with paragraphs inserted between column-width paragraphs would create an odd looking layout.

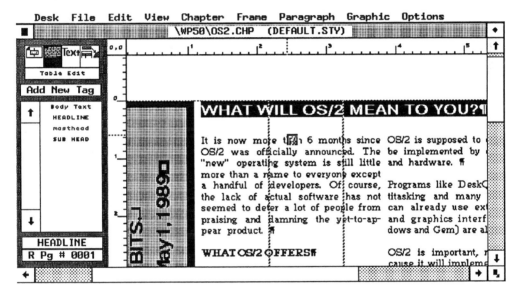

*Figure 8.16    Headline spreads across frame width.*

The next format is for the subheadings within the body of the article. Select a subheading paragraph.

> **Point** the mouse at OS/2 OFFERS
> **Click**

**Exercise 3:** Change the font to Swiss, 14-point bold. Try this on your own. The correct commands can be found under EX-3 at the end of the chapter.

You can enhance the column layout by inserting vertical lines between columns. Activate the Frame Setting mode. Enter

**[Ctrl/u]**

Select the Inter-Col. Rules option from the Frame menu's VERTICAL RULES dialog box.

---

**Point** the mouse at Frame
**Point** the mouse at Vertical Rules
**Click**
**Point** the mouse at Inter-Col. Rules
**Click**
**Drag** to On

---

Enter

⌐

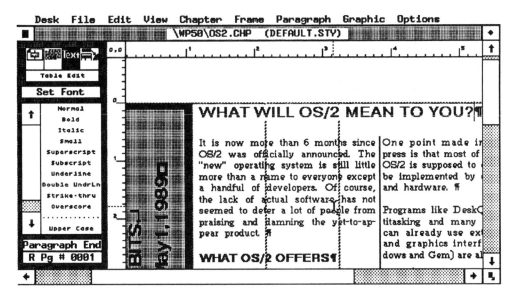

*Figure 8.17   Vertical lines added between columns.*

# ADDING OTHER ARTICLES

There are still two more articles to place on the first page of the newsletter.  Place Ventura in the reduced view mode.  Enter

**[Ctrl/r]**

You can divide the bottom of the screen between the two articles.  Activate the frame drawing mode.

> **Point** the mouse at Add New Frame
> **Click**

Draw a frame three columns wide in the lower left part of the page, as shown in Figure 8.18.

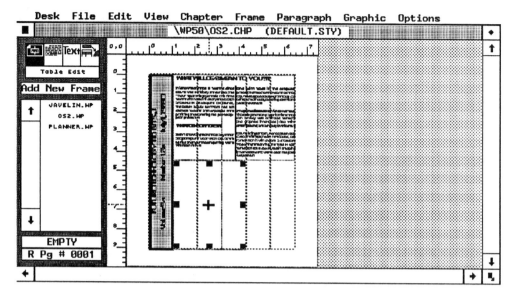

*Figure 8.18    Frame drawn in lower left part of the page.*

Insert the Javelin article into that frame.

---

**Point** the mouse at JAVELIN.WP
**Click**

---

This frame is filled with the text from the article.  The text is formatted into a single column with a width equal to the frame width.  Note that because the same paragraph tag names are used in each article, the headlines and subheadings are automatically formatted.

Add margins to this frame to separate the text from the surrounding frames.

---

**Point** the mouse at Frame
**Point** the mouse at Margins & Columns
**Click**

---

This frame has an overall width of 3.24". Enter margins of .1" for the top, left, and right sides of the frame. The bottom of the frame touches the bottom of the page, so no bottom margin is necessary. Enter

↓
**[Esc]**
**.1**
↓ (2 times)
**[Esc]**
**.1** ↓
**[Esc]**
**.1** ⏎

To separate this article from the one to its right, you can draw a vertical line down the right side of the frame. Ventura allows you to draw one or two vertical lines at specified locations within a frame. In this case, you want to draw a line on the right edge of the frame. Display the Frame menu's VERTICAL RULES dialog box.

> **Point** the mouse at Frame
> **Point** the mouse at Vertical Rules
> **Click**

In addition to the Inter-Col. Rules option you used previously, there are two additional rule line settings for specifying the location and width of the vertical ruling line.

This ruling line will be drawn down the entire vertical length of the frame. Keep in mind that the location value is the horizontal distance from the left edge of the page — not the frame.

In this case, you want to place the ruling line at the right edge of the current frame. You must calculate the correct location.

Recall that the master frame is divided into six 1.08"-wide columns. The current frame has its right edge aligned with the right edge of the fourth column in the master frame layout. The total width of the four columns is 1.08" × 4 = 4.32". Keep in mind that the page has a left margin of 1". If you add the left margin to the column widths, you arrive at 5.32". In placing a vertical rule, you need to select a horizontal position that is within the bounds of the selected frame. The right edge of the frame is at 5.32". The left edge is located one column past the margin at 2.08" (1" margin and a column width of 1.08"). Ventura will accept a position value that falls between those two values. Position values outside that range will fail to display a rule line because those locations would be outside the area of the selected frame.

Recall that you created a .1" right margin for this frame. If you subtract .05" from the edge location, 5.32", you will place the rule at 5.27" so that it will fall in the middle of that margin. Enter

**[Esc]**
**05.27** ↓

Set the width of the line to three points, .042". Enter

**[Esc]**
**.042** ⏎

Ventura draws the three-point line on the right side of current frame.

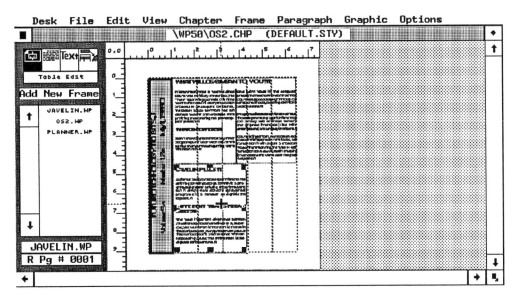

*Figure 8.19    Vertical ruling line positioned on right edge of frame.*

You will place the last article in the narrow column that remains in the lower right corner of the page.  Place Ventura into the frame drawing mode.

**Point** the mouse at Add New Frame
**Click**

Draw a frame that fills the remaining corner of the page, as shown in Figure 8.20.

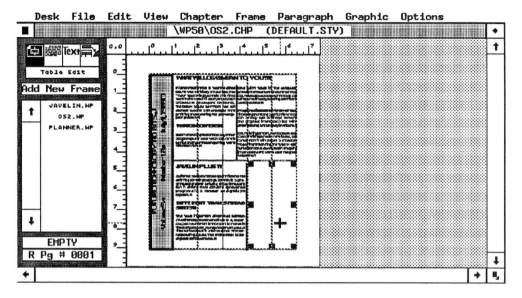

*Figure 8.20    Frame drawn for third article.*

Place the last text file, PLANNER.WP, into this frame.

---

**Point** the mouse at PLANNER.WP
**Click**

---

The text fills the selected frame.

> **Exercise 4:**    Add a top and left margin of .1" to the frame.  Try
> this on your own.  The correct commands can be
> found under EX-4 at the end of this chapter.

The first page of the newsletter should resemble Figure 8.21.

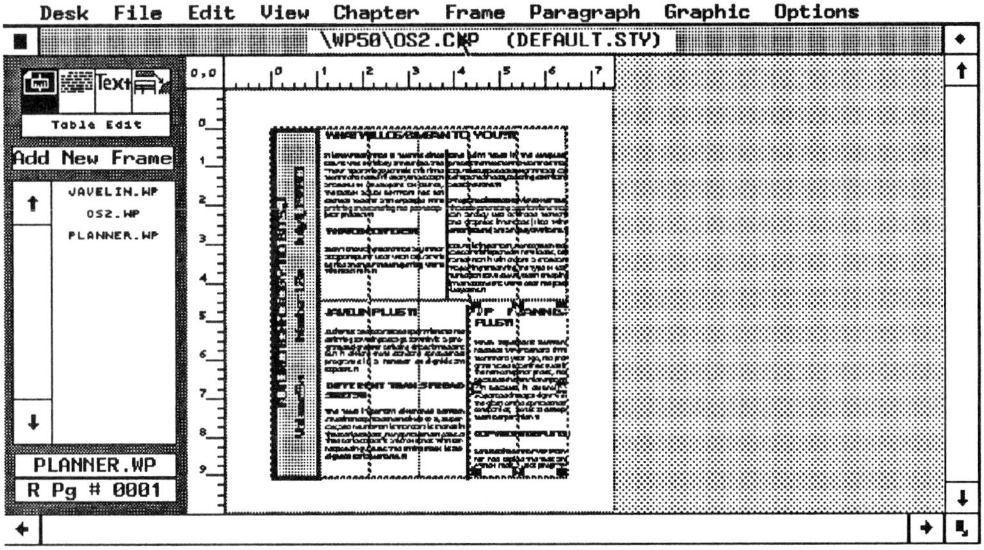

*Figure 8.21 First page of newsletter formatted.*

## DIVIDING A HEADING

The headline for the PLANNER.WP article is too long to fit on a single line. Ventura places the first two words on the top line and the third word on the next line. The headline might appear more balanced if only the first word, "VP," is on the top line and "PLANNER PLUS" appears on the second line.

This can be accomplished by inserting a line break character, [Ctrl/⏎], before the word PLANNER. Place Ventura into the Text Entry mode by entering

**[Ctrl/o]**

Position the text cursor in front of the letter "P" in the word "PLANNER."

> **Point** at "P" in "PLANNER"
> **Click**

Enter

**[Ctrl/⌐]**

The line break causes Ventura to display two words on the second line, creating a more balanced appearance. Inserting line breaks in headlines or headings often allows you to avoid awkward looking headline text.

## ADDING A SECOND PAGE

The layout so far has accommodated only part of each of the text files loaded into the frames because Ventura places in each frame only as much text as can fit. To display the full text of the documents, you will need to add more pages to the chapter and lay out additional frames on those pages.

You may have noticed that when text is added to frames other than the master frame, Ventura does not automatically create new pages for the text. In the multiple-page document in Chapter 6, the text file was inserted into the master frame, and Ventura automatically created as many pages as were needed for the text.

In this example, each text file was assigned to its own frame. Ventura displayed only the amount of text that would fit into the frames. The rest of the text will not appear until more frames appear, so you must add more pages to the chapter, using the Chapter menu's INSERT/REMOVE PAGE dialog box.

> **Point** the mouse at Chapter
> **Point** the mouse at Insert/Remove Page
> **Click**

Ventura displays the INSERT/REMOVE PAGE dialog box.

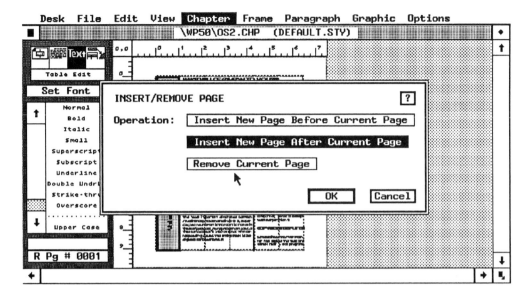

*Figure 8.22 INSERT/REMOVE PAGE dialog box.*

This dialog box allows you add a new page either before or after the current page. You can also remove a page. Be careful when removing pages because a page cannot be recalled once it has been removed. It is usually a good idea to save the document before you remove a page. In that case, if you make a mistake, you can abandon the change and reload the last saved copy of the chapter.

In this case, you want to add a new page following the current page. That option is the default setting and is already highlighted. Enter

⏎

Ventura displays a new blank page. When a blank page is added, it is considered an extension of the master frame, so the layout of the master frame repeats on the second page. You can see that the new page is divided into the same six-column layout as the first page of the document.

## REPEATING FRAMES

The second page of the newsletter begins as a blank page. In some cases, you might want to have one of the frames that you previously created repeat automatically on subsequent pages. For example, the masthead frame on page 1 could be repeated on each subsequent page of the newsletter.

Ventura allows you designate a frame as repeating on subsequent pages. This feature is useful for repeating logos, headlines, or graphics. Repeating frames work much like headers or footers. The advantage of a repeating frame is that the type of information repeated can be larger and more complex than can be inserted into the standard header or footer. Unlike headers or footers, repeating frames can contain several lines of text, with a variety of paragraph formatting and graphics.

In this example, you might want to repeat the masthead frame on each page. Return to page 1 by entering

**[PgUp]**

Select the masthead frame. Enter

**[Ctrl/u]**

> **Point** at the masthead frame
> **Click**

Display the REPEATING FRAME dialog box.

> **Point** the mouse at Frame
> **Point** the mouse at Repeating Frame
> **Click**

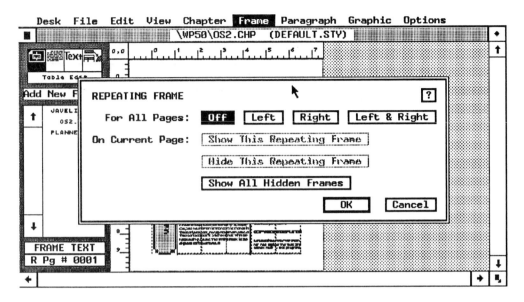

*Figure 8.23    REPEATING FRAME dialog box.*

The dialog box allows you to select repetition of a frame on left, right, or left and right pages.  Select **Left & Right**.

---

**Point** the mouse at Left & Right
**Click**

---

Enter

⏎

Display page 2 by entering

**[PgDn]**

The masthead frame appears on the second page. Note that Ventura automatically switches the location of the frame to the right edge of the page because page 2 is designated as a left page. If the document is eventually reproduced on both sides of the paper, this setting will cause the masthead to print on the same physical edge on both sides of the paper. If you are planning on reproducing the document on one side only, you should use the Chapter menu's PAGE SIZE & LAYOUT dialog box to select single-sided layout.

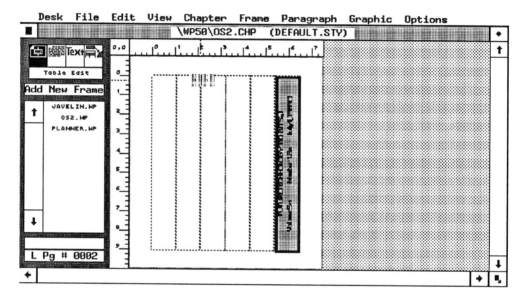

*Figure 8.24    Masthead repeated on page 2.*

## CONTINUING AN ARTICLE

Suppose you want to use the two left columns on this page to continue the OS2 article from the first page. All you need to do is to create a frame and then select the same text file from the list that was used on the previous page. Ventura will simply continue the text from where the last frame ended.

Ventura can flow text through as many different frames as you want until all of the text in the file appears. The end-of-file marker will appear when you have displayed all the text. Activate the frame drawing mode.

Point the mouse at Add New Frame
**Click**

Draw a frame that covers the left three columns and extends to the bottom of the page, as shown in Figure 8.25.

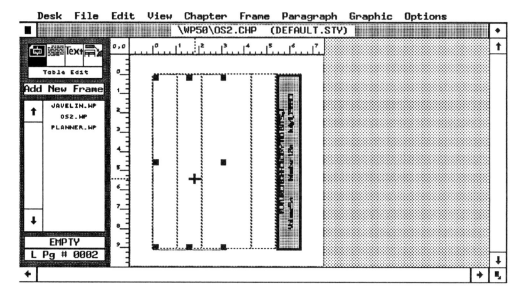

*Figure 8.25   Frame added to page 2.*

Insert the text from the OS2 document into this frame.

**Point** the mouse at OS2.WP
**Click**

This completes the OS/2 article.  You can tell that the text is complete because the end-of-file marker (a box) appears at the bottom of the text.  Create a .1" right margin for the frame.

---

**Point** the mouse at Frame
**Point** the mouse at Margins & Columns
**Click**

---

Enter

↓ (4 times)
**[Esc]**
**.1** ⏎

Add a vertical ruling line to the edge of the frame. Again, you must calculate. This frame's edge is the sum of three columns, 1.08" × 3 = 3.24, plus the 1" left margin = 4.24". Subtract .05" so that the line will fall in the right margin area, and you arrive at 4.19" as the location for the line. Draw a three-point (.042") line.

---

**Point** the mouse at Frame
**Point** the mouse at Vertical Rules
**Click**

---

Enter

**[Esc]**
**04.19** ↓
**.042** ⏎

The ruling line is drawn down the right edge of the frame.

## ADDING A FRAME CAPTION

You can use frame captions to identify the frame as the text from the OS2 article begun on page 1.

> **Point** the mouse at Frame
> **Point** the mouse at Anchors & Captions
> **Click**

Select a caption for above the frame.

> **Point** the mouse at Caption
> **Click**
> **Drag** to Above

You can now type in the caption. The text of the caption will tell the reader that this is the continuation of the OS2 story. To distinguish the caption from the text of the article, you can use the text attribute codes to display *italic* text. Enter

**<I> OS/2 from first page <D>** ⏎

The caption frame is added to the top of the frame you have drawn.

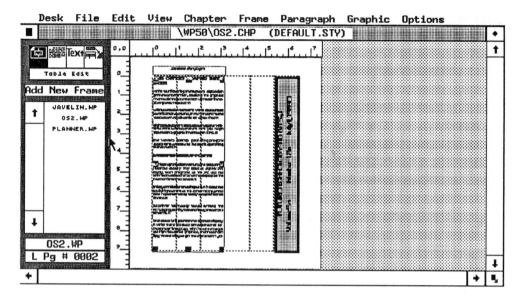

*Figure 8.26    Caption added to top of frame.*

Complete the second page by drawing a new frame over the remaining two columns and inserting the text from the JAVELIN.WP document into that frame. Place Ventura into the frame drawing mode.

---

**Point** the mouse at Add New Frame
**Click**

---

Draw a frame as shown in Figure 8.27.

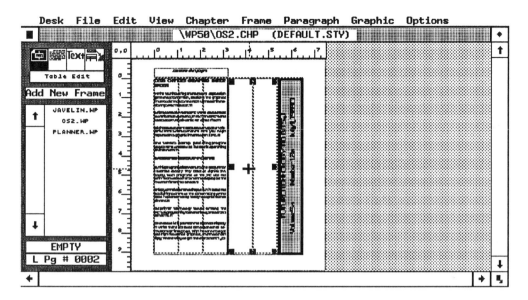

*Figure 8.27    New frame added to page 2.*

Insert more text from the JAVELIN.WP file.

---

**Point** the mouse at JAVELIN.WP
**Click**

---

Note that there is still more text for the Javelin article because the end-of-file marker has not appeared yet. Add the left and right margins and the caption for this frame.

---

**Point** the mouse at Frame
**Point** the mouse at Margins & Columns
**Click**

---

Enter

↓ (3 times)
**[Esc]**
**.1** ↓
**[Esc]**
**.1** ⏎

---

**Point** the mouse at Frame
**Point** the mouse at Anchors & Captions
**Click**
**Point** the mouse at Caption
**Click**
**Drag** to Above

---

Enter the text and format codes for the caption:

**<I>Javelin from first page<D>** ⏎

The completed second page should resemble Figure 8.28.

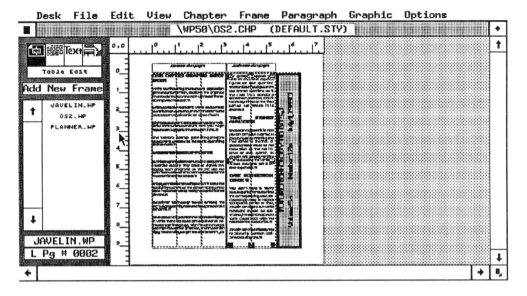

*Figure 8.28    Second page of newsletter complete.*

There is still more text to display, so you will need to add a third page to the newsletter.

---

**Point** the mouse at Chapter
**Point** the mouse at Insert/Remove Page
**Click**

---

Enter

⏎

To complete the layout, draw two new frames on the third page. The frames should divide the open area into two even rectangles, as shown in Figure 8.29.

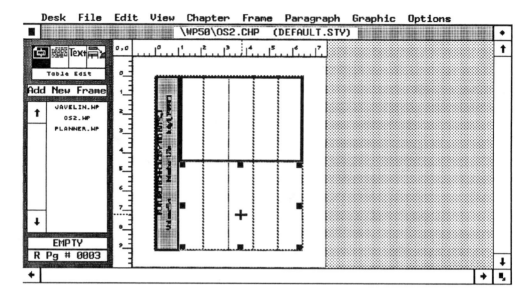

*Figure 8.29   Frames added to third page.*

Place the remainder of the PLANNER.WP text into the top frame.  Select that frame.

> **Point** at the top frame
> **Click**

**Exercise 5:**   Format the frame by creating two columns, a .1" gutter between the columns, and left and bottom margins of .1".  Try this on your own.  The correct commands can be found under EX-5 at the end of this chapter.

Create a caption for this frame.

> **Point** the mouse at Frame
> **Point** the mouse at Anchors & Captions
> **Click**
> **Point** the mouse at Caption
> **Click**
> **Drag** to Above

Enter

**< I > Vp Planner from first page < D >** ⏎

Place the text into the frame.

> **Point** the mouse at PLANNER.WP in the side bar
> **Click**

The top of the page now displays the remainder of the PLANNER.WP text.

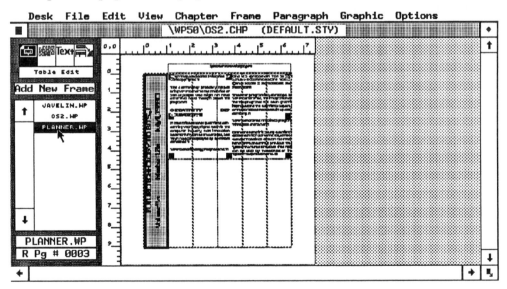

*Figure 8.30    Remainder of the PLANNER.WP file displayed.*

Select the frame on the bottom of the page.

```
Point at the bottom frame
Click
```

Exercise 6:    Format this frame exactly as you did the upper
frame on the page with the exception that only
a left margin will be needed. Try this on your
own. The correct commands can be found under
EX-6 at the end of this chapter.

Place the remaining text of the JAVELIN.WP file into the frame.

```
Point the mouse at JAVELIN.WP
Click
```

Note that when you created the caption for the bottom frame, it may have over-
lapped some of the text in the top frame. The bottom frame has only a small
amount of text, so you many need to reduce the bottom frame's size to make sure
that the end-of-file marker still appears in the top frame.

The completed final page of the newsletter should resemble Figure 8.31.

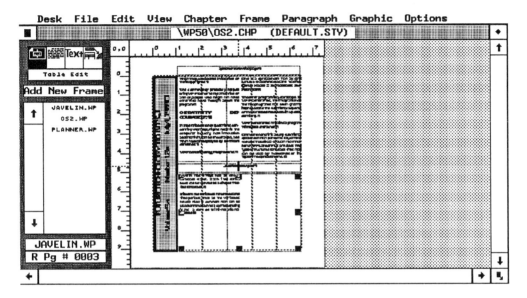

*Figure 8.31   Final page of the newsletter completed.*

## COLUMN BALANCING

When you are formatting the final frame of an article, you may notice that the columns do not fill the entire frame. The column on the left is full, but the column on the right is not. Ventura has an option called Column Balancing that attempts to make the columns all the same length if the text does not fill the entire frame.

Column balancing is handy for two reasons: First, it improves the appearance of column text when part of the column is left blank. Second, after the columns have been balanced, you can use the text as a guide to shortening the frame to eliminate the unneeded space.

To select balanced columns, you need to display the SIZING & SCALING dialog box.

---

**Point** the mouse at Frame
**Point** the mouse at Frame Typography
**Click**

---

The third item in the dialog box is **Column Balance**. Select balanced columns.

---

**Point** the mouse at Column Balance
**Click**
**Drag** to On

---

Enter

⏎

The text is balanced between the two columns.

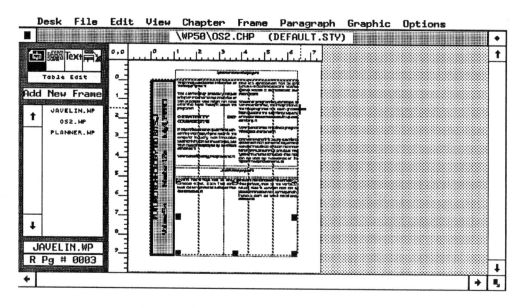

*Figure 8.32    Text balanced between columns.*

You might be wondering about the default setting, On, listed for the options on the Frame menu's TYPOGRAPHY dialog box. In Ventura there are three levels of settings — chapter, frame, and paragraph — for many of the options available. Of the three levels of operations, chapter and frame settings tend to be related to one another while paragraph settings are usually related to line and paragraph issues.

For example, consider column balancing. The chapter level setting is the one that determines the default setting for column balance whenever a new frame is added to the chapter. The frame level setting is used to set the balance for a specific frame.

If you want to change the column balance setting, you must decide if that change is to be made for all the frames in the chapter or just for specific frames. If you want to change the setting for all the frames, you use the Chapter menu's Typography option. If the change is to be made only for the currently selected frame, you would use the Frame menu's Typography option.

## SAVING AND PRINTING

Before you print, you should save the work you have done so far. First, save the style sheet under a new name.

---

**Point** the mouse at File
**Point** the mouse at Save as New Style
**Click**

---

Enter

**newslrt** ⏎

Ventura will automatically use the first document filename as the chapter name, which would make this chapter OS2.CHP. To change the name, use the File menu's Save As option.

> **Point** the mouse at File
> **Point** the mouse at Save As
> **Click**

Enter

**newsltr** ↵

You can print the chapter if you want.

> **Point** the mouse at File
> **Point** the mouse at To Print
> **Click**

To print all of the pages, change the Which Pages setting to All.

> **Point** the mouse at Which Pages
> **Click**
> **Drag** to All

Enter

↵

# SUMMARY

- **Newsletter Formats**. Creating newsletters involves variations on the basic techniques used in multiple-page and multiple-frame documents. Newsletters do not place any text directly into the master frame. Instead, the text is placed into a series of frames, which are then placed onto the master frame. The master frame helps you line up the columns correctly. The master frame is formatted for a column layout. The column snap feature ensures that frames placed on top of the master frame will line up correctly. Each frame placed on top of the master frame is used to display text from one of the articles in the newsletter.

- **Multiple-Frame Documents**. When a text file is displayed in a frame other than the master frame, Ventura shows only as much text as will fit into the frame. You can display the rest of the text from that file at another point in the chapter by adding a frame and selecting the same text file from the list of files in the side bar display. The process can be continued until the entire text is displayed in a series of frames.

- **Insert Page**. When text is added to frames other than the master frame, Ventura will not automatically add new pages to accommodate the document. In such cases, you must manually create additional pages by using the Insert/Remove Page command.

- **Alignment Width**. When frames are divided into columns, you can display a line that runs along the width of the frame rather than the width of the column by changing the overall width setting in the Alignment menu.

- **Rotated Text**. Ventura allows you to create paragraph formats in which the text is rotated 90, 180, or 270 degrees. The height of the rotated text is controlled by the Rotated Text Maximum Height setting.

- **Repeating Frames**. One or more frames can be designated as repeating frames, which can be used like a header or footer. The selected frame or frames will appear at the same position and with the same contents on all pages. If the Left & Right pages option is selected, Ventura will shift the location of the frames to match left or right pages. You can suppress a frame from being displayed on individual pages by using the Suppress Frame option in the REPEATING FRAME dialog box.

- **Column Balance**. If text in a multiple-column frame does not fill all columns equally, turning on column balance will cause Ventura to distribute the text to even lengths in all columns.

## Answers to Exercises

**EX-1 (see p. 524):** Create a new style sheet for the newsletter.

> **Point** the mouse at File
> **Point** the mouse at Load Diff.  Style
> **Click**
> **Point** the mouse at DEFAULT.STY
> **Double Click**

**EX-2 (see p. 545):** Change the font of the HEADLINE tag to Swiss, 18-point bold.

> **Point** the mouse at Paragraph
> **Point** the mouse at Font
> **Click**
> **Point** the mouse at Swiss
> **Click**
> **Point** the mouse at 18
> **Click**

Enter

⏎

**EX-3 (see p. 548):** Change the font of the SUB HEAD tag to Swiss, 14-point bold.

> **Point** the mouse at Paragraph
> **Point** the mouse at Font
> **Click**
> **Point** the mouse at Swiss
> **Click**
> **Point** the mouse at 14
> **Click**

**EX-4 (see p. 554):**  Add a top and left margin of .1" to the frame.

```
Point the mouse at Frame
Point the mouse at Margins & Columns
Click
```

Enter

↓
**.1**
↓ (2 times)
**.1** ↵

**EX-5 (see p. 568):**  Format the frame by creating two columns, a .1" gutter between the columns, and left and bottom margins of .1".

```
Point the mouse at Frame
Point the mouse at Margins & Columns
Click
Point the mouse at 2
Click
```

Enter

↓  (2 times)
**[Esc]**
**.1**
↓ (2 times)
**[Esc]**
**.1** ↓
**[Esc]**
**.1** ↵

**EX-6 (see p. 570):** Format the frame at the bottom of the page as you did the upper frame, but only include a left margin this time.

---

**Point** the mouse at Frame
**Point** the mouse at Margins & Columns
**Click**
**Point** the mouse at 2
**Click**

---

Enter

↓ (2 times)
**[Esc]**
**.1**
↓ (3 times)
**[Esc]**
**.1** ⏎

---

**Point** the mouse at Frame
**Point** the mouse at Anchors & Captions
**Click**
**Point** the mouse at Caption
**Click**
**Drag** to Above

---

Enter

**< I > Javelin from page 2 < D >** ⏎

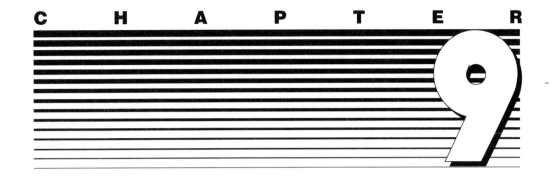

# THE VENTURA PROFESSIONAL EXTENSION

Version 2.0 of Ventura is sold in two forms. The standard Ventura 2.0 program contains all of the features discussed in Chapters 1-8. The Professional extension contains additional features that are not included in the standard program. This chapter will focus on four additional typesetting features included in the Professional Extension version of Ventura 2.0.

- **Tables**. The Professional Extension edition contains special commands that create and format information tables. This makes it much easier to prepare documents that contain tables with columns and rows.

- **Equations**. The standard edition of Ventura 2.0 contains a fraction formatting function, which is discussed in Chapter 7. In the Professional Extension edition, this feature is expanded to cover creation of mathematical equations of all types and complexities.

- **Vertical Justification**. This feature is used to create text columns in which the text is aligned flush with the tops and bottoms of columns and pages.

- **Cross-References**. The Professional Extension edition allows you to create document cross-references. This feature is useful in large documents in which references are made to specific information, tables, or figures located on different pages. It allows Ventura to automatically update references with accurate page numbers.

In addition to these features, the Professional Extension edition provides support for EMS expanded memory. If you have this type of additional memory installed in your computer, the Professional Extension edition will use expanded memory to allow for longer documents and/or the loading of a hyphenation dictionary into memory to support dictionary hyphenation of words. The dictionary feature requires 1.2 megabytes of EMS expanded memory.

Note that many AT computers have 640K of conventional memory and 384K of extended memory. **Extended** memory is not the same as EMS or **expanded** memory. Ventura cannot use extended memory for implementation of these features.

# TABLES

Many documents require table information that consists of rows and columns. The Professional Extension edition of Ventura contains numerous commands for creating tables of all types with a minimum of effort.

Load Ventura in the usual manner. If you have been working through this book, the six-column format used in Chapter 8's newsletter document is displayed as part of the NEWSLTR style sheet. Create a new style sheet called TABLE for table operations.

---

**Point** the mouse at File
**Point** the mouse at Load Diff. Style
**Click**
**Point** the mouse at DEFAULT.STY
**Double Click**

---

Create the new style sheet by saving this style sheet under a new name.

---

**Point** the mouse at File
**Point** the mouse at Save As New Style
**Click**

---

Enter

**table** ↵

The document you are about to prepare is a table for a cook book that details how certain spices can be used with certain foods.

Place Ventura into the Text Entry mode. Enter

**[Ctrl/o]**

Create a text document in the master frame.

> **Point** at the upper left corner of the column guides
> **Click**

This causes Ventura to create a text file. Note that **End of File** should appear above the page number in the side bar. Change to the normal display mode. Enter

**[Ctrl/n]**

Enter the following text.

**COOKING WITH HERBS AND SPICES** ⏎
**Today, herbs and spices cost mere pennies, so there's no reason not to try all of them. The chart below shows you how to use the most popular herbs.** ⏎

Next you will want to create the table into which your data will be placed. If you are using the Professional Extension edition, note that below the four mode icons in the side bar display is a box that contains the words **Table Edit**. This box represents a fifth operation mode for Ventura called the Table Edit mode. In this mode, it is possible to create, revise, expand, or contract a Ventura table layout. Enter the Table Edit mode.

> **Point** the mouse at Table Edit
> **Click**

As with the other four operational modes, the selection of Table Edit causes Ventura to change the information displayed in the side bar. This time, the options listed in the side bar refer specifically to table operations.

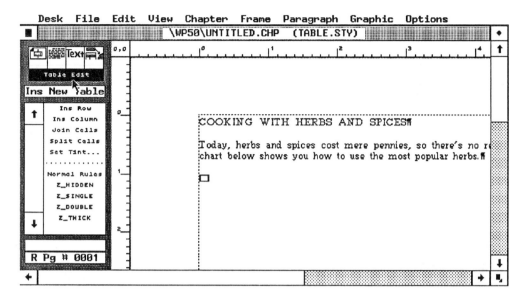

*Figure 9.1    Table Edit mode side bar display.*

The first step in table operations is to create a new table. Tables are treated differently from paragraphs. They can be inserted into any document that contains an end-of-file marker. To create a new table, you must first indicate where in the document you want to insert the table by pointing and clicking the mouse at a paragraph or at the blank space above the paragraph where you want the table inserted. For example, if you wanted to place the table between "COOKING WITH..." and "Today, herbs..." you would point at "Today" and click.

---

**Point** the mouse at Today
**Click**

---

Ventura draws a gray line above the paragraph.

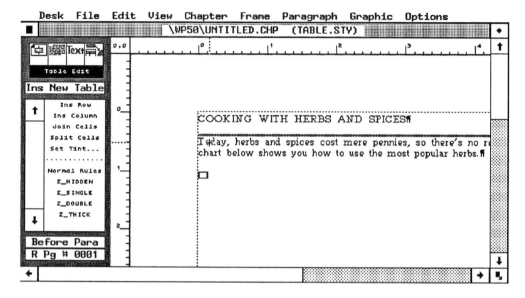

*Figure 9.2    Gray line indicates table placement.*

The gray line shows the location in which the table will be inserted. In this case, you want to insert the table below that paragraph. To move the gray line to the area following the paragraph, you need to point and click on the end-of-file symbol because there are no more paragraphs in the document.

---

**Point** the mouse at end-of-file symbol
**Click**

---

Note that the gray line now appears above the end-of-file symbol. The line is drawn only as wide as the paragraph, which, in this case, is the end-of-file symbol. The size of the line is not important and will have no effect on the size of the table. The only function of the gray line is to indicate the vertical location in which the table will be inserted.

To create the table at the selected position, select the Ins New Table box found in the side bar.

> **Point** the mouse at Ins New Table
> **Click**

Ventura displays the INSERT/EDIT TABLE dialog box.

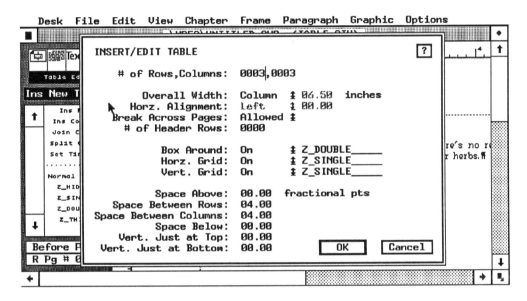

*Figure 9.3    INSERT/EDIT TABLE dialog box.*

This dialog box is used to specify the general layout of the table. The most important setting on this display is the **# of Rows, Columns** option, which determines the number of rows and columns that will be created for the table. Note that once a table is created, you can add or remove rows and columns at any time. The default setting for rows and columns is 3, meaning that the default table contains nine boxes arranged in three rows and three columns.

In the example table you are about to create, you will need to change that basic layout to five rows and four columns. Enter

5 ↓
4

The next section in the dialog box contains settings that affect the table as a whole.

- **Overall Width** and **Horz. Alignment**. The default layout for a table is to use the entire column width for the table. In this case, the master frame has a single column that is 6.5" wide. If you select custom width, you can enter a value for the width of the table and also enter a value for placement of the table relative to the left edge of the current column.

- **Break Across Pages** and **# of Header Rows**. These options determine how Ventura handles tables that are too long to fit on one page. If **Allowed** is selected, then the table is broken and continued on the next page. If not, the entire table is moved to the next page. When Allowed is selected, you can specify header rows. The header row or rows are automatically added to the continuation of a table when it is divided by a page break, so the table will always have column headings no matter how many pages it spans.

The next section of the dialog box refers to the drawing of ruling lines around the table and between the rows and columns. The default is to draw a double line around the entire table with a grid of single lines between each row and column.

To draw the table, enter

↵

Ventura draws the table with the specified number of rows and columns at the selected location.

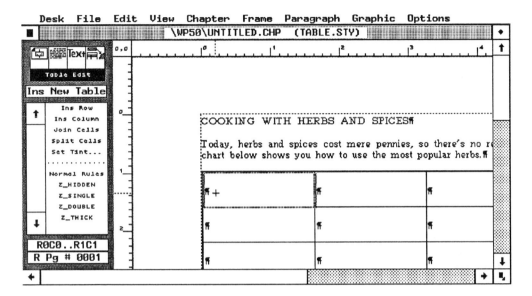

*Figure 9.4    Table layout created.*

To see the entire table, switch to the reduced view.  Enter

**[Ctrl/r]**

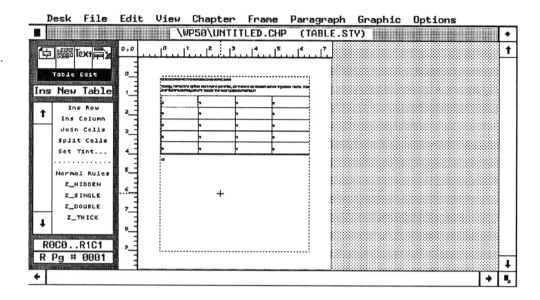

*Figure 9.5    Table layout in reduced view.*

Note that the table displays a paragraph-end symbol inside each of its **cells** (or **boxes**), which indicates that you can enter text into each of the cells. Ventura automatically creates three new tags when a table is created.

- **Table Text**. This tag is automatically assigned to all paragraphs inserted into the cells. The tag is given the same settings as the Body Text tag in the current style sheet. You can alter the format of Table Text or create or apply other style tags to vary the formatting of the cells. Note that different cells within a single table can have different formats as well.

- **Z_SINGLE**. This tag is used to create the format used to draw the single lines within the table.

- **Z_DOUBLE**. This tag is used to create the format used to draw the double lines within the table.

## Location Guides

When you are working in the Table Edit mode, Ventura uses a very different method of indicating selected text. Enlarge the display.

---

**Point** at the upper left corner of the table
**Click**

---

Enter


[Ctrl/n]


In the normal display mode, you can see that the first cell is outlined in gray, which indicates that this cell is **selected** in the same way that the white-on-black highlight indicates selection in the Text Entry or Paragraph Tagging modes. In addition, the location of the selection is indicated in the side bar, in the box above the page number. In this case, that box reads **R0C0..R1C1**. This notation is used to describe in row and column terms the area of the table that is selected.

Ventura does not number the table in terms of cells as spreadsheet programs do. Instead, it counts by the lines in the row and column grid. The top border of the table is R0 — row zero. The left-most edge of the table is C0 — column 0. The point at which these two lines intersect is called R0C0.

When the first cell in the table is selected, Ventura displays **R0C0..R1C1**. The location describes the upper left and lower right corners of the cell.


## Entering Text

Once a table is created, you can enter text into the cells. Place Ventura into the Text Editing mode. Enter


[Ctrl/o]

> **Point** inside the upper left cell
> **Click**

Entering text within a table is the same as entering text in normal paragraph. The only difference is that entering a return has no effect. Ventura assumes that each cell can contain only one paragraph. The paragraph end is already entered into the cell. Additional returns will be ignored. If you need to create a new line within a cell, you can use the [Ctrl/↵], line break, command.

You can move from cell to cell in the table by using the arrow keys or by clicking the mouse to change the location of the text cursor.

Before you begin entering text, change the display so that you can see the entire table. Remove the side bar by entering

**[Ctrl/w]**

Use the scroll bars to position the table as shown in Figure 9.6.

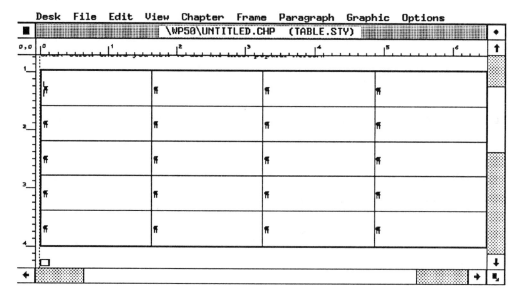

*Figure 9.6    Full table displayed in normal view mode.*

Enter

**Type of Food →**
**Basil →**
**Marjoram →**
**Oregano ↓**
← (3 Times)

Begin entering the next row of data.

**BEEF →**
**Stew or goulash: Add 1 teaspoon per 6 servings.**

Note that as you added text, Ventura automatically wrapped the lines and enlarged the height of the row to fit the expanded text entry. This is one of the major advantages of table operations; Ventura will ensure that all entries fit into the cells in which they are typed by adjusting the row heights automatically (see Figure 9.7).

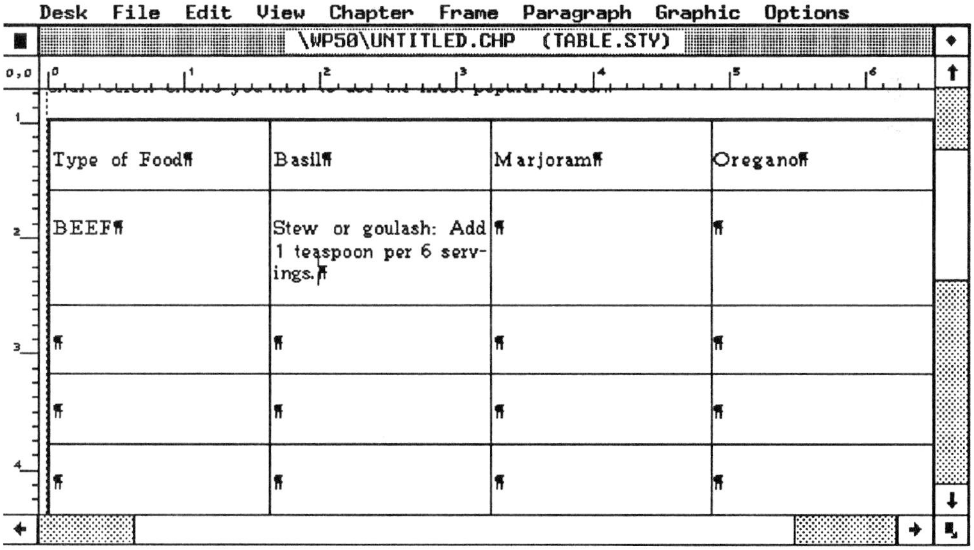

*Figure 9.7    Row height adjusted as text is entered.*

Enter the next type of food. This time, you will use a [Ctrl/⌐] to create a line break within a cell. Enter

↓
←
**PORK →**
**Scallopini: [Ctrl/⌐]**
**Crush a generous pinch and stir into tomato sauce.**

You can use any of Ventura's normal text formatting operations, such as bold, italic, underline, or font changes when entering text. You can even use special items such as fractions. Enter

→
**Roasts: [Ctrl/⌐]**
**Add [Space bar]**

In this case, you want to insert a fraction for half a tablespoon. You can perform the fraction operation in both editions of Ventura 2.0. In the Professional Extension edition, the screen display will be a bit different from the one in the regular version because fraction entry is integrated with the more complex operations of the equation editor. Activate the special item entry menu by entering

**[Ctrl/c]**

The special item menu appears, listing the special items that can be inserted into the text.

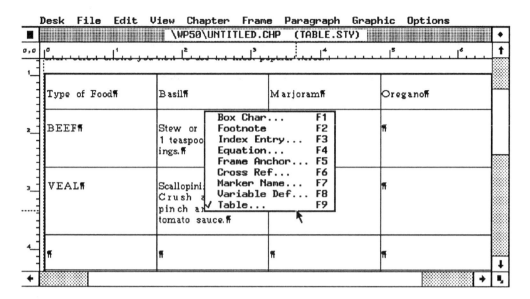

*Figure 9.8    Special item entry box.*

To create a fraction, select **Equation** by entering

**[F4]**

When you select the Equation option, Ventura clears the screen and displays a special screen for creating equations. The Professional Extension edition considers fractions a form of equation. Enter the characters for the fraction.

1/2

Shortly after you enter the characters, Ventura displays the fraction that will appear in the document.

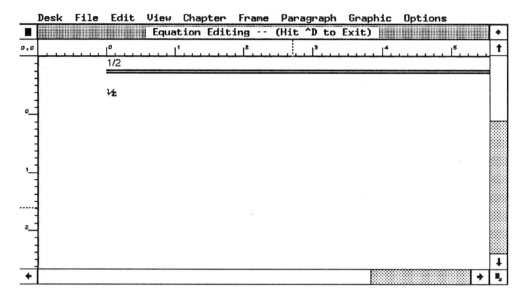

*Figure 9.9    Fraction displayed in equation display.*

When you have created the fraction, you will want to return to the document window by entering

**[Ctrl/d]**

The fraction is inserted into the text at the current cursor position. Continue entering the text. Note that you must move the cursor past the fraction to continue entry on that line. Enter

→
**[Space bar]**
**teaspoon to**
**[Space bar]**

Add another fraction — this time 2/3.  Enter

**[Ctrl/c]**
**[F4]**
**2/3**
**[Ctrl/d]**

There are now two fractions inserted into the text.

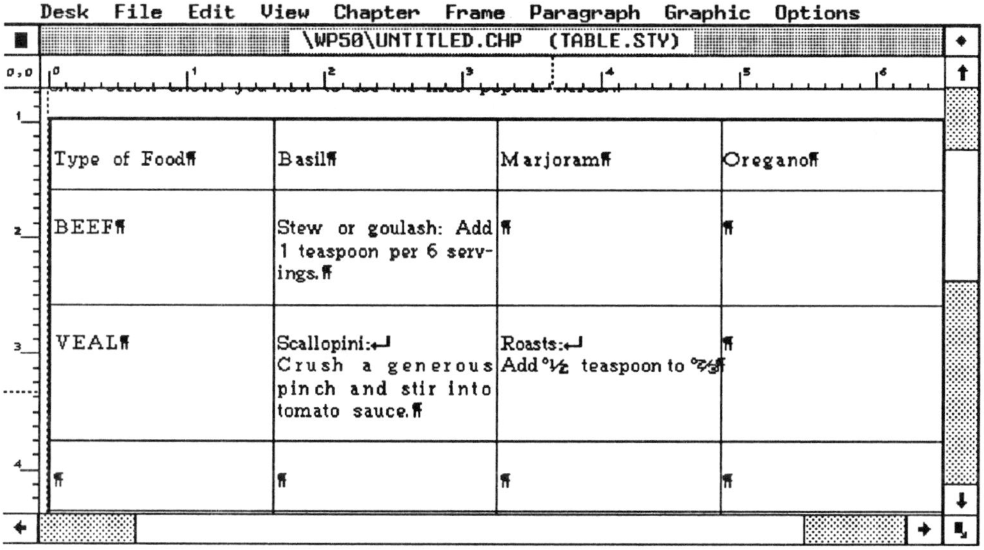

*Figure 9.10   Fractions added to document.*

Complete the item by entering

→
**[Space bar]**
**cup of flour and coat meat before roasting.**

## Changing Table Column Widths

You can adjust the widths of the columns by dragging the mouse with the [Alt] key held down. This [Alt/Drag] method is the same one used to position images within a graphics frame.

In this table, the first column contains only single words, such as "BEEF" and "VEAL." It does not need to be as wide as the other columns. To change the column width, return to the Table Edit mode. You must display the side bar to do so because there is no keystroke shortcut for the Table Edit mode. Enter

**[Ctrl/w]**

---

**Point** the mouse at Table Edit
**Click**

---

To change a column width, you must point and then [Alt/Drag] the vertical line that makes up the right edge of the column of cells. To change the width of the first column, you need to drag the line that runs between "Type of Food" and "Basil."

---

**Point** at line between "Type of Food" and "Basil"
**Hold down** the Alt key and mouse button
**[Alt/Drag]** to the left

---

As you drag, the mouse cursor will change to a four-directional arrow, and a shadow line will follow the mouse cursor to the left, as in Figure 9.11. The shadow line indicates the new location of the column edge.

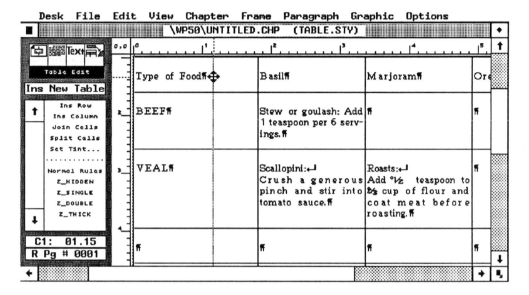

*Figure 9.11   Dragging column width.*

Continue dragging the line until it is about 1" from the edge of the master frame; then release the mouse button. Ventura will redraw the column to its new width. The three columns that were not manually altered will automatically adjust and evenly divide the additional space.

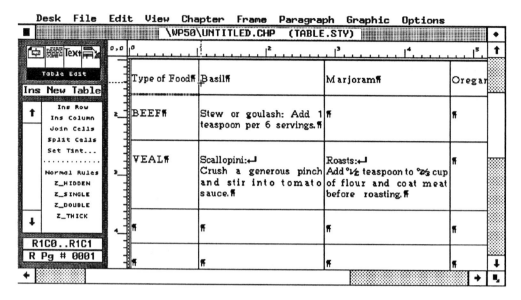

*Figure 9.12   First column reduced in width.*

## Rotating Text

Ventura permits you to create table items with rotated text.  Change to the Paragraph Tagging mode.  Enter

**[Ctrl/i]**

Select the "BEEF" cell.

> **Point** the mouse at "BEEF"
> **Click**

Create a new tag for this cell.

> **Point** the mouse at Add New Tag
> **Click**

Enter the new tag name:

**Food** ⌐

To rotate the text, use the ALIGNMENT dialog box.

> **Point** the mouse at Paragraph
> **Point** the mouse at Alignment
> **Click**

Change the rotation to 90 degrees.

> **Point** the mouse at Text Rotation
> **Click**
> **Drag** to 90

Before you return to the document, you will want to adjust the maximum height for the rotated text. The default value is 3". This would cause Ventura to increase the cell height to 3". Change it to 1". Enter

↓ ( 2 times)
**[Esc]**
**01** ⌐

The text is rotated inside the cell. Assign this format to another cell.

> **Point** the mouse at "VEAL"
> **Click**
> **Point** the mouse at Food
> **Click**

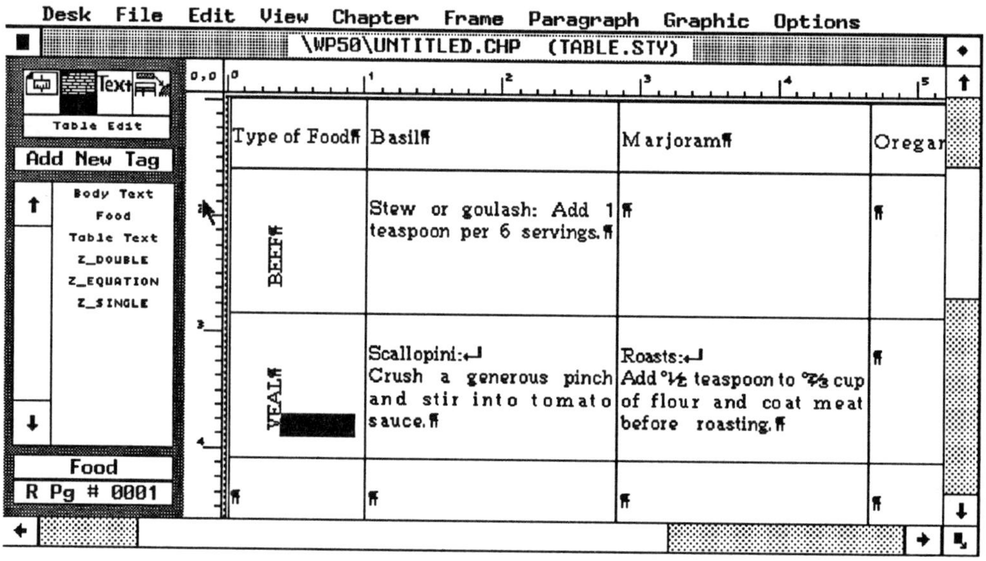

*Figure 9.13   Rotated text added to table.*

## Joining and Splitting Cells

Ventura's Table Edit mode also allows you to join two or more cells into one. The reason for performing this operation is to create a table in which some cells are larger than others. In the current example, the cell under "Marjoram" and next to "BEEF" is empty. The cell below it contains instructions on roasting veal with marjoram. It is possible that the same recipe would apply to both veal and beef. Instead of duplicating the text, you could join the two cells so the table layout would indicate that the same data applies to both items.

Activate the Table Edit mode.

> **Point** the mouse at Table Edit
> **Click**

You need to select the cells you want to join by pointing at the upper left corner of the first cell and dragging to the lower right corner of last cell to be joined.

Drag the mouse so that you highlight the cells shown in Figure 9.14. The location range in the side bar should show **R1C2..R3C3**.

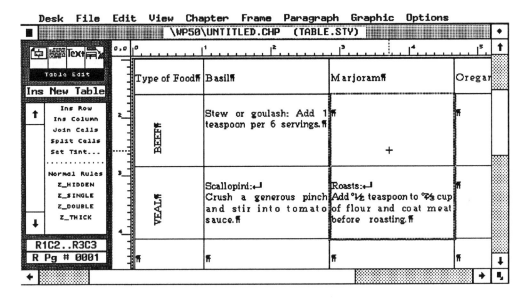

*Figure 9.14    Cells selected for joining.*

Join the cells by selecting the **Join Cells** option in the side bar.

> **Point** the mouse at Join Cells
> **Click**

The line between the cells is removed and both cells appear as an expanded cell, but something happened to the text.

When cells are joined, the text in the upper left cell is displayed in the joined cell. In this case, the upper left cell was empty, so the joined cells appear as empty. Note that the text that was in the lower cell is not erased, simply hidden. You can recall the text by splitting the cells back into their original form.

> **Point** the mouse at Split Cells
> **Click**

The cells return to the original layout. To have the text of both cells displayed when you join them, you must move the text of the lower cell into the top cell. Change to the Text Entry mode. Enter

**[Ctrl/o]**

> **Drag** the mouse from "Roasts" to "roasting."
> **Click**

Enter

**[Del]**

> **Point** the mouse at the upper left cell
> **Click**

Enter

**[Ins]**

You can now join the cells the way you had intended.

```
Point the mouse at Table Edit
Click
```

Select the two cells again as shown in Figure 9.14.

```
Point the mouse at Join Cells
Click
```

The cells are joined, and the text from both cells appears in the joined cell.

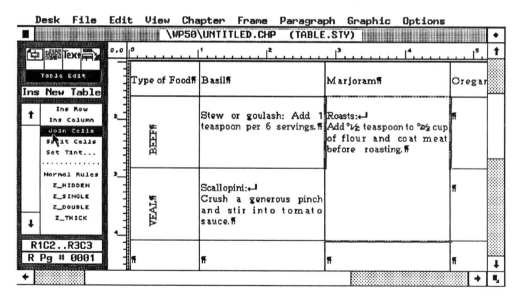

*Figure 9.15    Cells joined.*

## Shading Cells

Ventura allows you to select a shaded background for one or more cells in the table by using the **Set Tint** side bar option. As with the other cell operations, you must first select a cell. The joined cell is already selected, so you can place a shaded background in this cell.

> **Point** the mouse at Set Tint
> **Click**

Ventura displays a dialog box similar to the one used for frame backgrounds. Create a shaded background.

> **Point** the mouse at Color
> **Click**
> **Drag** to Black
> **Point** the mouse at Pattern
> **Click**
> **Drag** to 2

Enter

⏎

The selected cells now appear with a shaded background. Place Ventura into the reduced view mode by entering

**[Ctrl/r]**

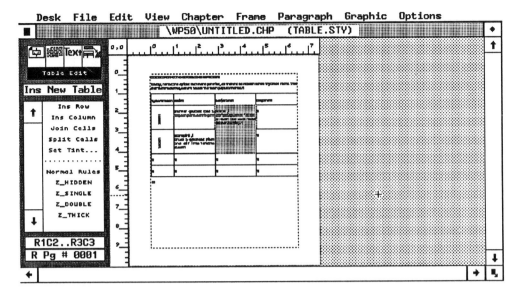

*Figure 9.16  Background shading added to cells.*

Save the chapter by entering

**[Ctrl/s]**
**table** ⏎

## Dialog Box Revisions

In addition to the techniques discussed in the previous section for altering an existing table, you can perform many operations through dialog boxes. Entering [Ctrl/d] will display the INSERT/EDIT dialog box in which you can change any of the settings you originally selected for the table.

To change a column width, you can call up the dialog box shown in Figure 9.17 by entering [Ctrl/c]. You can set the width of any of the columns by changing the number in the column number box to the column that you want to affect. The Width Setting option has two choices. The default is a variable-width column, which means that the column width will be calculated by evenly dividing the available space by the number of columns. This means that if you insert, delete, or change the width of columns, the variable width columns will adjust to the changes. A fixed width column will maintain an exact width no matter what insertions or deletions are made in the table.

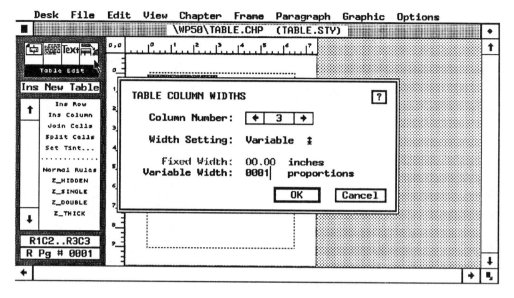

*Figure 9.17   TABLE COLUMN WIDTHS dialog box.*

## Text Editing for Tables

The previous section described how a table can be created and edited in Ventura's Professional Extension edition. However, as with other types of documents there are advantages in being able to specify the formatting in the text file. It is possible to create a column layout within a text file so that when it is loaded into Ventura, it will automatically be formatted into a table. Note that tables created in this way can still be edited in Ventura, using the procedures discussed earlier in this chapter.

Experienced users may find that preparing a table in a text file may be faster than entering table text in the Ventura document window.

In addition, many applications such as databases (e.g., dBASE III and dBASE IV) and spreadsheets (Excel but not Lotus 1-2-3), can convert data into text files. You can create Ventura tables from these files by adding table specifications.

How would you create a table layout in a text file? The first decision you need to make is the number of columns in the table. In the text format, it is not necessary to decide the number of rows in advance. That will be determined by the text, if you add any. Suppose that you wanted to create a four-column table within a text document. You would begin with the **@Z_TBL_BEG** — table begin — code.

The following code is used to begin a table using the default values that would be entered if you created the table in Ventura.

**@Z_TBL_BEG = COLUMNS(4), DIMENSION(IN), HGUTTER(.056), VGUT-**
**TER(.056), BOX(Z_DOUBLE), HGRID(Z_SINGLE), VGRID(Z_SINGLE),**
**KEEP(OFF)**

Note that when you enter this command it should be typed as a single paragraph with a return following only the last item, **KEEP(OFF)**. The tag requires the following eight parameters:

- **COLUMNS(*n*)**. This parameter requires a numeric value (*n*) for the number of columns in a table.

- **DIMENSION(*xx* )**. This option uses two letter codes (*xx*) to indicate the unit of measurement used to format the table. The default value is IN for inches.

- **HGUTTER(*n*)**. Requires a numeric value (*n*) for the horizontal gutter width between columns. The default is .056".

- **VGUTTER(*n*)**. Requires a numeric value (*n*) for the vertical gutter width between columns. The default is .056".

- **BOX(*tag name*)**, **HGRID(*tag name*)**, **VGRID(*tag name*)**. These settings select the tag to be used to format the box and the horizontal and vertical grid lines, respectively. The Z_DOUBLE and Z_SINGLE tags are used as the default values.

- **KEEP(ON/OFF)**. This sets the value for breaking the table between pages. The default is OFF, which allows the table to be split between pages if necessary.

Following the @_TBL+BEG code, you need to insert the @Z_TBL_BODY information, which requires a list of tag names to use for text in each column. There *must* be one tag name for each of the columns specified. The default is to assign all of the columns the TABLE TEXT tag. Following is an example of the code line for the four-column table.

**@Z_TBL_BODY = TABLE TEXT, TABLE TEXT, TABLE TEXT, TABLE TEXT**

Following that code, you can enter the text that is to be placed into the columns. Each row in the table is entered as a single line of text in which each of the column items is separated by a space and a comma. Keep in mind that a comma without a space following it will not be read correctly.

**CORRECT:**          Name, Company, City, Zip

**INCORRECT:**          Name,Company,City,Zip

Note that if you want to insert text, such as an address, that contains commas, enter double commas. Ventura will treat the double commas as part of a single column entry.

**CORRECT:**          Shrewsbury,, MA (Ventura sees single entry)

**INCORRECT:**          Shrewsbury, MA (Ventura sees two entries)

If no data is used for a column, a space must be placed into the line to show that an empty column is there.

**CORRECT:**          Name, , City, Zip

**INCORRECT:**          Name, City, Zip

The following lines will create three rows of data in the table. Note that there is not a setting that fixes the number of rows you can insert into a table. It is therefore easy to edit text to expand a table.

**Name, Company, City, Zip** ⏎
**Gerri Flynn, New England Telephone, Shrewsbury,, MA, 01625** ⏎
**Walter La Fish, La Fish Publications, Martinez,, CA, 94536** ⏎

After the data lines, you must enter a final table ending code. This code requires no parameters.

The following entries will create the table shown in Figure 9.18 when it is loaded into a Ventura frame:

**@Z_TBL_BEG = COLUMNS(4), DIMENSION(IN), HGUTTER(.056), VGUT-**
**TER(.065), BOX(Z_SINGLE), HGRID(Z_SINGLE), VGRID(Z_SINGLE),**
**KEEP(OFF)** ⏎
**@Z_TBL_BODY = TABLE TEXT, TABLE TEXT, TABLE TEXT, TABLE TEXT**
⏎
**Name, Company, City, Zip** ⏎
**Gerri Flynn, New England Telephone, Shrewsbury,, MA, 01625** ⏎
**Walter La Fish,La Fish Publications, Martinez,, CA, 94536** ⏎
**@Z_TBL_END =** ⏎

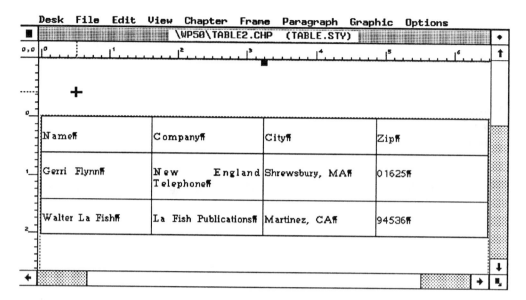

*Figure 9.18    Table created from text specifications.*

You can use the @Z_TBL_BODY command more than once in a table setup. This command enables you to change the formatting tags applied to the columns. For example, if a column contains numeric data, you might want to use a style tag that uses decimal or right alignment.

The following text shows the insertion of an additional @Z_TBL_BODY command, which changes the formatting of records 2 and 3, in columns 3 and 4. Once you insert a @Z_TBL_END command, the assigned tags will continue until another code is found or the end of the table is reached. You can insert as many @Z_TBL_END codes as needed to format the text the way you want.

@Z_TBL_BEG = COLUMNS(4), DIMENSION(IN), HGUTTER(.056), VGUT-
TER(.065), BOX(Z_SINGLE), HGRID(Z_SINGLE), VGRID(Z_SINGLE),
KEEP(OFF) ↵
@Z_TBL_BODY = TABLE TEXT, TABLE TEXT, TABLE TEXT, TABLE TEXT
↵
Name, Company, City, Zip ↵
@Z_TBL_BODY = TABLE TEXT, TABLE TEXT, CENTERED, NUMBERS ↵
Gerri Flynn, New England Telephone, Shrewsbury,, MA, 01625 ↵
Walter La Fish, La Fish Publications, Martinez,, CA, 94536 ↵
@Z_TBL_END = ↵

Joined cells can be indicated by entering a ^ character. The following lines of data would produce the joined cells in Figure 9.19.

**Gerri Flynn, New England Telephone, Shrewsbury,, MA, 01625 ⌐**
**Walter La Fish, ^, Martinez,, CA, 94536 ⌐**

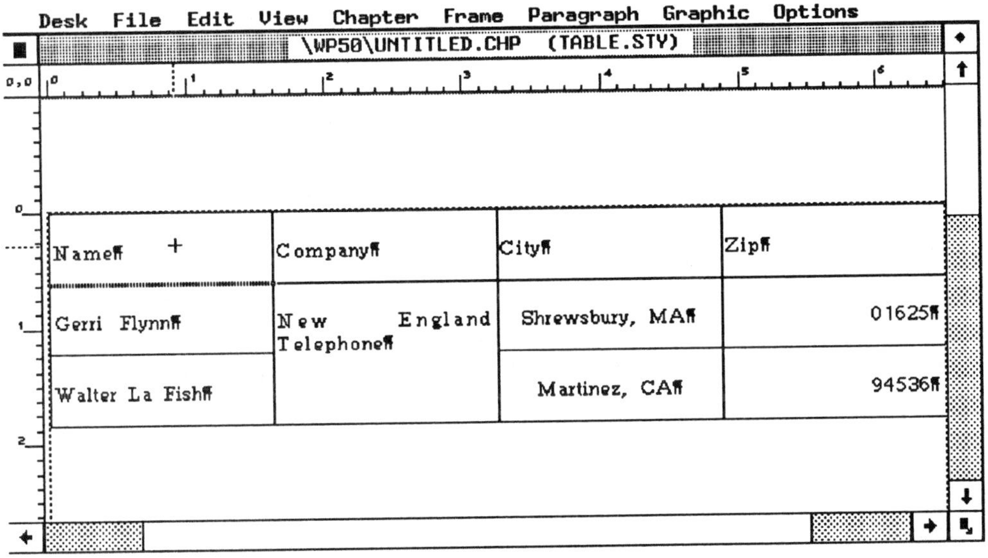

*Figure 9.19   ^ character used to create cell joining.*

## EQUATIONS

The equation editor was introduced earlier when you inserted fractions into the text of a document. The Professional Extension edition of Ventura has a sophisticated equation editing facility that makes it possible to create complex technical and scientific equations as part of a Ventura document. It is beyond the scope of this book to discuss scientific equations, but it might be useful to the average user to understand how to create simple mathematical expressions with the equation editor.

Begin with a clear document display. Place Ventura into the normal display mode.

> **Point** at the upper left corner of the master frame

Enter

**[Ctrl/n]**

Equations can be entered whenever you are editing text. Turn on the text editing mode by entering

**[Ctrl/o]**

> **Point** inside the master frame
> **Click**

You can now enter text into the master frame. To create an equation, enter

**[Ctrl/c]**

The special item menu is displayed. Enter

**[F4]**

The Equation Editing screen appears. It hides the document window for the moment.

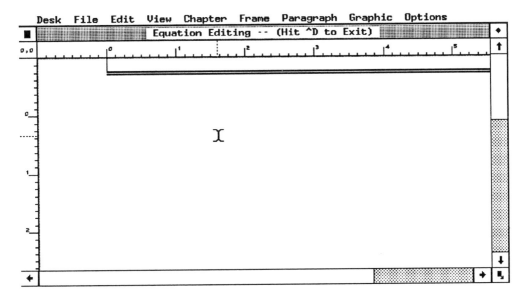

*Figure 9.20   Equation Editing display.*

Equations are created by entering a line of text that describes the equations you want to create. Ventura then interprets the line of text and creates the equation in the document. As you type, Ventura will wait for you to pause. If you do, in the bottom portion of the window, Ventura displays what you have entered so far as an equation.

To express certain mathematical notations, Ventura uses specific code words and symbols. Take, as an example, Einstein's famous equation. Enter

**E = mc sup 2**

The screen will display the equation as it appears in Figure 9.21.

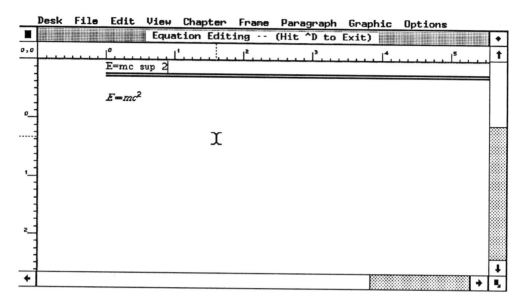

*Figure 9.21 Superscript exponent entered into the equation.*

The **sup** in the equation is one of the special code words used by the Professional Extension edition equation editor to signify a superscript exponent. To place the equation in the document, enter

**[Ctrl/d]**

The equation is inserted into the text. Return to the equation editor to try another example. Enter

↓
↵
**[Ctrl/c]**
**[F4]**

This time, try the Pythagorean theorem. Enter

**a sup 2 + b sup 2 = c sup 2**
**[Ctrl/d]**

A second equation is placed into the document.

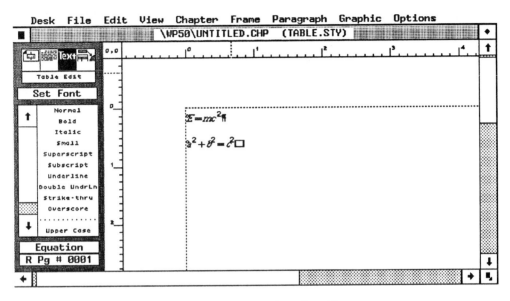

*Figure 9.22   Second equation placed into text.*

Note that the character font of the equation is the same as the font of the paragraph into which it was entered. The equation editor also has commands for changing fonts within an equation. Create a third equation. Enter

→
↵
**[Ctrl/c]**
**[F4]**

Suppose you wanted to write the first word in 24-point Swiss text. Normal text (not bold or italic) is set by the word **roman.** Fonts are selected by number according to the Ventura font system. For example, Swiss text is font #2. The {} indicate what part of the equation should be tagged with the specified font. Without the brackets, only the word immediately following the font change would be affected. Enter

**size 18 roman font 2 {Principal = (1 + rate) sup term}**

The equation appears in the specified font.

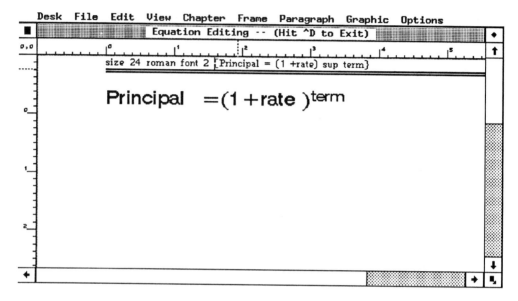

*Figure 9.23   Font change made in equation.*

Return to the document by entering

**[Ctrl/d]**

The three equations appear in the text.  Print the text.

Point the mouse at File
Point the mouse at To Print
Click

Enter

⏎

Clear the document window.

> **Point** the mouse at File
> **Point** the mouse at New
> **Click**
> **Point** the mouse at Abandon
> **Click**

Note that all equations created in the equation editor can be created in text files. Inserting the <$E...> code in the text will cause Ventura to create the specified equation when the text file is loaded, for example,

**<$Ea sup 2 + b sup 2 = c sup 2>**

## VERTICAL JUSTIFICATION

Another feature included in the Professional Extension edition is called **vertical justification**. Vertical justification refers to the process of adjusting the vertical spacing in a column to ensure that the bottom of the text is always flush with the bottom of the column.

Horizontal justification is common in word processing and is available in the standard edition of Ventura 2.0. This type of justification adds space between the words on a line to make sure that the end of the text falls exactly at the right column edge.

In creating vertically justified text, Ventura performs a similar type of adjustment by increasing the inter-line spacing within a column to ensure that the bottom of the column text is flush with the bottom edge of the column.

To see how vertical justification works, load the NEWSLTR chapter created in Chapter 8.

---

**Point** the mouse at File
**Point** the mouse at Open Chapter
**Click**
**Point** the mouse at NRESLTR.CHP
**Click**

---

Place Ventura into the reduced view mode. Enter

**[Ctrl/r]**

Examine the bottoms of the columns in the newsletter. There is blank space left at the bottom of most of the columns.

The JAVELIN article located on the bottom left of the first page leaves a gap between the last paragraph in the frame and the bottom of the frame column.

Place Ventura into the Frame Setting mode. Enter

**[Ctrl/u]**

---

**Point** the mouse at JAVELIN PLUS
**Click**

---

The frame is now selected. With the frame selected, you can display the FRAME TYPOGRAPHY SETTINGS dialog box.

> **Point** the mouse at Frame
> **Point** the mouse at Frame Typography
> **Click**

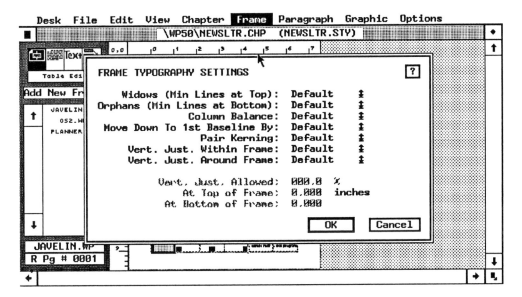

*Figure 9.24    FRAME TYPOGRAPHY SETTINGS dialog box.*

There are two types of vertical justification that can be used in Ventura.

- **Vert. Just. Within Frame**. This setting is the most obvious use of vertical justification. When set On, it allows Ventura to increase the spacing between lines of text to make text flush with the bottom of a column. There are two methods to choose from: feathering or carding. **Carding** is used to restrict the addition of interline space to Body Text formatted paragraphs only. **Feathering** adjusts all of the paragraphs to achieve the result. Carding is used in rare occasions when additional space in specially formatted paragraphs, e.g., ones with rotated text, needs to be avoided.

- **Vert. Just. Around Frame**. This use of justification refers to a situation in which the selected frame is a figure or chart placed within a column of text. This option can be set to fixed or moveable. **Fixed** causes Ventura to leave the frame at the exact same location on the page so space can only be added below that frame. **Moveable** allows Ventura to adjust the location of the frame in the column as part of the vertical justification process. Unless you have a specific reason for fixing the location of the frame, the moveable option will provide better vertical justification.

In this case, set the Vert. Just. Within Frame option to On.

> **Point** the mouse at Vert. Just. Within Frame
> **Click**
> **Drag** to Feathering

You must set the percentage of vertical justification allowed. For complete vertical justification, you would set the percentage to 100%, which is the usual procedure. If you have columns with gaps that are larger than normal, you might want to cut down on the amount of vertical justification allowed. Normal gaps would be those caused by paragraph spacing at the bottom of a column. Enter

**[Esc]**
**100 ⏎**

The text in the selected frame is spaced so that the text is justified on the bottom edge of the frame.

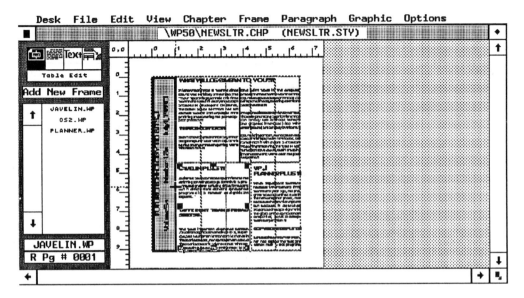

*Figure 9.25    Frame set for vertical justification.*

If you want to set all the frames in the document to vertical justification, use the same settings on the CHAPTER TYPOGRAPHY SETTINGS dialog box.

---

**Point** the mouse at Chapter
**Point** the mouse at Chapter Typography
**Click**
**Point** the mouse at Vert.  Just.  Within Frame
**Click**
**Drag** to Feathering

---

Enter

[**Esc**]
**100** ⏎

Now the text in all of the frames in the newsletter is vertically justified.

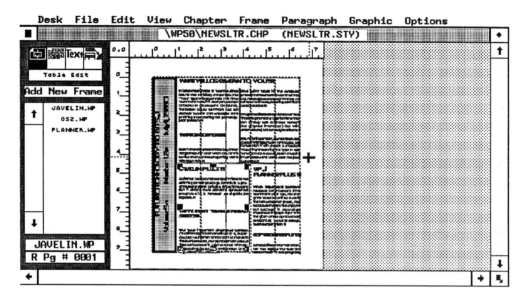

*Figure 9.26   Text in all frames vertically justified.*

Save the revised newsletter.

**[Ctrl/s]**

Clear the document window.

> **Point** the mouse at File
> **Point** the mouse at New
> **Click**

# CROSS-REFERENCES

In a large document it is often handy to refer to other parts of the text so that readers can jump to areas of interest without having to refer to the index or the table of contents.

The Professional Extension edition has the facility for creating cross-references within a chapter or group of chapters that belong to the same publication file.

A cross-reference consists of at least two items:

- **Reference Marker.** A marker is entered into a document to mark a special place in the text. Each marker must be given a unique name so that Ventura can locate any cross references made to that location. Setting markers has no visible effect on the text of the document.

- **Cross-Reference.** A cross-reference entry is placed into the text at a position in which you want the page number of the specified reference marker to appear. When you create a cross-reference, Ventura does not display anything in the text. For the page numbers to be created, you must run the chapter and any other related chapters through a multi-chapter operation called **renumber.**

Once a marker is created, you can have numerous references to that marker.

As an example, load the ANDORRA chapter created in Chapter 7.

> **Point** the mouse at File
> **Point** the mouse at Open Chapter
> **Click**
> **Point** the mouse at ANDORRA
> **Double Click**

When you enter markers and cross-references, it does not matter what order they are entered in. In this example, start by creating markers in the document. Move to page 2 by entering

**[PgDn]**

Place Ventura into the reduced view and Text Editing modes by entering

**[Ctrl/r]**
**[Ctrl/o]**

Just below the pie chart is the heading "HEALTH RATES."

> **Point** the mouse at "RATES"
> **Click**

To create a reference marker, enter

**[Ctrl/c]**
**[F7]**

The INSER/EDIT MARKER NAME dialog box appears.

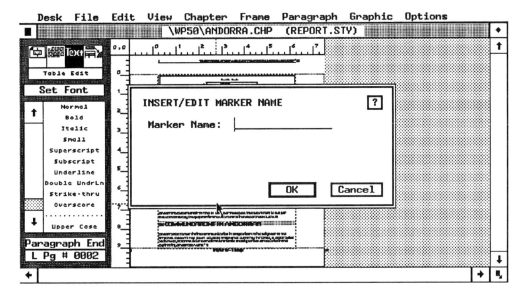

*Figure 9.27   INSERT/EDIT MARKER NAME dialog box.*

Enter a name to use as the reference marker.  The name can be any text from 1 to 16 characters in length.  Use a name that you are likely to remember exactly. Keep in mind that any cross-references made to that marker must match the spelling of the marker name exactly.  Enter

**health rates** ⅃

Go to page 4 of the document.  Enter

**[Ctrl/g]**
**4** ⅃

> **Point** the mouse at "ECONOMICS"
> **Click**

Enter a second reference marker:

**[Ctrl/c]**
**[F7]**
**economics** ⌐⌐

Return to the first page.  Enter

**[Home]**

Now you can enter references to the topics that you have marked.  In this case, place a reference to the health rates data at the end of the page.

> **Point** to the right of the last word on the page
> **Click**

Enter

**[Ctrl/n]**

Enter

**See Health Rate, p.**
**[Space bar]**

This is where the page number of the referenced data belongs.  Create a cross-reference to that page.  Enter

**[Ctrl/c]**
**[F6]**

The INSERT/EDIT REFERENCE reference dialog box appears. You need to enter the name of the reference marker. You can also use the **Refer to** option to place the page number, chapter number, figure number, table number, section number, or caption text at the reference location. Note that only chapter and page numbers will always appear. The other options depend on having a frame with the correct settings created in the document or in a related chapter.

You can also choose the numeric format in which the page or chapter number will appear. The default is Arabic numerals.

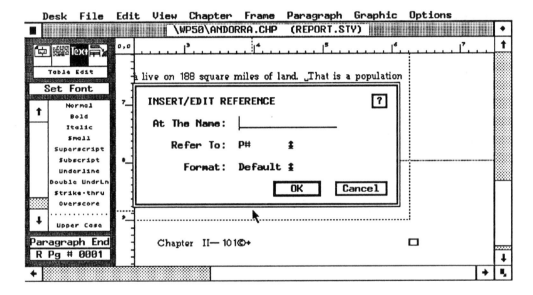

*Figure 9.28   INSERT/EDIT REFERENCE dialog box.*

Enter the name of the reference marker:

**health rates** ↵

A small circle appears to mark the location of the reference. Continue by adding a cross-reference to the other marker in the document. Enter

→
**[space bar]**
**also p.**

Insert a reference to "economics." Enter

**[Ctrl/c]**
**[F6]**
**economics** ↵

Note that these references do not display any actual page numbers yet. To fill these numbers in, you need to perform multi-chapter renumbering. Note that the renumber option on the Chapter menu — [Ctrl/b] — will not renumber cross-references. Only the renumber operation in the MULTI-CHAPTER dialog box can do that.

Display the ANDORRA mutli-chapter file.

---

**Point** the mouse at Options
**Point** the mouse at Multi-Chapter
**Click**

---

> **Point** the mouse at Renumber
> **Click**

The renumbering process may take a few minutes because Ventura must check and re-check the chapters to ensure that all the references are resolved.

When you have finished, return to the document window.

> **Point** the mouse at Done
> **Click**

The page numbers of the reference markers appear in the text.

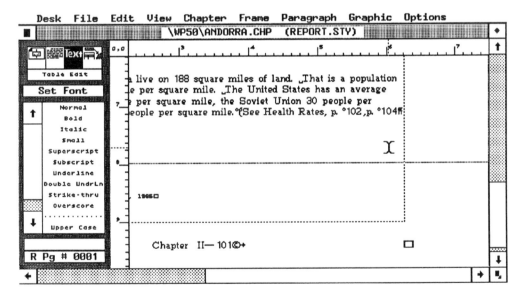

*Figure 9.29   Page numbers inserted for the reference markers.*

Save the revised chapter and exit Ventura. Enter

**[Ctrl/s]**

---

**Point** the mouse at File
**Point** the mouse at Quit
**Click**

---

## SUMMARY

- **Tables.** The Professional Extension edition contains special commands that create and format information tables. The Professional Extension edition includes a Table Edit mode in which table-oriented operations are carried out.

- **Equations.** In the Professional Extension edition, this feature is expanded to cover creation of mathematical equations of all types and complexities.

- **Vertical Justification.** This feature is used to create text columns in which the text is aligned flush with the tops and bottoms of columns and pages.

- **Cross-References.** The Professional Extension edition allows you to create cross-references in documents. This feature is useful in large documents in which references are made to specific information, tables, or figures located on different pages. It allows Ventura to automatically update references with accurate page numbers.

# ADDING PRINTER FONTS

One of the most fascinating features of Ventura is its ability to add fonts that will increase the variety of your formatting possibilities. Ventura supplies a basic set of fonts that can be used with your printer. The three basic font styles that are supplied with Ventura are as follows:

- **Times, Roman, or Dutch**. These fonts are the most commonly used and contain letters with lines that vary in thickness throughout different parts of the letter. They also include small extensions to the baseline, which are called **serifs** — from the French word for "foot."

- **Swiss or Helvetica**. These fonts are characterized by a uniform line width and a lack of serifs. The appearance of Swiss fonts is darker and cleaner than Dutch fonts. The name "Helvetica" is derived from the old Latin name for Swiss.

- **Courier**. This font is used to replicate the look of typical typewritten text produced on a monospaced typewriter.

## ADDING NEW FONTS

One of the best ways to add fonts to your Ventura system is to use the Bitstream Fontware program and purchase Bitstream fonts for your system. Bitstream supplies fonts for the Apple LaserWriter, AST TurboLaser, Cordata LP300X, HP LaserJet Plus and series II, and postscript printers.

Bitstream's program allows you to create both printer and screen fonts so your screen display will also show the new fonts you add.

One of the advantages of the Bitstream system is that you can create as many different point sizes as you want. Each font is supplied in a single file that is then used to create various point sizes. As of this writing, Bitstream offers more than 20 different fonts for Ventura. The price of each font is listed at $195.00, and a one-time purchase of an installation kit for all fonts is an additional $95.00.

The installation kit allows you to specify the type of screen display and printer you have, which is helpful if you have several computers that use different printers or monitor types. Suppose you had two printers, an HP LaserJet series II and a Cordata LP300X. The Bitstream program allows you to create fonts for both printers so you can get a consistent print output from both machines. Non-postscript printers have a limit on the point size of the largest font, usually 24- or 36-point. The Bitstream program will produce larger fonts, but Ventura will run out of memory if you try to use them.

The Bitstream program begins with a list of the fonts you can create.

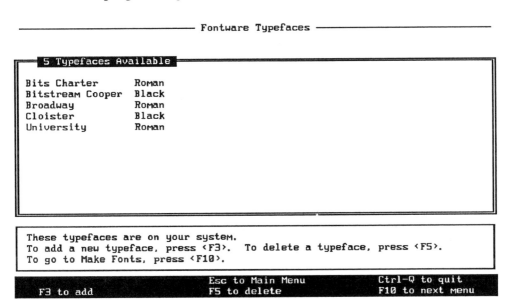

*Figure A.1    Typefaces listed in Fontware menu.*

You can select a series of fonts and the size that you want to use.

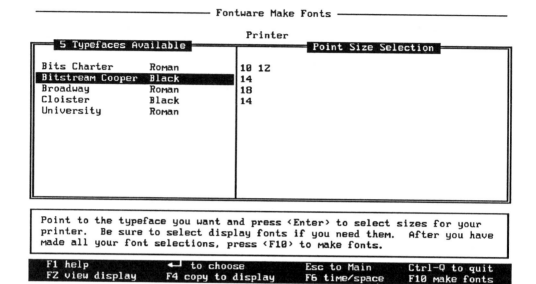

*Figure A.2    Printer font sizes.*

When using a program like Bitstream, you may want to generate small sets of fonts. You can later use Ventura to merge several of these small font sets into a large font set that will serve as your default printer font setup.

You also have the option to create screen fonts that match the printer fonts you have selected.

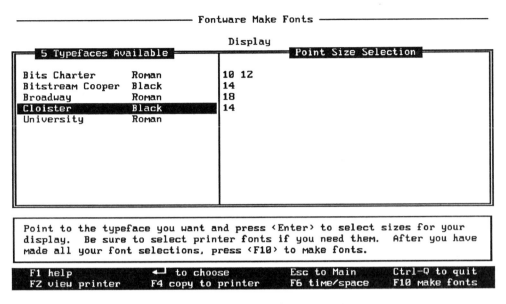

*Figure A.3    Display font selected.*

Font creation can take quite a bit of time. Bitstream will display an estimate of the time that it will take to create the fonts.

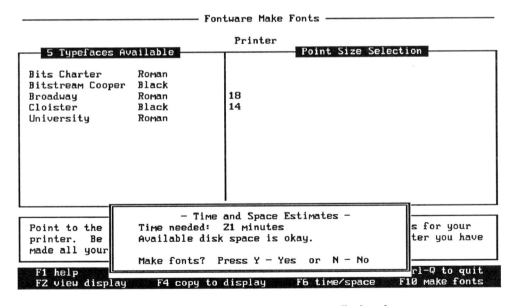

*Figure A.4    Time and space estimates displayed.*

As common sense would suggest, the larger the fonts, the longer they take to construct and the more disk space they will require. Printer fonts usually take up much more space than screen fonts. For example, a 24-point font file may take up 120 to 180 kilobytes. The equivalent screen font will take up about 10 to 12 kilobytes. You may need several megabytes of storage to hold all the fonts you want to create.

The Bitstream program produces two types of files that are needed to integrate the new fonts into Ventura.

**Printer font files** contain the printer information needed to create the characters on the printer. These files have a special naming structure that indicates the type of print they create. Following is an example of a font filename.

**CENT18BP.SFP**

The font is named CENT (short for Century); it is in 18-point, bold weight.

The other type of file is a **width table file**, which is the link between the font files and Ventura. It tells Ventura important information about the fonts that enables the program to display the new fonts for use with the program. Bitstream creates a width file for each group of fonts you create. Following is an example of a width table filename.

**HP_LJ000 WID**

Bitstream simply numbers the width tables HP_LJ001 WID, HP_LJ002 WID, etc. You may want to change the names to something more descriptive. You can simply use the DOS RENAME command to do this. Make sure that you use the WID extension, for example,

**RENAME HP_LJ000 WID HPOLDENG.WID**

Once you have created the necessary width and font files, you can integrate them into Ventura.

# LOADING DIFFERENT WIDTH TABLES

The Ventura Options menu has two commands that are used to add or change fonts. The first is the Set Printer Info option. The dialog box for this option resembles the following:

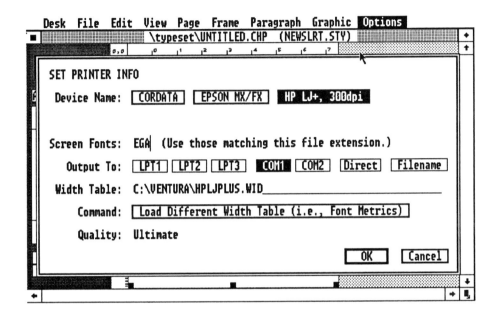

*Figure A.5    SET PRINTER INFO dialog box.*

The most significant entry on the screen is the name of the width table. In this example, the width table is HPJPLUS.WID. This file determines the fonts that are available when you use the font selection menus.

To load a different font table, select the Load Different Width Table option, which displays a list of WID files.

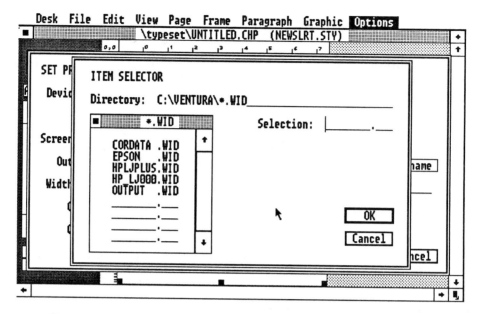

*Figure A.6    ITEM SELECTOR dialog box for selecting width table file.*

The file that you select determines the fonts available.  To see a list of fonts available, you can use the Add/Remove Fonts option on the **Options** menu.

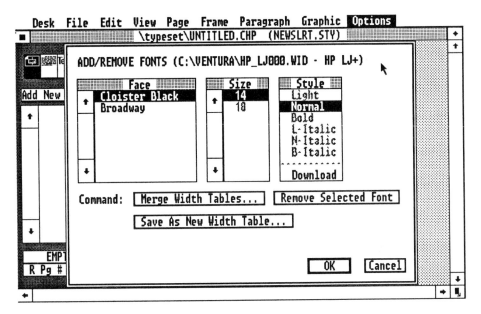

*Figure A.7    ADD/REMOVE FONTS dialog box.*

Figure A.7 shows two new fonts that were listed in the HP_LJ000 WID file. While that file is the active width file, you can select only from the fonts listed in that file. Figure A.8 shows how these fonts will appear on the screen.

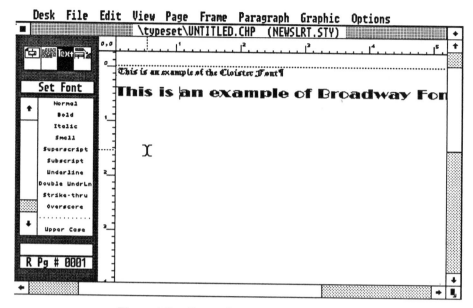

*Figure A.8    Screen fonts displayed in Ventura.*

Thanks to Bitstream's screen font generation, the new fonts appear on the screen as they will in the final printed document. This maintains Ventura's WYSIWYG (What You See Is What You Get) concept.

If you have a set of fonts, such as the one in this example, that you want to integrate into your standard font file, you can use the Merge Width Tables option in the ADD/REMOVE FONTS dialog box.

Suppose that in this case the standard font width table, the one that automatically is displayed in the SET PRINTER INFO dialog box, is HPLJPLUS.WID.

Select Merge Width Tables from the ADD/REMOVE FONTS dialog box. Ventura will display the list of WID (width) tables. Select HPLJPLUS.WID from the list. Ventura then adds all the fonts that would normally appear in the HPLJPLUS.WID file to the new width table file you loaded, which is called HP_LJ000.WID.

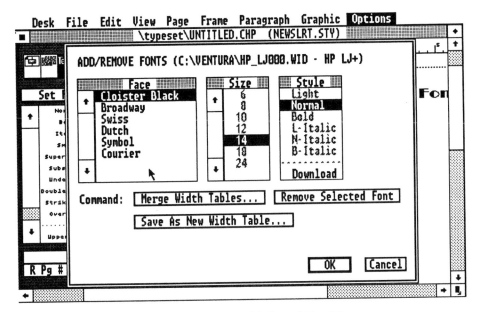

*Figure A.9    Fonts added to width table.*

If you want, you can save the new combined file under its own name, using the Save As New Width Table option.  You can also remove individual fonts from a width table if you don't want them by using the Remove Selected Font option.

With these commands, you can integrate and organize all the new fonts you acquire.

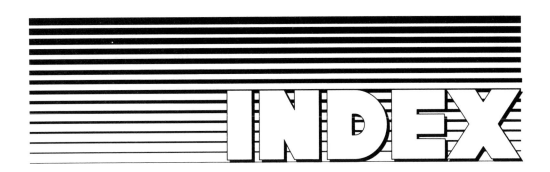

## H

Headers & footers, 400
  1st match, 402
  chapter #, 402
  chapter numbers, 409
  dialog box, 404
  frame, 419
  last match, 402
  page #, 402
  page numbers, 407
  suppressing, 414
  text attribute, 402
  turn on/off footer, 414
  turn on/off header, 414
  z_header tag, 405
Headers & footers dialog
  box, 401
Help, 13
Hide tabs & returns, 27
Home key, 394
Horz. alignment, 81

## I

Icons, 7
Image art, 335
Image files, 67
Images, 271
  illustration of, 338
Indents, 123
  ruling lines, 156
Index, 481
  completed dialog box, 484
  formatting of, 501
  z_index ltr, 503
  z_index main, 503
  z_index title tag, 503
Index items, 374

Insert graphics, 332
Insert new table, 584
Insert page, 556
Insert text, 73
Insert/edit table dialog box, 585
Insert/remove page, 556
  dialog box, 557
Installing Ventura, 2
Integrate graphics, 270
Inter-col lines, 308
Invite.wp document, 57
Invoice style sheet, 202
Italics, 41
Item selector dialog box, 56

## J

Javelin.wp document, 521

## K

Keep together, 420
Kerning, 111

## L

Letterhead, 204
Lift, 316
Lifts, 310
Line breaks, 130
Line endings, 34
Line snap, 280
Line spacing, 114
Line-art, 67, 335
Lines, 238
List files, 473
Load text into frame, 300, 298

# RELATED TITLES FROM MIS:PRESS

## WordPerfect 5.0

A comprehensive guide to WordPerfect, covering all the new desktop publishing features of version 5.0, including bit stream fonts, style sheets, various typefaces, and integrating graphics with text. This book addresses both new users and those already familiar with WordPerfect who are looking for upgrade information.

Rob Krumm   0-943518-97-0   $19.95

## WordPerfect for the Macintosh

For users who want to take full advantage of the power of WordPerfect for the Macintosh, this book documents, in step-by-step fashion, all the major features included in the Macintosh version of this best-selling word processor. It also includes an introductory section for PC and WordPerfect users coming to the Macintosh for the first time.

Rob Krumm   0-943518-91-1   $19.95

## Hard Disk Management

This new, revised edition is the practical guidebook for PC, PS/2, and compatible users. It reveals how to successfully use popular application software on hard disk systems, including how to master DOS, install programs, write menus, manage memory, and integrate software applications into a single powerful management tool. Covers fundamentals of DOS and OS/2 along with word processing, spreadsheets, and database management.

Ralph Blodgett and Emily Rosenthal   0-943518-82-2 $21.95

## Running DOS 4.0

This essential desktop reference is an invaluable resource for beginning and advanced PC- and MS-DOS users alike. It tells new users everything they need to know to use the system successfully. Power users will find it a comprehensive command reference and application development guide. Covering all major DOS commands, this book goes in depth on all the new 4.0 commands—including 4.0's new menu-driven shell.

Carl Siechert and Chris Wood   1-55828-005-7   $22.95

## DOS 4.0 Customizing The Shell

This sensational new book is written for users who want the freedom to "do it their own way." Author Thomas Goodell reveals DOS 4.0's arsenal of power-packed features and demonstrates how to master its new pull-down menu system. This book gives details on how to customize the Shell for specific applications; build, replace, and modify DOS menus; and go beyond the Shell to manipulate the DOS environment.

Thomas Goodell   1-55828-003-0   $22.95

## Microsoft Word 4.0 (Second Edition)

This book is a comprehensive guide to learning and using Microsoft Word 4.0. Describes how Word 4.0 interacts with desktop publishing systems, outlines commands and procedures for developing and using style sheets, and offers examples and illustrations.

Timothy Perrin   0-943518-31-8   $19.95

## Professional Programming Concepts

This book bridges the gap between amateur and professional programming. It takes readers from the BASIC language and introduces them to the professional C language, covering program development, programming techniques, and debugging. The logical and historical concepts of programming are also discussed.

Bud Pembroke   0-943518-87-3   $19.95

## dBASE IV
## Developer's Reference Guide

A must for anyone converting from dBASE III or III+ to IV. This invaluable sourcebook guides users through the newest version of America's best-selling database software and helps systems developers and programmers convert and upgrade program files. dBASE IV's extensive commands, functions, and language capabilities are detailed, along with a well-structured exploration of the dBASE IV Control Center and Menu Structure.

Clifford Philip, Jr.   1-55828-010-3   $26.95

*C*all free

**MANAGEMENT INFORMATION SOURCE, INC.**
P.O. Box 5277 • Portland, OR 97208-5277
(503) 222-2399

*M A N A G E M E N T   I N F O R M A T I O N   S O U R C E ,   I N C .*